The Talmud
of the
Land of Israel

Chicago Studies in the History of Judaism
Edited by Jacob Neusner

The University of Chicago Press
Chicago and London

The Talmud of the Land of Israel

*A Preliminary
Translation and
Explanation*

Volume 31   Sanhedrin and
                   Makkot

Translated by   Jacob Neusner

JACOB NEUSNER is University Professor and the Ungerleider Distinguished Scholar of Judaic Studies at Brown University. In addition to
editing and translating *The Talmud of the Land of Israel*, he is the au-
thor of many books, including *Judaism: The Evidence of the Mishnah*
and *Judaism in Society: The Evidence of the Yerushalmi.*

The University of Chicago Press, Chicago 60637
The University of Chicago Press, Ltd., London

Library of Congress Cataloging in Publication Data

Talmud Yerushalmi. Sanhedrin. English.
  Sanhedrin and Makkot.

  (The Talmud of the land of Israel; v. 31)
  Bibliography: p.
  Includes index.
  1. Talmud Yerushalmi. Sanhedrin—Commentaries.
2. Talmud Yerushalmi. Makkot—Commentaries. I. Neusner,
Jacob, 1932–   . II. Talmud Yerushalmi. Makkot.
English. 1984. III. Title. IV. Series: Talmud Yerushalmi.
English. 1982 ; v. 31.
BM498.5.E5   1982 vol. 31   296.1'2407s   [296.1'24]   83-18801
[BM506.S2E5]
ISBN 0-226-57691-4

For
Robert Alter

in friendship

Contents

Foreword

This translation into English of the Talmud of the Land of Israel ("Palestinian Talmud," "Yerushalmi") is preliminary and provisional, even though it is not apt to be replaced for some time. It is preliminary, first, because a firm and final text for translation is not in hand; second, because a modern commentary of a philological and *halakhic* character is not yet available; and third, because even the lower criticism of the text has yet to be undertaken. Consequently, the meanings imputed to the Hebrew and Aramaic words and the sense ascribed to them in this translation at best are merely a first step. When a systematic effort at the lower criticism of the extant text has been completed, a complete philological study and modern dictionary along comparative lines made available, and a commentary based on both accomplished, then the present work will fall away, having served for the interim. Unhappily, as I said, that interim is apt to be protracted. Text critics, lexicographers, and exegetes are not apt to complete their work on Yerushalmi within this century.

The purpose of this preliminary translation is to make possible a set of historical and religions-historical studies on the formation of Judaism in the Land of Israel from the closure of the Mishnah to the completion of the Talmud of the Land of Israel and the time of the composition of the first *midrashic* compilations. Clearly, no historical, let alone religions-historical, work can be contemplated without a theory of the principal document and source for the study, the Palestinian Talmud. No theory can be attempted, however tentative and provisional, without a complete, prior statement of what the document appears to wish to say and how its materials seem to have come to closure. It follows that the natural next steps, beyond my now-finished history of Mishnaic law and account of the Judaism revealed in that history, carry us to the present project. Even those steps, when they are taken, will have to be charted with all due regard to the pitfalls of a translation that is preliminary, based upon a text that as yet has not been subjected even to the clarifying exercises of lower criticism. Questions will have to be shaped appropriate to the parlous state of the evidence. But even if the historical and religions-historical program were to be undertaken in the Hebrew language, instead of in English, those who might wish to carry on inquiries into the history of the Jews and of Judaism in the Land of Israel in the third and fourth centuries would face precisely the same task we do. No one can proceed without a systematic account of the evidence and a theory of how the evidence may and may not be utilized. Further explanation of the plan and execution of this work will be found in volume 34, pages x–xiv.

Mr. Leonard Gordon checked my translation against the Leiden MS and the *editio princeps*, and saved me a great deal of tedious work in so doing. He also uncovered more than a few points requiring attention and correction. I am grateful for his hard and careful work.

Professor David Goldenberg of Dropsie University served as the critical reader for this volume. I am thankful for the many corrections and observations supplied by him and, still more, for his willingness to take time out to study this tractate and so improve my work on it. I retain full responsibility for whatever unsolved problems and deficiencies may remain. Professor Goldenberg kindly supplied an extensive commentary, which I have printed in *In the Margins of the Yerushalmi. Notes on the English Translation* (Chico, Calif.: Scholars Press for Brown Judaic Studies, 1983).

I completed this book during my tenure as a Guggenheim Fellow and during my coincident extraordinary research leave from Brown University. I am grateful to both the John Simon Guggenheim Memorial Foundation and Brown University for continued support for this research.

J.N.

Sanhedrin

1 Introduction to Sanhedrin

This tractate deals with two subjects: first, the organization of the Israelite government and court system; second, punishments administered to those convicted by the courts of having committed various crimes. The two topics are treated in sections of approximately equal length. The tractate provides a sizable repertoire of extremely well-organized facts, enlivened by narratives illustrating the workings of the courts and rules for conducting trials. But, the tractate asks no important questions about its facts, hardly attempts to show their complex potentialities, and undertakes no strikingly fresh intellectual initiatives. The framers are satisfied to paint a picture and tell a story. They may claim significant success only in the excellent way in which the tractate is organized.

Part of the reason for the tractate's logical and orderly treatment of its topic is that the framers choose to ignore the way Scripture handles the same set of themes. They make ample use of the facts they find in the Mosaic law codes. But these they lay out and organize entirely in their own way. When "Moses" does not provide information which their scheme of order and substance requires, they do not hesitate to make things up for themselves. These are the relevant verses, in the order in which the tractate calls upon them or upon information contained in them.

Deut. 16:18–20

You shall appoint judges and officers in all your towns which the Lord your God gives you, according to your tribes; and they shall judge the people with righteous judgment. You shall not pervert justice; you shall not show partiality; and you shall

not take a bribe, for a bribe blinds the eyes of the wise and
subverts the cause of the righteous. Justice, and only justice,
you shall follow, that you may live and inherit the land which
the Lord your God gives you.

Deut. 17:8–13

If any case arises requiring decision between one kind of homicide and another, one kind of legal right and another, or one
kind of assault and another, any case within your towns which
is too difficult for you, then you shall arise and go up to the
place which the Lord your God will choose, and coming to the
Levitical priests, and to the judge who is in office in those
days, you shall consult them, and they shall declare you the decision. Then you shall do according to what they declare to you
from that place which the Lord will choose; and you shall be
careful to do according to all that they direct you; according to
the instructions which they give you, and according to the decision which they pronounce to you, you shall do; you shall not
turn aside from the verdict which they declare to you, either to
the right hand or to the left. The man who acts presumptuously, by not obeying the priest who stands to minister there
before the Lord your God, or the judge, that man shall die; so
you shall purge the evil from Israel. And all the people shall
hear, and fear, and not act presumptuously again.

Ex. 23:21

Give heed to him and hearken to his voice, do not rebel against
him, for he will not pardon your transgression; for my name is
in him.

Num. 35:30

If anyone kills a person, the murderer shall be put to death on
the evidence of witnesses; but no person shall be put to death
on the testimony of one witness.

Deut. 17:6–7

On the evidence of two witnessses or of three witnesses he that
is to die shall be put to death; a person shall not be put to

death on the evidence of one witness. The hand of the witnesses shall be first against him to put him to death, and afterward the hand of all the people. So you shall purge the evil from the midst of you.

Lev. 21:10–12

The priest who is chief among his brethren, upon whose head the anointing oil is poured, and who has been consecrated to wear the garments, shall not let the hair of his head hang loose, nor rend his clothes; he shall not go in to any dead body, nor defile himself, even for his father or for his mother; neither shall he go out of the sanctuary, nor profane the sanctuary of his God; for the consecration of the anointing oil of his God is upon him: I am the Lord.

Deut. 17:14–20

When you come to the land which the Lord your God gives you, and you possess it and dwell in it, and then say, "I will set a king over me, like all the nations that are round about me"; you may indeed set as king over you him whom the Lord your God will choose. One from among your brethren you shall set as king over you; you may not put a foreigner over you, who is not your brother. Only he must not multiply horses for himself, or cause the people to return to Egypt in order to multiply horses, since the Lord has said to you, "You shall never return that way again." And he shall not multiply wives for himself, lest his heart turn away; nor shall he greatly multiply for himself silver and gold.

And when he sits on the throne of his kingdom, he shall write for himself in a book a copy of this law, from that which is in charge of the Levitical priests; and it shall be with him, and he shall read in it all the days of his life, that he may learn to fear the Lord his God, by keeping all the words of this law and these statutes, and doing them; that his heart may not be lifted up above his brethren, and that he may not turn aside from the commandment, either to the right hand or the left; so that he may continue long in his kingdom, he and his children, in Israel.

Deut. 21: 22–23

And if a man has committed a crime punishable by death and he is put to death, and you hang him on a tree, his body shall not remain all night upon the tree, but you shall bury him the same day, for a hanged man is accursed by God; you shall not defile your land which the Lord your God gives you for an inheritance.

Deut. 21:18–21

If a man has a stubborn and rebellious son, who will not obey the voice of his father or the voice of his mother, and, though they chastise him, will not give heed to them, then his father and his mother shall take hold of him and bring him out to the elders of his city at the gate of the place where he lives, and they shall say to the elders of his city, "This our son is stubborn and rebellious, he will not obey our voice; he is a glutton and a drunkard." Then all the men of the city shall stone him to death with stones; so you shall purge the evil from your midst; and all Israel shall hear, and fear.

Deut. 13:12–18

If you hear in one of your cities, which the Lord your God gives you to dwell there, that certain base fellows have gone out among you and have drawn away the inhabitants of the city, saying, "Let us go and serve other gods," which you have not known, then you shall inquire and make search and ask diligently; and behold, if it be true and certain that such an abominable thing has been done among you, you shall surely put the inhabitants of that city to the sword, destroying it utterly, all who are in it and its cattle, with the edge of the sword. You shall gather all its spoil into the midst of its open square, and burn the city and all its spoil with fire, as a whole burnt offering to the Lord your God; it shall be a heap forever, it shall not be built again. None of the devoted things shall cleave to your hand; that the Lord may turn from the fierceness of his anger, and show you mercy, and have compassion on you, and multiply you, as he swore to your fathers, if you obey the voice of the Lord your God, keeping all his commandments which I command you this day, and doing what is right in the sight of the Lord your God.

The outline of the tractate follows.

I. The court system (1:1–5:5)

A. *Various kinds of courts and their jurisdiction.* 1:1–6

1:1 Property cases are decided by three judges.
1:2 Various other sorts of cases which are decided by a court of three judges.
Continuation of the foregoing.
Cases involving the death penalty are judged by twenty-three judges.
1:3 Political crimes are judged by seventy-one judges, e.g., a tribe, a false prophet, a high priest.
1:4 The large court had seventy-one members, and the small one, twenty-three.

B. *The heads of the Israelite nation and the court system.* 2:1–5

2:1–2 The high priest judges and others judge him.
2:3 The king does not judge, and others do not judge him.
2:4–6 The prerogatives of the king.

C. *The procedures of the court system: property cases.* 3:1–8

3:1–4 Choosing the judges for a property case.
3:5 These are not valid to serve as judges or as witnesses.
3:6 These relatives are prohibited from serving as one's witnesses or judges.
3:7 Others who may not serve as judges or witnesses.
3:8 How do they examine the testimony of witnesses.
Procedures for reaching a decision.
3:9–10 Procedures for reaching a decision, continued.
3:11–12 Avenues of appeal.

D. *The procedures of the court system: capital cases.* 4:1–5:5

4:1–7 The difference of capital cases and their procedures from property cases.
4:8 The layout of the Sanhedrin, the places of the judges.
4:9 How they admonish witnesses in capital cases.
5:1 The points of interrogation of witnesses (in capital cases).
5:2 The more they interrogate witnesses, the more is one to be praised.
5:3 Contradictory testimony.

5:4   The foregoing continued. The discussion of the case. The possibility of appeal.

5:5   Reaching a decision. Voting procedures in capital cases.

II. The death penalty (6:1–11:6)

A. *Stoning*. 6:1–6

6:1–2   When the trial is over, they take the convicted felon out and stone him. Description of the penalty.

6:3   Appended homily.

6:4–10   Disposition of the corpse of the felon.

B. *Four modes of execution lie in the power of the court and how they are administered*. 7:1–3

7:1   Four modes of execution: stoning, burning, decapitation, and strangulation.

7:2   How burning is carried out.

7:3   How decapitation is carried out.

7:4   How strangulation is carried out.

C. *Those who are put to death by stoning*. 7:4–8:7

7:5   These are the ones who are put to death by stoning.

7:6–13   Continuation of the foregoing list and its exegesis.

8:1–6   Continuation of the foregoing list and its exegesis.

8:7–9   Appended homiletical materials.

D. *Those put to death through burning or decapitation*. 9:1–10:6

9:1–2   And these are the ones who are put to death through burning, decapitation.

9:3   Murderers.

9:4   Continuation of the foregoing.

9:5–6   He who is liable to be put to death through two different modes of execution is judged to be executed by the more severe.

9:7   Extrajudicial modes of punishment, e.g., of recidivists.

10:1–3   Homiletical expansion of M. 9:7: extrajudicial punishment, at the hands of Heaven. All Israelites share in the world to come except. . . .

10:6   Exegesis of M. 9:2 list for decapitation.

10:7–8   Homiletical continuation of the foregoing.

E. *Those put to death through strangulation.* 11:1–6

11:1 These are the ones who are to be strangled.
11:2 Continuation of the foregoing list and its exegesis.
11:3 Continuation of the foregoing list and its exegesis.
11:4 Continuation of the foregoing list and its exegesis.
11:5 Continuation of the foregoing list and its exegesis.
11:6 Continuation of the foregoing list and its exegesis.

Both units of the tractate are very carefully organized. There is, moreover, a careful and obvious effort to link the two, since M. 6:1ff. carry forward the narrative begun at M. 5:5, and it is only in the unfolding of the new materials that we realize a decisive shift in the topic has taken place. The tractate unpacks the opening topic, the court system, by describing, first, the several types of courts, I.A (I.B is important and can go nowhere else), then the procedures followed for the two distinct kinds of cases with which they deal, property litigation, I.C, and capital cases, I.D. This latter has to have its present position, for it serves as a prologue to the second unit. The important pericope in unit II is M. 7:1, which lays the foundations for all which follow. First, the four modes of execution are described. Then, still more important, those who are subjected to each of the four modes of execution are specified. The spelling out is at II.C, D, and E. As is clear, except for some inserted or appended homiletical materials, the entire construction systematically expounds the facts important for a full understanding of M. 7:1. I cannot imagine a more cogent or logically and formally coherent tractate than this one. The facts so elegantly put together are considerably less interesting than the way in which they are organized and given linguistic and syntactic form.

2 Yerushalmi Sanhedrin
Chapter One

1:1

[A]   [17d] *Property cases [are decided] by three [judges];*

[B]   *those concerning theft and damages, before three;*

[C]   *[cases involving] full compensation for damages, half compensation for damages [Ex. 21:35], twofold, fourfold, and fivefold restitution [Ex. 22:13], by three;*

[D]   *"cases involving him who rapes [Deut. 22:28–29], him who seduces [Ex. 22:16–17], and him who brings forth an evil name [Deut. 22:13–19], by three," the words of R. Meir.*

[E]   *And sages say, "He who brings forth an evil name is [tried] before twenty-three,*

[F]   *"for there may be a capital case."*

[I.A]   [18a] And whence shall we produce evidence from Scripture [for the factual statement of M. 1:1A]?

[B]   " 'And these things shall be for a statute and ordinance' (Num. 35:29).

[C]   "On the basis of this verse I draw the conclusion that [the reference to both statute and ordinance bears this meaning:] careful cross-examination of witnesses is required not only for capital cases but also for property ones.

[D]   "And then how do we know that property cases require three judges [and not twenty-three, as in the case of capital cases]?

[E]   " 'The owner of the house shall come near to the judges' (Ex. 22:8)—thus encompassing one judge.

[F]   " 'The case of both parties shall come before the judges' (Ex. 22:9)—thus encompassing a second judge.

[G]   " '. . . he whom the judges shall condemn shall pay . . .' (Ex. 22:9)—lo, here is yet a third," the words of R. Josiah.

[H]   R. Jonathan says, "The first [of the three verses] appears at the outset, and further exegetical meanings cannot be imputed to a verse in such a position [which is required simply to provide the information stated therein, as distinct from the later expressions of essentially the same idea]. [These later ones may serve to supply additional information, beyond the facts they contain, because they are superfluous in regard to their primary statements of facts.]

[I]   "But: '. . . before the judges . . . ,'—lo, one judge is required.

[J]   " '. . . whom the judges shall condemn . . .'—lo, two judges.

[K]   "Now a court cannot be made up of an even number of judges, so they add yet a third judge, so that there are three in all on the court."

[L]   Rabbi says, "The Scripture speaks of a plural of two ['judges']."

[M]   "You claim that the Scripture speaks of a plural. Perhaps it refers to only one?"

[N]   "When the Scripture says, '. . . whom the judges shall condemn,' Scripture states only that [thus providing for two judges]. Since there cannot be a court made up of an even number of judges, they add to the court yet a third, so lo, there are three judges."

[O]   R. Abbahu raised the question, "Now in accord with Rabbi, monetary cases should be decided by a court of five judges [for he has had two judges subject to discussion in the cited verses, above, J, and so there are two relevant verses, thus four judges, plus a fifth to create an odd number, hence five in all]. In this way the decision will be reached by three judges."

[P]   [Along these same lines] the following is available: R. Hezekiah taught, "Since the Torah has given instructions to carry out the death penalty at the decision of a majority, and to carry out the death penalty at the evidence of witnesses, just as there must be two witnesses, so too there must be a majority of two [to reach the decision, so four].

[Q]   "Since you cannot have a court of an even number of judges, they must add to the court yet one more, so there will be five [judges]."

[II.A]   Are not theft and damages [M. 1:1B] the same thing?

[B]   The following is available: R. Simeon b. Yohai taught, " 'And these are the ordinances which you shall set before them' (Ex. 21:1).

[C]   "Now [the purpose of the authority of M. who has treated property cases disjunctively, and not as a single group,] is to interpret the meaning of Scripture. [First come property cases, as at Ex. 21:2, buying a Hebrew slave, then come cases of theft and damages, damages at Ex. 21:12ff. and theft at Ex. 22:1ff.]"

[D]   This verse is in accord with the position of R. Yosé bar Halafta [who interprets the cited verse to mean that the judge must decide a case solely on the basis of the evidence in hand, as in the following case].

[E]   Two people came to him for judgment. They said to him, "It is on the condition that you render a judgment in accord with the law of the Torah."

[F]   He said to them, "I don't know what you mean by a 'judgment in accord with the law of the Torah,' [but I shall judge by what you testify before me]. And may He who understands what is in peoples' mind exact punishment from those men [you if you are guilty]. You must accept what I shall instruct you."

[G]   R. Aqiba, when someone came to him for judgment, would say to him, "Know before whom you stand, before Him who spoke and brought the world into being, as it is said, 'And both parties who have the controversy shall come before the Lord' (Deut. 19:17)—and not merely before Aqiba ben Joseph!"

[III.A]   It was taught: Forty years before the destruction of the Temple the right to judge capital cases was withdrawn, and it was in the days of Simeon b. Shatah that the right to judge property cases was withdrawn.

[B]   Said R. Simeon b. Yohai, "Blessed be the All-merciful that I am not a sage required to make court decisions."

[**IV**.A]   Samuel said, "Two who rendered a decision—their decision stands, but they are called a presumptuous court."

[B]   R. Yohanan and R. Simeon b. Laqish—both of them teach that even if two reached a decision, their decision does not stand.

[C]   There we have learned: *[If] one [person who was not an expert] judged a case, declaring the liable person to be free of liability, declaring the person free of liability to be liable, declaring what is clean to be unclean, declaring what is unclean to be clean, what he has done is valid. But he pays restitution from his own funds [M. Bekh. 4:4D–F].*

[D]   R. Ba in the name of R. Abbahu: "This applies when the parties to the dispute said to him, 'Lo, you are acceptable to us like two judges.' "

[E]   How shall we explain this statement?

[F]   If it is as a case in which one erred and made a decision based on his own reasoning [rather than the law of the Torah], in such a case do we hold that what is done is valid? [Obviously, not.]

[G]   If it is a case in which he erred even though he judged them in accord with the law of the Torah, in such a case must he pay compensation from his own house? [Obviously not.]

[H]   R. Ba in the name of R. Abbahu said, "It is a case in which they have said to him, 'Lo, you are acceptable to us like *three* judges, on condition that you render a judgment in accord with the law of the Torah.' But the man erred and made his decision on the basis of his own reasoning. What he has done is valid, because he has erred and made a decision on the basis of his own ruling. He must pay compensation out of his own property, for he dared to take upon himself the authority to give a judgement on his own in the case of a court decision based on Torah law."

[I]   For we have learned:

[J]   *Do not judge all by yourself, for only One judges all by Himself (Abot 4:8).*

[K]   Said R. Judah b. Pazzi, "Even the Holy One, blessed be He, does not give a decision all by himself, as it is said, 'And Micaiah said, "Therefore hear the word of the Lord: I saw the

Lord sitting on his throne, and all the host of heaven standing beside him on his right hand and on his left" (1 Kings 22:19).' These favor acquittal, and those favor conviction."

[L]   Even though [God] does not judge all by himself, he seals the decree all by himself, as it is said, "But I will tell you what is inscribed in the book of truth: there is none who contends by my side against these except Michael, your prince" (Daniel 10:21f.).

[M]   Said R. Yohanan, "Under no circumstances does the Holy One do a thing in his world without consulting with the heavenly court."

[N]   What is the Scriptural basis of this statement?

[O]   "And the word was true, and it was a great host" (Dan. 10:1).

[P]   Under what circumstances is the seal of the Holy One, blessed be He, truth? It is when he consults with the heavenly court.

[Q]   Said R. Eleazar, "Each passage in which it is stated, 'And the Lord,' means that at hand are He and his court.

[R]   "And the meaning of the matter is indicated by the principal source [describing the Lord and his court]: 'And the Lord has spoken evil concerning you' (1 Kings 22:23 and 2 Chron. 18:22). [That is, the court exacts justice, rather than dispensing mercy.]"

[S]   What is the seal of the Holy One, blessed be He?

[T]   R. Bibi in the name of R. Reuben:"It is truth."

[U]   What is the meaning of "truth"?

[V]   Said R. Bun, "It is that He is the living God and the everlasting King" (Jer. 10:10).

[W]   Said R. Simeon b. Laqish, "An *alef* stands at the beginning of the alphabet, a *mem* stands at the middle, and a *tau* stands at the end [both of the word and of the alphabet] to indicate, 'I am the first,' for I did not accept dominion by anyone else's authority. 'And besides me there is no god' (Is. 44:6), for I have no colleague. 'And I am the last' [Is. 44:6, in different order], for in the end I shall not hand over [dominion] to another."

[V.A]   R. Ba and R. Benjamin b. Yaphet had a case in the court of R. Isaac, and the decision went in favor of R. Benjamin. R. Ba came and wanted to cause trouble with R. Ami [because R. Isaac had decided the case all by himself]. [R. Ami] instructed him that an expert who sat down and gave a decision—his decision is valid.

[B]   R. Abbahu would go into session all by himself, as a judge in the synagogue at the gate of Caesarea. His disciples said to him, "And has not Rabbi taught us, 'Do not judge all by yourself'?" He said to them, "Since [people] see that I sit as a judge all by myself and [nonetheless] come to me, it is as if they accepted me [as a single judge to decide] their [case]."

[C]   And thus also has it been taught: "Under what [18b] circumstances [may one not judge all by himself]? When [the litigants] did not accept [the individual as sole judge] for their [case]. But if they did accept [the individual as sole judge] for their [case], it is proper even for an individual to judge all by himself."

[D]   R. Yohanan went to have a case judged before R. Hiyya the Great. [Hiyya] seated a disciple with him [so as not to judge all by himself].

[E]   But has it not been taught: **A father and his son, a master and his disciple—both of them are numbered as a single person [T. San. 7:2/0].**

[F]   We say that in this case it is an associate and a disciple, as in the case of R. Eleazar and R. Yohanan [in which case both count].

[G]   A court decision went forth from the court of Rab, when he was judging all by himself; from R. Aha, when he was judging all by himself; from R. Jonah and R. Yosé, when they were judging all by themselves.

[H]   There we have learned: *He who takes payment for judging—his judgments are null [M. Bekh. 4:6A].*

[I]   The meaning of the Mishnah law is this: **If one is suspect of collecting a salary in order to judge,** [his judgments are null]. [But if he accepts a salary only for the loss of time to earn a living, that is acceptable.] (T. Bekh. 3:8.)

[J]   A man came to seek a judgment before R. Huna. [Huna] said to him, "Bring me someone to till around my palm tree."

[K]   R. Huna was an ox herder, and he had evidence to give in behalf of someone in a suit. He said to him, "Come and give testimony in my behalf." He replied, "Pay me a salary [which I shall lose]."

[L]   And thus it has been taught: **They do pay a fee to a judge for his time, and a fee to the witness for his time [T. Bekh. 3:8C].**

[VI.A]   A man deliberately rendered a priest [cultically] unclean. The case came before R. Isaac, and he ordered the man to provide unconsecrated food for the priest to eat [since he could not eat cheaper food, in the status of heave offering, which he normally ate, by reason of his cultic uncleanness].

[B]   [The disciples] supposed that [the man] might deduct the cost of food in the status of heave offering from the penalty, [since the priest would have paid that lesser cost in any event]. [This would constitute a mediated agreement, which accounts for what follows.]

[C]   It was taught: **R. Eleazar, son of R. Yosé the Galilean, said, "He who arbitrates a case [after judgment has been passed, as at B] [—lo, this one] sins.**

[D]   **"And whoever praises the arbitrator—lo, this one is as if he curses the Omnipresent,**

[E]   **"as it is said, 'He who blesses the arbitrator blasphemes the Lord' (Ps. 10:3).**

[F]   **"But let justice pierce the mountain."**

[G]   **And so did Moses [say, "Let justice pierce the mountain"].**

[H]   **But Aaron would make peace between one person and another, as it is said, "He walked with me in peace and uprightness" (Mal. 2:6).**

[I]   It is taught: **R. Eleazar b. Jacob said, "Why does Scripture say, 'He who blesses a robber blasphemes the Lord'?**

[J]   **"They made an analogy. To what is the matter to be compared? To someone who stole a *seah* of wheat, ground it into wheat, baked it into bread, and separated dough offering** from the bread [for the priest], and then fed the bread to his children. How is such a person to say a blessing. It is no blessing but a curse" [T. San. 1:2].

[K]   R. Meir says, "Why does Scripture say, 'He who praises the one who gets unlawful benefit (boṣeʿa) blasphemes the Lord'?—

[L]   "These are the brothers of Joseph, who said, 'What profit (beṣaʿ) do we have if we kill our brother' (Gen. 37:26)."

[M]   R. Joshua b. Qorha says, "It is a religious duty to arbitrate, as it is said, 'Execute the judgment of truth and peace in your gates' (Zech. 8:16).

[N]   "Now is it not so that in any case in which there is a judgment of truth, there is no peace, and in any case in which there is peace, there is no judgment of truth?

[O]   "So what is the judgment of truth which also contains peace?

[P]   "You have to say, This is arbitration" [T. San. 1:3].

[Q]   (Rabbi says,) "[If] one has judged a case, declaring the guiltless to be guiltless and imposing liability on the guilty party,

[R]   "Scripture credits him for he has done charity with the one who is liable,

[S]   "for he removes the stolen goods from his possession.

[T]   "And he does justice to the innocent party, for he restores to him what belongs to him" [T. San. 1:5].

[U]   Said R. Abbahu, "Judgment is mentioned twice in the same passage: ['You shall not be partial in judgment; . . . you shall not be afraid before man, for judgment belongs to God' (Deut. 1:17).] [This indicates that there are two sorts of judgment, one a decision, one arbitration. Thus:] 'Execute the judgment of truth and peace in your gates' (Zech. 8:16)."

[V]   R. Zechariah asked before R. Ami, "Do they carry out the law in practice in accord with the opinion of this Tanna [who maintains that it is a religious duty to arbitrate]?"

[W]   It was taught: R. Simeon b. Menassia says, "Sometimes one should arbitrate, and sometimes he should not arbitrate.

[X]   "How so?

[Y]   "Two who came before someone to judge [their case]—

[Z]   "before he has heard what they have to say,

[AA]   "or if he has heard what they have to say but does not know in which direction the case should turn,

[BB]   "he has the right to say to them, 'Go out and seek arbitration.'

[CC]   "But once he has heard what they have to say and knows in which direction the case should turn,

[DD]   "he has no right to say to them, 'Go out and seek arbitration.'

[EE]   "Just as it is written, 'The beginning of strife is as when one lets out water; therefore, before the matter is laid bare, leave off contention' (Prov. 17:14)—

[FF]   "Before the ruling is clear, you are free to abandon it.

[GG]   "Once the decision is clear, you do not have the right to abandon it" (T. San. 1:6).

[HH]   R. Mattenaiah said, "Also arbitration requires [the judge to] make up his mind."

[II]   R. Judah b. Laqish would say, "Two who came before someone for judgment—

[JJ]   "one strong and one weak—

[KK]   "before one has heard what they have to say,

[LL]   "or if one has heard what they have to say but does not yet know in which direction the case should turn,

[MM]   "he has the right to say to them, 'I am not going to be subject to you [and to take your case],'

[NN]   "lest the weaker [Talmud: stronger] party turn out to be liable, and the stronger one go after him [Talmud: the stronger become his enemy].

[OO]   "But once he has heard what they have to say and knows in which direction the case should turn,

[PP]   "he has not got the right to say to them, 'I am not going to be subject to you [and to take your case].'

[QQ] "For it is said, 'You shall not be afraid before man, for judgment is God's' (Deut. 1:17)" [T. San. 1:7].

[RR] Said R. Joshua b. Qorha, "[How do we know that] if one was sitting before a judge and knew something for the case of the poor man and something against the case of the rich man, you are not free to keep silent?

[SS] "Scripture says, 'You shall not be afraid before man, for judgment is God's' (Deut. 1:17).

[TT] "Do not hold back what you have to say because of man" [T. San. 1:8].

[UU] The judges should know Whom they judge, and before Whom they judge, and Who it is Who judges with them.

[VV] And the witnesses should know about Whom they give testimony, and before Whom they give testimony, and with Whom they give testimony, and Who it is Who is a witness with them. It is He who spoke and brought the world into being,

[WW] since it is said, "Then both the men between whom the controversy is shall stand before the Lord" (Deut. 19:17).

[XX] And it is said, "God stands in the congregation of God and in the midst of judges he judges" (Ps. 82:1).

[YY] And so does Jehoshaphat say to the judges, "Consider what you do, for you judge not for man but for God" (2 Chron. 19:6).

[ZZ] Now is it possible for mortal man to judge his creator?

[AAA] But the Holy One, blessed be He, said, "It was I who declared [on the New Year] that Reuben should have a hundred *denars,* and that Simeon should have nothing. Yet you have taken them from this one and [in false judgment] hand them over to that one! It is my task to pay him and to exact payment from that man [who causes a miscarriage of justice]."

[BBB] It was taught: Rabban Simeon b. Gamaliel says, "Just as judgment is by three [judges], so arbitration is by three arbitrators.

[CCC] "The force of arbitration is greater than the force of a court decision.

[DDD]   **"How so?**

[EEE]   **"Two who made a judgment have the power to retract. Two who effected an arbitration do not have the power to react"** **[T. San. 1:9].**

[**VII**.A]   *"Cases involving him who rapes, seduces, [and brings forth an evil name, by three judges," the words of R. Meir. And sages say, "He who brings forth an evil name is tried before twenty-three, for there may be a capital case]."*

[B]   R. Mana said, "The dispute concerns a betrothed maiden. [If she is found guilty,] R. Meir says, 'She loses the right to collect her marriage settlement on the decision of a court of three judges, and she is put to death by stoning on the decision of a court of twenty-three.' And sages say, 'in the same court in which she is condemned to death by stoning, there she is sentenced to the loss of the right to collect her marriage settlement.'

[C]   "But as to one who brings forth an evil name, all parties concur that in the same court in which perjurers are sentenced to death by stoning, there the husband is condemned to be flogged and to pay a hundred *selas*. [So the Mishnah rule refers not to the court which will try the man, but to the one which will try the woman. The husband's trial is both separate and later. First comes that of the woman, and her trial court is what is subject to discussion. Meir surely could not refer to a case of seduction, in which case the woman is on trial for her life.]"

[D]   Said to him R. Yosé b. R. Bun, "Lo, the Mishnah pericope has been taught with its own division, and you divide it in your own way. Rather, [as the layout of M. makes clear,] the division of opinion [between R. Meir and sages] concerns one who brings forth an evil name. R. Meir maintains, 'The husband is sentenced to flogging and to pay a fine of a hundred *selas* by a court made up of three judges. If witnesses [are on trial for perjury in such a case], they are sentenced to death by the decision of a court of twenty-three judges.' And sages teach that in the court in which the witnesses are sentenced to death by stoning, there the husband is tried for the penalty of flogging and for paying a fine of a hundred *selas*.

[E]   "But as to a betrothed maiden, all parties concur that in the court in which she is tried on the count of stoning, there she is tried on the count of losing the claim of her marriage settlement."

[F] Now the view of R. Mana is in accord with the opinion of R. Zeira, and the opinion of R. Yosé b. R. Bun is in accord with the opinion of R. Abbahu. [That is, there is a parallel to the dispute concerning whether the trial of the accused and that of the perjured witnesses takes place before an equivalent court, or whether there will be different courts for the different cases, one of three, the other of twenty-three, as the prospective penalty will require. This is as follows:]

[G] R. Abbahu raised the question, "As to an ox which is brought to trial under penalty of stoning, in accord with the view of R. Meir should the owner be sentenced to pay the monetary fine by the decision of a court of three judges and the ox be sentenced to stoning by the decision of a court of twenty-three?"

[H] Said to him R. Yosé b. R. Bun, "The trial of an ox which is to be stoned is wholly a matter of a property claim. But the Scripture's decree is that it should be stoned [and consequently, the court should consist of only three judges, and that is for a trial on both counts, compensation and stoning]."

Most of the Talmud's discussion of the present Mishnah pericope consists of an assembly of relevant sayings rather than a sustained and analytical discussion of Mishnah's logic and implications, of its relationships to other rules, both obviously relevant and otherwise, and of its potentialities for extension and amplification. In other words, before us is a theory of what is expected *as* Talmud quite different from that operative in such tractates as Shebuot and Horayot. Unit **I** simply presents set-piece exegeses, supporting some of Mishnah's statements of facts. Unit **II** takes up the relationship of Mishnah's language to that of Scripture. I see no reason for the introduction of unit **III** at all, unless it is as a prologue to the protracted repertoire of didactic materials on why a judge should not make a decision alone. That rather diffuse discussion covers the whole of **IV** and **V**. Unit **VI** is yet another massive set-piece construction, dealing with a topic not found in the Mishnah at all, namely arbitration. Only unit **VII** brings us to a close and careful analysis of a segment of Mishnah's law and language.

1:2

[A] *[Cases involving the penalty of] flogging [Deut. 25:2–3] are before three.*

[B] *In the name of R. Ishmael they said, "Before twenty-three."*

[C] *[The decision to] intercalate the month is before three.*

[D] *"[The decision to] intercalate the year is before three," the words of R. Meir.*

[E] *Rabban Simeon b. Gamaliel says, "With three do they begin, with five they debate the matter, and they reach a final decision with seven [judges].*

[F] *"But if they reached a decision [to intercalate the year] with three judges, [the year is validly] intercalated."*

[G] *"The laying of hands [on a community sacrifice] by elders and the breaking of the heifer's neck [Deut. 21:1–9] are done by three judges," the words of R. Simeon.*

[H] *R. Judah says, "By five."*

[I] *The rite of removal of the shoe [breaking the levirate bond] (Deut. 25:7–9) and the exercise of the right of refusal are done before three judges.*

[J] *[The evaluation of] fruit of fourth-year plantings [which is to be redeemed (Lev. 19:23–25)] and of second tithe (Deut. 14:22–26), the value of which [must be set but] is not known is done before three judges.*

[K] *[Assessment of the value, for purposes of redemption,] of things which have been consecrated is done before three judges.*

[L] *[Property pledged as security for] vows of valuation (Lev. 27:2–8), in the case of movables, is evaluated by three judges.*

[M] *R. Judah says, "One of them must be a priest."*

[N] *And [evaluation of property pledged as security for vows of valuation] in the case of real estate is done by nine and a priest.*

[O] *And so for [the valuation-vow covering] men.*

[P] *Cases involving the death penalty are judged before twenty-three judges.*

[Q]   The beast who commits or is subjected to an act of sexual relations with a human being is judged by twenty-three,

[R]   since it is said, "And you will kill the woman and the beast" (Lev. 20:16),

[S]   and it says, "And the beast you will slay" (Lev. 20:15).

[T]   An ox which is to be stoned is judged by twenty-three,

[U]   since it is said, "And the ox will be stoned, and also its master will be put to death" (Ex. 21:29).

[V]   Just as [the case of the master], leading to the death penalty, [is adjudged,] so is the [case of] the ox, [leading to] the death penalty.

[W]   The wolf, lion, bear, panther, leopard, and snake—a capital case affecting them is judged by twenty-three.

[X]   R. Eliezer says, "Whoever kills them first acquires merit."

[Y]   R. Aqiba says, "Their capital case is judged by twenty-three."

[I.A]   R. Abbahu raised the question [with regard to the view of Ishmael that cases involving flogging are to be before not three judges but twenty-three, M. 1:2B], whether [the reason of Ishmael] might be that cases involving the penalty of flogging are before twenty-three judges, since there are occasions on which the convicted party may die from the flogging.

[B]   On this account, lo, there is a capital crime [under judgment, hence requiring twenty-three judges].

[II.A]   Bar Qappara derived [the Scriptural basis] for all of the [number of judges required to intercalate the year, in Simeon b. Gamaliel's opinion, M. 1:2E–F], from the following:

[B]   " 'May the Lord bless you and keep you' (Num. 6:24)—on this basis, we learn that they begin the process of intercalating the month with a court of three judges.

[C]   " 'The Lord make his face to shine upon you and be gracious to you' (Num. 6:25)—on this basis, we learn that they discuss the matter among five judges.

[D]   " 'The Lord lift up his countenance upon you and give you peace' (Num. 6:26)—on this basis, we learn that they complete the transaction with seven judges."

[E]   R. Joshua b. Levi derived [the Scriptural basis] for all of the [number of judges required to intercalate the year, in Simeon b. Gamaliel's opinion, M. 1:2E–F], from the following:

[F]   " 'And the captain of the guard took . . . the three keepers of the threshold . . . ,' (2 Kings 25:18)—on this basis, we learn that they begin with three judges.

[G]   " 'And five men of the king's council . . . ,' (2 Kings 25:19)—on this basis, we learn that they discuss the matter with five.

[H]   " 'And the captain of the guard took . . . seven men of the king's council' (Jer. 52:24–25)—on this basis, we learn that they complete the transaction with seven judges."

[I]   Said R. Jonathan, "On the following basis, we learn that the great Sanhedrin for the entire people of Israel [is made up of seventy judges]:

[J]   " 'And the captain of the guard took Seraiah, the chief priest, and Zephaniah, the second priest' (Jer. 52:24)—lo, two;

[K]   " 'and seven men of the king's council' (Jer. 52:25)—lo, nine;

[L]   'and sixty men of the people of the land' (Jer. 52:25)—lo, seventy, except for one;

[M]   " 'and from the city he took an officer' (Jer. 52:25)—lo, seventy."

[N]   Now there is a Tanna who teaches that the court is made up of seventy-one:

[O]   "And the captain of the guard took . . . the three keepers of the threshold . . ."; "and seven men of the king's council . . ."; "and sixty [18c] of the men of the people of the land" (Jer. 52:24–25); "and from the city he took an officer . . ." (Jer. 52:25)—lo, seventy-one.

[P]   Now why do they call [the officer] one who has been cut ["eunuch"]?

[Q]   For he cuts deep into the heart of the law.

[R]   We notice that one verse refers to five men of the king's council (2 Kings 25:19), and another verse refers to seven men of the king's council (Jer. 52:25).

[S]   The latter makes provision also for the scribes of the judges.

[**III**.A] [When the month is intercalated on the thirty-first day,] in fact there is no intercalation of the month [there being no proclamation to that effect, but merely] the *sanctification* of the new month.

[B] Samuel said, "The sanctification of the new month takes place in an assembly of no fewer than ten."

[C] Associates [of the court, that is, apprentice judges]—what is the law as to their being counted for the sanctification of the new month?

[D] R. Hoshaiah said, "When I was an apprentice, I came up with R. Samuel bar R. Isaac, for the sanctification of the new month, but I do not know whether [in court] I counted in the required number or not."

[E] It is self-evident that he did not count [since if he did, he would have known].

[F] What the reason was [is at issue].

[G] Is it because he was [Samuel's] son-in-law [and therefore a relative and not suited to sit on the same court]? Or is it because apprentices do not enter into the court of those required for the sanctification of the new month?

[H] Said R. Kahana, "I was an apprentice, and R. Tanhum bar Hiyya brought me up for the sanctification of the new month, and I did count toward the required number."

[I] This indicates that apprentices do enter into the count of those required for the sanctification of the new month.

[J] What is the law as to including apprentices in the count of those required for the intercalation of a new month into the year?

[K] Let us derive the answer to that question from the following.

[L] An incident happened with Rabban Gamaliel who said, "Let them call for me . . . seven elders to the upper room. But eight came in."

[M] He said, "Who is the one who came in without permission?"

[N] Samuel the Small arose and said, "I came in without permission. I had need of asking a question about a matter of law, so I came in to ask about it."

[O]   Rabban Gamaliel said to him, "Now as to Eldad and Medad, whom all Israel knows that they are two, I have said that you are one of them [and of their status, so surely you are worthy to intercalate the years]."

[P]   Nonetheless, in fact they did not intercalate the year that day. The reason is that they differed on laws connected with the right, and so they intercalated the year on the following day.

[IV.A] It was taught: A Sanhedrin which witnessed someone commit a murder—

[B]   there is a Tanna who teaches: Two serve as witnesses and give testimony before the remainder [of the court].

[C]   There is a Tanna who teaches: All of them are witnesses and give testimony before [a court made up of] others.

[D]   R. Judah bar Pazzi in the name of R. Zeira: "Just as they differ in this case, so they differ in regard to witnessing the new moon [if the entire court witnessed the new moon]."

[E]   [The reason that the latter authority rejects having the court serve as judges is that] one party may stand up [and give testimony] and take his seat, and another may do the same [so that the court in fact serves as both witness and judge].

[F]   But the present case [of witnessing the new moon] is different, for in any event a witness cannot serve as a judge.

[G]   [Parallel to these matters,] R. Huna knew evidence in the case of a certain man. The man came to judgment before R. Huna and denied [the claim of the other, even while R. Huna had evidence in behalf of that claim].

[H]   Said R. Samuel bar R. Isaac, "Since you know that R. Huna is a great man, you deny [the case concerning which he has contrary testimony].

[I]   "What is the law as to his going and giving testimony concerning you before a different court?"

[J]   Said to him R. Huna, "And do they do such a thing?"

[K]   He answered him, "Yes."

[L]   Then R. Huna exempted himself from that case and went and gave evidence [in that case] before another court.

[**V**.A]   R. Simeon b. Yohai taught, " 'And you will sanctify the fiftieth year' (Lev. 25:10). Years do you sanctify, and not months."

[B]   And have we not learned [in the following Mishnah]: *The head of the court declares, "It is sanctified"? (M. R.H. 2:7A).*

[C]   What is the meaning of "it is sanctified"? It is confirmed [without the court's declaration].

[D]   It was taught: **"For the sanctification of the month, they begin with the senior member of the court"** [= T. San. 7:2].

[E]   Said R. Hiyya bar Ada, "The Mishnah itself has said the same: *'The head of the court declares, 'It is sanctified.' "*

[F]   It was taught: For the intercalation of the year, they begin [with the opinion of] the one sitting on the side.

[G]   Said R. Zebida, "But that household below [the partiarchate] is not accustomed to do so.

[H]   Now has [that household] not heard that which R. Hiyya bar Mareh, R. Jonah, R. Ba bar Hiyya in the name of R. Yohanan, have said: "For the intercalation of the month they begin from the senior judge. For the intercalation of the year, they begin from the side"?

[I]   Now, further, R. Yohanan entered the court, and he was the youngest of all of them. They said to him, "Say, 'Lo, the year is sanctified in its intercalation.' He said, 'Lo, the year is sanctified in its intercalation.' "

[J]   Said R. Jonathan, "Notice the language which the son of the blacksmith [Yohanan] has taught us. If he had said 'in its fullness,' I should have said that the reference is to the eleven days by which the solar year is longer than the lunar year. But by saying 'in its *intercalation*,' he indicates that the sages have added thirty days to the year."

[K]   R. Jacob bar Aha, R Yasa in the name of R. Yohanan: "For purposes of intercalation, they follow the order in which judges were appointed [to the court].

[L]   "For purposes of [study in] the meetinghouse, they follow the order of those who are better able [to teach the law].

[M]   And that is the case when everyone has the power to speak in his own place and to complete [his statement in sequence after the one who spoke before him].

[N]   For instance: R. Haninah opened the discourse, R. Yohanan and R. Simeon b. Laqish completed it. R. Ba bar Zabedi opened the discourse, R. Yasa and R. Ami completed it. R. Haggai opened the discourse, R. Jonah and R. Yosé completed it."

[O]   R. Kahana was appointed [to the court] before R. Jacob bar Aha, but R. Jacob bar Aha came in before him for purposes of the vote on intercalation.

[P]   [Kahana] said, "So the master responsible for the teaching [that they follow the order in which they were appointed to the court (K)], does not carry it out?!"

[Q]   R. Hiyya bar Va was standing and saying his prayer. R. Kahana came in and stood behind him and prayed. R. Hiyya completed the prayer but could not take his seat because he did not want to pass in front of the other [who was still praying]. R Kahana began to tarry at his prayer. Once he finished, the other said to him, "Is that your (pl.) customary behavior, to cause trouble for your master?"

[R]   He said to him, "Rabbi, I come from the house of Eli, concerning whom it is written, 'Therefore I swear to the house of Eli that the iniquity of Eli's house shall not be expiated by sacrifice or offering for ever' (1 Sam. 3:14). That is to say, through sacrifice and offering it will not be expiated, but it will be expiated through prayer."

[S]   He prayed in his behalf, and the latter had the merit of living so long that his fingernails turned red like those of an infant.

[T]   They gave an old man precedence over R. Simeon b. Laqish in the intercalation of the year [who was unworthy of that privilege], and [at the end] they removed him from their gate. [Simeon] said, "Thus may be their reward [that is, it serves them right, that they put that unqualified man in before me]."

[U]   Now did they not hear that account which R. Qeripeseda told in the name of R. Yohanan:

[V]   M'SH W: Three herdsmen intercalated the year [so why did the court expel the unqualified elder?].

[W]   One of them said, "[If] the early and late sowing sprout together, [the month is Adar]."

[X]   One of them said, "[If the morning] frost is strong enough to kill an ox, but at noon the ox [lies] in the shade of the fig tree and scratches its hide, [then it is Adar. If not, it is not Adar]."

[Y]   One of them said, "[When the strong] east wind is blowing and your breath can overcome it, [it is Adar. If not, it is not Adar]."

[Z]   Now we see that, in that particular year, none of these signs was discerned, yet they intercalated the year by reason of [the herdsmen's] statements.

[AA]   Said R. Helbo, "Now did the court [actually] concur with their [decision]?

[BB]   "And did not R. Zeira say, '[And the rule that intercalation is called for] applies when all [judges] concur on a single ground [for invoking intercalation, and not for three distinct reasons]'?"

[CC]   Since each [set of signs of intercalation] coincided with the others, it was as if all of them concurred on the basis of a single ground [for the intercalation].

[DD]   [Returning to the point at which we began, namely, R. Simeon b. Laqish's pique at being excluded from the court by the presence of an unqualified person,] why is it that R. Simeon b. Laqish took umbrage at such a matter?

[EE]   He scrupled concerning that which R. Eleazar said, for R. Eleazar said, " 'My hand shall be against the prophets who see delusive visions and who give lying divinations; [they shall not be in the council of my people, nor be enrolled in the register of the house of Israel, nor shall they enter the land of Israel]' (Ez. 13:9).

[FF]   " 'They will not be in the council of my people'—this refers to intercalation.

[GG]   " 'Nor be enrolled in the register of the house of Israel'—this refers to appointment [to a court].

[HH]   " 'Nor shall they enter the land of Israel'—this refers to the Land of Israel."

[II]   R. Eleazar, when he came up here [from Babylonia to the Holy Land], he said, "Lo, I have [attained] one [of the specified rights in Ezekiel's statement]."

[JJ]   When they appointed him [to a court], he said, "Lo, I have attained the second."

[KK]   When he joined the court for the purpose of intercalation, he said, "Lo, I have attained the third."

[VI.A]   [R. Eliezer b. Sadoq says, "If the moon did not appear at its proper time, they need not declare it sanctified, since Heaven already has sanctified it" (M. R.H. 2:7)]. R. Ba bar Zabeda in the name of Rab: "The reason for the opinion of R. Eliezer b. R. Sadoq is [that] when the court above sees that the court below sanctify the month, they too sanctify it."

[B]   R. Eliezer in the name of R. Hanina: M'SH B: Twenty-four villages' [representatives], from the domain of Rabbi, came together to intercalate the year in Lud. The evil eye entered them, and all of them died on a single occasion. From that time they removed the intercalation of the year from Judah and permanently established the rite in Galilee.

[C]   They considered removing even the declaration [of the intercalation, from Judea to Galilee].

[D]   Said to them R. Simon, "Shall we then not leave in the land of Judea even a memorial [to the rite]? And lo, we find that they declared the year to be sanctified in Baalat [in Judea]."

[E]   Now as to that town of Baalat—sometimes it is included in the frontiers of Judea, and sometimes in Dan. Specifically: Alteqa, Gibaton, and Baalat, lo, they belong to Dan. Baalah, Iyyim, and Esem, lo, they belong to Judea.

[F]   Now, lo, do we not find that they sanctified the year in Baalah?

[G]   One must say, the houses are in the territory of Judea, but the fields are in the territory of Dan.

[H]   R. Jeremiah raised the question before R. Zeira, "Now is not Lud itself in the territory of Judea [so why do they have to make reference to a precedent for the rite in some other location]?"

[I]   He said to him, "Yes."

[J]   "And on what account do they not intercalate [the year] in that town of Lud?"

[K]   He said to him, "Because the people there are arrogant and ignorant of Torah."

[L] He turned around and saw [rabbis from Lud standing behind him, specifically,] R. [18d] Aha and R. Judah b. Pazzi.

[M] He said to him, "Now what have you done? You have treated rabbis discourteously."

[VII.A] On account of three signs do they intercalate the year, because of the [premature state of] the grain, because of the [condition of the] produce of the tree[s], and because of the [lateness of the spring] equinox.

[B] On account of two of these they will intercalate the year, but on account of only one of them they will not intercalate the year.

[C] But if they declared the year to be intercalated, lo, this is deemed intercalated.

[D] If the [premature state of] the grain was one of them, they would rejoice.

[E] R. Simeon b. Gamaliel says, "Also on account of the [lateness of the spring] equinox" [T. San. 2:2].

[F] On account of [evidence of conditions in] three regions do they intercalate the year: Judea, TransJordan, and Galilee.

[G] On account of [evidence produced in] two of them they intercalate the year, but on account of [evidence deriving from only] one of them they do not intercalate the year.

[H] But if they declared the year to be intercalated, lo, this is [Y.: not] deemed intercalated.

[I] And if the land of Judea was one of the two regions, they would rejoice,

[J] because of the first fruits of grain which would [have to] come from there [for the altar] [T. San. 2:3].

[K] They do not intercalate the year by reason of cold or rain, and if they did intercalate the year on such an account, lo, it is not intercalated.

[L] They do not intercalate the year because [the season of the] kids, lambs, or pigeons has not yet come, or because of the condition of the sucking lamb.

[M] But in the case of all of them, they regard it as a support [for intercalating] the year.

[N]   But if they declared the year to be intercalated [on the basis of their condition], lo, this is deemed intercalated [T. San. 2:4].

[O]   R. Yannai says in the name of R. [Simeon b.] Gamaliel who said [in Aramaic], "The pigeons are tender and the spring lambs thin,

[P]   "and it is proper in my view [and in that of my colleagues], so I have added thirty days to this year" [T. San. 2:5].

[Q]   It was taught, R. Judah said: MᶜSH B: Rabban Gamaliel and sages were in session on the steps of the Temple.

[R]   And Yohanan, that scribe, was before them.

[S]   Rabban Gamaliel said to [Yohanan], "Write:

[T]   "[In Aramaic:] 'To our brethren, residents of the upper south and residents of the lower south, May your peace increase! We inform you that the time for the removal has come, to set apart the tithes from the sheaves of grain.'

[U]   "[In Aramaic:] 'To our brethren, residents of Upper Galilee and residents of Lower Galilee, May your peace increase! I inform you that the time for the removal has come, to set apart the tithes from the olive vats.'

[V]   "[In Aramaic:] 'To our brethren, residents of the Exile of Babylonia, and residents of the Exile of Media, and of all the other Exiles of Israel, May your peace increase! We inform you that the pigeons are still tender, the lambs are thin, and the springtide has not yet come. So, as it is proper in my view and in the view of my colleagues, we have added thirty days to this year' " [T. San. 2:6].

[W]   They intercalate the year only if the equinox is distant by the better part of a month.

[X]   And how much is the better part of a month? Sixteen days.

[Y]   R. Judah says, "Two thirds of a month, twenty-one days" [T. San. 2:7].

[Z]   Said R. Samuel bar Nahman, "[The opinion stated at W–X] applies if the ᶜomer [of new grain] is offered on the end of Nisan [that is, within Nisan] in which the day marking the passage of the seasons falls."

[AA]   Said R. Yosé, "Up to Passover. [The cited authority requires that the day marking the conclusion of the previous season be before Passover.]"

[BB]   Said R. Mattenaiah [with regard to R. Judah's opinion, Y, above],"And [Judah's rule] applies if one should take up the *lulab* [in celebration of Tabernacles] by the end of Tishré in which the day marking the passage of the seasons falls."

[CC]   **They do not intercalate the year by less than a month or by more than a month.**

[DD]   **And if they intercalated it [by less or by more than a month], it is not deemed to have been intercalated [T. San. 2:8].**

[EE]   **They do not intercalate the year either in the case of the Seventh Year or in the case of the year after the Seventh Year. And if they did so, lo, this is intercalated.**

[FF]   **When are they accustomed to intercalate the year? In the year before the Seventh Year [T. San. 2:9].**

[GG]   Said R. Zeira in the name of R. Abbahu, "This statement which has been made [that they do not intercalate the year in the Seventh Year] applies to the case before Rabbi permitted purchasing vegetables from abroad for use in the land. But once Rabbi had permitted purchasing vegetables from abroad for use in the land, there was no longer any difference between the Seventh Year and the other years of the septennate."

[HH]   [As to the statement, T. San. 2:9, that they do not intercalate the year in a time of famine,] **R. Meir says, "Lo, Scripture says, 'And there came a man from Baal Shalisha, and he brought the man of God bread of the first fruits, twenty loaves of barley, and fresh ears of corn in his sack' (2 Kings 4:42). [And is it not so that there is no place in which the produce ripens earlier in the land of Israel than in Baal Shalisha? And even so, only that species which he had brought to the man of God had ripened. Is it possible that he brought it before the 'omer had been offered (the sixteenth of Nisan, so allowing the consumption of the new year for the first time)? Scripture says, 'And he said, Give to the people, so that they may eat' (2 Kings 4:43).] So it follows that the year was suitable for intercalation.**

[II]   **"Now why did Elisha not intercalate it?**

[JJ]   "Because it was a year of famine, and the whole people was running around to the threshing floors" [T. San. 2:9].

[KK]   There is a Tanna who teaches, They do not intercalate the year when there is uncleanness.

[LL]   R. Yosé says, "They do so. For so we find that Hezekiah the King intercalated the year when there was uncleanness, for it it said, 'For a multitude of the people, even the men of Ephraim and Manasseh, Issachar and Zebulun, had not cleaned themselves, yet they ate the Passover otherwise than it is written. For Hezekiah prayed for them, saying, The good Lord pardon every one' (2 Chron. 30:18)" [T. San. 2:10].

[MM]   R. Simeon says, "Even though they intercalated the month of Nisan, treated as intercalated is only the month of Adar. [That is, they do intercalate by reason of uncleanness, but this is done only in Adar.]"

[NN]   R. Simeon b. Judah says in the name of R. Simeon, "Hezekiah made the congregation celebrate a second Passover" [T. San. 2:11].

[OO]   There is a Tanna who teaches: "They do intercalate the year because of uncleanness."

[PP]   There is a Tanna who teaches: "They do not intercalate the year [on that account]."

[QQ]   Now the one who says that they do not intercalate the year [on that account] derives proof for his position from [the cited verse]. "They ate the Passover not in accordance with what is written." [So Hezekiah prayed for forgiveness, because he had intercalated the year by reason of uncleanness.]

[RR]   And the one who says that they do intercalate the year [on account of uncleanness]—how does he interpret [the cited verse], "Not in accordance with what is written"? [Hezekiah prayed for forgiveness] because he had intercalated the year in Nisan, and they intercalate the year only in Adar.

[SS]   Now this view [that the year was intercalated by reason of uncleanness affecting the people prior to Passover] accords with that which R. Simon bar Zebid said, "The skull of Arnon the Jebusite they found beneath the altar [of the Temple]."

[TT]   "[For Hezekiah had prayed for them, saying, 'The good Lord pardon every one who] sets his heart to seek God, [the Lord the God of his fathers, even though not according to the sanctuary's rules of cleanness]' " (2 Chron. 30:18–19)—and to do and to teach in Israel ordinances and judgments.

[UU]   [Now what is the meaning of this reference to "not according to the sanctuary's rules of cleanness"?] R. Simon bar Zebid and R. Samuel bar Nahman—

[VV]   one said, "Even though he carried out any number [of deeds] for the sake of the cleanness of Holy Things, he did not fully carry out what is required for the cleanness of Holy Things."

[WW]   And the other said, "Even all those many good deeds which people do for the sake of the cleanness of Holy Things—one does not thereby carry out the obligation involved in attaining the cleanness of Holy Things."

[XX]   It is written, "They began to sanctify on the first day of the first month, and on the eighth day of the month they came to the vestibule of the Lord; then for eight days they sanctified the house of the Lord, and on the sixteenth day of the first month they finished" (2 Chron. 29:17).

[YY]   Now is it not so that in a single day they were able to burn every idol which was there, [so why did it take so many days to clean and sanctify the Temple]?

[ZZ]   Said R. Idi, "Because of the Chaldean idols which had been engraved with vermilion."

[AAA]   Six things did King Hezekiah do. In three of them [sages] agreed with him, and in three of them they did not agree with him.

[BBB]   He dragged his father's bones on a rope bier, he pulverized the brazen serpent, and he hid away the notebook of remedies and they agreed with him.

[CCC]   He closed off the waters of Upper Gihon, he cut [the gold off] the doors of the Temple, and he intercalated the month of Nisan in Nisan itself [calling Nisan the second Adar after Nisan had already begun], and they did not agree with what he had done.

[VIII.A]   **They do not intercalate the year prior to the New Year, and if they did so, the year is not deemed intercalated.**

[B]   But if it is a matter of urgency [e.g., because people fear they will not be able to do so later], they do intercalate the year immediately after New Year.

[C]   Nonetheless, intercalated is only the month of Adar [T. San. 2:7].

[D]   Rabbi says, "Nisan has never been intercalated [that is, the new moon of Nisan has never been designated on the thirty-first day of Adar]."

[E]   And have not we learned:

[F]   [How so for the heave offering of *sheqels?*

[G]   All public offerings are offered on the first of Nisan.]

[H]   If the new *[sheqels]* come on time, [(the public offerings) are offered (from beasts purchased from) the new (heave offering of the *sheqels*)].

[I]   And if not, they are offered (from beasts purchased) from the old (heave offering of the *sheqels*)] [T. R.H. 1:4 = T. Sheq. 2:7]. [The point is that the money for the purchase of the public offerings on the first of Nisan should come from newly contributed funds. Now if the new funds come in on time, they are used. The assumption then is that the money comes in on the thirtieth day, in which case that money is used for beasts to be offered on the next day. If they intercalated the month and treated the new moon of Nisan as the thirty-first day of Adar, the daily whole offering of that date would come from the newly contributed funds. If not, they would use the funds contributed in the prior year. What this set of rules indicates in any event is that there are occasions on which the new moon of Nisan will be celebrated on the thirty-first of Adar, and this is stated as, "If . . ."]

[J]   [But that proves nothing. For it says,] "If it should come . . ." But it never came in that way.

[K]   Rab said, "Tishré has never been intercalated [that is, beginning on the thirty-first day of Elul]."

[L]   And have we not learned: *[If a man slaughtered a heifer and divided it among purchasers on the first day of the eighth year,] if the month was intercalated, [the debt incurred by them who buy the meat is canceled; but if the month was not intercalated, it is not canceled (M. Sheb. 10:2)]*. [As above, I, this would indicate that it is possible that Tishré indeed was intercalated.]

[M]   [But that proves nothing. For it says,] "If it should come . . ." But it never came in that way.

[N]   **Now when they sanctified the year in Usha, on the first day R. Ishmael b. R. Yohanan b. Beroqah passed [before the ark] and said it in accord with the view of R. Yohanan b. Nuri.**

[O]   **Said Rabban Simeon b. Gamaliel, "That was not the custom which we followed in Yabneh."**

[P]   **On the second day R. Hanina, son of R. Yosé the Galilean, passed [before the ark] and said the prayer in accordance with the opinion of R. Aqiba.**

[Q.]   **Then said Rabban Simeon b. Gamaliel, "Now *that* was the custom which we followed in Yabneh!" [T. R.H. 2:11].**

[R]   Now thus it is taught that they declared [the day] holy on the first and on the second [and this calls into question Rab's statement that Tishré has never been intercalated].

[S]   R. Zeira in the name of R. Hisdai: "That year things were miscalculated."

[T]   What is the meaning of "in the first . . . ," and "in the second . . ."?

[U]   Raba in the name of Rab: "In the first year, in the second year."

[V]   And has it not been taught: **They declared it sanctified on the first day . . . on the second; day . . .?** [So the above answer is impossible.]

[**IX**.A] [If the court] declared the month to be sanctified before its proper time or after its intercalation, is it possible that the month should be deemed sanctified?

[B]   Scripture states, "[The appointed feasts of the Lord] *which* [you shall proclaim as holy convocations, my appointed feasts, are these]" (Lev. 23:2).

[C]   That is, *these* are my appointed feasts, these others are not my appointed feasts. [So if one has sanctified the new month] prior to its proper time, on the twenty-ninth day, or after its intercalation, on the thirty-second day of the month, [it is not sanctified].

[D] Now how do we know that they in any event intercalate the year on account of those who dwell in Exile but have not yet reached their homes and so cannot carry out the Passover at the right time]?

[E] Scripture states, "Say to the people of Israel, The appointed feasts [of the Lord which you shall proclaim as holy convocations]" (Lev. 23:2)—

[F] that is to say, "Declare appointed feasts in such a way that all Israelites may carry them out."

[G] Said R. Samuel bar Nahman, "And that is so that the Israelites may reach the Euphrates River [en route home]."

[X.A] **They intercalate the year only in Judah,**

[B] **and if they intercalated it [in Galilee], lo, it is deemed to have been intercalated.**

[C] **Hananiah of [19a] Ono gave testimony [before Rabban Gamaliel] that if they cannot intercalate the year in Judah, they intercalate the year in Galilee, and it is deemed to have been intercalated [T. San. 2:13].**

[D] They do not intercalate the year abroad, and if they did so, it is not intercalated.

[E] Now you see that in Galilee they do not intercalate. So that they intercalate abroad [hardly seems likely].

[F] [The point is this]: In Galilee they do not intercalate the year. And if they did so, it indeed is intercalated. Abroad they do not intercalate, and if they did so, it is *not* intercalated.

[G] [This rule applies] when they are able to intercalate in the Land of Israel.

[H] But if they are not able to intercalate in the Land of Israel, then they do intercalate the year abroad.

[I] Jeremiah intercalated the year abroad. Ezekiel intercalated the year abroad. Baruch b. Neriah intercalated the year abroad. Hananiah, nephew of R. Joshua, intercalated the year abroad.

[J] Rabbi sent him three letters with R. Isaac and R. Nathan.

[K] In one he wrote, "To his holiness, Hananiah."

[L] And in one he wrote, "The lambs that you have left behind have become rams."

[M] And in one he wrote, "If you do not accept our authority, go out to the thorny wilderness, and there you be the slaughterer [of the sacrifice], with Nehunyon, the sprinkler [of blood upon the altar]."

[N] He read the first and did obeisance, the second and did likewise. But when he read the third, he wanted to disgrace the messengers.

[O] They said to him, "You cannot, for you have already treated us with honor."

[P] R. Isaac stood up and read in the Torah, "These are the festivals of Hananiah, the nephew of R. Joshua."

[Q] He said, " 'These are the festivals of the Lord' (Lev 23:4) [is what is written]."

[R] He replied, "They are with us, [and your calendar is not legitimate, because you have intercalated abroad, and that is not to be done]."

[S] R. Nathan arose and read in the prophetic passage, "For from Babylonia will Torah go forth, and the word of the Lord from Nehar Peqod."

[T] They said to him, "[It is written,] 'For from Zion will Torah go forth, and the word of the Lord from Jerusalem' " (Is. 2:3).

[U] He said to them, "[The Torah is] with us. [Your decrees are not authoritative.]"

[V] [Hananiah] went and complained about them to R. Judah b. Batera in Nisibis. He said to them, " 'After them . . . after them . . .' [meaning, one must accept the authority of the majority]."

[W] He said to him, "Do I not know what is over there? What tells me that they are masters of calculating [the calendar] like me? Since they are not so well informed as I am in calculating the calendar, let them listen to what I say."

[X] [He replied,] "And since they [now] are masters of calculation as much as you, you must listen to them."

[Y]   He rose up and mounted his horse.

[Z]   Places which he reached, he reached, [and there he retracted his intercalation,] and the ones he did not reach observed the holy days in error.

[AA]   It is written, "[These are the words of the letter which Jeremiah the prophet sent from Jerusalem] to the rest of the elders of the exiles" (Jer. 29:1).

[BB]   Said the Holy One, blessed be He, "The elders of the exile are most valuable to me. [Yet] more beloved to me is the smallest circle which is located in the Land of Israel, more than a great Sanhedrin located outside of the land."

[CC]   It is written, ". . . and the craftsmen and the smiths, one thousand" (2 Kings 24:16)—and you say this! [Namely, how can you say that the smallest circle in the Land is more beloved than the important Sanhedrin abroad? The craftsmen and smiths are assumed to be disciples of sages, and they are many and important in Babylonia.]

[DD]   R. Berekhiah in the name of R. Helbo and rabbis:

[EE]   R. Berekhiah in the name of R. Helbo said, "The craftsmen were one thousand, and the smiths one thousand in number."

[FF]   And rabbis say, "All of them together added up to a thousand."

[GG]   R. Berekhiah in the name of Rabbi: "These are apprentices [to the courts]."

[HH]   And rabbis say, "They are councillors."

[XI.A]   R. Hoshaiah, when he would receive testimony [concerning the new moon] would do so very graciously. He would say to them, "You must realize how important is the testimony which you provide, how great a sum of money for rental of houses depends on your evidence."

[B]   Said R. Abuna, "And if so, then even capital cases [depend on the testimony of the witnesses to the new moon].

[C]   "[For example:] In the case of a girl three years and one day old, if someone has sexual relations with her [if she is betrothed], lo, this one is subject to the death penalty by stoning. But if the court should decide to intercalate the month, and such a one should have sexual relationships with the same girl [now not yet three years and one day old], he is not subject to the death penalty by stoning."

[D]   Said R. Abin, " 'I cry to God Most High, to God who fulfills his purpose for me' (Ps. 57:2). As to a girl three years and one day old, if the court decides to intercalate [the month or the year], the signs of virginity return, and if not, the signs of virginity do not return."

[XII.A]   *"The laying of hands [on a community sacrifice] by elders and the breaking of the heifer's neck are done by three judges," the words of R. Simeon. R. Judah says, "By five" [M. San. 1:2G–H].*

[B]   What is the Scriptural basis for the opinion of R. Simeon? [Scripture specifies,]

[C]   "And [the elders] shall lay on hands . . ." (Lev. 4:15). So there are two [elders], and since there cannot be a court with an even number of judges, they add to their number one more, lo, three.

[D]   What is the Scriptural basis for the position of R. Judah?

[E]   "And (they) shall lay hands . . ."—two.

[F]   ". . . the elders . . ."—two.

[G]   There cannot be a court with an even number of judges, so they add one more to their number, lo, five in all.

[H]   Now with reference to the heifer whose neck is broken, what is the Scriptural basis for the position of R. Judah?

[I]   [". . . then your elders and your judges shall come forth . . ." (Deut. 21:2).]

[J]   "Your elders" are two, and "your judges" are two, and there cannot be a court with an even number of judges, so they add one more to their number, lo, five in all.

[K]   And what is the Scriptural basis for the position of R. Simeon?

[L]   "Your elders and your judges" are two, and there cannot be a court with an even number of judges, so they add to their number yet one more, lo, three.

[M]   Said Rabbi, "The opinion of R. Judah appears preferable in the case of the heifer whose neck is broken, for he does not effect an exegesis for 'And they shall go forth . . .' And the opinion of R. Simeon appears preferable in the case of laying hands on a sacrificial beast, for he does not effect an exegesis for '. . . and (they) 'shall lay hands . . .' "

[N]   If you say that the position of R. Judah is preferable in the case of the heifer whose neck is broken, then, just as he effects an exegesis for ". . . and they will lay hands . . . ," let him effect an exegesis for ". . . and they will go forth"

[O]   Then it will turn out that you will say, "And they will go forth . . ."—two. "Your elders . . . ," two, and "your judges . . . ," two. There cannot be a court with an even number of judges, so they add one more—lo, seven in all.

[P]   How does R. Simeon interpret the language, "Your elders . . . and your judges . . ."?

[Q]   This refers to "your elders" who also are your judges.

[R]   It was taught: R. Eliezer b. Jacob said, " 'Your elders'—this refers to the high court. 'And your judges . . .'—this refers to the king and high priest."

[XIII.A]   It was taught: Ordination (SMYKWT) requires three judges.

[B]   Is not laying on of hands (SMYKH) the same as ordination (SMYKWT)?

[C]   There [in Babylon] they call appointment to a court "ordination."

[D]   Said R. Ba, "At first each one would appoint his own disciples [to the court]. For example, R. Yohanan b. Zakkai appointed R. Eliezer and R. Joshua; R. Joshua appointed R. Aqiba; and R. Aqiba, R. Meir and R. Simeon."

[E]   He said, "Let R. Meir take his seat first."

[F]   R. Simeon's face turned pale.

[G]   R. Aqiba said to him, "Let it be enough for you that I and your Creator recognize your powers."

[XIV.A]   They went and paid honor to "this house" [the patriarchate].

[B]   They made the rule, "A court which made an appointment without the knowledge and consent of the patriarch—the act of appointment is null.

[C]   "And a patriarch who made an appointment without the knowledge and consent of the court—his appointment is valid."

[D]   They reverted and made the rule that the court should make an appointment only with the knowledge and consent of the patriarch, and that the patriarch should make an appointment only with the knowledge and consent of the court.

[XV.A]   [With regard to M. 1:2I,] it was taught: **At first they would write a deed of ḥaliṣah: In session of Mr. So-and-so and Mr. Such-and-such, Mrs. So-and-so, daughter of Mr. So-and-so, carried out the rite of ḥaliṣah with Mr. So-and-so, son of Mr. So-and-so, in our presence. She came before us, removed his sandle from his right foot, spat before him a drop of spit which could be seen by us on the ground, and stated, "Thus will it be done to the man who does not build the house of his brother"** Deut. 25:9) [= T. Yeb. 12:15].

[B]   [With regard to M. 1:2I,] it was taught: **At first they would write a document of the exercise of the right of refusal: In the presence of Mr. So-and-so and Mr. Such-and-such, Mrs. So-and-so, daughter of Mr. So-and-so, effected the right of refusal of Mr. So-and-so, son of Mr. So-and-so. In our presence [she stated], "I do not want him. I will not stay with him. I do not want to be married to him"** [= T. Yeb. 13:1].

[XVI.A]   [With regard to M. San. 1:2J, K,] said R. Yohanan: "A consecrated item which one had redeemed for more than its true value—lo, this is redeemed. But produce in the status of second tithe which one has redeemed for more than its true value—lo, this is not redeemed."

[B]   What is the difference between that which has been consecrated and produce in the status of second tithe?

[C]   Said R. La, "For that which has been consecrated, there is a demand, while for produce in the status of second tithe, there is no demand."

[D]   R. Jonah raised the question, "This reason is valid from the viewpoint of one who said that it is not in the status of the man's property. But in accord with the opinion of the one who says, 'It is indeed in the status of the man's property,' what is the difference between that which has been consecrated and that produce in the status of a second tithe?"

[E]   Said R. Yosé, "Now has the answer not been given already: 'For that which has been consecrated there is a demand, while for produce in the status of second tithe there is no demand'!"

[F]   R. Zeira raised the question before R. Ami, "If we should examine that man, if he should say, 'That was not my intent,' what is the law?"

[G]   He said to him, "When he is examined, [we accept what he says, but if he is not examined, we invoke the stated criterion]."

[H]   Said R. Yohanan, "A consecrated object which one has redeemed, and for which one did not add the required added fifth—lo, this is deemed redeemed. But as to produce in the status of second tithe which one redeemed and for which one did not add the added fifth, lo, it is not deemed to have been redeemed."

[I]   What is the difference between produce in the status of second tithe and a consecrated object?

[J]   Said R. La, "For it is common for a man to be generous about things which he has consecrated."

[K]   R. Jonah raised the question: "Now that answer is from the viewpoint of the one who said that it is not in the status of the man's own property. But in accord with the one who said that it is in the status of one's own property, what is the difference between a consecrated object and second tithe?" [That is to say, if one says that second tithe belongs to the Most High, then on that account the man did not add the fifth, so as not to increase the amount of funds which must be spent in Jerusalem. But if one says that the produce in the status of second tithe, belongs to the farmer, why should he not add the money? Whatever he gave is for the sake of redeeming the produce. The answer is the same:]

[L]   Said R. Yosé, "Now have you not already stated a reason, that it is common for a man to be generous about things which he has consecrated?"

[XVII.A]   [Assessment of the value [19b] for purposes of redemption] of things which have been consecrated is done before three judges (M. San. 1:2K). [Property pledged as security for vows of valuation, in the case of movables, is evaluated by three judges. . . . And in the case of real estate it is done by nine and a *priest (M. San. 1:2L–N). Note also M. Meg. 4:3J–K: And in the case of assessing the value for redemption of dedicated immovable property, the assessment is made by nine and a priest; in the case of the valuation vow of man, the law is the same.]*

[B]   [Following the text supplied by PM:] This rule [that we require for immovable property nine and a priest] applies when one has consecrated his field itself.

[C]   But if one has said, "The *value* of my field is incumbent upon me," what is the law? [Do we invoke the analogy of the law covering valuations of movables, on the basis of his dedicating funds? Or do we deem the language to encumber actual real estate which must be assessed?]

[D]   Let us derive the law from the following: *[Property pledged as security for] vows of valuation, in the case of movables, is evaluated by three judges (M. San. 1:2L).*

[E]   Now, by definition, is there such a thing as valuation vows which do not cover movables? [Obviously not, since those vows, by definition, cover persons or movables. So the stated language covers a statement such as, "The value of my field is incumbent upon me."]

[F]   R. Jacob bar Aha, R. Simeon bar Va in the name of R. Haninah: "He who says, 'My valuation is incumbent upon me,' and one came to arrange for his [payment]: If from real estate— they assess the value in a court of ten. But if the valuation is to be paid from movables, it is with a court of three."

[G]   [From the foregoing statement, we draw the following inference:] He who says, "My valuation is incumbent on me" is not in the status of him who says, "The valuation of my field is incumbent on me."

[H]   But if he said, "Lo, incumbent on me is a *maneh* for the sanctuary," they assess [whatever he presents in payment] in a court of three.

[I]   But if he should get rich, they assess him for all he can pay.

[**XVIII**.A] It was taught: Slaves, bonds, and movables are not subject to a deed of inspection [issued by a court announcing the sale of these items in order to attract bidders and so discover an exact market value for such items. Such a deed is issued to provide advance notice of the forthcoming auction, thirty days for

property accruing to orphans, sixty days for property accruing
to the sanctuary. But no such deed is announced in the stated
types of property].

[B]   R. Judah b. Pazzi said, "It is an announcement."

[C]   [The reason that these three items are not publicly advertised
prior to auction,] Ulla bar Ishmael said, "is this: In the case of
slaves, that they not flee; in the cases of bonds and movables,
that they not be stolen [under the pretext of advance
inspection]."

[D]   R. Ba bar Kahana raised the question before R. Yosé: "Does
this rule not imply that slaves are to be redeemed by the assessment of three judges [for slaves are in the status of movables in
general, so that slaves will not hear they are to be sold, and so
flee]?"

[E]   He said to him, "Yes."

[F]   [He said to him,] "And yet we have learned: *Immovable property is assessed by nine and a priest, and in the case of . . .
man, the law is the same* (M. San. 1:2N–O; M. Meg. 4:3J–K).
[So ten, not three, are required.]"

[G]   He said to him, "But here the reference is to a free man [who
is subject to valuation, and not to a slave. A slave will be evaluated by three]."

[H]   [With reference to M. Ket. 11:5A–B, *If the estimate of the
value made by judges was a sixth too little or a sixth too much,
their act of sale is void. Rabban Simeon b. Gamaliel says,
"Their act of sale is confirmed . . . ,"*] Hananiah bar Shelameh
said in the name of Rab. "A case came before Rabbi, and he
considered applying the law in accord with the position of
rabbis.

[I]   "Said to him R. Eleazar b. Parta, son of the son of R. Eleazar
b. Parta, 'Rabbi! Did you not teach us in the name of your
forefathers, *But if they issued a deed of inspection, [the sale is
valid]*? [That is, Rabbi's forefather, Simeon b. Gamaliel, took
the position that whether or not there is a deed of inspection,
the sale is valid. Rabbis' position, then, is as stated.]'

[J]   "He said to him, 'Yes.'

[K]   "And he retracted and decided the case in accord with the position of R. [Simeon b.] Gamaliel."

[**XIX**.A] *Cases involving the death penalty are judged before twenty-three judges [M. San. 1:2P].*

[B] R. Abbahu asked, "As to an ox which is to be stoned, in accord with the opinion of R. Meir [who assesses with a court of three judges penalties involving fines], should the monetary fine be imposed by a court of three judges, but a decision as to stoning by a court of twenty-three judges [in line with M. 1:1.**VII**]?"

[C] Said to him R. Yosé b. R. Bun, "A case of an ox on trial for stoning is wholly a case involving monetary damages. But it is Scripture's decree that the ox should be stoned."

[D] Agentos the *hegemon* asked R. Yohanan b. Zakkai, " 'The ox will be stoned, and also its master will die' (Ex. 21:29)—[what has the ox done to be liable to the death penalty]?"

[E] He said to him, "The accomplice of a brigand is like a brigand [and also culpable]."

[F] When he had left, his disciples said to him, "Rabbi, this one you drove away with a mere reed. But what have you got to say to us?"

[G] He said to them, "It is written, 'The ox will be stoned, and also its master will die.' The death of the ox must be like the death of the master, for the death of the master is tied to the death of the ox.

[H] "Just as the master is tried by a process of careful investigation of the testimony against him and in a court of twenty-three judges, so the death of the ox will come about through a trial characterized by careful investigation of the testimony against the ox and in a court of twenty-three judges."

This long passage of Talmud, serving an equally long passage of the Mishnah, presents little analysis. It is an anthology of materials, only tangentially relevant for the most part. Where what is in the Talmud is not relevant to the Mishnah, it is joined to a passage which intersects with a topic mentioned in the Talmud, particularly the matter of intercalation. The anthology provides supplementary information, appropriate to the character of the Mishnah pericope, which itself is essentially a compilation of facts. Unit **II** provides a Scriptural pretext for

Mishnah's law. Unit **III** begins with the clarification of the
Mishnah's language and proceeds to supplement the Mishnah's
information by determining who may participate in the decision
on the intercalation of the month or year. It is at this point that
the vast essay on intercalation takes over. Unit **IV** is relevant
because of **IV.D**, and unit **V** carries forward that same topic.
Unit **VI** presents yet another repertoire of sayings and stories
on the intercalation of the month, and, as we see, unit **VII** is a
set piece of Toseftan materials, a rich essay on intercalating the
year, intersecting only in its fundamental topic with what is at
Mishnah. Units **VIII, IX, X,** and **XI** follow suit, although, as
we see, unit **X** moves in a direction suggested by its own materials, in no way relevant to Mishnah. Only at unit **XII** do we
revert to the wider range of Mishnah's materials, as indicated.
Unit **XII** is a familiar kind of exercise; unit **XIII** is merely informative. Since the issue of ordination is not included in Mishnah at all, **XIII** and **XIV** are joined because "laying on of
hands" on sacrificial beasts, to which Mishnah does refer, calls
to mind "laying on of hands" on candidates for judgeships, to
which it does not. In the end, therefore, **XV, XVI, XVII**
(drawing in its wake **XVIII**), and **XIX** present the sole truly
systematic exegeses of Mishnah. Most of what is in the Talmud
for the present Mishnah can have appeared in entirely other
contexts. Only the opening and closing sections may truly be
deemed Talmud for the present Mishnah pericope in particular. The rest of the units present set-piece materials, fully complete along lines of their own interests, and inserted whole; all
of them, in any event, present facts, not analyses.

1:3

[A]   *They judge a tribe, a false prophet [Deut. 18:20], and a high
priest, only on the instructions of a court of seventy-one
members.*

[B]   *They bring forth [the army] to wage an optional war only on
the instructions of a court of seventy-one.*

[C]   *They make additions to the city [of Jerusalem] and to the courtyards [of the Temple] only on the instructions of a court of seventy-one.*

[D]   *They set up Sanhedrins for the tribes only on the instructions of a court of seventy-one.*

[E]   *They declare a city to be "an apostate city" [Deut. 13:12ff.] only on the instructions of a court of seventy-one.*

[F]   *And they·do not declare a city to be "an apostate city" on the frontier,*

[G]   *[nor do they declare] three [in one locale] to be apostate cities,*

[H]   *but they do so in the case of one or two.*

[I.A]   One should take note of the following: two individuals [namely, the false prophet and the high priest] are not judged [by an ordinary court]. Is it not an argument *a fortiori* that an entire tribe [should not be judged by an ordinary court, but only by one of seventy-one members]?

[B]   Said R. Mattenaiah, "The Mishnah pericope refers to the patriarch of a tribe [and not a whole tribe, for that is an obvious fact]. [The point is that the patriarch of a tribe is judged only by a Sanhedrin with seventy-one members.]"

[C]   Said R. Eliezer, "The Mishnah speaks of a tract of forest between the territory of two tribes [and makes the point that, if there is a suit involving such territory, then even though it is a property case, it is settled by a court of seventy-one, just as, to begin with, the Land was divided up in accord with the instructions of such a court]."

[II.A]   Said R. Zira, " 'Presumptuously' ["The man who acts presumptuously, by not obeying the priest . . . shall die" (Deut. 17:12)] is stated in one context, and 'presumptuously' ["But the prophet who presumes to speak a word in my name which I have not commanded him to speak, . . . the prophet has spoken it presumptuously . . ." (Deut. 18:20, 22)] is stated in another context.

[B]   "Just as in the reference to presumptuousness in the latter passage Scripture speaks of a false prophet, so in the reference to presumptuousness in the former passage, Scripture speaks of a false prophet."

[C]   Said R. Hezekiah, " 'Speaking' is mentioned in the one context ["According to the instructions which they give you, and according to the decision which they pronounce to you, you shall do" (Deut. 17:11)], and later on it is stated, '. . . when a prophet speaks in the name of the Lord . . .' (Deut. 18:22).

[D] "Just as in the latter usage Scripture speaks of a false prophet, so in the former instance, the same usage indicates that Scripture speaks of a false prophet."

[**III**.A] *They bring forth the army to wage an optional war only on the instructions of a court of seventy-one (M. San. 1:3B). [They make additions to the city . . . only on the instruction of a court of seventy-one (M. San. 1:3C).] [The following serves M. Sheb. 2:2B–F: They add to the city and courtyards only on the instructions of the king and prophet, the Urim and Thummim, and the Sanhedrin of seventy-one members, with two thank offerings and singing. The court goes along with the two thank offerings behind them, and all the Israelites after them. The one offered inside is eaten, and the one offered outside is burned. And any area which is not treated wholly in this way (with the proper rites)—he who enters that area—they are not liable on that account.]*

[B] R. Judah says, "At the outset [of designating the holy ground of Jerusalem], 'So David went up at Gad's word' (2 Sam. 24:19)—thus the king and prophet [of M. Sheb. 2:2].

[C] " 'Then Solomon began to build the house of the Lord in Jerusalem on Mount Moriah, where the Lord had appeared [to David his father]' (2 Chron. 3:1)—thus the Urim and Thummim.

[D] " 'To David, his father'—this refers to the Sanhedrin.

[E] " 'Ask your father, and he will show you your elders, and they will tell you' (Deut. 32:7)—[this refers to consecrating the new territory] with song.

[F] " 'And after them went Hoshaiah and half of the princes of Judah' (Neh. 12:32)—[this refers to the requirement of bringing] thank offerings."

[G] "And I appointed two great companies which gave thanks and went in procession. One went to the right upon the wall to the Dung Gate" (Neh. 12:31).

[H] Said R. Samuel bar Yudan, "Why is it written, 'moved in procession' (MHLKWT), not 'walked in procession'

(THLWKWT)? The meaning is that the thank offerings were carried by another person [and did not go on foot]."

[I]   R. Huna bar Hiyya in the name of Rab derived from the Torah itself [proof that the king, prophet, Urim and Thummim, and Sanhedrin are required to add to the city]: "According to all that I show you concerning the pattern of the tabernacle, and of all its furniture, so you shall make it" (Ex. 25:9).

[J]   "Thus you shall make it"—for generations to come.

[K]   "Moses stands for the king and prophet.

[L]   "And Aaron stands for the Urim and Thummim.

[M]   " 'And the Lord said to Moses, Gather for me seventy men of the elders of Israel' (Num. 11:16)—this refers to the Sanhedrin.

[N]   " 'Ask your father and he will show you your elders, and they will tell you' (Deut. 32:7)—[this refers to consecrating the new territory] with song.

[O]   " 'And after them went Hoshaiah and half of the princes of Judah' (Neh. 12:32)—[this refers to the requirement of bringing] thank offerings.

[P]   " 'And I appointed two great companies which gave thanks and went in procession. One went to the right upon the wall to the Dung Gate' (Neh. 12:31)."

[Q]   Said R. Samuel bar Yudan, "Why is it written, 'moved in procession' and not, 'walked in procession'? The meaning is that the thank offerings were carried by another person [and did not go on foot]."

[R]   How were they borne?

[S]   R. Hiyya the Elder and R. Simeon bar R. Rabbi—one said, "One opposite the other," and the other said, "One behind another."

[T]   Both of them interpret the same biblical verse: "The other company of those who gave thanks went to the left [lmw'l, (lmwl)] and I followed them" (Neh. 12:38).

[U]   The one who says they came opposite one another [cites as evidence]: "They are dwelling opposite me" [mmwly] (Num. 22:5).

[V]   The one who says they came one after another [cites as evidence]: "He shall wring its head from behind its neck [*mmwl*]" (Lev. 5:8).

[W]   The one who says that they came toward one another maintains that it so happened that every place was atoned for with a single thank offering.

[X]   The one who said they came one after the other maintains that it turned out that every place was atoned for through two thank offerings.

[Y]   The one who maintains that they came one after the other finds no difficulty in that which we have learned: **The inner one [nearest the court] is eaten, and the outer one is burned [T. San. 3:4E].**

[Z]   But the one who maintains that they came toward one another—which of the two thank offerings will be the inner one?

[AA]   It is the one which is the nearer to the house [the Temple].

[BB]   R. Yasa in the name of R. Yohanan: "At the instruction of a prophet is the thank offering [offered on the occasion of the consecration of the city] to be eaten.

[CC]   Said R. Zira, "There we learn: 'If the prophet is here, then what need have I for the Urim and Thummim?' "

[DD]   He found it taught: R. Judah says, "There is need for Urim and Thummim."

[IV.A] Said R. Abbahu, "R. Yohanan and R. Simeon b. Laqish differed.

[B]   "One said, 'First they build, then they consecrate.'

[C]   "The other said, 'First they consecrate, then they build.' "

[D]   As to the view of him who said, "First they build and then they consecrate"—do they not regard the walls [of the Temple] as if they were burnt offerings [so how will it be possible to continue the building process once the Temple has been consecrated]?

[V.A]   [If] they wished to add to the courtyards, with what [offerings] do they [commemorate] the additions?

[B]   With two loaves of [leavened] bread.

[B]   "Just as 'congregation' referred to at the latter point is made up of ten individuals, so 'congregation' referred to at the former likewise is made up of ten individuals."

[C]   Said R. Simon, "Here it is written, 'within,' ["And I shall be sanctified within the people of Israel" (Lev. 22:32),] and there it is written, 'within,' ["Thus the sons of Israel came to buy among ('within') the others who came . . .'" (Gen. 42:5)].

[D]   "Just as 'within' stated in the latter context refers to ten, so 'within' stated in the former refers to ten."

[E]   Said to him R. Yasa b. R. Bun, "If from the usage of 'within' you wish to derive the matter, then there are many usages of 'within' which refer to more than ten.

[F]   "But here (Lev. 22:32), 'sons of Israel' is mentioned, and elsewhere, 'sons of Israel' is mentioned. Just as 'sons of Israel' stated there, 'And the sons of Israel came to buy . . .' (Gen. 42:5), refers to ten, so here the same language refers to ten."

[II.A]   *And how do we know that we should add three more, etc. (M. San. 1:4K):* **It was taught: Said Rabban R. Simeon b. Gamaliel, "At first only priests, Levites, or Israelites suitable for marriage into the priesthood would sign as witnesses on the marriage contracts of women."**

[B]   **Said R. Yosé, "At first there were dissensions in Israel only in the court of seventy in the hewn-stone chamber [in Jerusalem].**

[C]   **"And there were other courts of twenty-three in the various towns of the Land of Israel, and there were other courts of three judges each in Jerusalem, one on the Temple mount, and one on the Rampart.**

[D]   **"[If] someone needed to know what the law is, he would go to the court in his town.**

[E]   **("[If] there was no court in his town, he would go to the court in the town nearest his.)**

[F]   **"If they had heard the law, they told him. If not, he and the most distinguished member of that court would come on to the court which was nearest to his town.**

[C]   And do they consecrate [Temple space] on a festival day? [Where will they get leavened bread?]

[D]   But: it is done with the show bread [after it is removed from the altar].

[E]   And do they consecrate on the Sabbath [when that bread is put out]?

[F]   But: it is done by night.

[G]   But do they consecrate by night?

[H]   Said R. Yosé b. R. Bun, "[They consecrate] with a meal offering which is baked in the oven [which may be eaten in the courtyard]."

[I]   This view is suitable for the case in which they came up from the Exile, in which case they made an offering, and afterward they consecrated the Temple.

[J]   But when they entered the Land, how did they consecrate?

[K]   Said R. Yosé b. R. Bun, "With two thank offerings which come from Nob and Gibeon."

[VI.A]   **Abba Saul says, "There were two valleys in Jerusalem, a lower one and an upper one.**

[B]   **"The lower one was sanctified with all these procedures, but the upper one was not sanctified.**

[C]   **"And when the Exiles came up, without a king, without Urim, without Thummim, in the lower one, which had been consecrated completely, the people of the land would eat Lesser Holy Things and second tithe, and associates would eat Lesser Holy Things but not second tithe.**

[D]   **"And in the upper one, which had not been consecrated completely, the people of the land would eat Lesser Holy Things and not second tithe, while the associates [would eat] neither Lesser Holy Things nor second tithe.**

[E]   **"And on what account did they not sanctify it? Because it was a weak point in Jerusalem, and it was easily conquered" [T. San. 3:4].**

[VII.A]   *They set up sanhedrins for the tribes only [on the instructions of a court of seventy-one] (M. San. 1:3D).*

[B]   Scripture says, "[You shall appoint judges and officers in all your towns which the Lord your God gives you, according] to your tribes; and they shall judge the people" (Deut. 16:18).

[VIII.A]   *They declare a city to be an apostate city, etc. (M. San. 1:3E–H).*

[B]   R. Yohanan in the name of R. Hoshaiah: "There are three authorities [who differ in this regard].

[C]   "One said, 'One they do declare to be apostate, two they do not declare to be apostate' (cf. M. San. 1:3F–H).

[D]   "Another said, 'Those that are contiguous they declare apostate cities, those that are scattered about they do not declare apostate cities.'

[E]   "And the third said, 'Those that are scattered they do not declare apostate cities at all, lest gentiles break in and enter the Land of Israel.' "

[F]   [19c] And there is he who proposes to state, "Lest the enemy break in and it will come to depopulation."

Following two rather routine exercises, units **I, II,** the Talmud concentrates its attention on M. 1:3C. But here too the point of interest is not the pericope before us but, rather, M. Sheb. 2:2, as cited. Clearly, **III**.E–H, N–Q, require attention. It seems to me that S carries forward N–Q, E–H break into the discourse established by A–D, I–M, so it is the former appearance which must be deleted. Units **IV, V,** and **VI** enrich the discussion of consecrating Jerusalem and the Temple area; here too the appropriate pericope is at M. Shebuot. So we are left with **I, II,** and, at the end, **VII, VIII,** all of them brief and essentially descriptive pericopae. Here is no Talmud worthy of the name.

1:4

[A]   *The great Sanhedrin was [made up of] seventy-one members,*

[B]   *and the small one was twenty-three.*

[C]   *And how do we know the great Sanhedrin was to have seventy-one members?*

[D]   *Since it is said, "Gather to me seventy men of the elders of Israel" (Num. 11:16).*

[E]   *Since Moses was in addition to them, lo, there were seventy-one.*

[F]   *R. Judah says, "It is seventy."*

[G]   *And how do we know that a small one is twenty-three?*

[H]   *Since it is said, "The congregation shall judge," and "The congregation shall deliver" (Num. 35:24, 25)—*

[I]   *One congregation judges (that is, condemns), and one congregation delivers (that is, acquits), thus there are twenty.*

[J]   *And how do we know that "a congregation" is ten? Since it is said, "How long shall I bear with this evil congregation" [of the twelve spies] (Num. 14:27)—excluding Joshua and Caleb.*

[K]   *And how do we know that we should add three more?*

[L]   *From the implication of that which is said, "You shall not follow after the majority to do evil" (Ex. 23:2), I derive the inference that I should be with them to do good.*

[M]   *If so, why is it said, "After the majority to incline" [lhṭwl] (Ex. 23:2)?*

[N]   *Your verdict of guilt is not equivalent to your verdict of acquittal.*

[O]   *Your verdict of acquittal may be on the vote of a majority of one, but your vote for guilt must be by a majority of two.*

[P]   *Since there cannot be a court of an even number of members [twenty-two], they add yet another—thus twenty-three.*

[Q]   *And how many residents must there be in a town so that it may be suitable for a Sanhedrin?*

[R]   *One hundred twenty.*

[S]   *R. Nehemiah says, "Two hundred and thirty, equivalent in number to the chiefs of groups of ten [Ex. 18:21]."*

[I.A]   R. Ba, R. Yasa in the name of R. Yohanan: "Here it is stated 'Congregation' (Num. 35:24, 25), and there it is stated, 'How long shall I bear with this evil congregation' (Num. 14:27).

[G]   "If they had heard the law, they told them. And if not, they and the most distinguished member of that group would come to the court which was on the Temple mount.

[H]   "If they had heard, they told them, and if not, these and those would go to the high court which was on the Rampart.

[I]   "If they had heard, they told them, and if not, these and those would go to the high court which was in the hewn-stone chamber."

[J]   For from there Torah spreads forth over all Israel, as it is said, "Then you shall do according to what they declare to you from that place which the Lord will choose" (Deut. 17:10).

[K]   "The court which was in the hewn-stone chamber, even though it consists of seventy-one members, may not fall below twenty-three.

[L]   "[If] one of them had to go out, he looks around to see whether there would be twenty-three left [after he departs]. If there would be twenty-three left he goes out, and if not, he does not go out—

[M]   "unless there would be twenty-three left.

[N]   "And there they remained in session from the time of the daily whole offering of the morning until the time of the daily whole offering at twilight.

[O]   "On Sabbaths and on festivals they came only to the study house which was on the Temple mount.

[P]   "[If] a question was brought before them, if they had heard the answer, they told them.

[Q]   "If not, they stand for a vote.

[R]   "[If] those who declare innocent turn out to form the majority, they declared the man innocent. [If] those who declare guilty form the majority, they declared the man guilty.

[S]   "[If] those who declare unclean turn out to form the majority, they declared the matter unclean. [If] those who declare the matter clean form the majority, they declared the matter clean.

[T]   "From there did the law go forth and circulate in Israel.

[U]   "From the time that the disciples of Shammai and Hillel who had not served their masters so much as was necessary become numerous, dissensions became many in Israel.

[V]   "And from there they send for and examine everyone who is wise, prudent, fearful of sin, and good of repute, in whom people found pleasure.

[W]   ("They make him a judge in his town.)

[X]   "Once he has been made a judge in his town, they promote him and seat him on the Rampart's court, and from there they promote him and seat him in the court of the hewn-stone chamber."

[III.A]   *The Sanhedrin was arranged like the half of a round threshing floor so that all might see one another. [M. San. 4:3A].*

[B]   Said R. Eleazar b. R. Sadoq, "When Rabban Gamaliel sat in session in Yavneh, my father and his brother were at his right hand, and elders were at his left hand."

[C]   (And why does one sit at the right hand of an elder?) Because of the honor due an elder [T. San. 8:1].

[IV.A]   And how many are the judges of Israel? They are 78,600 [calculated as follows]:

[B]   Heads of thousands are six hundred.

[C]   Heads of hundreds are six thousand.

[D]   Heads of troops of fifty are twelve thousand.

[E]   Heads of troops of ten are sixty thousand.

[F]   It thus turns out that the judges of Israel [heads of all units] are seventy-eight thousand six hundred.

[G]   What is the reason of *R. Nehemiah [who says, "Two hundred and thirty, equivalent in number to the heads of groups of ten"]? [M. San. 1:4S].*

[H]   It is so that there should be in the town a court of twenty-three judges [one out of ten male residents]: those who are on trial, the witnesses against them, witnesses capable of proving that the witnesses are perjurers, witnesses capable of proving that those witnesses themselves are perjurers, the chief of the court, their scribes, and a beadle.

[I]   And what is the reason of rabbis [who say that the town should have a minimum of one hundred twenty male residents]?

[J]   It is so that there should be twelve sanhedrins for the twelve tribes.

[V.A]   *And Moses was in addition to them (M. San. 1:4E).*

[B]   Moses carried out a wise arrangement when the Holy One, blessed be He, said to him, "Number all the firstborn males of the people of Israel, [from a month old and upward, taking their number by names. And you shall take the Levites for me . . . instead of all the firstborn among the people of Israel. . . . And all the firstborn males . . . were twenty-two thousand two hundred and seventy-three. . . . And for the redemption of the two hundred and seventy-three of the firstborn of the people of Israel, over and above the number of the male Levites, you shall take five *shekels* apiece" (Num. 3:40–47, *pass.*)].

[C]   He reflected, "Who will accept upon himself the burden of handing over five *shekels* a head?"

[D]   What did he do? He took twenty-two thousand slips and wrote on them, "Son of Levi." And on two hundred seventy-three he wrote, "Five *shekels.*'"

[E]   He put them into an urn.

[F]   He said to the people, "Come and take your slips."

[G]   To whoever turned up in his hand, "Son of Levi," he would say, "A son of Levi already has redeemed you."

[H]   And to whoever turned up in his hand, "Five *shekels*," he would say, "What can I do for you? It is from Heaven."

[I]   R. Judah and R. Nehemiah—one Tanna said to his fellow [complaining against this procedure]: "[Still there would be conflict, so:] 'If you have written me as "Levi," I would have succeeded.' [That is, the two hundred seventy-three complained that if 'Levi' had been written, they would have succeeded in the drawing. Since only twenty-two thousand slips were marked, 'Levi,' they have lost out. So Moses did not succeed in avoiding conflict.]"

[J]   But thus did he do: He took twenty-two thousand slips and wrote "Levi" on each of them, and two hundred seventy-three

and wrote on them, "Levi," and on two hundred seventy-three, he wrote, "Five shekels."

[K]   He then put them into the urn.

[L]   He said to them, "Come and pick your slip."

[M]   To whoever turned up in his hand, "Levi," he said, "Levi already has redeemed you."

[N]   And to whoever turned up in his hand, "Five shekels," he would say, "What can I do for you? It is from Heaven."

[O]   A second time one Tanna objected to his fellow: "Take note, for [what if] all of them came up, 'Levi'!"

[P]   He replied, "It was a miracle, and the differently marked slips came up alternately."

[Q]   Said R. Samuel, "In the opinion of the latter Tanna, it was a miracle. In the opinion of the former Tanna, it was no miracle."

[R]   [Abbahu] said to him, "In the opinion of all, the matter was miraculous, and they came up alternately."

[S]   Antoninus the *Hegemon* asked Rabban Yohanan ben Zakkai, "In general [when numbered all together] they were found wanting, but in detail [when added up one by one] they were found excessive."

[T]   He said to him, "Those three hundred extras were the firstborn sons of the priesthood, and the holy [that is, the firstborn Levite] cannot redeem the holy [that is, the firstborn non-Levite]." [This is spelled out at Num. R. 3:14, trans. J. J. Slotki, as follows: "At the command of the Lord, by their families, all males from a month old and upward, were twenty and two thousand" (Num. 3:39). you will find that the tribe of Levi, in the detailed numbering, consisted of twenty-two thousand and three hundred. For there were three families—Gershon, Kohath, and Merari. Now if you take each family separately and compute the figures in it—seven thousand and five hundred for Gershon, eight thousand and six hundred for Kohath, six thousand and two hundred for Merari—the total for all amounts to twenty-two thousand and three hundred. Yet when the Levites were counted all together, their numbers are given as twenty-two thousand. Where were the three hundred? The detailed numbers were in fact given in order to make known how many there were in each family. But a sum total of twenty-two thousand, a reduction of three hundred from the real figure, is given because this numbering was in order to compare them with the number of firstborn for the purposes of redeeming the firstborn Israelites. He deducted from their number three hundred who were firstborn belonging to the Levites, because one firstborn cannot redeem another firstborn. For this reason there are twenty-two thousand and three hundred in the numbering of the families, and twenty-two thousand in the total used for the redemption of the firstborn Israelites.]

[U]   Along these same lines: "And the Lord said to Moses, 'Gather for me seventy men of the elders of Israel' " (Num. 11:16).

[V]   Said Moses, "If I take six from each tribe, I shall have seventy-two in hand.

[W]   "If I take ten from six tribes and two from five, which tribe will agree to be diminished in such a way?"

[X]   What did he do?

[Y]   He took seventy slips and wrote on them, "Elder," and two he left blank, and he put them into an urn.

[Z]   He said to them, "Come and pick your slip."

[AA]   To whoever turned up in his hand a slip marked, "Elder," he would say, "They have chosen you in Heaven."

[BB]   And to whoever turned up in his hand a blank slip, he would say, "What can I do for you? It is from Heaven."

[CC]   R. Judah and R. Nehemiah: One Tanna objected to his colleagues, "[Moses did not succeed in avoiding strife. For the claim still could be made,] 'If you had written "Elder" for me, I should have succeeded too.'

[DD]   "But this is what he did. He took seventy-two slips and wrote on them, 'Elder,' and two blank ones, and he put them into an urn.

[EE]   "He said to them, 'Come and take your slip.'

[FF]   "To whoever turned up in his hand a slip marked, 'Elder,' he said, 'They have indeed chosen you in Heaven.'

[GG]   "To whoever turned up in his hand a blank slip, he would say, 'What can I do for you? It is from Heaven.' "

[HH]   Objected one Tanna to his fellows: "But what if all of them came up marked, 'Elder'?"

[II]   He said to him, "It was a miracle, and the ballots came up in alternate order [so that two blank ones were chosen]."

[JJ]   Said R. Samuel, "I argued before R. Abbahu, 'In the opinion of the latter Tanna, it was a miracle. In the opinion of the former Tanna, it was no miracle.' "

[KK]   He said to him, "It indeed was a [19d] miracle. They came up in alternate order."

[VI.A]   [The translation which follows is by Baruch A. Levine:] Antonius the *Hegemon* engaged in polemics with Rabban Yohanan ben Zakkai: "Either your teacher Moses was an embezzler or he was inexpert in keeping accounts, for it is written, '[The silver of those of the community who were recorded came to one hundred talents and seventeen hundred seventy-five *sheqels* by the sanctuary weight] a half-*sheqel* a head [half a *sheqel* by the sanctuary weight, for each one who was entered in the records]' (Ex. 38:25–26). Now if you reckon the *centenarius* as one hundred *libras*, Moses misappropriated one-sixth [of the silver], and if you reckon the *centenarius* at sixty *libras*, as is normal, he misappropriated one half." [The regular talent was sixty *minas*, or fifteen hundred *sheqels*, or three thousand half-*sheqels*. Thus, the approximately six hundred thousand half-*sheqels* is equal to two hundred talents. But Scripture states that approximately one hundred talents were reported. Therefore half the silver was *not* reported. At one hundred *minas* to the talent, the misappropriation would have amounted to one-sixth of the silver, since at that rate a talent was equal to twenty-five hundred *sheqels*, five thousand half-*sheqels*. Thus 100 × 5,000 = 500,000, which leaves the silver collected for 100,000 people unreported. For the population, see Ex. 38:26].

[B]   Rabban Yohanan ben Zakkai replied, "Moses our teacher was a trustworthy treasurer and expert in keeping accounts. And," he continued, "is it not written, 'And the copper from the wave offering was seventy talents and twenty-four hundred *sheqels*' (Ex. 38:29)? Observe that these twenty-four hundred *shekels* amount to ninety-six *libras*. [One *libra* is twenty-five *sheqels*], and yet Scripture did not convert them into *libras* [which would have been convenient]." [This is taken as proof that these *libras* did not have the usual weight of twenty-five *sheqels* each, but twice that weight, which was the standard of the sanctuary. Otherwise they would have been converted. Now if the sanctuary weight was indeed twice the regular standards, Moses misappropriated nothing whatsoever.]

[C] To this the *Hegemon* countered, "[The reason Scripture did not convert the *sheqels* into *libras* is] that the *centenarii* do not amount to a talent. But if you insist that they do, [I maintain that Scripture was interested only in the round total of seventy talents and therefore did not convert the relatively small amount of twenty-four hundred *sheqels*]. Moses thus misappropriated half." [At sixty *libras* per *centenarius*, twenty-four hundred *sheqels* would amount to one talent and nine hundred *sheqels*. At one hundred *libras* per *centenarius*, twenty-four hundred would not amount to a full talent, which would be twenty-five hundred *sheqels*.]

[D] Rabban Yohanan ben Zakkai replied, "Is it not written, 'And of the one thousand seven hundred seventy-five [sheqels] he made hooks for the posts' (Ex. 38:28)? You observe that these *sheqels* amount to seventy-one *libras*, yet Scripture reported them specifically as *sheqels* [and did not convert them into *libras*]."

[E] [The *Hegemon* repeated his earlier objection] saying to Rabban Yohanan ben Zakkai, "It is because the *centenarii* did not amount to a talent. Moses was [consequently] guilty of misappropriation." [At one hundred *libras* per *centenarius*, twenty-five hundred *sheqels* would amount to a full talent, and here we have only one thousand seven hundred seventy-five.]

[F] Rabban Yohanan ben Zakkai argued further, "Is it not written, 'The *sheqel* is twenty *gerah*, and twenty and twenty-five and fifteen *shekels* are one *mina* for your purposes' (Ezek. 45:12)? The Holy One, blessed be He, ordained a talent of twice the regular weight." [The usual *mina* (= *libra*) amounts to twenty-five *sheqels*, but the sanctuary weight of a *mina* in the Torah was fifty *sheqels*. In Ezekiel's time, ten *sheqels* were added, making sixty.]

[G] The *Hegemon* finally conceded, "Verily, [Moses your teacher] was a trusted treasurer and expert in keeping accounts."

Once more the Talmud presents a series of set pieces, most of them tangential to our pericope of the Mishnah. Unit **I** goes over Mishnah's own proofs for the count of ten for a congregation. Unit **II** presents a vast corpus of Tosefta's materials relevant to the great Sanhedrin, but in no other way pertinent to the rule of this passage of Mishnah. Unit **III** does the same. Unit **IV** actually turns to the Mishnah and complements its information. Units **V** and **VI** in no way pertain. Clearly, **V.B–R** and U–KK impose precisely the same discourse on two different verses of Scripture. I am inclined to find the latter somewhat easier to follow. Unit **VI** is tacked on because it is thematically congruent to unit **V**.

3 Yerushalmi Sanhedrin Chapter Two

2:1

[A] *A high priest judges, and [others] judge him;*

[B] *gives testimony, and [others] give testimony about him;*

[C] *performs the rite of removing the shoe [Deut. 25:7–9], and [others] perform the rite of removing the shoe with his wife.*

[D] *[Others] enter levirate marriage with his wife, but he does not enter into levirate marriage,*

[E] *because he is prohibited to marry a widow.*

[F] *[If] he suffers a death [in his family], he does not follow the bier.*

[G] *"But when [the bearers of the bier] are not visible, he is visible; when they are visible, he is not.*

[H] *"And he goes with them to the city gate," the words of R. Meir.*

[I] *R. Judah says, "He never leaves the sanctuary,*

[J] *"since it says, 'Nor shall he go out of the sanctuary' (Lev. 21:12)."*

[I.A] It is understandable that he judges others.

[B] But as to others judging him, [is it appropriate to his station?]

[C] Let him appoint a mandatory.

[D] Now take note: What if he has to take an oath?

[E] Can the mandatory take an oath for his client?

65

[F]   Property cases involving [a high priest]—in how large a court is the trial conducted?

[G]   With a court of twenty-three judges.

[H]   Let us demonstrate that fact from the following:

[I]   **A king does not sit in the sanhedrin, nor do a king and a high priest join in the court session for intercalation [T. San. 2:15].**

[J]   [In this regard,] R. Haninah and R. Mana—one of them said, "The king does not take a seat on the Sanhedrin, on account of suspicion [of influencing the other judges].

[K]   "Nor does he take a seat in a session for intercalation, because of suspicion [that it is in the government's interest to intercalate the year].

[L]   "And a king and a high priest do not take a seat for intercalation, for it is not appropriate to the station of the king [or the high priest] to take a seat with seven judges."

[M]   Now look here:

[N]   If it is not appropriate to his station to take a seat with seven judges, is it not an argument *a fortiori* that he should not [be judged] by three?

[O]   That is why one must say, Property cases involving him are tried in a court of twenty-three.

[II.A]   [What follows is verbatim at M. Hor. 3:1:] Said R. Eleazar, "A high priest who sinned—they administer lashes to him, but they do not remove him from his high office."

[B]   Said R. Mana, "It is written, 'For the consecration of the anointing oil of his God is upon him: I am the Lord' (Lev. 21:12).

[C]   [Here omitted:] ("That is as if to say: 'Just as I [stand firm] in my high office, so Aaron [stands firm] in his high office.' ")

[D]   [Here omitted:] (Said R. Abun, " 'He shall be holy to you [for I the Lord who sanctify you am holy]' (Lev. 21:8).)

[E]   "That is as if to say, 'Just as I [stand firm] in my consecration, so Aaron [stands firm] in his consecration.' "

[F]   R. Haninah Ketobah, R. Aha in the name of R. Simeon b. Laqish: "An anointed priest who sinned—they administer lashes
to him [by the judgment of a court of three judges]."

[G]   "If you rule that it is by the decision of a court of twenty-three
judges [that the lashes are administered], it turns out that his
ascension [to high office] is descent [to public humiliation,
since if he sins he is publicly humiliated by a sizable court]."

[III.A] R. Simeon b. Laqish said, "A ruler who sinned—they administer lashes to him by the decision of a court of three judges."

[B]   What is the law as to restoring him to office?

[C]   Said R. Haggai, "By Moses! If we put him back into office, he
will kill us!"

[D]   R. Judah the Patriarch heard this ruling [of R. Simeon b. Laqish's] and was outraged. He sent a troop of Goths to arrest R.
Simeon b. Laqish. [R. Simeon b. Laqish] fled to the Tower,
and, some say, it was to Kefar Hittayya.

[E]   The next day R. Yohanan went up to the meetinghouse, and
R. Judah the Patriarch went up to the meetinghouse. He said
to him, "Why does my master not state a teaching of Torah?"

[F]   [Yohanan] began to clap with one [20a] hand [only].

[G]   [Judah the Patriarch] said to him, "Now do people clap with
only one hand?"

[H]   He said to him, "No, nor is Ben Laqish here [and just as one
cannot clap with one hand only, so I cannot teach Torah if my
colleague, Simeon b. Laqish, is absent]."

[I]   [Judah] said to him, "Then where is he hidden?"

[J]   He said to him, "In a certain tower."

[K]   He said to him, "You and I shall go out to greet him
tomorrow."

[L]   R. Yohanan sent word to R. Simeon b. Laqish, "Get a teaching of Torah ready, because the patriarch is coming over to see
you."

[M]   [Simeon b. Laqish] came forth to receive them and said, "The
example which you [Judah] set is to be compared to the para-
digm of your Creator. For when the All-Merciful came forth to
redeem Israel [from Egypt], he did not send a messenger or an

angel, but the Holy One, blessed be He, himself came forth, as it is said, 'For I will pass through the Land of Egypt that night' (Ex. 12:12)—and not only so, but he and his entire retinue.

[N] [Here omitted:] ([" 'What other people on earth is like thy people Israel, whom God went to redeem to be his people' (2 Sam. 7:23).] 'Whom God went' (sing.) is not written here, but 'Whom God went' (plural) [—meaning, he and all his retinue]."）

[O] [Judah the Patriarch] said to him, "Now why in the world did you see fit to teach this particular statement [that a ruler who sinned is subject to lashes]?"

[P] He said to him, "Now did you really think that because I was afraid of you, I would hold back the teaching of the All-Merciful? [And lo, citing 1 Sam. 2:23f.,] R. Samuel b. R. Isaac said, '[Why do you do such things? For I hear of your evil dealings from all the people.] No, my sons, it is no good report [that I hear the people of the Lord spreading abroad]. [Here omitted:] (If a man sins against a man, God will mediate for him; but if a man sins against the Lord, who can intercede for him? But they would not listen to the voice of their father, for it was the will of the Lord to slay them' (1 Sam. 2:23–25). [When] the people of the Lord spread about [an evil report about a man], they remove him [even though he is the patriarch]."）

[IV.A] [The reference to tearing above in M. Hor. 3:3A is at issue: *A high priest tears his garment [on the death of a close relative] below [at the bottom hem], and an ordinary one, above [at the hem of his garment nearest his shoulder].*] R. Eleazar in the name of Kahana: " 'Above' means above the binding [therefore separating the binding], and 'below' means below the binding [therefore not separating the binding]."

[B] R. Yohanan said, " 'Below' means what it says, literally [near the ground]."

[C] R. Yohanan went up to visit R. Hanina. When he was yet on the road, he heard that he had died. He sent word and said to send to him his best Sabbath garment, and [he went and] tore it [in mourning on account of this news]. [Thus he holds that one tears a garment at the demise of someone who is not a close relative.]

[D]   R. Yohanan differs from R. Yudan in two matters. [First, that he maintains one has to tear the garment as a sign of mourning for any master who has died, not merely for the one from whom one learned most; second, that one does the tear above the binding.]

[E]   The teaching of R. Eleazar in the name of Kahana is in accord with R. Judah [who does not distinguish among relationships to the deceased].

[F]   And if he is in accord with R. Judah, [the high priest] should not perform the act of tearing at all [since R. Judah holds that "any tear which does not separate the binding . . . is a worthless act of tearing" (I), and R. Eleazar holds that " 'below' means below the binding" (A)].

[G]   This [Mishnah] deals with the [death of] his father or mother and follows the view of R. Meir, for it has . . . been taught in a Tannaitic teaching:

[H]   "For no dead does he undo the binding, except for his father and his mother," the words of R. Meir.

[I]   R. Judah says, "Any tear which does not separate the binding, lo, this is a worthless act of tearing."

[J]   What is the rule [for the high priest]?

[K]   It is a more strict ruling in the case of the high priest, that he should not undo the binding, [but he rips through the fabric].

[V.A]   *"A high priest makes an offering while he is in the status of one who has yet to bury a close relative, but he does not eat* [the priestly portion]," **the words of R. Meir** (M. Hor. 3:3B; T. Zeb. 11:3].

[B]   **R. Judah says, "That entire day."**

[C]   **R. Simeon says, "He completes all the act of sacrifice which is his responsibility and then he goes along [and leaves the altar]."**

[D]   The difference between the view of R. Meir and R. Simeon is one point, [specifically: in Simeon's view, when the priest hears the news, while he is performing the rite, that a close relative has died, he completes the entire rite for which he is responsible. But if he has not begun the rite, he should not do so. And after he has completed the rite, he should not begin another. In

Meir's view, he may carry on an act of service, without condition.]

[E]   The difference between the view of R. Judah and R. Simeon is one point, [specifically: in Judah's view, the priest makes offerings that entire day, while in Simeon's, once he has completed the rite in which he is involved, he leaves the altar.]

[F]   The difference between the view of R. Meir and R. Judah is [whether or not the priest who has not yet buried his close relative] enters [the Temple at all. Meir maintains that if he has not gone out of the sanctuary, he is permitted to make an offering. But if he has gone out, he does not enter the sanctuary. Judah maintains that that entire day the priest is permitted even to enter the sanctuary and to undertake offerings.]

[G]   R. Jacob bar Disai [says, "Whether or not the priest at the altar] interrupts [his act of service] is what is at issue between [Meir and Simeon]."

[H]   R. Meir says, "[If, when the priest heard the news], he was inside, he would go out [of the sanctuary]. [If] he was outside [the sanctuary], he would [not] go back in."

[I]   R. Judah says, "[If, when he heard the news, the priest] was inside, he would go in [and, for the entire day on which he heard, carry out an act of service, as is his right], but if he was outside, he would not go in [to perform an act of service]."

[J]   **R. Simeon says, "He completes all the act of service which is his responsibility and then he goes along."**

[VI.A]   R. Yosé b. R. Bun in the name of R. Huna: "The following Mishnah saying [belongs] to R. Simeon: " 'And from the sanctuary he will not go forth' (Lev. 21:12)—with [the bearers of the bier] he does not go forth, but he does go forth after them."

[B]   *"When [the bearers of the bier] are not visible, he is visible, when they are visible, he is not. And he goes with them to the city gate," the words of R. Meir.*

[C]   *R. Judah says, "He never leaves the sanctuary, since it says, 'Nor shall he go out of the sanctuary' (Lev. 21:12)"* [M. San. 2:1G–J].

[D]   If he did go out, he should not come back.

[E] R. Abbahu in the name of R. Eleazar: "The word 'mourning' applies only to the corpse alone, as it is written, 'And her gates shall lament and mourn' (Is. 3:26)."

[F] Hiyya bar Adda replied, "And is it not written, 'The fishermen shall mourn and lament' (Is. 19:8)?"

[VII.A] Said R. Hanina, "So does the Mishnah [teach, that] the consideration of uncleanness by reason of mourning applies only on the account of the corpse [and not on account of hearing of the death. The day of the death, along with the night, imposes the status of the one who has yet to bury his close relative]."

[B] It has been taught in a Tannaitic tradition: At what point does the status of the one who has yet to bury his close relative apply?

[C] "It applies from the moment of death to the moment of burial," the words of Rabbi.

[D] And sages say, "It applies for that entire day [on which the deceased dies]."

[E] You may then discern both a lenient and a strict side to the ruling of Rabbi, and a lenient and a strict side to the ruling of rabbis.

[F] What is the difference between their two positions [for strict and lenient rulings]?

[G] If one dies and is buried at the proper time—

[H] in accord with the position of rabbis the mourner [in such a case] is subject to prohibitions applying to mourning for that entire day. In accord with the position of Rabbi the mourner is subject to prohibitions only in the period of the day down to that hour [of burial] alone.

[I] If one dies and is buried three days later—

[J] in accord with the opinion of rabbis, the prohibitions applying to the mourner are valid throughout that entire day [but not for the next two].

[K] In accord with the position of Rabbi, the prohibitions applying to the mourners pertain for all three days.

[L] R. Abbahu came [to teach] in the name of R. Yohanan, [and] R. Hisda—both of them teach: "Rabbi concurs with sages [in the case of I] that the prohibition applies only to that day alone." [The dispute concerns only M–N.]

[M] That is in accord with the following teaching on Tannaitic authority:

Rabbi says, "You should know that the status of first-day mourning by the authority of the Torah does not apply to the night, for lo, they have said, 'A first-day mourner may immerse and eat his Passover offering in the evening [of the fifteenth of Nisan, having suffered a bereavement on the fourteenth].' "

[N] And lo, they have said that the laws of first-day mourning do apply by the authority of the Torah!

[O] R. Yosé b. R. Bun in the name of R. Huna, "You may solve the contradiction by referring [Rabbi's ruling, M] to the case in which the [death was during the day and] burial took place in the last rays of sunlight [and Rabbi, M, holds that to that following night the status of first-day mourning does not apply by the authority of the Torah]."

Since the main point of M. Hor. 3:1E–H is that the high priest retains his consecrated status for all time, the Talmud's first question is the source for that ruling. Unit I provides ample exegetical proof. The second unit is devoted to the case of the punishment of a ruler. I have followed the version of the story as it appears at Y. San. 2:1. Unit IV is relevant to M. Hor. 3:3A. From that point the interest is in the relationship of the opinions of Yohanan to those of the Tanna, Judah. Unit V takes up M. Hor. 3:3B. The Talmud brings Mishnah's position into relationship with a richer account of the same matter supplied by Tosefta. The exegesis then is of Tosefta's version. Unit VI serves M. San. 2:1, which is cited verbatim. Unit VII's interest, in the point at which the prohibitions applicable to one who has suffered a bereavement but has yet to bury his dead, is relevant to M. Hor. 3:3B.

2:2

[A] *And when he gives comfort to others—*

[B]   *the accepted practice is for all the people to pass one after an-*
       other, and the appointed [prefect of the priests] stands between
       him and the people.

[C]   *And when he receives consolation from others,*

[D]   *all the people say to him, "Let us be your atonement."*

[E]   *And he says to them, "May you be blessed by Heaven."*

[F]   *And when they provide him with the funeral meal,*

[G]   *all the people sit on the ground, while he sits on a stool.*

[I.A] [The statement at M. San. 2:2G] implies: A stool is not subject
       to the law of mourners' overturning the bed.

[B]   [But that is not necessarily so. For] the high priest [to begin
       with] is subject to that requirement of overturning the bed
       [and, it follows, no conclusion can be drawn from M.].

[II.A] It was taught: They do not bring out the deceased [for burial]
       at a time near the hour of reciting the *Shema*, unless they did
       so an hour earlier or an hour later, so that people may recite
       the *Shema* and say the Prayer.

[B]   And have we not learned: *When they have buried the dead and*
       returned, [if they can begin the Shema and finish it before
       reaching the row of mourners, they begin it; but if they cannot,
       they do not begin it] [M. Ber. 3:2]. [Thus they do bring out
       the deceased for burial at a time quite close to that for reciting
       the *Shema*.]

[C]   Interpret [the cited pericope of Mishnah] to deal with a case in
       which the people thought that they had ample time for burying
       the corpse but turned out not to have ample time for that pur-
       pose [prior to the time for reciting the *Shema*].

[D]   It is taught: **The person who states the eulogy and all who**
       are involved in the eulogy interrupt [their labor] for the pur-
       pose of reciting the Shema, but do not do so for saying the
       Prayer. MᶜSH W: Our rabbis interrupted for the purposes of
       reciting the Shema and saying the Prayer (T. Ber. 2:11).

[E]   Now have we not learned, *If they can begin and finish . . . ?*
       [As above, B. Now here we have them interrupt the eulogy!]

[F]   The Mishnah refers to the first day [of the death, on which
       they are exempt from saying the *Shema*], and the Tosefta peri-

cope to the second [day after death, on which they are liable to say the *Shema*].

[G]   Said R. Samuel bar Abedoma, "This one who entered the synagogue and found the people standing [and saying] the prayer, if he knows that he can complete the Prayer before the messenger of the congregation [who repeats the whole in behalf of the congregation] will begin to answer, 'Amen,' [to the Prayer of the community], he may say the Prayer, and if not, he should not say the Prayer."

[H]   To which "Amen" is reference made?

[I]   Two Amoras differ in this regard.

[J]   One said, "To the *Amen* which follows, 'The Holy God.' "

[K]   And the other said, "to the *Amen* which follows, 'Who hears prayer' on an ordinary day."

[III.A]   It was taught: **R. Judah says, "If there is only a single row [of mourners], those who are standing as a gesture of respect are liable [to say the Shema], and those who are standing as a gesture of mourning are exempt [from the obligation to say the Shema]. If they proceed to the eulogy, those who see the face [of the mourners] are exempt [from having to say the Shema,] and those who do not see their face are liable [T. Ber. 2:11].**

[B]   Note that which we have learned: *When he gives comfort to others, the accepted practice is for all the people to pass after one another, and the appointed [prefect of the priests] stands between him and the people [M. San. 3:3A–B].*

[C]   This is in accord with the earlier practice [Mishnah] [to be cited below].

[D]   And as to that which we have learned: *[Of those who stand in the row of mourners], the ones on the inner line are exempt from reciting the Shema, and the ones on the outer row are liable [M. Ber. 3:2]—*

[E]   this is in accord with the later Mishnah [to be cited below].

[F]   Said R. Haninah, "At first [the former Mishnah = B], the families would stand and the mourners would pass before them. R. Yosé ordained that the families would pass and the mourners would stand still [the later Mishnah = D].

[G]   Said R. Samuel of Sofafta, "The matters were restored to their original condition."

By introducing the materials of M. Ber. 3:2, the Talmud succeeds in drawing together diverse discussions of mourning rites. But the present pericope figures only modestly in the discussion, which is primary to M. Ber. 3:2 and, at best, tangential to the present location.

2:3

[A]   *The king does not judge, and [others] do not judge him;*

[B]   *does not give testimony, and [others] do not give testimony about him;*

[C]   *does not perform the rite of removing the shoe, and others do not perform the rite of removing the shoe with his wife;*

[D]   *does not enter into levirate marriage, nor [do his brothers] enter levirate marriage with his wife.*

[E]   *R. Judah says, "If he wanted to perform the rite of removing the shoe or to enter into levirate marriage, his memory is a blessing."*

[F]   *They said to him, "They pay no attention to him if he expressed the wish to do so."*

[G]   *[Others] do not marry his widow.*

[H]   *R. Judah says, "A king may marry the widow of a king.*

[I]   *"For so we find in the case of David, that he married the widow of Saul,*

[J]   *"For it is said, 'And I gave you your master's house and your master's wives into your embrace' (2 Sam. 12:8)."*

[I.A]   [The king] does not judge [M. San. 2:3A]. And has it not been written: "[So David reigned over all Israel;] and David administered justice and equity to all his people" (2 Sam. 8:15).

[B]   And yet do you say [that the king does not judge]?

[C]   [From this verse of Scripture, we draw the following picture:] He would indeed judge a case, declaring the innocent party to be innocent, the guilty party to be guilty. But if the guilty party was poor, he would give him [the funds needed for his penalty] out of his own property. Thus he turned out doing justice for this one [who won the case] and doing charity for that one [who had lost it].

[D]   Rabbi says, "[If] a judge judged a case, declaring the innocent party to be innocent, and the guilty party to be guilty, [the cited verse of Scripture indicates that] the Omnipresent credits it to him as if he had done an act of charity with the guilty party, for he has taken out of the possession of the guilty party that which he has stolen."

[II.A]   *And [others] do not judge him [M. San. 2:3A].* This is in line with the verse [in the Psalm of David], "From thee [alone] let my vindication come!" (Ps. 17:2).

[B]   R. Isaac in the name of Rabbi: "King and people are judged before Him every day, as it is said, '. . . and may he do justice for his servant and justice for his people Israel, as each day requires' (1 King 8:59)."

[III.A]   *R. Judah says, "If he wanted to perform the rite of removing the shoe or to enter into levirate marriage, his memory is a blessing" [M. San. 2:3E].*

[B]   They said to him, "If you rule in this way, you turn out to diminish the honor owing to the king."

[IV.A]   *Others do not marry the widow [M. San. 2:3G]* or the woman divorced by a king.

[B]   This is by reason of that which is said: "So [David's concubines] were shut up until the day of their death, living as if in widowhood" (2 Sam. 20:3).

[C]   R. Yudah bar Pazzi in the name of R. Pazzi in the name of R. Yohanan: "This teaches that David [treating them as forbidden though in law they were not] would have them dressed and adorned and brought before him every day, and he would say to his libido, 'Do you lust after something forbidden to you?' By your life! I shall now make you lust for something which is permitted to you."

[D]   Rabbis of Caesarea say, "They were in fact forbidden [20b] to him [and it was not merely that he treated the women whom

Absalom had raped as forbidden to him, but the law deemed them prohibited].

[E]   "For if a utensil belonging to an ordinary man used by an ordinary man is prohibited for use of a king, a utensil belonging to a king which was used by an ordinary man—is it not an argument *a fortiori* that the king should be forbidden to make use of it?"

[V.A]   *R. Judah says, "The king may marry the widow of a king. For we find in the case of David that he married widows of Saul, for it is said, 'And I gave you your master's house and your master's wives into your embrace' (2 Sam. 12:8)" [M. San. 2:3H–J].*

[B]   This refers to Rispah, Abigail, and Bath Sheba.

[C]   [The reference to Abigail, 1 Sam. 25, calls to mind Nabal and his origins:] Hezron had three sons, as it is written, "The sons of Hezron that were born to him: Yerahmeel, Ram, and Kelubai" (1 Chron. 2:9)

[D]   The first [son] was Yerahmeel, but he married a gentile woman to be crowned through her [royal ancestry], as it is written, "Yerahmeel also had another wife, whose name was Atarah [crown]" (1 Chron. 2:26).

[E]   "She was the mother of Onam" (1 Chron. 2:26), for she brought mourning *(aninah)* into his household.

[F]   "Ram was the father of Amminadab, and Amminadab was the father of Nahshon, [prince of the sons of Judah]. Nahshon was the father of Salma, Salma of Boaz, [Boaz of Obed, Obed of Jesse]" (1 Chron. 2:10–12). And Boaz married Ruth.

[G]   Lo, Nadab came from Kelubai.

[H]   Nabal said, "In all Israel there is no son better than I."

[I]   This is in line with that which is written, "And there was a man in Maon, whose business was in Carmel. The man was very rich" (1 Sam. 25:2).

[J]   Now he was a Kelubaite (1 Sam. 25:3), for he came from Kelubai.

[K]   "David heard in the wilderness that Nabal was shearing [his sheep. So David sent ten young men; and David said to the young men, 'Go up to Carmel, and go to Nabal, and greet him in my name]. And thus shall you salute the living one: 'Peace be to you, [and peace be to your house, and peace be to all that you have' " (1 Sam. 25:4–6).

[L]   Said R. Yusta bar Shunam, "They became a whole camp."

[M]   "And Nabal answered David's servants, ['Who is David?']" (1 Sam. 25:10).

[N]   How do we know that *in capital cases they begin from the side* [the youngest members of the court] [M. San. 4:2]?

[O]   Samuel the Elder taught before R. Aha: " 'And David said to his men, [Gird every man his sword, and every man girded on his sword, and David also girded on his sword' (1 Sam. 25:13)." David thus is the last to express his opinion.]

[P]   " 'And he railed at them' (1 Sam. 25:14)—what is the meaning of 'And he railed at them'?

[Q]   "He incited them with words" [But see QH].

[R]   "Now therefore know this and consider what you should do; [for evil is determined against our master and against all his house, and he is so ill-natured that one cannot speak to him" (1 Sam. 25:17).

[S]   "And as she rode on the ass . . . behold, David and his men came down toward her;] and she met them" (1 Sam. 25:20).

[T]   She showed her thigh, and they followed out of desire for her.

[U]   " '. . . she met them'—all of them had [involuntary] ejaculations" (PM).

[V]   "Now David said, 'Surely in vain have I guarded [all that this fellow has in the wilderness . . . and he has returned me evil for good. God do so to the enemies of David . . . if by morning I leave so much as] one who pisses against the wall of all who belong to him' " (1 Sam. 25:21–22).

[W]   [This reference to one who pisses on a wall is to a dog.] Now what place is there for referring to a dog, who pisses on the wall? The meaning is that even a dog will get no pity.

[X]   "When Abigail saw David, [she made haste, and alighted from the ass, and fell before David on her face, and bowed to the ground]" (1 Sam. 25:23).

[Y]   She said to him, "My lord, David, as to me, what have I done? And my children—what have they done? My cattle—what have they done?"

[Z]   He said to her, "It is because [Nabal] has cursed the kingdom of David."

[AA]   He said to him, "And are you [now] a king?"

[BB]   He said to her, "And has not Samuel anointed me as king?"

[CC]   She said to him, "Our lord Saul's coinage still is in circulation."

[DD]   "But I your handmaid . . ." (1 Sam. 25:25)—this teaches that he demanded to have sexual relations with her.

[EE]   Forthwith she removed her stained [sanitary napkin] and showed it to him [indicating that she was in her menses and forbidden to have sexual relations on that account].

[FF]   He said to her, "Can one examine stains at night?"

[GG]   They said to him, "And let your ears hear what your mouth speaks. They do not examine sanitary napkins by night—and do they judge capital cases by night [as David was judging Nabal]!"

[HH]   He said to her, "The trial concerning him was complete while it was still day."

[II]   She said to him, " '[And when the Lord has done to my lord according to all the good that he has spoken concerning you . . .] my lord shall have no causes of grief, [for pangs of conscience, for having shed blood without cause]' " (1 Sam. 25:30–31).

[JJ]   Said R. Eliezer, "There were indeed doubts [riddles] there."

[KK]   R. Levi was reviewing this pericope. R. Zeira told the associates, "Go and listen to R. Zeira, for it is not possible that he will lay out the pericope without saying something fresh about it."

[LL]   Someone went in and told them that that was not so.

[MM]   R. Zeira heard and said, "Even in matters of biblical stories there is the possibility of saying something fresh:

[NN] " '. . . have no doubts . . .'—that is, there were indeed causes [riddles] there."

[OO] [Continuing Abigail's speech to David:] "When word of your cause of grief goes forth, people will say about you, 'You are a murderer (1 Sam. 25:31), and you are destined to fall *(ibid.)* into sin, specifically to err through the wife of a man. It is better that there should be but one such case, and not two.

[PP] "A much greater sin is going to come against you than this one. Do not bring this one along with the one which is coming."

[QQ] "For having shed blood" (1 Sam. 25:31)—"You are going to rule over all Israel, and people will say about you, 'He was a murderer.'

[RR] "And that which you say, 'Whoever curses the dominion of the house of David is subject to the death penalty,'

[SS] "but you still have no throne."

[TT] "[And when the Lord has dealt well with my lord], then remember your handmaid" (1 Sam. 25:31).

[UU] This indicates that she treated herself as available [to David by referring to herself as his handmaid], and since she treated herself as available, Scripture itself treated her as diminished.

[VV] For in every other passage you read, "Abig*ail*," but in this one: "And David said to Avig*al*" (1 Sam. 25:32).

[WW] "And David said . . . , 'Blessed be your discretion, and blessed be you, who have kept me this day from bloodguilt' " (1 Sam. 25:33)—in two senses, in the sense of the blood of menstruation, and in the sense of bloodshed [for she kept him from both kinds of bloodguilt].

After a fairly systematic glossing of Mishnah, the Talmud presents a substantial passage unrelated to Mishnah's interests. The reference to Abigail surely is the reason that unit **V** is tacked on.

2:4

[A] *[If the king] suffers a death in his family, he does not leave the gate of his palace.*

[B]   R. Judah says, "If he wants to go out after the bier, he goes out,

[C]   "for thus we find in the case of David, that he went out after the bier of Abner,

[D]   "since it is said, 'And King David followed the bier' (2 Sam. 3:31)."

[E]   They said to him, "This action was only to appease the people."

[F]   And when they provide him with the funeral meal, all the people sit on the ground, while he sits on a couch.

[I.A]   Does [M. San. 2:4F] indicate that a couch is subject to the rule of overturning as a sign of mourning?

[B]   The king is not subject to the rule of overturning the bed [and therefore the passage does not prove the case, one way or the other].

[II.A]   There is a Tanna who teaches that the women go first [in the mourning procession], and the men after them.

[B]   And there is a Tanna who teaches that the men go first, and the women afterward.

[C]   The one who said that the women go first invokes as the reason that they caused death to come into the world.

[D]   The one who said that men go first invokes the reason that it is to preserve the honor of Israelite women, so that people should not stare at them.

[E]   Now is it not written, "And King David followed the bier" (2 Sam. 3:31)? They said to him, "This action was only to appease the people" (M. San. 2:4D–E).

[F]   Once he appeased the women, he went and appeased the men [in the view of A].

[G]   Or: Once he appeased the men, he went and appeased the women [in the view of B].

[III.A]   "And David returned [to bless his household. But Michal the daughter of Saul came out to meet David, and said, 'How the king of Israel honored himself today, uncovering himself today before the eyes of his servants' maids, as one of the vulgar fellows shamelessly uncovers himself!']" (2 Sam. 6:20).

[B]   What is the meaning of "one of the vulgar fellows"?

[C]   Said R. Ba bar Kahana, "The most vulgar of them all—this is a dancer!"

[D]   She said to him, "Today the glory of father's house was revealed."

[E]   They said about Saul's house that [they were so modest] that their heel and their toe never saw [their privy parts].

[F]   This is in line with that which is written, "And he came to the sheepfolds [by the way, where there was a cave; and Saul went in to relieve himself]" (1 Sam. 24:3).

[G]   R. Bun bar R. Eleazar: "It was a sheepfold within yet another sheepfold."

[H]   "And Saul went in to relieve himself" ["cover his feet"]: [David] saw him lower his garments slightly and excrete slightly [as needed].

[I]   [David] said, "Cursed be anyone who lays a hand on such modesty."

[J]   This is in line with that which he said to him, "Lo, this day your eyes have seen [how the Lord gave you today into my hand in the cave; and some bade me kill you, but it spared you]" (1 Sam. 24:10).

[K]   It is not written, "I spared you," but "It spared you"—that is, "Your own modesty is what spared you."

[L]   And David said to Michal, "But by the maids of whom you have spoken, by them I shall be held in honor" (2 Sam. 6:22).

[M]   For they are not handmaidens ('amahot), but mothers ('immahot).

[N]   And how was Michal punished? "And Michal the daughter of Saul had no child to the day of her death" (2 Sam. 6:23).

[O]   And is it now not written, ". . . and the sixth was 'Ithream of Eglah, David's wife" (2 Sam. 3:5)?

[P]   She lowed like a cow (Eglah) and expired [giving birth on the day of her death].

[Q]   You have no Israelite who so lowered himself in order to do religious deeds more than did David.

[R]   On what account did he lower himself for the sake of religious deeds?

[S]   For the people were staring at the ark and dying, as it is written, "And he slew some of the men of Beth Shemesh, [because they looked into the ark of the Lord; he slew seventy men, and fifty thousand men, of them, and the people mourned because the Lord had made a great slaughter among the people]" (1 Sam. 6:19).

[T]   R. Haninah and R. Mana: one said, " 'And he smote of the people seventy men'—this refers to the Sanhedrin.

[U]   " 'And fifty thousand men'—for they were comparable in worth to fifty thousand men."

[V]   And one of them said, " 'He smote of the people seventy men'—this is the Sanhedrin.

[W]   " 'And fifty thousand'—of the ordinary people as well."

[X]   It is written, "A song of ascents of David: O Lord, my heart is not lifted up" (Ps. 131:1)—"when Samuel anointed me."

[Y]   "My eyes are not raised too high" (Ps. 131:1)—"when I slew Goliath."

[Z]   "And I do not occupy myself with things too great [or too marvelous for me]" (Ps. 131:1)—"when I brought the ark up."

[AA]   "Or too wondrous for me"—"when they put me back on my throne."

[BB]   "But I have calmed and quieted my soul, like a child quieted at its mother's breast" (Ps. 131:2)—"Like a child which gives up goes down from its mother's belly, so my soul is humbled for me."

Once more the Talmud has little to say about the rule of Mishnah. I.A goes over familiar ground. Unit II is not relevant to Mishnah, and unit III is added to fill out the picture of David, mentioned tangentially in the discussion of unit II.

2:5

[A]   *[The king] calls out [the army to wage] an optional war [fought by choice on the instructions of a court of seventy-one.*

[B]   *He [may exercise the right of eminent domain in order to] open a road for himself, and [others] may not stop him.*

[C]   *The royal road has no required measure.*

[D]   *All the people plunder and lay before him [what they have grabbed], and he takes the first portion.*

[I.A]   [The rule of M. San. 2:5A is in line with] that which is written, "At his word they shall go out, and at his word they shall come in, [both he and all the people of Israel with him, the whole congregation]" (Num. 27:21).

[II.A]   *He [may exercise the right of eminent domain in order to] open a road for himself and others may not stop him [. . . and he takes the first portion] (M. San. 2:5B–D).*

[B]   This is in line with that which is written, "And the people drove those cattle before him, and said, 'This is David's spoil' " (1 Sam. 30:20).

[III.A]   "He was with David at Pas-dammim, [when the Philistines were gathered there for battle. There was a plot of ground full of barley, and the men fled from the Philistines. But he took his stand in the midst of the plot and defended it, and slew the Philistines; and the Lord saved them by a great victory]" (1 Chron. 11:13–14). [Note also 2 Sam. 23:11f.: "And next to him was Shammah, the son of Agee the Hararite. The Philistines gathered together at Lehi, where there was a plot of ground full of lentils; and the men fled from the Philistines. But he took his stand in the midst of the plot and defended it, and slew the Philistines; and the Lord wrought a great victory."]

[B]   R. Yohanan said, "It was a field as red as blood [so the place-name is taken literally]."

[C]   And R. Samuel said, "[It was so called] for from that place the penalties ceased [as will be explained below]."

[D]   "When the Philistines were gathered [there for battle, there was a plot of ground full of barley." R. Jacob of Kepar Hanan said, "They were lentils, but their buds were as fine as those of barley [which accounts for the divergence between 1 Chron. 11:12 and 2 Sam. 23:11]."

[E]   Said R. Levi, "This refers to the Philistines, who came standing up straight like barley, but retreated bent over like lentils."

[F]   One Scripture says, "There was a plot of ground full of barley" (1 Chron. 11:13), and it is written, ". . . full of lentils" (2 Sam. 23:11).

[G]   [20c] R. Samuel bar Nahman said, "The event took place in a single year, and there were two fields there, one of barley, the other of lentils."

[H]   [To understand the following, we must refer to 2 Sam. 23:15–16: "And David longed and said, 'O that someone would give me water to drink from the well of Bethlehem which is by the gate!' And the three mighty men broke through the host of the Philistines and drew water out of the well of Bethlehem that was by the gate." Now "water" here is understood to mean "learning," "gate" the rabbinical court, and David is thus understood to require instruction. At issue is the battlefield in which the Philistines had hidden themselves, that is, as at Pasdammim. What troubled David now is at issue.] David found it quite obvious that he might destroy the field of grain and pay its cost (DMYM).

[I]   Could it be obvious to him that he might destroy the field and *not* pay its cost [to its Israelite owners]? [It is not permissible to rescue oneself by destroying someone else's property, unless one pays compensation. So that cannot be at issue at all.]

[J]   [If he did have to pay, as he realized, then what he wanted to know "at the gate" was] which of them to destroy, and for which of the two to pay compensation [since he did not wish to destroy both fields such as, at G, Samuel posits were there].

[K]   [These are then the choices] between the one of lentils and the one of barley.

[L]   The one of lentils is food for man, and the one of barley is food for beast. The one of lentils is not liable, when turned into flour, for a dough offering, and the one of barley is liable, when turned into flour, for dough offering. As to lentils, the *omer* is not taken therefrom; as to barley the *omer* is taken therefrom. [So these are the three choices before David, and since there were two fields, he wanted to know which to burn and for which to pay compensation.]

[M] [This entire picture of the character of the battlefield is rejected by rabbis,] for rabbis say there was one field, but the incident took place [twice, in a period of] two years [and hence, in one year, it was planted with one crop, in the other year, the other].

[N] David then should have learned from the rule prevailing in the preceding year. But they do not derive a rule from one year to the next.

[O] One verse states, "They took their stand in the midst of the plot and defended it" (1 Chron. 11:14).

[P] And the other Scripture states, ". . . and he defended it" (2 Sam. 23:12).

[Q] What this teaches is that he restored the field to its owner, and it was as precious to him as a field planted with saffron.

[IV.A] It is written, "And David said longingly, 'O that some one would give me water to drink from the well of Bethlehem [which is by the gate']" (1 Chron. 11:17).

[B] R. Hiyya bar Ba said, "He required a teaching of law."

[C] "Then the three mighty men broke through [the camp of the Philistines]" (1 Chron. 11:18).

[D] Why three? Because the law is not decisively laid down by fewer than three.

[E] "But David would not drink of it; [he poured it out to the Lord, and said, 'Far be it from me before my God that I should do this. Shall I drink the lifeblood of these men? For at the risk of their lives they brought it']" (1 Chron. 11:18–19).

[F] David did not want the law to be laid down in his own name.

[G] "He poured it out to the Lord"—establishing [the decision] as [an unattributed] teaching for the generations [so that the law should be authoritative and so be cited anonymously].

[H] [Delete:] *He may exercise the right of eminent domain in order to open a road for himself, and others may not stop him.)*

[I] Bar Qappara said, "It was the festival of Sukkot, and the occasion was the water offering on the altar, and it was a time in which high places were permitted [before the centralization of the cult in Jerusalem]. [So the view that David required a legal teaching is not accepted; it was literally water which David wanted and got.]"

[J]   "And three mighty men broke through . . ."—Why three? One was to kill [the Philistines]; the second was to clear away the bodies; and the third [avoiding the corpse-uncleanness] was to bring the flask for water in a state of cultic cleanness.

[K]   One version of the story states, ". . . He poured it out to the Lord . . ." (1 Chron. 11:18).

[L]   And the other version of the story states, "He spilled it . . ." (2 Sam. 23:16).

[M]   The one which states "spilled" supports the view of R. Hiyya bar Ba [who treats the story as figurative], and the one which stated, "poured it out to the Lord" supports the picture of Bar Qappara [who treats it as a literal account].

[N]   Huna in the name of R. Yosé, "David required information on the laws covering captives."

[O]   R. Simeon b. Rabbi says, "What he thirsted after was the building of the house for the sanctuary [the Temple]."

Once more the Talmud to the Mishnah pericope is brief and scarcely informative; there are no analytical initiatives at all.

2:6

[A]   *"He should not multiply wives to himself" (Deut. 17:17)—only eighteen.*

[B]   *R. Judah says, "He may have as many as he wants, so long as they do not entice him [to abandon the Lord] (Deut. 17:17)."*

[C]   *R. Simeon says, "Even if there is only one who entices him [to abandon the Lord]—lo, this one should not marry her."*

[D]   *If so, why is it said, "He should not multiply wives to himself"?*

[E]   *Even though they should be like Abigail [1 Sam. 25:3].*

[F]   *"He should not multiply horses to himself" (Deut. 17:16)—only enough for his chariot.*

[G]   *"Neither shall he greatly multiply to himself silver and gold" (Deut. 17:17)—only enough to pay his army.*

[H]   *"And he writes out a scroll of the Torah for himself" (Deut. 17:18)—*

[I]   *When he goes to war, he takes it out with him; when he comes back, he brings it back with him; when he is in session in court, it is with him; when he is reclining, it is before him,*

[J]   *as it is said, "And it shall be with him, and he shall read in it all the days of his life" (Deut. 17:19).*

[K]   *[Others may] not (1) ride on his horse, (2) sit on his throne, (3) handle his sceptre.*

[L]   *And [others may] (4) not watch him while he is getting a haircut, or (5) while he is nude, or (6) in the bathhouse,*

[M]   *since it is said, "You shall surely set him as king over you" (Deut. 17:15)—that reverence for him will be upon you.*

[I.A]   R. Kahana: "[The limitation to eighteen wives] is by reason of the following: 'And the sixth, Ithream, of Eglah, David's wife. These were born to David in Hebron' (2 Sam. 3:5). And what is stated further on? '. . . I would add to you as much more . . .' (2 Sam. 12:8). [This indicates that there would be yet two more groups of six wives, eighteen in all.]"

[B]   "He should not multiply horses to himself (Deut. 17:16), only enough for his chariot" (M. San. 2:6F).

[C]   This is in line with the following: "And David hamstrung all the chariot horses, but left enough for a hundred chariots" (2 Sam. 8:4).

[D]   "Neither shall he greatly multiply to himself silver and gold" (Deut. 17:17)—only enough to pay his army (M. San. 2:6G).

[E]   R. Joshua b. Levi said, "But that provides solely for the wages for a given year alone [and not wages for several consecutive years]."

[II.A]   Said R. Aha, "Said Solomon, '[I said of laughter, it is mad' (Qoh. 2:2)]. 'Three things the attribute of justice ridiculed and I profaned:

[B] " 'He should not multiply wives to himself' (Deut. 17:17).

[C] "And it is written, 'Now King Solomon loved many foreign women' (1 Kings 11:1)." [This pericope resumes below, I.]

[D] R. Simeon b. Yohai said, "He loved them literally, that is, he fornicated with them."

[E] Hananiah, nephew of R. Joshua, says, "[He actually married them and violated the precept,] 'You shall not marry with them' (Deut. 7:3)."

[F] R. Yosé says, "It was to draw them to the teachings of Torah and to bring them under the wings of the Indwelling Presence of God."

[G] R. Eliezer says, "It was by reason of the following verse: 'Did not Solomon king of Israel sin on account of such women? . . . nevertheless foreign women made even him to sin' (Neh. 13:26)."

[H] It turns out that R. Simeon b. Yohai, Hananiah, and R. Eliezer maintain one viewpoint, and R. Yosé differs from all three of them.

[I] " 'He should not multiply horses to himself' (Deut. 17:16).

[J] "And it is written, 'Solomon had forty thousand stalls of horses for his chariots and twelve thousand horsemen' (1 Kings 4:26).

[K] "They were unemployed, [there being peace in Solomon's days].

[L] "But one who is not a king is permitted in these [that is, having many wives and horses, and much gold and silver] (PM.QH).

[M] "And it is written, 'And the king made silver to be in Jerusalem as stones' (1 Kings 10:27)."

[N] Was none of them stolen?

[O] Said R. Yosé b. Haninah, "They were stones of a measure of ten cubits or eight cubits, and so they were [too large to be so stolen]."

[P] R. Simeon b. Yohai taught, "Even the weights in the time of Solomon were not of silver but of gold."

[Q]   What is the Scriptural basis for this statement? "None was of silver; it was accounted as nothing in the days of Solomon" (1 Kings 10:21).

[R]   It is written, "I said of laughter, 'It is mad' (Qoh. 2:2)."

[S]   Said the Holy One, blessed be He, to Solomon, "What is this crown [doing] on your head? Get off my throne."

[T]   R. Yosé b. Hanina said, "At that moment an angel came down and took the appearance of Solomon and removed Solomon from his throne and took the seat in his stead."

[U]   Solomon went around the synagogues and schoolhouses, saying, "I, Qohelet, have been king over Israel in Jerusalem" (Qoh. 1:12).

[V]   But they showed him the king sitting in his basilica, and [said to him,] "Do you say, 'I Qohelet'?" And they beat him with reeds and placed before him a dish of grits.

[W]   At that moment he wept and said, "This was my portion from all my labor" (Qoh. 2:10).

[X]   There are those who say they beat him with a staff, and there are those who say they beat him with a reed, and some say that they beat him with a belt of knotted rope.

[Y]   Now who caused Solomon's downfall [= was his adversary]?

[Z]   Said R. Joshua b. Levi, "It was the *yud* in the word, 'increase' (YRBH) which served as his adversary."

[AA]   R. Simeon b. Yohai taught, "The book of Deuteronomy went up and spread itself out before the Holy one, blessed be He.

[BB]   "It said before him, 'Lord of the world! You have written in your Torah that any convenant part of which is null is wholly nullified.'

[CC]   "Now lo, Solomon wishes to uproot a *yud* [as above] of mine.'

[DD]   "Said to him the Holy One, blessed be He, 'Solomon and a thousand like him will be null, but not one word of yours will be nullified.'

[EE]   R. Huna in the name of R. Aha: "The *yud* which the Holy One, blessed be he, removed from our matriarch, Sarah, [when her name was changed from Sarai,] half of it was given to Sarah, and half of it was given to Abraham."

[FF]   R. Hoshaiah taught, "The *yud* went up and prostrated itself before the Holy One, blessed be he, and said, 'Lord of the world! You have uprooted me from the name of that righteous woman!'

[GG]   "The Holy One, blessed be he, said to him, 'Go forth. In the past you were set in the name of a woman, and at the end of the name [Sarai]. By your life, I am going to put you in the name of a male, and at the beginning of the name.' "

[HH]   This is in line with that which is written, "And Moses called Hoshea b. Nun, 'Joshua' " (Num. 13:16).

[**III**.A]   *And he writes for himself a scroll of the Torah (Deut. 17:18)*—

[B]   **for his own use, that he not have to make use of the one of his fathers, but rather of his own [T. San. 4:7].**

[C]   And they correct his scroll by comparing it to the scroll of the Temple courtyard, on the authority of the Sanhedrin of seventy-one members.

[D]   *When he goes forth to war, it goes with him,* as it is said, "And it shall be with him, and he shall read in it all the days of his life" (Deut. 17:19) [Cf. M. San. 2:6I–J].

[E]   **Lo, it is a matter of an argument *a fortiori:* Now if a king of Israel, who is taken up with the needs of Israel, is told, "And he shall read in it all the days of his life," an ordinary person, how much the more so [must he read in the Torah all the days of his life].**

[F]   **Along these same lines, concerning Joshua it is written, "This book of the law shall not depart out of your mouth, but you shall meditate on it day and night" (Joshua 1:8).**

[G]   **Lo, it is a matter of an argument *a fortiori:* Now if Joshua, who is taken up with the needs of Israel, is told, "You shall meditate in it day and night," an ordinary person, how much more so [must he meditate in the Torah all the days of his life] [T. San. 4:8–9].**

[**IV**.A]   A king of Israel: *Others may not ride on his horse, sit on his throne, or handle his crown, sceptre (M. San. 2:6K),* or any other of his possessions.

[B]   And when he does, all of them are to be burned in the presence of his corpse, as it is said, "You shall die in peace. And as spices were burned for your fathers, the former kings who were before you, so men shall burn spices for you and lament for you" (Jer. 34:5).

[C]   *And others may not see him while he is nude, or when he is getting a haircut, or in the bathhouse (M. San. 2:6L).*

[D]   This is in line with the following verse: "Your eyes will see the king in his beauty" (Is. 33:17).

[E]   R. Haninah went up to R. Yudan the Patriarch. He came out to greet him, dressed in his undershirt.

[F]   He said to him, "Go and put on your woolen cloak, on the grounds of 'Your eyes will see the king in his beauty' (Is. 33:17)."

[G]   R. Yohanan went up to call on R. Yudan the Patriarch. He came forth to receive him in a shirt made of cotton.

[H]   He said to him, "Go back and put on your cloak of wool, on the grounds of: 'Your eyes will see the king in his beauty.' "

[I]   When R. Yohanan was leaving, [R. Yudan the Patriarch] said to him, "Bring refreshment for the mourner [bring good cheer]."

[J]   He said to him, "Send and get Menahem, the cake baker, for it is written, 'The teaching of kindness is on her tongue' (Prov. 31:26)."

[K]   As he was leaving, [Yohanan] saw R. Haninah bar Sisi chopping wood.

[L]   He said to him, "Rabbi, this occupation is not consonant with your status."

[M]   He said to him, "And what shall I do? For I have no one who serves me as a disciple."

[N]   He said to him, "If you have no one to serve you as a disciple, you should not accept upon yourself appointment [to a court]."

[V.A]   Yosé Meoni interpreted the following verse in the synagogue in Tiberias: " 'Hear this, o priests!' (Hos. 5:1): Why do you not labor in the Torah? Have not the twenty-four priestly gifts been given to you?

[B]   "They said to him, 'Nothing at all has been given to us.'

[C]   [20d] " 'And give heed, O House of Israel!' (Hos. 5:1).

[D]   " 'Why do you not give the priests the twenty-four gifts concerning which you have been commanded at Sinai?'

[E]   "They said to him, 'The king takes them all.'

[F]   " 'Hearken, O house of the king! For the judgment pertains to you' (Hos. 5:1).

[G]   "To you have I said, 'And this shall be the priests' due from the people, from those offering a sacrifice . . . : they shall give to the priest the shoulder, the two cheeks, and the stomach' (Deut. 18:3).

[H]   "I am going to take my seat with them in court and to make a decision concerning them and blot them [the kings] out of the world."

[I]   R. Yudan the Patriarch heard [about this attack on the rulers] and was angry.

[J]   [Yosé] feared and fled.

[K]   R. Yohanan and R. Simeon b. Laqish went up to make peace with [the Patriarch].

[L]   They said to him, "Rabbi, he is a great man."

[M]   He said to them, "Is it possible that everything which I ask of him, he will give to me?"

[N]   They said to him, "Yes." [So Yosé was called back.]

[O]   [The Patriarch] said to [Yosé], "What is the meaning of that which is written: 'For their mother has played the harlot' (Hos. 2:5)?

[P]   "Is it possible that our matriarch, Sarah, was a whore?"

[Q]   He said to him, "As is the daughter, so is her mother.

[R]   "As is the mother, so is the daughter.

[S]   "As is the generation, so is the patriarch.

[T]   "As is the patriarch, so is the generation.

[U]   "As is the altar, so are its priests."

[V]   Kahana said likewise: "As is the garden, so is the gardener."

[W]   He said to them, "Is it not enough for him that he dishonors me one time not in my presence, but also in my presence he does so these three times [Q–T]!"

[X]   He said to him, "What is the meaning of that which is written, 'Behold, everyone who uses proverbs will use this proverb about you, 'Like mother, like daughter' (Ez. 16:44).

[Y]   "Now was our matriarch, Leah, a whore?

[Z]   "As it is written, 'And Dinah went out' (Gen. 34:1) [like a whore, thus reflecting on her mother]"

[AA]   He said to him, 'It is in accord with that which is written, 'And Leah went out to meet him' (Gen. 30:16).

[BB]   "They compared one going out to the other [and Leah went out to meet her husband, and Dinah learned from this that it was all right to go out, so she went out to meet the daughters of the land, but got raped]." [This was an acceptable reply to Yudan.]

[VI.A] R. Hezekiah was going along the way. A Samaritan met him. He said to him, "Rabbi, are you the rabbi of the Jews?"

[B]   He said to him, "Yes."

[C]   He said to him, "Note what is written, 'You will surely set a king over you' (Deut. 17:15).

[D]   "It is not written 'I shall set . . . ,' but 'You shall set . . . ,' for you yourself set him over you."

Unit **I** systematically cites and lightly glosses the Mishnah, as indicated. But, as usual, the Talmud cannot resist the theme of the Davidic (here: Solomonic) materials, which are taken up and amply interpreted. The cited verses of Scripture, however, make this exercise considerably more *à propos* than their counterparts in the earlier units. The segments of the story about Solomon's deposition are separated from one another but are readily restored. Unit **III** then returns to the Mishnah, and up to **IV**.D we have a fairly straightforward set of materials, parallel to unit **I**. But the remainder of unit **IV** develops ideas relevant to the proof text cited at the outset, Is. 33:17. I assume that unit **V** is inserted because of its materials on the hostility of sages to the patriarch, in line with the stories of unit **IV**.

Still, since the Mishnah's basic theme is the law of the king, the materials are pertinent in general if not in detail, and that is probably why they are inserted. In all, here again the Talmud has the quality of an anthology of topical materials.

4 Yerushalmi Sanhedrin
Chapter Three

3:1

[A]   [21a] *Property cases are [decided by] three [judges] (M. 1:1A).*

[B]   *"This litigant chooses one [judge], and that litigant chooses one judge, and then the two of the [litigants] choose one more," the words of R. Meir.*

[C]   *And sages say, "The two judges choose one more."*

[I.A] [The basic theory,] said R. Zira, is that, since the litigant chooses the judge, he takes for granted that his choice will seek out cause in his own behalf.

[B]   What is the reasoning of R. Meir [who maintains that the third judge is chosen with the knowledge and consent of the litigants]?

[C]   It is so that the third (lit., three) of them will be chosen with the concurrence [of the litigants].

[D]   What is the reasoning of rabbis [who do not require the knowledge and consent of the litigants]?

[E]   [One party will say to the other,] "You have not got the power to choose and seat the one of your choice. Rather, you and I will choose and seat one of our choice." [Thus there can be no end to the matter.]

[F]   But there is a problem to the position of sages [who exclude the intervention of the litigants]: if one of the two judges who choose the third judge should die [and the litigant whose choice has died should choose a replacement, it turns out that the third judge will have been chosen with the knowledge and consent of the two litigants]. [For the new judge has had no role in choosing him. So the third judge will remain on the court, even though the newly chosen judge does not concur in the matter. It must follow that the litigants must agree (PM).] It turns out that all three judges have been selected with the knowledge and consent of the litigants.

The Talmud provides a thorough account of the reasoning behind the Mishnah's law and dispute.

3:2

[A]   *"This party has the right to invalidate the judge chosen by that one, and that party has the right to invalidate the judge chosen by this one," the words of R. Meir.*

[B]   *And sages say, "Under what circumstances?*

[C]   *"When he brings evidence about them, that they are relatives or [otherwise] invalid [to serve as judges].*

[D]   *"But if they are valid [judges] or experts recognized by a court, he has not got the power to invalidate them."*

[I.A]   Thus the Mishnah teaches that this one may invalidate the judge chosen by the other. Lo, [he then may not invalidate] the judge he himself has chosen [even though he has reason to retract].

[B]   R. Simeon b. Laqish said, "Meir's rule applies to court archives in Syria [made up of amateurs]. But lo, to courts set up in accord with the law of the Torah [made up of experts], [what he has said does] not [apply]. [The archival courts are made up of unqualified people, not experts. If they are experts, then Meir concurs that there can be no disqualification. Thus he agrees with M. 3:2B–D.]"

[C]   R. Yohanan said, "Even in the case of courts set up in accord with the law of the Torah [and made up of experts, Meir maintains the same position]. [Thus he differs from M. 3:2B–D.]"

[II.A]   Thus do they say:
    Two men had a case in Antioch. One of them said to his fellow, "That which R. Yohanan will rule [in this case] do I accept for myself."

[B]   R. Yohanan heard and ruled: "He does not have the power to compel his antagonist [to go to Tiberias for the trial]. But [the court in Antioch] will hear the claims of both parties there. Then if there is need, they may write up the particulars of the case and send the case to the rabbis."

[C]   R. Eleazar said, "This one says, 'In Tiberias,' and that one says, 'In Sepphoris'—they accept the position of the one who said, 'In Tiberias.' "

[D]   [With regard to the statement of Meir, M. 3:2A,] may this one continue to invalidate the judges whom the other brings?

[E]   Said R. Zira, "The rule has been taught with reference to a supererogatory court [made up of amateurs]."

[F]   Said R. La, "And as to that which R. Eleazar has stated, 'This one says, 'In Tiberias,' and that one says, 'In Sepphoris'— they accept the position of the one who said, 'In Tiberias'—
       "that statement applies to a case in which the two live in the same neighborhood in town, [so that] from here to there [for both parties] will be the same distance, e.g., of seven *mils* or of nine *mils*."

[G]   Said R. Yosé, "You may derive from the law a further consideration. If there are two men at litigation with one another in Tiberias, and this one says, 'In the major court,' and the other one says, 'In the minor court' [of the same town], they accept the statement of the one who said, 'In the major court.' "

Unit **I** presents the two possibilities for interpreting Mishnah. I see no connection between **II**.A–B and unit **I**. The tie is thematic, namely, further information on conflicts over the choice of judges. C is relevant to B. **II**.D–E seem to me to go over the ground of **I**.B, that is, Zira says the same thing as Simeon b. Laqish; then D–E are wildly out of place. **II**.F clearly relates directly to **II**.C, and the same is so of **II**.G. The main point of unit **II**, then, is that the choice of judges may involve the location of the court as much as the identities of the members of the court, a valuable addition to M.

3:3

[A]   "*This party invalidates the witnesses brought by that one, and that party invalidates the witnesses brought by this one,*" *the words of R. Meir.*

[B]   *And sages say, "Under what circumstances?*

[C]   *"When he brings evidence about them, that they are relatives or otherwise invalid.*

[D]   *"But if they are valid [to serve as witnesses], he has not got the power to invalidate them."*

[I.A]   R. Simeon b. Laqish said, "Thus the Mishnah [concerning Meir, M. 3:3A] teaches: 'His witness' [one of those brought by the antagonist]. Lo, two of his witnesses [one may not invalidate]."

[B]   R. Yohanan said, "Even the two witnesses he has brought [may the antagonist invalidate]."

[C]   This is in line with that which is taught:

[D]   **Under all circumstances they continue adding judges until the court process has been completed. And the witnesses too may retract [their originally stated position until the court process has been completed]. . . . Once the court process has been completed, they cannot retract [T. San. 6:4].** [This shows one may invalidate *both* witnesses of the other party prior to judgment.]

[E]   R. Yohanan concedes that if there are there only those witnesses, they [the contrary litigants] cannot invalidate them [since now the action is against the essence of the case of the other party].

[F]   Said R. Zeira, "And he and an outsider [from the marketplace] may join together to invalidate this testimony [if the latter, not party to the case, does have testimony against the witness himself]."

[G]   R. Hanina raised the question: "[How is it possible to invalidate a single witness, even in the event that the contrary litigant has access to other witnesses? Will this not permit one party to the dispute to invalidate the essence of the case of the other, prior to hearing what is at issue? For even if a single witness has not got the power to impose on the defendant a monetary claim,] he does have the power to require him to take an oath." [Now this question applies to Yohanan and Simeon b. Laqish, but in context, it is addressed to Zeira: Even if the intent is to invalidate only a single witness, how can we permit this procedure?]

[H]   Said R. Zeira, "As to one invalid to give testimony, he must be invalidated in court. As to a relative, it is not necessary to invalidate him in court. [In the case under discussion, it is necessary to invalidate the witness solely on factual grounds that he is a relative. If the evidence against the proposed witness deals with the suitability of the man to testify at all, not merely with the fact of his relationship, then the action must be taken in court and with proper judicial safeguards. Consequently, we do not have a case in which one party invalidates the essence of the case of the other.]"

[II.A]   [With reference to the following passage of T. San. 6:3K–P: **And how many do they add? Step by step, two at a time. [When] they add to the judges, [if] they rule, "He is innocent," he is innocent. If they rule, "He is guilty," he is guilty. [If] one says, "He is innocent," and one says, "I don't know," they add to the judges, for up to that point the court has been evenly divided. [If] one says, "He is liable," and one says, "He is innocent," and one says, "I don't have an opinion," they add to the judges, for up to now they have added only one judge at a time (T. San. 6:3K–P). Under all circumstances they continue adding judges until the court process has been completed (T. San. 6:4A),**] said Raba bar Buna in the name of Rab, "[They add to the court only when one ruled for one party, one for the other, and one declined to rule. When they added the same situation pertained. But if to begin with two have ruled for one party and one for the other, and when they added to the court, one ruled for one party and one declined to rule, there now are three judges who hold a single position. Consequently,] when three [concur], it is the completion of the trial, [and a decision has been reached]."

Unit **I** does a good job of analyzing the Mishnah's rule. The important point comes at **I.E**, which generates the discussion and clarification provided by **I.F–H**. One party cannot invalidate the witnesses of the other if that means the other party has no case at all. This now has to be clarified. G points out that such an action will affect even a single witness, not only two. H then works out the needed clarification. Unit **II** takes up a segment of the passage of Tosefta cited for the purposes of unit **I**. It has nothing to do with our problem.

3:4

[A]   *[If] one litigant said to the other, "I accept my father as reliable," "I accept your father as reliable," "I accept as reliable three herdsmen [to serve as judges],"—*

[B]   *R. Meir says, "He has the power to retract [after the decision]."*

[C]   *And sages say, "He has not got the power to retract [after the decision]."*

[D]   *[If] one owed an oath to this fellow, and this fellow said, "[Instead of an oath,] take a vow to me by the life of your head,"*

[E]   *R. Meir says, "He has the power to retract [after the decision]."*

[F]   *And sages say, "He has not got the power to retract [after the decision]."*

[I.A]   [If] one said to him, "Your father is acceptable to me" [and if] he accepted [his father as witness or judge] before two individuals, he has the power to retract.

[B]   If he did so before three, he does not have the power to retract [in the opinion of sages, for the three constitute a court].

[C]   Samuel said, "[The dispute of the Mishnah pericope] applies in a case in which one has not taken the disputed object from one party and given it to the other. But if one has taken it from one party and given it to the other, the one who made the statement no longer has the power to retract, [for the transaction has been completed in the transfer of the disputed object, and the winning party has effected possession of the object]. [Even Meir now must concur that there can be no further retraction.]"

[D]   Both R. Yohanan and R. Simeon b. Laqish said, "Even if [the court] has taken [the disputed object] from this party and given it to that party, [in Meir's view] he can retract."

[II.A]   [WM'SH B: **Someone owed his fellow an oath in court and**] **vowed to him by the life of a certain object, and [the person to whom the oath was owed] accepted it [T. San. 5:M]**—the latter can retract. [The vow is null.]

[III.A]   [Leiden MS and *editio princeps*: 3:5] "The argument of Meir and sages applies,]" said R. Hiyya bar Ba, "in a case in which [the plaintiff] said to [the defendant], 'Let your father say to me, And I have no claim against you.' But if [the defendant] said to [the plaintiff], 'Let your father say, And I accept upon me,' it is a mere pretext which he gave since he wanted [the father] to concur with [the defendant]. [That is, the claimant says, 'If your father says that matters are thus-and-so, then I have no further claim against you. But if the defendant said to him, 'Let your father say that matters are such-and-so, as you have stated,' this is of no weight at all. The defendant merely hoped the father would support his case, not the son's case; the statement of the defendant then has no bearing.]"

[B]   R. Yosé b. Haninah said, "And even if [the plaintiff] said, 'Let your father say so, and I shall accept [your claim] against me,' [that statement is null,] for we do not find valid testimony which a relative may give [in any such case at all]. [So the whole is null.]"

The dispute of unit **I** is fundamental: to what point in the procedure does the Mishnah's dispute apply? Samuel maintains that, once a valid act of acquisition has taken place, there can be no further retraction. Unit **II**, clarifying M. San. 3:4D–F, deals with an informal vow, which is null. Sages' position is expanded. Unit **III** presents yet a further important clarification of the Mishnah, filling out the language of M. San. 3:4A by explaining circumstances in which one may accept the testimony of the father and when, under such circumstances, said testimony has effect (**III.A**).

3:5 [In Leiden MS and *editio princeps*: 3:6]

[A]   *And these are those who are invalid [to serve as witnesses or judges]:*

[B]   *(1) he who plays dice; (2) he who loans money on interest; (3) those who race pigeons; (4) and those who do business in the produce of the Seventh Year.*

[C]   *Said R. Simeon, "In the beginning they called them, 'Those who gather Seventh Year produce.' When oppressors became many [who collected taxes in the Seventh Year], they reverted to call them, 'Those who do business in the produce of the Seventh Year.' "*

[D]   *Said R. Judah, "Under what circumstances? When [the after-named (B)] have only that as their profession. But if they have a profession other than that, they are valid [to serve as witnesses or judges]."*

[I.A]   These are they who are invalid [M. San. 3:5A]: *He who plays dice [M. San. 3:5A–B(1)]—*

[B]   this refers to one who plays with blocks of wood.

[C]   All the same are one who plays with blocks of wood, and one who plays with nutshells or pomegranate shells—

[D]   under no circumstances do they accept the testimony of such a person unless he undertakes to break his blocks of wood and to carry out a complete reformation.

[E]   *One who lends on interest [M. San. 3:5B(2)]* do they not accept [as a witness] unless he tears up bonds of indebtedness owing to him, and [undertakes] to carry out a complete reformation.

[F]   *Those who race pigeons [M. San. 3:5B(3)]—*

[G]   this refers to one who trains pigeons.

[H]   All the same are the one who trains pigeons and the one who trains any other sort of domesticated beast, wild beast, or bird—

[I]   under no circumstances do they accept the testimony of such a person unless he undertakes to break his stages (or rinse) and to carry out a complete reformation.

[J]   *Those who do business in the produce of the Seventh Year [M. San. 3:5B(4)]—*this is a merchant in the produce of the Seventh Year.

[K]   **What is such a merchant? This is one who sits idle during the other six years of the septennate. Once the Seventh Year comes, he begins to do business in produce of the Seventh Year.**

[L]   **Under no circumstances do they accept such a person until another year of release arrives, and one may test him and find that he has reformed himself completely.**

[M]   (It was taught: R. Yosé [says], "Two septennates.")

[N]   **R. Nehemiah says, "It must be a reform through property, not merely a reform through what he has said.**

[O]   **"How so?**

[P]   **"[He must say,] 'These two hundred *denars* I collected from the sale of produce of transgression.' Then [he must] hand them out to the poor"** [T. San. 5:2].

[Q]   They added to the list of those named-above shepherds, thugs, robbers, and anyone with a shady reputation in financial matters. Their testimony is null.

[R]   Said R. Abbahu, "This applies to shepherds of small cattle [but not large ones]."

[S]   R. Huna said, "Who taught that pigeon racers [are unacceptable as witnesses]?" It is R. Eliezer, as it has been taught, *Pigeon racers are invalid as witnesses [M. Ed. 2:7].*

[T]   Said R. Mana in the presence of R. Yosé, "And further, is this teaching in respect to Sanhedrin also in accord [only] with R. Eliezer?"

[U]   He said to him, "It is the opinion of all parties, in the present matter [of oaths]."

[V]   Said R. Yosé [continuing T–U], "We knew that such a one was invalid to serve as a witness in a monetary case. Concerning what did [R. Eliezer] come to give testimony? But just as he is invalid to give testimony in a monetary case, so he is invalid to give testimony in a capital case.

[W]   "And witnesses to the appearance of the new moon are in the status of witnesses to capital cases."

[X]   For we have learned:

[Y]   *This is the general principle: In the case of any sort of testimony which a woman is not valid to give, also they are not valid to give [M. R.H. 1:8].*

[Z]   Who taught this rule? It is the rabbis [since Eliezer cannot concur, for S leaves no room for Y's exception].

[AA]   Now do the rabbis accord with R. Eliezer? Do they teach in accord with his opinion *and* differ from him?

[BB]   R. Jonah said, in the name of R. Huna: "The entire passage is in accord with the opinion of R. Eliezer [who concurs that those listed at M. San. 3:5B and M. Sheb. 7:4C and M. R.H. 1:8 may testify of matters about which women may testify]."

[CC]   The disputes of these [Eliezer, rabbis] are parallel to the disputes of those [Yosé, Meir], as it has been taught:

[DD]   **"A witness [shown to have conspired against another party and so to have] perjured [himself] is invalid for giving evidence in every matter covered by the Torah,"** the words of R. Meir.

[EE]   **Said R. Yosé, "Under what circumstances? When such a person has been perjured in a capital case.**

[FF]   **"But if he was perjured in a case involving a monetary claim, he is invalid only for the purpose of giving that particular testimony alone"** [T. Mak. 1:11].

[GG]   Now the opinion of R. Yosé is in accord with that of rabbis, and the opinion of R. Meir is in accord with that of R. Eliezer.

[II.A] *Said R. Simeon, "In the beginning they called them, 'Those who gather Seventh Year produce.' When oppressors became many [who collected taxes in the Seventh Year], they reverted to call them, 'Those who do business in the produce of the Seventh Year.' " Said R. Judah, "Under what circumstances? When they have only that as their profession. But if they have a profession other than that, they are valid [to serve as witnesses or judges]" [M. San. 3:5C–D].*

[B]   What would be a concrete example [of Judah's position]?

[C]   **It is one who sits idle during the other six years of the septennate. Once the Seventh Year comes, he stretches out his hands and legs and does business in produce of the Seventh Year [T. San. 5:2K].**

[D]   [But] if he has yet another profession, he is valid, and [only] if not is he invalid.

[E]   But if he carried out his own profession through all the years of the septennate, and once the Seventh Year arrives, he then stretches out his hands and does business in produce of the Seventh Year, even though such a person has no other profession [in the Seventh Year itself], he [too] is valid.

[F]   R. Ba bar Zabeda, R. Abbahu in the name of R. Eleazar: "The law is in accord with the opinion of R. Judah in the present pericope of the Mishnah [M. San. 3:5D]."

[G]   R. Ba bar Zabeda was praised because he stated this tradition in the name of someone [Abbahu] who was younger than he.

[H]   R. Hiyya taught this tradition [of Judah's views] in a strict way [as we shall now see].

[I]   What would be a concrete example [of a strict ruling]?

[J]   [If] one was sitting and occupied [21b] with his normal profession all the years of the septennate, and [only] once the Seventh Year began, he began to stretch out his hands and do business in the produce of the Seventh Year, even though he has some other profession along with [this activity], he is invalid [for giving testimony].

[K]   [What follows is dependent on M. Sheb. 4:2: *A field that has been cleared of thorns in the Seventh Year may be sown in the eighth year; but one that has been prepared or used by cattle may not be sown in the eighth year.* Now in that context it is stated that sages permitted ploughing once in the Sabbatical Year to pay taxes, but if one did so two times, he then is penalized by sages and not permitted to sow in the eighth year. In this context it is stated:] Is it not in this case that R. Ba bar Zabeda, R. Abbahu in the name of R. Eleazar, said, "The law is in accord with R. Judah of the Mishnah [that one is invalid as a witness if he has no other profession"? In R. Hiyya's view he is always invalid. It must follow that sages did not permit on any occasion that one do business with produce of the Seventh Year. Why is it stated here that the field has been prepared or improved as a special case? There is no need for such a specification (PM)].

[L]   There [they praised] R. Ba bar Zabeda who stated the tradition in the name of one who is younger than he. Therefore that is the law. Here too the law should be the same.

[M]   Said R. Yosé b. R. Bun, "There the government did not force [the people to farm in the Seventh Year], but here they did force them [to farm in the Seventh Year in order to pay taxes]. [Where the person who does business in the produce of the Seventh Year is prohibited from testifying is a case in which the government did not force him to do what he was doing. But where he is permitted to testify, it is because he had no choice. Then sages permitted one sowing, for purposes of raising crops to pay taxes.]"

[N]   When the government first became oppressive, R. Yannai gave instructions that the people might plough one time. There was an apostate to idolatry, who transgressed the laws of the Seventh Year. When he saw them throw up the ploughed clods, he said to them, "Oh! that perversion of the law! You have been given permission to plough [in the Sabbatical Year, because of the government's edict], but have you been permitted to throw up the ploughed clods?" [Cf. Jastrow I.328B, s.v. H'SṬW.]

[O]   [As to Yannai's permitting the people to plough in the Seventh Year,] said R. Jacob bar Zabedi, "I asked before R. Abbahu, 'Did not Zeira and R. Yohanan in the name of R. Yannai say, [or] R. Yohanan in the name of R. Simeon b. Yehosedeq: "They voted in the upper room of the house of Nitzeh in Lud:

[P]   " ' "In regard to the Torah, how do we know that if an idolater should say to an Israelite to transgress any one of all of the religious duties which are stated in the Torah, except for idolatry, fornication, and murder, that he should transgress and not be put to death . . . ?'

[Q]   " ' "Now that rule applies to some matter which is done in private.

[R]   " ' "But if it is a matter of public desecration, then even for the most minor religious duty one should not obey him. [So how could Yannai have permitted the people to plough in the Seventh Year?]

[S]   " ' "For example, there is the case of Papus and Lulianos, his brother, to whom they gave water in a colored glass flask [bearing an idol's name], and they did not accept it from them." ' "

[T]   [Yannai] said, "[The case is different here. For] they do not have in mind to force the Jews to commit apostasy [which is not the issue], but solely to pay taxes. [In such a case it is permitted publicly to violate the laws of the Torah.]"

[U]   How many are present for the case to involve public desecration?

[V]   Rabbis of Caesarea say, "Ten, as it is written, 'I will be sanctified among the people of Israel' (Lev. 22:32)."

[W]   They saw R. Bina the Younger running after an ass on the Sabbath [at the instance of idolaters].

[X]   R. Yonah and R. Yosé gave instructions to bake bread for Ursicinus on the Sabbath.

[Y]   Said R. Mani, "I asked before R. Jonah, 'Father, now did not R. Zeira, R. Yohanan in the name of R. Yannai, R. Jeremiah, R. Yohanan in the name of R. Simeon b. Yehosedeq say: "They voted in the upper room of the house of Nitzeh, etc. [as above O–R]." ' [So how can you permit Jews to bake bread in public on the Sabbath?]"

[Z]   He did not intend to force them to apostasize; he intended only to eat warm bread.

[AA]   How many are present for the case to involve public desecration?

[BB]   Rabbis of Caesarea say, "Ten, as it is written, 'I will be sanctified among the people of Israel' (Lev. 22:32)."

[CC]   R. Abuna raised the question to R. Ami: "As to idolaters, what is the law as to their being commanded to sanctify the Name?"

[DD]   He said to him, " 'I will be sanctified among the people of Israel' (Lev. 22:32). Israelites are commanded to sanctify God's name, and idolaters are not commanded to sanctify God's name."

[EE]   R. Nisi in the name of R. Eleazar derived the same rule from the following: " 'In this matter may the Lord pardon your servant [Naaman]: [when my master goes into the house of Rimmon to worship there, . . . and I bow myself in the house of Rimmon, when I bow myself in the house of Rimmon, the Lord pardon your servant in this matter]' (2 Kings 5:18).

[FF]   "This indicates that Israelites are commanded concerning the sanctification of God's name [through not publicly or privately practicing idolatry, as in the cited instance], but idolaters are not commanded concerning the sanctification of God's name."

[GG]   R. Ba bar Zamina was employed in sewing clothes by someone in Rome. [The Roman] brought him carrion meat.

[HH]   He said to him, "Eat."

[II]   He said to him, "I am not going to eat."

[JJ]   He said to him, "Eat, or I'll kill you."

[KK]   He said to him, "If you want to kill me, kill me, but I'm not going to eat carrion meat."

[LL]   He said to him, "Who told you [that my intention was to test you], for had you eaten the meat, I would have killed you. If you are going to be a Jew, be a Jew. If you are going to be a Roman, be a Roman [Aramaean]."

[MM]   Said R. Mana, "Had R. Ba bar Zamina heard the teaching of the rabbis, [who said that it is all right to transgress in private,] he would have eaten in this case."

[NN]   As to clearing a field in the Seventh Year in this time, [in which case the rabbis' applied penalty that one who does so in the Seventh Year is penalized and may not sow in it in the year after the Seventh Year,] what is the law? [That is, does the rule of sages still apply?]

[OO]   R. Jeremiah thought to say, "Once the [Roman] law is annulled, then the rabbis' decree also is nullified."

[PP]   R. Yosé thought to say, "The decree of the rabbis remains valid indefinitely, until another court will be called into session and nullify it."

[QQ]   And similarly the [two authorities, Jeremiah and Yosé, differ in the following case]:

[RR]   At what point does one effect acquisition of produce of his in the Seventh Year?

[SS]   R. Jeremiah thought to say, "Once he has put the produce into his baskets."

[TT]   R. Yosé thought to say, "Even if they are put into his baskets, he has not acquired possession of them. For he will be thinking that at that point they belong to him, but they do not belong to him at all."

[UU]   When Perocles came to Sepphoris, R. Mana instructed the bakers to put out [bread] in the marketplace on the Sabbath.

[VV]   Rabbis of Naveh gave instructions [to the bakers] to bake leavened bread on Passover.

[WW]   Said R. Yosé b. R. Bun, " 'Keep I the king's command, and because of your sacred oath be not dismayed' (Qoh. 8:2)—the command of the King of kings do I keep, who said to me at Sinai, 'I am the Lord your God' (Ex. 20:2).

[XX]   "And as to that commandment, 'You shall have no other gods before me,' this refers to the oath of God: 'You shall not take the name of the Lord your God in vain.' "

[YY]   [As to the name of Nebuchadnezzar: In all other matters you are king, as to taxes and corvées, but in this matter, you are] like an empty pot [and] the barking [of a dog]. That man [you] and a dog are equal [to us, for we do not obey you].

[III.A]   R. Judah in the name of Rab: "The law is in accord with R. Judah."

The opening units, appearing also at M. Shebi. 7:4 and R.H. 1:8, amplify Mishnah's materials on those invalid to give testimony. Unit II, which takes up Judah's ideas, stresses the matter of right conduct in the Seventh Year. There are two pictures of Judah's view, as indicated. Once the solution to the apparent conflict between Judah's ruling and the established law for the Seventh Year requires us to invoke the consideration of state intervention, a fresh and interesting question follows. It is whether we distinguish diverse causes for violating the law. The trend of the discussion is to distinguish, in particular, the state's forcing Jews to violate the Torah essentially for reasons neutral to Judaism, e.g., the state's own service or convenience, and Jews being forced to apostasize and so violate the law and so to disgrace God and the Torah. It is this latter kind of pressure, but not the former, which Jews must resist at all costs. That is the main point which flows from the exposition of Judah's view, in the light of, and in comparison with, the matter of M. Shebu. 4:2. We notice in this present unit a number of problems of lower criticism, e.g., the repetition of F–G at L, but this is with good reason. U–V clearly should not be repeated by AA–BB. UU–VV also belong together with W–X. There are contradictory trends in the materials, as is self-evident, and the proposed distinction falls away at WWf. I do not understand why YY is included, unless the intent is to underline the distinction between state-enforced idolatry, which is to be resisted, and state-enforced violation of the law of the Torah for some legitimate public purpose, which is not to be resisted.

3:6 [In Leiden MS and *editio princeps: 3:7]*

[A]   *And these are relatives [prohibited from serving as one's witnesses or judges]: (1) one's father, (2) brother, (3) father's brother, (4) mother's brother, (5) sister's husband, (6) father's sister's husband, (7) mother's sister's husband, (8) mother's husband, (9) father-in-law, and (10) wife's sister's husband—*

[B]   *they, their sons, and their sons-in-law;*

[C]   *but the stepson only [but not the stepson's offspring].*

[D]   *Said R. Yosé, "This is the version of R. Aqiba. But the earlier version [is as follows]:*

[E]   *"His uncle, the son of his uncle [Lev. 25:49], and anyone who stands to inherit him [M. B.B. 8:1]."*

[F]   *And anyone who is related to him at that time.*

[G]   *[If] one was a relative but ceased to be related, lo, that person is valid.*

[H]   *R. Judah says, "Even if his daughter died, if he has sons from her, lo, [the son-in-law] is deemed a relative."*

[I.A]   Since we have learned that his brother [is deemed invalid as a relative], what need is there to teach, "The brother of his father"?

[B]   It is to indicate that [included as relatives are] the son and son-in-law of the son-in-law of his father's brother.

[C]   Since we have learned that the brother of his father [is deemed invalid as a relative], what need is there to teach, "The brother of his mother"?

[D]   It is to indicate that [included as relatives are] the son and the son-in-law of the son-in-law of his mother's brother.

[E]   Since we have learned that the husband of his sister [is deemed invalid as a relative], what need is there to teach, "The husband of his father's sister"?

[F]   It is to indicate that [included as relatives are] the son and the son-in-law of the son-in-law of the husband of his father's sister.

[G]   Since we have learned that the husband of his father's sister [is deemed invalid as a relative], what need is there to teach, "The husband of his mother's sister"?

[H]   It is to indicate that [included as relatives are] the son and the son-in-law of the son-in-law of the husband of his mother's sister.

[II.A]   But we have learned, *The stepson only [M. San. 3:6C].* [This would exclude the stepson's wife, who may testify.]

[B]   Rab said, "If the son-in-law of his mother-in-law is forbidden, the husband and his stepdaughter all the more so [are forbidden]. [Since the father-in-law and son-in-law are forbidden, and since a woman is in the status of her husband, then the son-in-law of his father-in-law also is forbidden. This then would include the son-in-law from the first husband. That is, the husband's daughter by another woman and the wife's daughter from another husband are married to two men. One then is the son-in-law of the mother-in-law of the other, even though the wives are merely related as stepdaughters. Nonetheless, the two men may not testify in one another's behalf (PM).]"

[C]   [That is not the case.] Interpret the rule to speak of a case in which the woman has sons and sons-in-law from his father-in-law.

[III.A]   As to the wife's sister's husband [of M. 3:6A(10)], there is a Tanna who teaches that his sons and sons-in-law also are prohibited to serve as witnesses.

[B]   There is a Tanna who teaches that his sons and sons-in-law are permitted to serve as witnesses.

[C]   The one who maintains that the sons and sons-in-law are subject to the prohibition of testimony regards them as deriving from the sister of his wife [and hence are related through the mother].

[D]   The one who maintains that the sons and sons-in-law are not subject to the prohibition of testimony regards them as deriving from some other source [than the sister of his wife]. [That is, they are the children of some other woman entirely who married his wife's sister's husband.]

[IV.A]   Rab went out to look over a property for R. Hiyya the Elder. He passed through a certain place and found R. Yohanan in session and raised the following question:

[B]   "We have learned, 'The stepson only.'

[C]   "What is the law as to the wife of the stepson? [Is she valid to testify, in light of Mishnah's statement?] What is the law as to the husband of one's stepdaughter?

[D]   "Do we maintain that a woman is in the status of her husband, and a husband is in the status of his wife? [In this case the wife of the stepson or husband of the stepdaughter also is prohibited from testifying.]

[E]   "And the matter was settled that, indeed, the wife of his stepson is in the status of his stepson, [or] the husband is in the status of the wife [and what is excluded by Mishnah's language is the sons and sons-in-law of the stepson]."

[V.A]   R. Hisda raised the question: "What is the law concerning the third generation's being permitted to testify in respect to the wife of the first generation?

[B]   "As to Moses, what is the law as to his being permitted to testify concerning the wife of Phineas [his grandson] [and, further, do we invoke the rule that the wife is in the status of the husband in the third generation as in the first]?"

[C]   R. Simeon b. Laqish said, "They accept the testimony of the second and third generation when it is out of necessity."

[D]   R. Yohanan said, "Even if there is ample [testimony, that of the named parties also is acceptable]."

[VI.A]   [If one was a relative but ceased, that person is valid (M. San. 3:6G).] This is in line with the following case: The wife's sister's husband of R. Huna had a suit against a certain person.

[The former wife's sister's husband of Huna] said, "Whatever R. Huna says I accept [as valid evidence in this case]."

[B]   R. Huna heard and said the same. [That is, he maintained the same position, that he was then valid to testify for his former wife's sister's husband.]

[C]   "[For," he continued,] "I know that just as they said that that rule applies to the earlier generation [e.g., if one's daughter had died,] so it applies to the later generation [e.g., if the wife's sister's husband becomes free to testify in behalf of his former wife's sister's brother."

[D]   R. Jeremiah in the name of Rab: "The law is in accord with the statement of R. Judah [at M. San. 3:6H, that is, contrary to C, the foregoing statement]."

The secondary exposition of M. San. 3:1A now turns to exclusions by reason of family ties. The basic entry, M. 3:6A–C, is clear as given. The earlier version, E, simply excludes all male relatives who stand to inherit. The second clarification, after Yosé's is at M. 3:6F–H. F–G take account of the possibility of one's ceasing to be related, e.g., if one's wife died. The exegesis of Mishnah at unit I systematically extends the stated prohibition to the sons-in-law. This simply exemplifies the rule that the husband is in the status of the wife, and vice versa, even when not specified. So, we see, the extended family is worked out through the lines of marriage as well. Unit II takes up the specification of M. 3:6C, "the son-in-law only," as does unit IV. I am not clear as to the meaning of the materials of unit II. Unit IV, by contrast, is readily accessible. Unit III poses no problems. Unit V moves beyond the limits of Mishnah by asking about grandchildren. The matter is not amply treated. Unit VI, finally, exemplifies the possibilities of M. 3:6G.

3:7 [In Leiden MS and *editio princeps*: 3:8]

[A]   *"One known to be a friend and one known to be an enemy— [are prohibited to serve as a judge or a witness].*

[B]   *"One known to be a friend—this is the one who served as his groomsman;*

[C]   *"one known to be an enemy—this is one who has not spoken with him for three days by reason of outrage."*

[D]   *They said to [Judah], "Israelites are not suspect for such considerations."*

[I.A]   R. Tablai, R. Abina in the name of Rab: "[The law covering the groomsman applies not only on the day of the wedding, but also] throughout the seven days of the wedding celebration. [For that period the groomsman may not testify. But thereafter he may do so.]"

M. 3:7 is generally understood to continue Judah's saying. He now adds two items to the original list, and his additions are rejected for the stated reason, but only after B–C, a rather fullsome exposition of their own.

3:8 [In Leiden MS and *editio princeps*: 3:9]

[A]   *How do they test the witnesses?*

[B]   *They bring them in and admonish them.*

[C]   *Then they take all of them out and keep back the most important of the group.*

[D]   *And they say to him, "Explain: How do you know that this one is liable to that one?"*

[E]   *If he said, "He told me 'I owe him,'*

[F]   *[or] 'So-and-so told me that he owes him,' " he has said nothing whatsoever,*

[G]   *unless he says, "In our presence he admitted to him that he owes him two hundred 'zuz.' "*

[I.A]   [With regard to M. San. 3:8E, F,] R. Yosé in the name of R. Yohanan: "If [the defendant] clearly intended to hand on solid testimony [as to his guilt, not merely a remark made casually], then the testimony to that effect given by witnesses indeed is valid."

[II.A] **How do they carry out a judgment?**

[B]   **The judges seat themselves, and the litigants remain standing before them.**

[C]   **Whoever brings claim against his fellow is the one who opens the proceedings [T. San. 6:3],**

[D]   as it is said, ". . . Whoever has a complaint, let him go to them [Aaron and Hur, as judges]" (Ex. 24:14).

[E]   And how do we know that the one who lays claim against his fellow bears the burden of proof?

[F]   R. Qerispa in the name of R. Hananiah b. Gamaliel: " '. . . let him go to them . . . ,' [meaning,] Let him bring his evidence to them."

[G]   R. Yohanan raised the question, "In the case of a childless sister-in-law, who brings claim against whom?"

[H]   R. Eleazar replied, "And is it not written, '. . . then the brother's wife shall go up to the gate to the elders' (Deut. 25:7)?"

[I]   R. Yohanan said, "Well did R. Eleazar teach one."

[J]   [Resuming A–C] R. Berekhiah and R. Helbo, R. Ba in the name of R. Yannai: "The plaintiff makes his claim, and the defendant replies, and then the judge makes his decision."

[K]   Said R. Simon, "The judge has to rehearse the claims [of the plaintiff and the defendant], as it is said, 'Then the king said, "The one says, 'This is my son that is alive, and your son is dead'; [and the other says, 'No, but your son is dead, and my son is the living one]' " ' (1 Kings 3:23)."

[III.A]   [21c] R. Huna, when he would see witnesses using identical language, would undertake a strict examination. And when he did so, it turned out that he was right [that there had been a prior rehearsal on what the witnesses were to say].

[B]   R. Huna would ridicule a judge who [began the proceedings, e.g., by asking,] "Do you accept the testimony of one witness?" But [he maintained that the litigants] must open the proceedings.

[C]   R. Huna, when he knew reason to acquit someone in court, and [the litigant] could not properly present his argument, he [R. Huna] would argue for [the litigant]—on the basis of "Open your mouth for the dumb, for the rights of all who are left desolate; open your mouth, judge righteously . . ." (Prov. 31:9).

[IV.A]   R. Abbahu in the name of R. Yohanan: "He who hides his witnesses behind a wall [to entrap another party] has not accomplished anything."

[B]   It is in line with the following: There was a man who wanted to join at a banquet.

[C]   [The host] said to him, "Will you give me what you owe me?"

[D]   He said to him, "Yes."

[E]   After they got up from the banquet, [the unwanted guest] said to him, "I don't owe you anything at all."

[F]   [The host] said to him, "I have witnesses [that you confessed to the debt]."

[G]   [The defendant] said to him, "I only said that because I didn't want to ruin your banquet."

[H]   The case came before R. Ammi, who ruled, "This is in line with that which R. Yohanan has stated, 'He who hides his witnesses behind a wall has not accomplished anything.' "

The Talmud presents a fairly ample picture of the Mishnah's meaning and amplifies on the theme of Mishnah. Unit I is an important clarification. Unit II moves on to the general matter of court procedure. Then units III and IV take up the theme of cross-examining witnesses and the sorts of witnesses whose testimony is acceptable to begin with—in all, a model of what is needed.

3:9 [In Leiden MS and *editio princeps:* 3:10]

[A]   *And afterward they bring in the second and test him in the same way.*

[B]   *If their testimony checks out, they discuss the matter.*

[C]   *[If] two [judges] say, "He is innocent," and one says, "He is guilty," he is innocent.*

[D]   *[If] two say, "He is guilty," and one says, "He is innocent," he is guilty.*

[E]   *[If] one says, "He is innocent," and one says, "He is guilty," and one says, "I do not know,"*

[F]   *they have to add to the judges.*

[G]   *And even if two declare him innocent and two declare him guilty—*

[H]   *but one of them says, "I don't know,"*

[I]   *they [still] have to add to the judges.*

[I.A]   The smallest number of goats (Lev. 16:5: "Two male goats for a sin offering") is two. Why then does Scripture specify "two"? To indicate that the two of them should be equivalent to one another.

[B]   The smallest number of lambs (Lev. 14:10) is two. Why then does Scripture specify "two"? To indicate that the two of them should be equivalent to one another.

[C]   The smallest number of birds is two. Why then does Scripture specify "two" ["two living clean birds" (Lev. 14:4)]? To indicate that the two of them should be equivalent to one another.

[D]   The smallest number of trumpets (Num. 10:2) is two. Why then does Scripture specify "two"? To indicate that the two of them should be equivalent to one another.

[E]   [The foregoing is relevant because of the following:] R. Haggai objected to R. Yasa, "And is it not written, 'If a malicious witness raises against any man to accuse him of wrongdoing, then both parties to the dispute shall appear before the Lord . . .' (Deut. 19:16–17)?

[F]   "Shall we now say: 'The smallest number of men is two'? Why then does Scripture specify, 'the two parties'? Is it to say that both of them must be equivalent to one another? But has it not been written [to the contrary, indicating that they need not be equivalent to one another], 'You shall not pervert the justice due to the sojourner or to the fatherless' (Deut. 24:17)? Lo, a sojourner may enter into a case with one who is not a sojourner, an orphan enters into a case with one who is not an orphan.

[G]   "If so, why has it been written, 'two'?

[H]   "It is a superfluous word, left available for drawing an analogy therefrom or for constructing an argument on the foundation of similarities.

[I]   "[This argument, specifically, is as follows:] Here is it stated, 'two,' and below it says, 'Now two men remained in the camp, one named Eldad, and the other named Medad, and the spirit rested upon them' (Num. 11:26).

[J]   "Just as in the cited passage the reference is to men, not women, so here [with regard to testimony] the meaning is to permit [two] men, but not women or children [to testify].

[K]   "Thus we have learned that a woman does not judge or give testimony in court."

[L]   R. Yosé b. R. Bun in the name of R. Joseph: "Here 'two' is said, and elsewhere 'two' is said.

[M]   "Just as elsewhere, the meaning is that by the evidence of two witnesses a case is decided (Deut. 19:15), so here, on the basis of two witnesses a case is decided.

[N]   "If so, why does Scripture specify, 'Two'?"

[O]   "The meaning is that [they must be treated equally, so] one may not stand while the other is sitting, one may not state his case as is fitting, while the other is told, 'Cut it short.' "

[P]   **Said R. Judah, "I heard that if the judge wanted to have the two of them sit down together, he may do so."**

[Q]   **R. Ishmael says, "They say to him, 'Dress just as the other party is dressed, or give him garments equivalent to yours' "** [T. San. 6:2H–J].

[R]   Said R. Ba in the name of R. Huna, "The witnesses have to stand when they give testimony, since it is said, 'And the two parties to the dispute shall stand before the Lord' (Deut. 19:17)."

[S]   R. Jeremiah in the name of R. Abbahu: "Also those who are subject to trial must stand when they receive the judgment pertaining to them, since it said, 'Then both parties to the dispute shall appear before the Lord' (Deut. 19:17)."

[II.A]   It is written, "The fathers shall not be put to death for the children" (Deut. 24:16).

[B]   And has it not also been stated, "Every man shall be put to death for his own sin" (Deut. 24:16)?

[C]   Why does Scripture then state, "The fathers shall not be put to death for the children"?

[D]   The fathers shall not be put to death by the testimony of the children, and the children shall not be put to death by the testimony of the fathers.

[E]   How then do we know [further] that witnesses may not be related to the litigants, and how do we know that witnesses may not be related to one another [= M. 3:6]?

[F]   Take note that, if they should be declared to be conspiring witnesses, is it not by their own testimony that they are put to death [in which case relatives turn out to testify against one another, which is not permitted]?

[G]   And how do we know that witnesses may not be related to the judges?

[H]   Take note that if one of the witnesses is declared a conspiratorial witness, is he put to death before his fellow also is so declared? [Of course not.] If you say so, will he not be put to death by his testimony? [That is, the judges will turn out to inflict the death penalty on their own relatives.]

[I]   And how do we know that the judges may not be related to one another?

[J]   The Torah has declared that one should be put to death on the testimony of witnesses, and one should be put to death at the decision of judges. Just as witnesses may not be related to one another, so judges may not be related to one another.

[K]   I know that [these rules apply] only to fathers and children. How do I know that they supply to other relationships?

[L]   Said R. Zeira, "*And* children"—the use of "and" serves to encompass other relatives.

[M]   This explanation is suitable for R. Aqiba [who deems the use of the word "and" to bear meaning as indicated]. How is the question to be answered within the exegetical techniques associated with the name of R. Ishmael?

[N]   R. Ishmael teaches, " 'Then the congregation shall judge . . . then the congregation shall rescue . . .' (Num. 35:24, 25).

[This rule teaches that the congregation] may not be made up of relatives either of the one who has administered the blow or the one who has received it."

[O]   Said R. Yosé, "If you say so [that the court may be related to the one receiving the blow], you turn out to rule that a court may be made up of avengers of the blood [and Num. 35:24 clearly differentiates between the court and the avenger of the blood]."

[P]   "On this basis we learn that the judges may not be related to the accused."

[Q]   And how do we know that the witnesses may not be related to the accused?

[R]   The Torah has said that one should administer the death penalty on the testimony of witnesses, and one should administer the death penalty on the testimony of judges. Just as judges may not be related to the accused, so the witnesses may not be related to the accused.

[S]   And how do we know that the witnesses may not be related to one another?

[T]   Take note that if they should be declared conspiring witnesses, is it not by their now testimony that they are put to death?

[III.A]   *[The law governing an oath of testimony applies to men and not to women, to those who are not related and not to those who are related,] to those who are suitable to bear witness, and not to those who are not suitable to bear witness [M. Sheb. 4:1A].*

[B]   This is in line with that which is said, "If he does not speak, he shall bear his iniquity" (Lev. 5:1).

[C]   [This applies to] him who gives evidence, so that his fellow will have to pay out money. It thus excludes one who is unfit to give testimony, for even if he does tell what he knows, his fellow is not going to have to pay out money.

[D]   *Before a court [and not before a court:]* This excludes the case of a single witness [without a corroborating witness], in a case in which they said to him, "Lo, you are acceptable for us as two witnesses."

[E]   Is it possible to suppose that, in the stated case, such a one
       should be liable [to the oath of testimony]?

[F]   Scripture has stated, ". . . whether he has seen or come to
       know the matter, yet does not speak" (Lev. 5:1)—this refers to
       one who is suitable to give testimony valid by the law of the
       Torah, excluding a lone witness, who is not valid to give testi-
       mony by the law of the Torah.

[G]   *And not before a court:* "If he does not speak, he shall bear his
       iniquity" (Lev. 5:1)—[the oath thus applies to] the one who re-
       ports what he has seen and [his fellow] pays what he owes, ex-
       cluding a case outside of a court, in which even if one reports
       what he knows, his fellow is not going to have to pay out
       compensation.

[H]   And how do we know that the law applies to two witnesses?
       Scripture says, "And he . . . a witness . . . ," lo, here are two
       witnesses.

[I]   And this is in accord with R. Ishmael (PM).

[J]   R. Ishmael has said, "In any case in which it is written in the
       Torah, 'Witness,' without further explanation, lo, under dis-
       cussion in fact are two witnesses, unless Scripture informs you
       explicitly that it means to speak of only a single witness." Thus
       R. Ishmael has found two witnesses [to be liable] (PM).

[K]   As to a single witness [who swears he has no knowledge], what
       is the law as to declaring him liable for taking a rash oath?

[L]   Is it possible to say so? Since it is possible to join another wit-
       ness to his testimony and to impose on [both of them] liability
       for an oath of testimony, how can you [ever] impose upon him
       liability for a rash oath?

[M]   [Along these same lines,] what is the law as to imposing liabil-
       ity upon a relative for a rash oath [since he cannot testify in
       court]?

[N]   [Is the answer to this question] in line with the following,
       which R. Ba bar Samuel stated, "[If one said,] 'I swear that
       Mr. So-and-so has given a *maneh* to Mr. So-and-so,' and it
       turns out that he never gave him the money [he is exempt from
       liability, for the oath was invalid], since he has not got the
       power to speak about the future [in an oath], he also has not
       got the power to speak about what has happened in the past"?

[So the answer to M is negative, since the relative cannot govern matters in the future.]

[O]   Or [is the answer to the question raised in line with the following]?

[P]   If one said to him, "Where is my ox," and he said to him, "I do not know what you're talking about," and the case was that the ox had died or broken its leg or been captured or been lost,
"I impose an oath on you,"
and the other said, "Amen,"—
the latter is exempt [from punishment for having taken a false oath] [M. Shebu. 8:2].

[Q]   Rab said, "He is exempt by reason of taking a false oath of bailment, but he is liable by reason of taking a rash oath." [Likewise the answer to M is affirmative.]

[R]   Said R. Yohanan, "Since it is a religious duty to appease him, he is not liable on the count of having taken a rash oath."

[S]   In the view of Rab, is it not a religious duty to appease his fellow? One appeases him by telling the truth, but he does not appease him by a lie.

[T]   [Concurring that where there is no oath of testimony, there still is a rash oath, which has been violated and must be expiated,] R. Ishmael taught, " '. . . he shall bear his iniquity' (Lev. 5:1) [by bringing] an offering."

[U]   How do we know that [the denial nonetheless must take place] before a court [even in the case of a relative or someone else who is not suitable for testimony in court]?

[V]   We derive the matter from "telling."

[W]   [That is to say,] just as "telling" in this context [Lev. 5:1] involves doing so in court, so "telling" mentioned in connection with the rebellious elder [Deut. 17:9] involves doing so in court.

[IV.A]   (As to the following:) The evidence of witnesses is not combined [so that we have the testimony of two witnesses] unless the two of them saw the incident simultaneously—

[B]   R. Joshua b. Qorha says, "Even if they saw it sequentially."

[C]   R. Jeremiah in the name of Rab: "Sages concede to R. Joshua b. Qorha in the matter of witnesses to the claim of one to be the firstborn, and in the case of witnesses to the claim of one to have established rights of ownership through usucaption, [that successive, not simultaneous, witness, is acceptable]."

[D]   R. Ba in the name of R. Jeremiah: "Also in the case of testimony as to the presence of the signs [of puberty] the fact is the same."

[E]   This is indeed self-evident. [If] one says, "I saw two hairs in his privy parts," and the other said, "I saw two hairs on his body" [the two statements are not acceptable as joined testimony that the person is now mature (PM)].

[F]   [If] one says, "I saw a single hair on his privy parts," and one says, "I saw a single hair on his belly," it is as nothing [the statements are not acceptable as joined testimony]—is it not so that all the more so [we deem one statement regarding] his privy parts and one [regarding] his body [as unacceptable for joined testimony] (PM).

[G]   [If] two say, "We saw a single hair on his privy parts," and two say, "We saw a single hair on his belly"—

[H]   R. Yosé and R. Hoshaiah [21d] bar R. Shimi—one said, "He is unfit [not yet mature]," and the other said, "He is fit."

[I]   The one who said that he is unfit deems the testimony to be equivalent to that of one who testifies concerning the appearance of only part of the required sign [of maturity]. The one who said he is valid [maintains], "I say that [there were two, but one of them] may have fallen out."

[J]   [If] one party says, "I saw two hairs on his privy parts," and one says, "I saw two hairs on his belly,"

[K]   R. Ba said, "In the opinion of all parties, he is now valid, [since there is sure evidence that there are the requisite two pubic hairs]."

[L]   Said R. Haggai, "In the opinion of all parties he is invalid."

[M]   R. Yosé says, "The matter is still subject to dispute."

[N]   Said R. [Yosé] to R. Haggai, "Lo, R. Yudan [my student] ruled in accord with my view of the matter."

[O]   He said to him, "Now since I differ from his master, all the more so do I disagree with him!"

[P]   Said R. Mana, "R. Haggai's ruling is quite sound. For if we
       have a bond which bears four seals, and one party gives testi-
       mony concerning two of them, while another gives testimony
       concerning two of them, and someone cavils at the value of the
       bond, is the bond of any value whatsoever? [Hardly!] For does
       not each seal require the validation of two witnesses? Here too
       each sign [of maturity] requires the validation of two
       witnesses."

[Q]   R. Hinena derived the same facts from the case of [attesting to
       full use and enjoyment of a property] throughout the years of
       usucaption [to which testimony must be brought]. [That is, if
       one wishes to establish the claim of title through usucaption, he
       must bring evidence that he has held and used the property for
       a given number of years.] "Now if one witness testified that he
       had enjoyed usucaption for the first, second, and third years,
       and one witness testified that he had enjoyed usucaption for the
       fourth, fifth, and sixth years, is it possible that such [joined]
       testimony is worth a thing? Is it not so that each year of usu-
       caption must be attested by two witnesses? Here too each sign
       [of maturity] requires the validation of two witnesses."

[V.A] [What follows does not occur at Y. Sheb. 4:1 but, nonetheless,
       carries forward IV.A–B above.] [In regard to Joshua b. Qorha's
       view that the evidence of witnesses is combined even if they
       saw the matter to which they testify sequentially, note the fol-
       lowing:] They accept the testimony of witnesses only when
       they come at the same time [and testify in the same
       proceeding].

[B]   R. Nathan says, "They accept the testimony of the first, and
       when the second comes, they accept his testimony as well."

[C]   When R. Jonathan was in session, he asked, "Is it possible that
       anyone here has heard that the law accords with the teaching of
       R. Nathan?"

[D]   Said to him R. Yosé bar Haninah, "Lo, R. Simeon b. Yaqim
       [has]."

[E]   He said to him, "Go up forward."

[F]   Once he had gotten up, he said to him, "Have you heard that
       the law accords with the teaching of R. Nathan?"

[G]   He said to him, "I have heard: R. Joshua b. Qorha concurs
       with the position of R. Nathan."

[H]   He said to him, "Now is that what we needed? [That is perfectly obvious]. [If Joshua b. Qorha does not require the witnesses to see the fact at the same time, he obviously will not expect them to testify at the same time.]"

[I]   He said to him further, "But R. Yosé bar Haninah intended only to bring R. Simeon b. Yaqim forward, since he is a great man, [and Yosé wanted to be sure that he got full recognition such as was coming to him]."

[VI.A]   R. Hisda raised the question: "What is the law as to accepting the testimony of witnesses not in the presence of a litigant?"

[B]   R. Yosé in the name of R. Shabbetai: "They accept the testimony of witnesses not in the presence of a litigant, and they issue a court decree. If thereafter he comes and objects, his objections may be sustained. [That is, the court then hears his contrary evidence and may act on it.]"

[C]   [In the case of] a man whom the court summoned three times and who did not come to court—

[D]   R. Joshua b. Levi said, "They accept [contrary] testimony in the absence of that litigant, and they issue a court decree."

[E]   This is in line with the following: Kahana died, and left his estate to R. Josiah. R. Eleazar accepted testimony [in behalf of Josiah] in [Josiah's] absence and issued a decree favoring R. Josiah.

[F]   And not only so, but [Kahana] left sacred scrolls. R. Eleazer wrote to the heirs, "Scrolls of which the Land of Israel has established possession do they not remove [from the Land and take] abroad. [The scrolls, therefore, will not be exported to heirs living overseas.]"

[G]   R. Nisi in the name of R. Eleazar, "If one wrote them on condition that he take them abroad, he may take them abroad."

[H]   R. Hiyya bar Ba raised the question before R. Yosé: "What is the law as to taking them abroad?"

[I]   He said to him, "Are you raising this question to me because of a concrete case?"

[J]   He said to him, "No."

[K]   And R. Zeira *[sic!]* was displeased that he had not raised the question in order to make a practical decision, for he indeed knew what one must rule.

[L]   R. Jeremiah had a matter under litigation with someone, and the court accepted testimony in the absence of R. Jeremiah, and they declared R. Jeremiah to be liable [and decided against him].

[M]   R. Jeremiah was sitting and sorrowful: "Is it possible that they accept testimony in the absence of a litigant?"

[N]   R. Huna, R. Pinhas, R. Hezekiah [delete: HWQWQ] did not go into the schoolhouse for the lesson on that day. R. Huna made his way in and found R. Jeremiah in a state of sorrow, and [Jeremiah] said to him, "Is it possible that they accept testimony in the absence of a litigant, even if the litigant is there with them in the same town?"

[O]   He said to him, "I have seen that the rabbis indeed hold that position."

The Talmud for the present pericope of Mishnah through unit **IV** is located at Y. Sheb. 4:1. Unit **II** serves M. San. 3:6–7. The main point of unit **III** is that the oath of testimony is effective in court, and one who cannot give testimony in court therefore will not be liable should he take an oath of testimony and turn out to violate it or to have lied. That fact explains why units **I–II** have been associated with the present Mishnah pericope and the whole made to serve two distinct pericopae. The element of interest in unit **III** comes at the end, Kff., the question of punishing those unsuitable to give testimony in court if they should take an oath, on the grounds that, if it is not an oath of testimony, such an oath *is* a rash oath. Units **V** and **VI** provide information in general relevant to the theme of accepting testimony and acting on it in court. But M.'s concrete principles in no way are elucidated. **VI**.F–K are joined to E, but hardly relate to the present discourse.

3:10 [In Leiden MS and *editio princeps:* 3:11]

[A]   *[When] they have completed the matter, they bring them back in.*

[B]   *The chief judge says, "Mr. So-and-so, you are innocent," "Mr. So-and-so, you are guilty."*

[C]   *Now how do we know that when one of the judges leaves [the court], he may not say, "I think he is innocent, but my colleagues think he is guilty, so what can I do? For my colleagues have the votes!"*

[D]   *And it is said, "He who goes about as a talebearer reveals secrets, [but he that is faithful conceals the matter]" (Prov. 11:13).*

[I.A] Said R. Yohanan, "They force a judge who has taken the position that the accused is guilty to sign the decree of innocence with them, [if that is the position of the majority]."

[B]   R. Simeon b. Laqish said, "The judge who deems the accused to be guilty writes, 'Guilty,' and the judge who deems the accused to be innocent writes, 'Innocent.' "

[C]   The Mishnah pericope [surely] stands at variance with the position of R. Simeon b. Laqish: *How do we know that when one of the judges leaves the court, he may not say, "I think he is innocent, but my colleagues think he is guilty"? [M. San. 3:10C].*

[D]   Now how does R. Yohanan deal with this same matter? [That is, why does he require all the judges to sign the decision, even if they differed from it?]

[E]   [If a judge does not sign with them, people will assume that he did not concur.] [So Yohanan makes provision] so that there will not be anyone to say, "If I had my choice, I would have declared So-and-so to be innocent, but they did not let me do so."

[F]   What is the reasoning of R. Simeon b. Laqish?

[G]   [The minority judge makes provision,] "so that someone else should not come along and maintain the same view as I do, [but since I have signed the decree, contrary to my views,] he will think that even [I], So-and-so, was there on the court, and even he erred in this same matter." [So Simeon b. Laqish allows a judge to keep the record straight as to his opinions.]

The Talmud explores the full possibilities of Mishnah's rule by having Yohanan and Simeon b. Laqish fill out the picture. Yohanan takes Mishnah to mean that the court must be represented as unanimous. Simeon b. Laqish, for good and sufficient reasons, wants minority opinion to register, as against M. 3:10C.

3:11 [In Leiden MS and *editio princeps:* 3:12]

[A] *So long as [a litigant] brings proof, he may reverse the ruling.*

[B] *[If] they had said to him, "All the evidence which you have, bring between this date and thirty days from now,"*

[C] *[if] he found evidence during the thirty-day period, he may reverse the ruling.*

[D] *[If he found evidence] after the thirty-day period, he may not reverse the ruling.*

[E] *Said Rabban Simeon b. Gamaliel, "What should this party do who could not find the evidence during the thirty-day period but found it after thirty days?"*

[I.A] Said R. Oshaiah, "[As to the comparison of this rule, dealing with a case in which the judges are in doubt as to their decision and are willing to consider further evidence, with the situation prevailing when one of the judges cannot make up his mind, in which case they add to the court, we may ask why they do not add to the court here as well.] There [where they add to the court, it is because] it is possible for them to add judges in pairs, but here it is not possible to add more judges [since the full complement has been reached]. [Consequently further evidence is admissible.]"

[B] R. Yohanan and R. Laqish both teach that even here it is possible to add to the court. [For they hold that the point of adding judges is not the need of the available judges for more decisive evidence, as Oshaiah thinks. It is that the judges differ as to the legal principles. Here the *sole* doubt is as to the evidence, not as to the legal principles.]

The Talmud's discourse is somewhat puzzling since, if **I.A** were not located here, it is difficult to see how we might have read Oshaiah's opinion in the present context; but that is precisely the reply of **I.B.**

3:12 [In Leiden MS and *editio princeps:* 3:13]

[A]   *[If] they had said to him, "Bring witnesses,"*

[B]   *and he said, "I don't have witnesses,"*

[C]   *[if] they had said, "Bring proof,"*

[D]   *and he said, "I don't have proof"*

[E]   *and after a time he brought proof, or he found witnesses—*

[F]   *this is of no weight whatsoever.*

[G]   *Said Rabban Simeon b. Gamaliel, "What should this party do, who did not even know that he had witnesses on his side, but found witnesses? Or who did not even know that he had proof, but who found proof?"*

[H]   *[If] they had said to him, "Bring witnesses,"*

[I]   *and he said, "I have no witnesses,"*

[J]   *"Bring proof," and he said, "I have no proof,"*

[K]   *[if] he saw that he would be declared liable in court and [only then] said, "Let Mr. So-and-so and Mr. Such-and-such [now] come along and give evidence in my behalf,"*

[L]   *or if [on the spot] he brought proof out of his pocket—*

[M]   *lo, this is of no weight whatsoever.*

[I.A]   R. Yohanan in the name of R. Hoshaiah [said, "There are] three masters [who differ on the interpretation of this rule].

[B]   "One said, 'At any time at which one brings proof, he may reverse the decision.'

[C]   "One said, 'If he brought contrary evidence in thirty days, he may reverse the decision. If he did so after thirty days, he cannot do so.'

[D]   "And one said, 'Under no circumstances can he overturn the judgment, unless he brings proof that he had no knowledge at all [at the time of the trial, that this further evidence in his behalf was available].' "

[E]   And [with reference to the position of C,] have we not learned: *Rabban Simeon b. Gamaliel said, "What should this party do, who did not even know that he had witnesses on his side, but found witnesses? Or who did not even know that he had proof, but found proof?"* [M. San. 3:12G].

[F]   [With regard to the position of D, that the litigant had no prior knowledge of the availability of the evidence which he now wishes to introduce,] R. La and R. Zira—One said, "This evidence may be introduced unless the other party can disprove the evidence. [The evidence may be presented, so long as the other party cannot disprove it.]"

[G]   The other said, "This evidence may be introduced unless the other party [merely] denies the evidence. [Once the other party points out that he has no pertinent evidence, the losing party cannot reverse the court decision.]"

[II.A]   R. Levi had a case with a litigant in a matter of houses, and they came to court before R. Eleazar.

[B]   After the trial was over, he brought evidence.

[C]   [Eleazar] asked R. Yohanan, who said to him, "So long as he brings proof, he may reverse the decision."

[D]   R. Abemakhis had a litigation with someone concerning mill-stones, and they came to court before R. Eleazer. After the trial was over, he brought witnesses.

[E]   [Eleazar again] asked R. Yohanan, who said to him, "Are you still [in doubt] about this matter? So long as he brings proof, he may reverse the decision."

[F]   Now why was it necessary to cite two cases?

[G]   In the case of R. Levi, the court decision had not yet been issued, while in the case of R. Abemakhis, the court decision had already been issued, [so these were two quite separate situations].

[III.A]   As to the court's validation [of a document in which the signature of the witnesses and judges are not recognized], what is the law as to requiring court action? [That is, do we have to validate all the signatures on a bond before a court, or perhaps, since the bond itself has been validated, it is not necessary to revalidate all the signatures.]

[B]   R. Hoshaiah in the name of Samuel, R. Benai in the name of Samuel:

[C]   One said, "It must be validated either through the signatures of the witnesses or through the signatures of the judges."

[D]   And one said, "It may be validated even by the signature of one witness and a single judge." [So both require revalidation of some of the signatures. But a witness and a judge join together for purposes of validation.]

Unit **I** glosses the Mishnah and provides an exegesis of its materials; unit **II** adds a set of precedents and their interpretation. Unit **III** then may be seen to expand on the established theme, namely, validating evidence not necessarily in hand at the time of a trial. In all, this is a model of a brief Talmudic discussion.

5 Yerushalmi Sanhedrin Chapter Four

4:1

[A] *[22a] All the same are property cases and capital cases as to examination and interrogation [of witnesses],*

[B] *as it is said, "You will have one law" (Lev. 24:22).*

[C] *What is the difference between property cases and capital cases?*

[D] *Property cases [are tried] by three [judges], and capital cases by twenty-three.*

[E] *In property cases they begin [argument] with the case either for acquittal or for conviction, while in capital cases they begin only with the case for acquittal, and not with the case for conviction.*

[I.A] Said R. Yohanan, "In order to protect an Israelite's assets, they say [to a witness in a property case], 'How do you know that this one owes to that one?' " [This explains why witnesses are cross-examined in property cases.]

[B] R. Hiyya bar Ba raised the question before R. Yosé, "How do they apply the law in practice?"

[C] He said to him, it is in accord with R. Yohanan.

[D] "For R. Yohanan said, 'In order to protect Israel's assets, they say [to a witness in a property case], 'How do you know that this one owes money to that one?' "

[II.A] Zeira bar Hinena in the name of R. Haninah, and R. Judah: One said, " '. . . Then you shall inquire and make search and ask diligently' (Deut. 13:14). [That is why there must be a careful cross-examination.]"

133

[B]   And the other said, " 'Justice, justice will you pursue' (Deut. 16:20). [That is why there need not be so careful a cross-examination, so long as justice is done.]"

[C]   Lo, how are [the two conflicting verses to be interpreted]?

[D]   If you see that [solely through close cross-examination] the decision will go forth in accord with the truth, then execute a full cross-examination into it, and if not, then justify [straighten] it out [without elaborate cross-examination, which is not needed].

[E]   When R. Huna would see witnesses using identical language, he would undertake a strict examination. And when he did so, it turned out that he was right [that there had been a prior rehearsal on what the witnesses were to say] (M. 3:8, **III**.A).

[**III**.A]   How do they begin the argument with the case for acquittal?

[B]   [Judges] say, "Is it possible that this man killed someone?"

[C]   Said R. Yosé, "If so, [the court itself will disrupt the case. For] one of the witnesses may say that he has arguments in favor of acquittal, and his fellow will come along and support him, in which case the testimony is amply supported. If you say so, does it come out that you impose guilt on the judges themselves [for disrupting the case]?"

[D]   And are there witnesses for such a liar? [That is, if a witness turns around and repudiates his original testimony and declares the man innocent, will yet a second party support such a reversion?]

[**IV**.A]   Said R. Yohanan, "Whoever does not know how to argue through one hundred arguments that a dead creeping thing is clean and that it is unclean has not got the right to begin the argument for acquittal at all."

[B]   How do they construct such an argument in regard to a dead creeping thing?

[C]   Said R. Yannai, "[An example of an argument to prove that a dead creeping thing is cultically clean is as follows:] Now if a snake, which kills, is clean, a mouse, which does not have the power to kill, all the more so should be cultically clean.

[D]   "Or, turning matters around: a mouse, which cannot kill, is cultically unclean. A snake, which can kill, all the more so should be cultically unclean."

[E]   Replied R. Pinhas, "Lo, there is the scorpion, which kills, and lo, it is clean. [So this argument is null.]"

[F]   It is found to be taught: He said, "The snake is in the same category as the scorpion."

[G]   Said Rabbi, "R. Meir (Leiden MS and *editio princeps* read: Rabbi) had an advanced disciple, who could bring arguments to prove a hundred times over that a dead creeping thing was clean and also that it was unclean."

[H]   They say that that disciple did not know how to teach [anything of substance, but only to create fanciful arguments].

[I]   Said R. Jacob bar Disai, "That disciple was cut off from Mount Sinai [and did not receive a share in the revelation of the Torah]."

Unit **I** deals with why there should be cross-examination of the witnesses at all in a property case, as M. 4:1A specifies is the law. Unit **II** focuses upon the same matter, now asking whether cross-examination is invariably required. It is left to the discretion of the judges. Unit **III** then jumps to M. 4:1E, treating cross-examination as part of the argument for acquittal, and unit **IV** continues the inquiry into the argument for acquittal.

4:2

[A]   *In property cases they decide by a majority of one, whether for acquittal or for conviction,*

[B]   *while in capital cases they decide by a majority of one for acquittal, but only with a majority of two [judges] for conviction.*

[I.A]   Said R. Yannai, "If the Torah were handed down cut-and-dried [so that there were no possibility for disagreement in reasoning about the law and no need to make up one's mind], [the world] wouldn't have a leg to stand on. [RYDBZ: We should not know how to decide a case.]"

[B]   What is the Scriptural basis for that statement?

[C]   "And the lord spoke to Moses . . . ," [telling him the diverse arguments relevant to each law (PM)].

[D]   [Moses] said to him, "Lord of the World! Teach me the [prac-
       tical] law [so that there will be no doubts about it]."

[E]   He said to him, " '. . . follow the majority to incline the law'
       [to a decision, that is, make a decision in the law by a majority
       of the judges' opinions] (Ex. 23:2).

[F]   "[If] those who declare innocent form the majority, declare the
       accused innocent. [If] those who declare the accused to be
       guilty, declare him to be guilty."

[G]   [This is] so that the Torah may be expounded in forty-nine
       ways on the side of a decision of uncleanness, and in forty-nine
       ways in favor of a decision of cleanness. ["Now if I reveal the
       law to you in all its finality, there will be no possibility for such
       a range of argument."] [And forty-nine is the] numerical equiv-
       alent of WDGLW [Song of Songs 2:4].

[H]   And so it says, "The promises of the Lord are promises that
       are pure, silver refined in a furnace on the ground, purified
       seven times seven" (Ps. 12:6). [That is why there must be
       forty-nine arguments, G.]

[I]   And it says, "Rightly do they love you" (Song of Songs 1:4).
       [In argument to work out a right decision, they express their
       love for God.]

       The Talmud presents its theory of why diverse opinions in de-
       cisions are to be deemed praiseworthy. None of this relates to
       the present pericope in particular.

       4:3

[A]   *In property cases they reverse the decision whether in favor of*
       acquittal or in favor of conviction,

[B]   *while in capital cases they reverse the decision in favor of ac-*
       quittal, but they do not reverse the decision in favor of
       conviction.

[I.A] Lo, if one went forth from court having been declared inno-
       cent, and they found reasons for finding him guilty, might I
       suppose that they should bring him back into court?

[B]   Scripture says, "One who has been found righteous you must not put to death" (Ex. 23:7).

[C]   Lo, if he went forth from court having been declared guilty, and they found grounds for finding him innocent, might I suppose that they should *not* bring him back into court?

[D]   Scripture says, [22b] "Do not slay the innocent" (Ex. 23:7).

[E]   "Is it possible that if he should turn out to be righteous in your court, he also will be righteous in my court?"

[F]   Scripture says, "For I will not acquit the wicked [even if you do]" (Ex. 23:7).

[**II**.A]   Said R. Isaac, "R. Yosé said to me, '[Under certain circumstances], there is no difference [between the two kinds of decisions]. For if he was declared innocent by a [gross] error, they indeed do bring him back to court.' "

[B]   [Leiden MS and *editio princeps:* 4:4] R. Ammi raised the question before R. Yohanan: "And even in the case of an adulterer and an adulteress?"

[C]   He said to him, "Your patch is peeling off. [That is, your ignorance is revealed in such a question. Of course the law applies in such a case.]"

The Talmud's treatment of Mishnah is to find Scriptural grounds for the rule of M. 4:3B.

4:4 [In Leiden MS and *editio princeps:* 4:5]

[A]   *In property cases all [judges and even disciples] argue either for acquittal or conviction.*

[B]   *In capital cases all argue for acquittal, but all do not argue for conviction.*

[C]   *In property cases one who argues for conviction may argue for acquittal, and one who argues for acquittal may also argue for conviction.*

[D]   *In capital cases, the one who argues for conviction may argue for acquittal, but the one who argues for acquittal has not got the power to retract and to argue for conviction.*

[**I**.A] Rabbi said, "[But the rule, D, that people may not switch sides applies] only in a case in which what is now lacking is [merely the reading of the verdict,] saying 'So-and-so, You are innocent,' or '. . . you are guilty.'

[B] "But if they lacked yet the full working out of the arguments in the case, it is not in such a case [that a judge is forbidden from switching sides]."

[C] R. Yosé b. Haninah said, "Even if they are still lacking in the full working out of the arguments in the case, in such a case a judge is forbidden from changing sides [once he has spoken up]."

The Talmud clarifies M. 4:4D.

4:5 [In Leiden MS and *editio princeps:* 4:6]

[A] *In property cases they try the case by day and complete it by night.*

[B] *In capital cases they try the case by day and complete it [the following] day.*

[**I**.A] What is the source of this rule [that the completion of a property case may take place after dark]?

[B] "And let them judge the people at all times" (Ex. 18:22).

[C] And is it [possible to interpret the verse only] with reference to that which already has taken place, [that is, to assume that the verse speaks of completing the trial and giving the decision after dark on the same day on which the trial has taken place]? [Perhaps it speaks of commencing a trial, not completing the court process.]

[D] Said R. Samuel bar R. Isaac, "Thus does the Mishnah law [intend to teach], that if the judges erred and reached a decision by night, the decision is valid, [for] it is taught, 'And let them judge the people at all times.' "

[E] He said [to him], "That indeed is a valid explanation" (PM).

The intent seems to be to treat M. 4:5A in a somewhat more restrictive sense, as at D. That is, even in property litigations, in general the court should not issue its decree by night.

4:6 [In Leiden MS and *editio princeps*: 4:7]

[A]   *In property cases they come to a final decision on the same day [as the trial itself], whether it is for acquittal or conviction.*

[B]   *In capital cases they come to a final decision for acquittal on the same day, but on the following day for conviction.*

[C]   *Therefore they do not judge [capital cases] either on the eve of the Sabbath or on the eve of a festival.*

[I.A]   It was taught: **A witness does not give an argument either for acquittal or for conviction [cf. M. San. 5:4C] [T. 9:4C].**

[B]   How do we know it?

[C]   As it is said, "And [one witness will not [suffice to] give testimony [to put the accused] to death" (Num. 35:30).

[D]   And how do we know that he may not give arguments either for acquittal or conviction?

[E]   Scripture says, "*And* [he] will not [suffice to] give testimony [to put the accused] to death" (Num. 35:30).

[F]   [Giving a reason based on law, not Scripture,] R. Simeon b. Laqish said, "There are times at which a person will see himself in danger of being rendered a perjured witness, [and to avoid that possibility,] he will exaggerate his evidence so that the accused is not put to death [thus avoiding the possibility that he too, in danger of perjury, may be put to death]. [Consequently, the witness has a vested interest in acquitting the man, and, it follows, he may not give arguments of that character.]"

[II.A]   And how do we know [M. San. 4:6C] that we require two consecutive days [for the completion of a capital trial]?

[B]   R. Hezekiah, R. Ahi in the name of R. Abbahu: "It is forbidden to undertake a trial for a property case on a Friday."

[C]   Now the following Mishnah is at variance with this statement: *Therefore they do not judge capital cases either on the eve of the Sabbath or on the eve of a festival [M. San. 4:6C].*

[D]   Lo, property cases may be tried [on those days]!

[E]   And R. Hiyya [also] taught so: "They judge property cases on the eve of the Sabbath, but they do not judge capital cases on the eve of the Sabbath."

[F]   He [B's authority] said, "The one rule is for purposes of legal theory, but the other governs what is actually done. [Hiyya's statement is the legal theory. But if such a case is tried on a Friday, it is not retried]."

[G]   And let the court try the accused on a Friday, complete the court process and issue the decision on the Sabbath, and put the convicted criminal to death on Sunday.

[H]   If you rule in that way, it turns out that the man's trial is prolonged, [and this constitutes torture to the accused, which is not permitted].

[I]   R. Simeon b. Laqish raised the question: "Then let him be judged on the Sabbath, and let the decision be reached on the Sabbath, and let him be put to death on the Sabbath.

[J]   "Now if the conduct of the Temple cult overrides the Sabbath, carrying out the religious duty of executing the murderer surely should override the Sabbath, for it is said, 'But if a man willfully attacks another to kill him treacherously, you shall take him from my altar, that he may die' (Ex. 21:14). [Thus the judgment of the murderer overrides the sanctity of the priestly labor at the altar.]

[K]   "Now since the Temple liturgy overrides [the Sabbath], is it not logical that the religious duty of executing the murderer will override the Sabbath?"

[L]   R. La in the name of R. Yannai, "On the basis of the following verse of Scripture we may prove that courts are not to go into session on the Sabbath.

[M]   "What is the relevant verse?

[N]   "Here it is said, '[You shall kindle no fire] in all your habitations on the Sabbath day' (Ex. 35:3).

[O]   "Further on it is said, 'And these things shall be for a statute
        and ordinance to you throughout your generations in all your
        dwellings' (Num. 35:29).

[P]   "Just as, later on, Scripture speaks of a court, so here Scrip-
        ture speaks of a court [and so the verse at Ex. 35:3 indicates
        that one should not carry out the business of the court on the
        Sabbath]."

Unit **I** is more appropriately situated at M. San. 4:4, but,
again, even in that setting, it is relevant only in theme. No
contribution is made to the exegesis of Mishnah. Unit **II**, by
contrast provides an elaborate treatment of M. 4:6C, taking up
the two questions left open by Mishnah: first, whether property
trials may take place on Friday; second, why capital cases may
not take place on the Sabbath.

4:7 [In Leiden MS and *editio princeps:* 4:8]

[A]   *In property cases [and] cases involving questions of uncleanness
        and cleanness they begin [voting] from the eldest. In capital
        cases they begin from the side [with the youngest].*

[B]   *All are valid to engage in the judgment of property cases, but
        all are not valid to engage in the judgment of capital cases,*

[C]   *except for priests, Levites, and Israelites who are suitable to
        marry into the priesthood.*

[I.A]   Rabbi says, " 'Do not answer in a suit (RYB)' (Ex. 23:2)—It is
        written, RB [meaning, Rab:] One should not answer after the
        master but before him [so that, in capital cases, the younger
        judges will be able to exercise independent judgment only if
        they speak before the master has given his opinion]."

[B]   R. Yosé b. Haninah said, " 'Do not answer in a suit'—RB is
        written, meaning, One should not answer before the master but
        only after him [in monetary cases]."

[C]   Rab said, "Do not answer, even after a hundred" [delete: the
        words of R. Pinhas].

[II.A] R. Hilqiah in the name of R. Simon: "R. Yohanan and R. Si-
        meon b. Laqish differed.

[B]   "One said, 'Our conduct of trials is like their conduct of trials.'

[C]   "And the other said, 'Our conduct of trials is not like their conduct of trials.' "

[D]   The one who said, "Our conduct of trials is like their conduct of trials," has no problems.

[E]   But the one who said, "Our conduct of trials is not like their conduct of trials," [must interpret the meaning of] the following verse: "Then Judah said to his brothers, ['What profit is it if we slay our brother and conceal his blood?']" (Gen. 37:26). [Thus Judah spoke first, even though he was not the oldest brother. This was before the Torah was given, so in what is deemed a capital case, it is merely a matter of reason that they do not begin from the eldest.] "Then Memucan said in the presence of the king and the princes . . ." (Est. 1:16). [Here too Memucan spoke first in the trial of Vashti. Thus in biblical times they did begin in capital cases with the youngest—Memucan being the last mentioned—and it is indeed a matter of reason to do so. Now if one says that in biblical times the law was different from what it became, how are these verses to be explained? For they indicate that the practice was the same, and that is because it is reasonable and obvious.]

[F]   [The person who holds that the way we conduct trials is not like the way they conducted trials explains these verses as follows:] They saw the correctness of the opinion of Judah, they saw the correctness of the opinion of Memucan.

[III.A]   And how do we know that in capital cases they begin from the side [with the youngest]?

[B]   Samuel the Elder taught before R. Aha: " 'And David said to his men, "Every man gird on his sword!" . . . [David also girded on his sword]' (1 Sam. 25:13). And afterward they went into session concerning Nabal. [David came last in the discussion.]"

[C]   R. Tema bar Pappias in the name of R. Hoshaiah: "Also in a case involving the invalidation of a family [for marriage into the priesthood] they begin on the side."

[IV.A]   *All are valid to judge property cases [M. San. 4:7B].*

[B]   R. Judah says, "Even *mamzerim.*"

[C]   [Delete: R. Judah says, "They do not apply the law punctiliously in the case of libation-wine."]

[V.A]   [Leiden MS and *editio princeps:* 4:9] It is written, "You shall not be partial to a poor man in *his* suit" (Ex. 23:6) [so a majority of two is required].

[B]   In *his* suit you do not show partiality, but you show partiality in the case of an ox [who may be convicted by a majority of only one vote].

[C]   R. Abbahu in the name of R. Yohanan, "But that is so only in regard to the differences between property cases and capital cases. [The ox is tried by twenty-three judges, but in all other ways it is a property case.]"

[D]   And how many are the [differences between capital and property procedures]?

[E]   We have learned, They are nine [such as are listed in the present pericopae of the Mishnah].

[F]   R. Hiyya taught, "They are eleven."

[G]   And what are the two additional ones [added by Hiyya]?

[H]   **A eunuch and whoever has never had children is valid to judge property cases but not capital cases [T. San. 7:5A].**

[I]   R. Abbahu in the name of R. Yohanan: "Also one who is younger than twenty, and who has not yet produced two pubic hairs, is valid to judge property cases and not capital cases, and he may sit in on the case involving an ox."

[J]   R. Yosé b. Haninah said, "They are thirteen."

[K]   What are the additional two?

[L]   They judge two property cases in a single day, **and they do not judge two capital cases in a single day.**

[M]   Said R. Abin, "**And even the case of an adulterer and an adulteress**" (T. San. 7:2A–B).

Unit **I** takes up the Scriptural basis for M. 4:7A. If **I**.A and B do not simply conflict, then A speaks of capital and B of property cases. What C wishes to say I do not know. Without the deleted attributive, we have Rab in concurrence with Rabbi

(PM). The dispute at unit **II** concerns whether trials in the time of the rabbis of the Talmud follow the procedures laid down in Scriptures. If one maintains that that is the case, then the Mishnaic law clearly accords with the cited biblical precedents. If not, however, then there is a conflict, as E specifies, between Scripture's picture of the conduct of trials and that of the Mishnah. Unit **III** reverts to the same matter, finding a Scriptural basis for the Mishnah's rule. The purpose of inserting the materials marked as unit **IV** is clear—a gloss of the Mishnah by Judah. What unit **V** contributes is unusual. It is a summation of the whole set of discussions of M. San. 4:1–7, that is, the differences between the procedures for property and capital trials. The summary is accomplished in a rather indirect way, by beginning with the matter of the trial of the ox. The ox is tried by a court of twenty-three, but it is still a property case, a proposition already familiar to us. Then, on the basis of this pretext, what is accomplished is to point up the many other ways in which property cases differ from capital ones. Hence—reverting to the pretext for introducing the whole—in all these ways the trial of the ox will be conducted along the lines of any other property case. In fact, a count of the Mishnah's points of difference yields ten differences, down to M. 4:7B. But in one of these, the court of twenty-three, the ox's trial is like that of a human being. So the Mishnah's count is followed in the Talmud's subtle and significant exercise of summation by enumeration.

4:8 [In Leiden MS and *editio princeps:* 4:10]

[A]   *The Sanhedrin was [arranged] in the shape of a half of a round threshing floor [that is, as an amphitheater],*

[B]   *so that [the judges] should see one another,*

[C]   *and two judges' clerks stand before them, one at the right and one at the left.*

[D]   *And they write down the arguments of those who vote to acquit and of those who vote to convict.*

[E]   *R. Judah says, "Three: one writes the opinion of those who vote to acquit, one writes the opinion of those who vote to convict, and the third writes the opinions both of those who vote to acquit and of those who vote to convict."*

[F]   *And three rows of disciples of sages sit before them.*

[G]   *Each and every one knows his place.*

[H]   *[If] they found need to ordain [a disciple to serve on the court],*

[I]   *they ordained one who was sitting in the first row.*

[J]   *[Then] one who was sitting in the second row joins the first row, and one who was sitting in the third row moves up to the second row.*

[K]   *And they select for themselves someone else from the crowd and set him in the third row.*

[L]   *[The new disciple] did not take a seat in the place of the first party [of the third row who had now joined the second row] but in the place that was appropriate for him [at the end of the third row].*

[I.A]   R. Ba bar Yasa in the name of R. Yohanan: "Here 'Congregation' is stated, and there 'Congregation' is stated" (Num. 35:24, 14:27) [proving that a court has twenty-three members]." [cf. M. San. 1:4 I A.]

[B]   Rab introduced this [same proof text in the context of the present] Mishnah pericope [to explain M. 4:8H–L, that is, adding to the court when there was need].

[II.A]   The Mishnah has stated, *"Be a tail to lions, and not a head of foxes"* [M. Abot 4:15].

[B]   The proverb says, "Be a head of foxes, not a tail to lions."

[C]   For we have learned, *"If they found need to ordain a disciple to serve on the court, they ordained one who was sitting in the first row"* [M. San. 4:8H–I].

The Talmud takes up the procedure of M. 4:8F–L, the requirement of twenty-three judges, unit **I**, and how it is met, unit **II**.

4:9 [In Leiden MS and *editio princeps:* 4:11]

[A]   *How do they admonish witnesses in capital cases?*

[B]   *They would bring them in and admonish them [as follows]:*
"Perhaps it is your intention to give testimony on the basis of
supposition, of hearsay, or of what one witness has told
another;

[C]   *"[or you may be thinking,] 'We heard it from a reliable*
person.'

[D]   *"Or, you may not know that in the end we are going to interro-*
gate you with appropriate interrogation and examination.

[E]   *"You should know that the laws governing a trial for property*
cases are different from the laws governing a trial for capital
cases.

[F]   *"In the case of a trial for property cases, a person pays money*
and achieves atonement for himself. In capital cases [the ac-
cused's] blood and the blood of all those who were destined to
be born from him [who was wrongfully convicted] are held
against him [who testifies falsely] to the end of time.

[G]   *"For so we find in the case of Cain who slew his brother, as it*
is said, 'The bloods of your brother cry' (Gen. 4:10).

[H]   *"It does not say, 'The blood of your brother,' but, 'The bloods*
of your brother'—his blood and the blood of all those who were
destined to be born from him."

[I]   *Another matter: "The bloods of your brother"—for his blood*
was spattered on trees and stones.

[J]   *Therefore man was created alone, to teach you that whoever de-*
stroys a single soul is deemed [by Scripture] as if he had de-
stroyed a whole world.

[K]   *And whoever saves a single soul is deemed by Scripture as if he*
had saved a whole world.

[L]   *And it was also for the sake of peace among people, so that*
someone should not say to his fellow, "My father is greater
than your father."

[M]   *And [it was also on account of the "minim,"] so that the*
"minim" should not say, "There are many powers in Heaven."

[N]   *And it was to portray the grandeur of the Holy One, blessed be*
he. For a person mints many coins with a single seal, and they
are all alike one another. But the King of kings of kings, the
Holy One, blessed be he, minted all human beings with that

seal of his with which he made the first person, yet not one of them is like anyone else. Therefore everyone is obligated to maintain, "On my account the world was created."

[O]   *Now perhaps you [witnesses] would like now to say, "What business have we got with this trouble?"*

[P]   *But it already has been written, "He being a witness, whether he has seen or known, if he does not speak it, then he shall bear his iniquity" (Lev. 5:1).*

[Q]   *And perhaps you might want to claim, "What business is it of ours to convict this man of a capital crime?"*

[R]   *But has it not already been said, "When the wicked perish there is rejoicing" (Prov. 11:10).*

[I.A]   **What is considered "supposition" [M. San. 4:9B]?**

[B]   **So that [the witnesses] should not say, "We saw him running after his fellow, with a sword in his hand. [The victim] ran in front of him into a ruin, and then the other went after him into the ruin. We went in after them and found the victim slain [on the floor]. We saw him leaving with a knife in the hand [of the murderer], dripping blood."**

[C]   **[Y. omits:] Now lest you say, "If not, then who killed him?"—[you must be admonished that this is not valid evidence].**

[D]   **Said Simeon b. Shatah, "May I [not] see consolation, if I did not see someone run after his fellow, [with a sword in his hand,] and [the pursued man] went before him into a ruin, and the [pursuer] ran in after him, and then I came in right after him, and found [the victim] slain, and this one was leaving with a knife in the hand of the murderer, dripping blood, and I said to him, '[You evil person! Who killed this one?]' May I [not] see consolation [if I did not see him (run in here)]. [Either] you killed him [or I did!] But what can I do to you? For your blood is not handed over to me. [For lo, the Torah has said, 'At the testimony of two witnesses, or at the testimony of three witnesses, shall he who is on trial for his life be put to death' (Deut. 17:6).]**

[E]   **" 'But He who knows the thoughts of man will exact punishment from that man.'**

[F]   "He did not move from the spot before a snake bit him, and he died" [T. San. 8:3].

[G]   [Leiden MS and *editio princeps*: 4:12] **A man was created one and alone,**

[H]   because of [proud] families, so that families should not quarrel with one another. For if now, that they come from one father, they quarrel with one another, if they were from two, how much more so! [Cf. M. 4:5L].

[I]   [And why was he created one and alone in the world?] So that the righteous should not say, "We are the sons of the righteous one," and so that the evil ones should not say, "We are the sons of the evil one." [Because of the thieves and robbers. And if now, that he was created one and alone, people steal and rob, had there been two, how much the more so!] [T. San. 8:4].

[J]   **Another matter: Why was he created one and alone?**

[K]   [Leiden MS and *editio princeps*: 4:13] *To portray the grandeur of the king of the kings of kings, blessed be he [M. San. 4:9N].*

[L]   **For with a single seal he created all seals and not one is like the other [Tosefta: from a single seal all those many (diverse) seals have come forth],**

[M]   as it is said, "It is changed as clay under the seal, and all these things stand forth as in a garment" (Job 38:14) [M. 4:9N, T. San 8:5].

[N]   And on what account are faces not like one another?

[O]   [Talmud: On account of imposters,]

[P]   so no one should jump into his neighbor's field or jump in bed with his neighbor's wife,

[Q]   [Talmud omits: as it is said, "And from the wicked their light is withheld and the strong arm is broken" (Job. 38:15).]

[R]   It was taught: R. Meir says, "The omnipresent has varied people in three aspects: [22a] appearance, intelligence, and voice—

[S]   "appearance and intelligence, because of robbers and thieves, and voice, because of the possibilities of licentiousness" [T. San. 8:6].

[T]   R. Isaac said, "Even dates and wheat are unlike one another."

[U]   The [first] man was created on the eve of the Sabbath so that he might immediately take up the doing of a religious duty [T. San. 8:8D].

[V]   Another matter: Why was he created last? [So that he might enter the banquet at once with everything ready for him.]

[W]   They have made a parable: To what is the matter comparable?

[X]   To a king who built a palace and dedicated it and prepared a meal and [only] afterward invited the guests.

[Y]   [And so Scripture says,] "The wisest of women has built her house" (Prov. 9:1).

[Z]   This refers to the Holy One, blessed be he, who built his world [in seven days] by wisdom, as it is said, "The Lord through wisdom founded the world" (Prov. 3:19).

[AA] "She has hewn out her seven pillars" (Prov. 9:1)—these are the seven days of creation.

[BB] "She has killed her beasts and mixed her wine" (Prov. 9:2)— these are the oceans, rivers, deserts, and all the other things which the world needs.

[CC] [And afterward: "She has sent forth her maidens, she cries on the high places of the city], 'Who is simple—let him turn in hither, [and he who is void of understanding]' (Prov. 9:3–4)—these refer to Adam and Eve [T. San. 8:9].

[II.A] [Leiden MS and *editio princeps*: 4:14] *And perhaps you might want to claim, "What business is it of ours to convict this man of a capital crime?"* [M. San. 4:9Q].

[B]   It is written, "And about sunset a cry went through the army" (1 Kings 22:36).

[C]   What is this cry (HRYNH)?

[D]   Lo, it is a song (HRY RYNH), [as it is said, "When the wicked perish, there is a song" (Prov. 11:10).

[E]   But, on the contrary, it also is said, "That they should praise (PM) as they went out before the army [and say, 'Give thanks unto the Lord, for his mercy endures for ever']" (2 Chron. 20:21).

[F]   [Omitting the words, "for he is good,"] is to teach you that
       even the downfall of the wicked is no joy before the
       Omnipresent.

Unit **I** vastly enriches the Mishnah's materials for M. 4:9J, and
unit **II**, for M. 4:9R. But clearly, the Talmud has nothing distinctive about itself and does nothing with Tosefta's materials.
Once more the Talmud provides an anthology on a theme of
the Mishnah.

6 Yerushalmi Sanhedrin Chapter Five

5:1

[A]   *They interrogated [the witness] with seven points of interrogation:*

[B]   *(1) In what septennate? (2) In what year? (3) In what month? (4) On what day of the month? (5) On what day [of the week]? (6) At what time? (7) In what place?*

[C]   *R. Yosé says, "(1) On what day? (2) At what time? (3) In what place? (4) Do you know him? (5) Did you warn him [of the consequences of his deed]?"*

[D]   *[In the case of] one who worships an idol: Whom did he worship, and with what did he worship [the idol]?*

[I.A] We do not learn in the Mishnah pericope [that they ask concerning] which Jubilee.

[B]   For the Jubilee is uncommon [coming only once in fifty years, and if someone committed an act of murder in one Jubilee, it would be unlikely that the witnesses would wait fifty years to testify].

[C]   [But] there is also a tradition which teaches: R. Simeon b. Yohai says, "Also, 'In which Jubilee?' "

[D]   And we may explain this inquiry to apply in a year in which one Jubilee is beginning and another ending.

[II.A] How do we know that there are to be seven points of interrogation?

[B]   Samuel the Elder taught before R. Aha: " 'Then you shall inquire [1], and make search [2], and ask [3] diligently [4], and behold [5], if it be true [6] and certain [7] [that such an abominable thing has been done . . .]' (Deut. 13:14). [The seven words in the verse thus signify seven points of interrogation.]"

[C]   He said to him, "You should not continue counting words in the same verse [or you will have an eighth, namely, *thing*].

[D]   "Rather: 'Then you shall inquire, and make search, and ask diligently' (Deut. 13:14) [yielding four]; and '. . . and it is told you and you hear it, then you shall inquire diligently' (Deut. 17:4), [yielding three more, both in the case of idolatry].

[E]   "The use of 'diligently' in both instances serves to establish an analogy between them and to permit invoking each usage in all contexts: hearing, asking, inquiring, and making a search."

[F]   R. Isaac raised the question [whether all seven points of interrogation are invariably required, for lo, if] they caught a thug in Tiberias, [they may have occasion to] say, "[We saw] this one killed, and that one do the killing." [In such a case, what need is there for all these points of interrogation?]

[G]   And how do we then know that in such a case all seven points of interrogation are required [anyhow]?

[H]   Issi said, "[The reason is that] so long as these witnesses might be perjured [by the interrogation of the seven elements and they are not so interrogated], the accused killer cannot be put to death on their testimony. Accordingly, the questions must be addressed to the witnesses, to make sure that they cannot be subjected to the charge of perjury. That is so, even if the act of murder took place on that very day and in their presence; still they must be shown to be honest witnesses, and that is what Scripture requires before the death penalty may be invoked.]"

[III.A]   [Do the interrogators also ask,] "Do you know whether he was an idolater or an Israelite?"

[B]   Let us derive the answer from the following: R. Yohanan said, "If he was killed between Tiberias and Sepphoris, it is taken for granted that he was an Israelite. [Accordingly, the character of the deceased also is to be established.]"

[IV.A]   *"Did you warn him [of the consequences of his deed]?"* [M. San. 5:1C(5)].

[B]   And how do we know [that the Torah requires] an act of warning [of the consequences of the deed]?

[C]   Samuel bar Nahman in the name of R. Jonathan: " 'If a man takes his sister, a daughter of his father or a daughter of his mother, and sees her nakedness, and she sees his nakedness, it is a shameful thing' (Lev. 20:17). [The reference to "seeing" indicates that the matter depends upon the prior act of others' seeing the man in action and warning him of the consequent death penalty.]"

[D]   [The reference to *hesed*, translated, "shameful thing" or "act of love," as the context requires, calls to mind a different context entirely.] Said R. Bun, "Cain married his sister, Abel married his sister, [so how can it be deemed a shameful thing]?"

[E]   [God answers:] "It was an act of love (*hesed*) which I did with the former generations, through whom the world would be built up: 'For I said, "The world will be built upon merciful love" (Ps. 89:2).' "

[F]   [Yet another answer to the question of the biblical basis for the requirement of a warning is as follows:] It was taught: R. Simeon b. Yohai says, " 'On the evidence of two witnesses or of three witnesses he that is to die (lit., the dead one) shall be put to death' (Deut. 17:6).

[G]   "Now can a 'dead one' die? [Of course not. So the reference is to the one engaged in the act of murder, and it is] to inform him by what form of the death penalty he will be put to death [if he should engage in the contemplated action, and that is the meaning of 'warning.']"

[H]   It was taught: R. Judah b. R. Ilai says, " 'But if a man willfully attacks another to kill him knowledgeably' (Ex. 21:14)—that the witness must make him knowledgeable about what mode of the death penalty [he will suffer, should he engage in the contemplated action]."

[I]   If the form of death [22d] for the crime about to be committed was a severe one, and the witnesses gave warning of a form of the death penalty which was a lenient one, the accused has the right to claim that, had he known that the form of death for the proposed crime was so severe, he would never have done such a thing. [That is self-evident.]

[J]   [But what is the law if] the form of death was a lenient one, and they warned him that the form of death was a more severe one?

[K]   In the theory of R. Judah b. R. Ilai, who maintains that the
witnesses must make the man knowledgeable about what form
of death he will suffer if he commits the contemplated action,
[the man cannot claim what he may say in the contrary situa-
tion]. [He knows about the death penalty and commits the
deed. He has no further defense in this aspect.]

[L]   **[If] they warn him and he was silent,**

[M]   **or if they warn him and he nods his head,**

[N]   **even though he says, "I know"—**

[O]   **he is exempt—**

[P]   **unless he will say, "I know it, and it is with that very stipulation that I am doing what I am doing!" [T. San. 11:2].**

[Q]   **[If] they saw him killing somebody, and said to him, "You
should know that that man is subject to the [divine] covenant, and it is said, 'Whoever sheds the blood of man by
man shall his blood be shed' (Gen. 9:6)—**

[R]   **even though he said, "I know it"—**

[S]   **he is exempt,**

[T]   **unless he says, "I know, and it is with that very stipulation
that I am doing what I am doing!" [T. San. 11:4].**

[U]   **[If] they saw him profaning the Sabbath,**

[V]   **[and] said to him, "You should know that it is the Sabbath
today, and Scripture says, 'Those who profane it will certainly die' (Ex. 31:14)"—**

[W]   **even though he said, "I know"—**

[X]   **he is exempt,**

[Y]   **unless he says, "I know, and it is with that very stipulation
that I am doing what I am doing!" [T. San. 11:3].**

[V.A]   R. Hiyya bar Gamda asked, "One who gathers wood—on what
count is he liable [for violating the Sabbath]? Is it because he
plucks up the wood, or is it on the count of harvesting?"

[B]   Let us learn the answer from the following verse: "While the
people of Israel were in the wilderness, they found a man gathering sticks on the Sabbath . . ." (Num. 15:32).

[C]   This teaches that they found him plucking up twigs from the ground.

[D]   R. Hiyya bar Gamda asked, "One who gathers wood—by what form of capital punishment is he put to death? It is by stoning. [That they found out from Heaven. So how could they have warned him?]"

[E]   Let us derive the answer from the following:

[F]   [The reason that they brought the case to Moses, who awaited a message from the Lord, which was that the man should be stoned (Num. 15:35)], was that they knew that he was to be executed, but did not know how he was put to death. [It follows that warning of the particular form of the death penalty is not required.]

[G]   The following teaching is to be found: R. Hiyya taught, "The Lord said to Moses, 'Bring out of the camp him who cursed; and let all who heard him lay their hands upon his head, and let all the congregation stone him' (Lev. 24:13–14).

[H]   "How was he to be put to death? Through stoning."

[VI.A]   "Whom did he worship? And with what did he worship [an idol]?" [M. San. 5:1D].

[B]   "Whom did he worship," Peor or Mercury?

[C]   "And with what did he carry out the act of worship?" Was it with the act of worship paid to such an idol? Or was it with the act of worship normally paid to the Most High?

[D]   Let us derive the answer from the following:

[E]   M'SH S: Two witnesses came and stated, "We saw this one performing an act of worship to an idol, but we do not know whether it was Peor or Mercury." [The testimony was valid, so we need not know what act was carried out, or to which idol.]

[F]   [Now in accord with your reasoning,] do they judge the accused on both counts, and declare him innocent on whichever count he turns out to be innocent?

The Talmud provides an ample account of the present pericope. Unit I excludes a possible question. Unit II goes over the Scriptural foundations for the Mishnah's law. Once, unit IV, we reach the matter of a proper warning, we proceed to a fairly full account of that issue. First comes the expected exercise in Scriptural exegesis. Then we have an important initiative, specifying the sort of warning which is required. G and H indicate that the form of death must be specified to the person before he commits the crime. **IV.**I–K take up and expand on this matter. Then there is a vast insertion from Tosefta, which gives a rich picture of the required form of warning. At unit **V**, we have a contrary view, that the particular form of death need not be specified. Unit **VI**, at the end, takes up the matter of the specification demanded of testimony about idolatry.

5:2

[A]   *The more one expands the interrogation, the more is he to be praised.*

[B]   *M^{c}SH W: Ben Zakkai examined a witness as to the character of the stems of figs [under which the incident took place].*

[C]   *What is the difference between interrogation and examination?*

[D]   *In the case of interrogation, [if] one witness says, "I don't know the answer," the testimony of the witnesses is null.*

[E]   *[In the case of] examination, [if] one of the witnesses says, "I don't know," or even if both of them say, "We don't know," their testimony nonetheless stands.*

[F]   *All the same are interrogation and examination [in the following regard]: When [the witnesses] contradict one another, their testimony is null.*

[I.A]   [With regard to a violation of the Sabbath, Yohanan ben Zakkai interrogated the witnesses who testified that one had gathered dates:] "With what did he collect them?"

[B]   "With their stems he collected them."

[C]   "With what did he eat them?"

[D]   "With their pits did he eat them."

[II.A]   There we learned:

[B]   *He concerning whom two groups of witnesses gave testimony—*

[C]   *these testify that he took a vow to be a Nazir for two spells,*

[D]   and those testify that he took a vow to be a Nazir for five spells—

[E]   The House of Shammai say, "The testimony is at variance, and no Naziriteship applies here at all."

[F]   And the House of Hillel say, "In the sum of five are two spells, so let him serve out two spells of Naziriteship" [M. Naz. 3:7].

[G]   Rab said, "As to a general number [the Houses] are in disagreement, [that is, as to whether he has taken the Nazirite vow at all]. But as to a specific number, all parties agree that (the testimony is at variance). [Following the versions of Y. Yeb. 5:5, Naz. 3:7: the sum of five includes two, as at M. 5:2F.]"

[H]   R. Yohanan said, "As to spelling out the number of vows there is a difference of opinion, but as to a general number all parties concur that (within the general principle of five spells of Naziriteship there are two upon which all parties concur). [Following the parallels: the testimony is at variance.]"

[I]   What is meant by the "general number," and what is meant by "counting out the number of specific vows" [the man is supposed to have taken]? [Examples of each are as follows:]

[J]   The general number—One party has said, "Two," and one party has said, "Five."

[K]   Counting out the number of vows one by one is when one said, "One, two, " and the other said, "Three, four, [five]."

[L]   Rab said, "If the essence of the testimony is contradicted, the testimony is not null."

[M]   And R. Yohanan said, "If the essence of the testimony is contradicted, the testimony has been nullified."

[N]   All parties concede, however, [that] if testimony has been contradicted in its nonessentials [that is, in elements occurring after the essential part of the testimony,] the testimony [of the first set of witnesses] is not nullified.

[O]   The full extent of the position taken by R. Yohanan is seen in the following case:

[P]   For R. Ba bar Hiyya in the name of R. Yohanan: "The assumption [that a loan has taken place is] confirmed [by testimony] that one has counted out [coins].

[Q]   "If this witness says, 'From the pocket did he count out the money,' and that one says, 'From the pouch did he count out the money,'

[R]   "we have a case in which a testimony is contradicted in its essentials [within the same pair of witnesses, who thus do not agree]. [This is null.]"

[S]   Here even Rab concedes that the testimony is null.

[T]   Concerning what do they differ?

[U]   Concerning a case in which there were two *groups* of witnesses.

[V]   One states, "From the pocket did he count out the money," and the other says, "From the the pouch did he count out the money."

[W]   Here we have a case in which testimony is contradicted in its essentials. The effect of the testimony [in Yohanan's view] is null.

[X]   But in the view of Rab, the effect of the testimony is not null.

[Y]   If one witness says, "Into his vest did he count out the money," and the other says, "Into his wallet,"

[Z]   in the opinion of all parties, the testimony is contradicted in its nonessentials and therefore the testimony is not nullified. [This testimony is not about the essence of the case.]

[AA]   If one party says, "With a sword did he kill him," and the other party says, "With a staff did he kill him," we have a case in which testimony has been contradicted on its essentials [just as in a property case, so in a capital one].

[BB]   Even Rab concedes that the effect of the entire testimony is null.

[CC]   In what regard did they differ?

[DD]   In a case in which there were two sets of two witnesses:

[EE]   One group says, "With a sword . . . ," and the other says, "With a staff . . ."

[FF]   Here we have a case in which the testimony has been contradicted in its essentials, and the effect of the testimony is null.

[GG]   But in the view of Rab, the effect of the testimony is not null.

[HH]   One witness says, "[The murderer] turned toward the north [to flee]," and the other witness says, "He turned toward the south." In the opinion of all parties, the testimony [of one group] has been contradicted in its nonessentials and the testimony has not been nullified.

[II]   The full force of Rab's opinion is indicated in the following, which we have learned there:

[JJ]   *[If one woman says, "He died," and one says, "He was killed," R. Meir says, "Since they contradict one another [in details of their testimony], lo, these women may not remarry."] R. Judah and R. Simeon says, "Since this one and that one are in agreement that he is not alive, they may remarry" [M. Yeb. 15:5B–D].*

[KK]   Now did he not hear that which R. Eleazar said, "R. Judah and R. Simeon concur in the matter of witnesses [that where they contradict one another in essentials their testimony is null]?"

[LL]   If so, what is the difference between such contradiction when it comes from witnesses and the same when it comes from co-wives?

[MM]   They did not treat the statement of a co-wife concerning her fellow-wife as of any consequence whatsoever.

[NN]   Said R. Yohanan, "If R. Eleazar made such a statement, he heard it from me and said it."

[OO]   The Mishnah pericope is at variance with the position of Rab: *All the same are interrogation and examination in the following regard: When the witnesses contradict one another, their testimony is null [M. San. 5:2F].* [Rab does not deem it invariably null, as we have seen.]

[PP]   Now how does Rab interpret that passage [which contradicts his position]?

[QQ]   Said R. Mana, "Rab interprets the Mishnah rule to speak of a case in which one witness contradicts another [but not in which a *set* of witnesses contradicts another such set in some minor detail]."

[RR]   Said R. Abin, "Even if you interpret the passage to speak of contradictions between one set of witnesses and another, still Rab will be able to deal with the matter. For a capital case is subject to a different rule, since it is said, 'Justice, and only justice, will you pursue' " (Deut. 16:20). [Thus capital trials are subject to a different set of rules of evidence from those applicable in property cases of which Rab spoke above at L.]

Unit **I** makes sense of M. 5:2B. The vast discussion of unit **II** takes up the matter of witnesses contradicting one another, as at M. 5:2F. But the sole point of relevance to this pericope in particular is at **II**.OO–RR. The issue otherwise is not pertinent.

5:3

[A]   *[If] one [of the witnesses] says, "It was on the second of the month," and one of the witnesses says, "It was on the third of the month," their testimony stands,*

[B]   *for one of them may know about the intercalation of the month, and the other may not know about the intercalation of the month.*

[C]   *[If] one of them says, "On the third," and one of them says, "On the fifth," their testimony is null.*

[D]   *[If] one of them says, "At two," and one of them says, "At three," their testimony stands.*

[E]   *[If] one of them says, "At three," and one of them says, "At five," their testimony is null.*

[F]   *R. Judah says, "It stands."*

[G]   *[If] one of them says, "At five," and one of them says, "At seven," their testimony is null.*

[H]   *For at five the sun is at the east, and at seven the sun is at the west.*

[I.A]   To what extent [do we attribute an error to one's not having known that the month was intercalated (M. San. 5:3B)]?

[B]   R. Yasa in the name of R. Yohanan: "Up to the greater part of the month."

[C]   Said R. Yohanan, "For instance, these villagers [who are uninformed about the intercalation, would fall under the stated rule]."

[D]   And sages say, "They are nothing out of the ordinary [but all fall under the rule]."

[E]   And said R. Yasa, "Take me for example! For in my entire life I have never said the Additional Prayer [of the New Month], when I did not know when the new month commences [exactly]" (PM).

[II.A]   [The following discussion takes for granted knowledge of M. Pes. 1:4: *R. Meir says, "They eat leaven throughout the fifth hour on the fourteenth of Nisan (the eve of Passover), and they burn it at the beginning of the sixth hour." And R. Judah says, "They eat leaven through the fourth hour, keep it in suspense throughout the fifth hour, and burn it at the beginning of the sixth hour."*] [Now what is the issue between the two?] R. Meir says, "From the sixth hour and beyond [leaven is prohibited] by reason of [the scribes'] decree [but not the law of the Torah]."

[B]   R. Judah says, "[The prohibition of leaven] from the sixth hour onward is by reason of the authority of the Torah. [That is why they may eat leaven only up to the end of the fourth hour, to make sure the Torah law is not violated.]"

[C]   What is the Scriptural basis for R. Meir's position? "But on the first day you shall put away leaven out of your houses" (Ex. 12:15).

[D]   Is it possible that that requirement [to remove leaven] applies only when night falls?

[E]   Scripture states, "But . . ."

[F]   The intention is to make a sharp distinction.

[G]   How so?

[H]   Apply the prohibition at least one hour prior to sunset.

[I]   What is the Scriptural basis for the position of R. Judah?

[J]   "But on the first day . . ." refers to the fourteenth of Nisan [not the fifteenth].

[K]   Is it possible that this applies to the whole of the day?

[L]   Scripture states, "But . . ."

[M]   The meaning is to divide the day: half of that day is for the eating of leaven, and the other half is for the eating of unleavened bread.

[N]   The opinion attributed to R. Meir contradicts [another which is assigned to him, for] there he has said, "But . . ." serves to encompass [and expand the range of the law to the hour before dark], while he here maintains that the function of "But" is to limit and serve as an exclusionary phrase.

[O]   Said R. Samuel bar Abudimi, "It serves to exclude that which does not fall under the category of leavening. [One may eat leaven on the fourteenth.]"

[P]   R. Meir says, " 'You shall eat no leavened bread with it' (Deut. 16:3)—this applies [only] to the eating of it [which must be without leaven at hand]."

[Q]   R. Judah says, " 'You shall eat no leavened bread with it'—this applies to preparing it [that is, even preparing the Passover must be done without leaven at hand]."

[R]   R. Judah maintains that there is both a positive and a negative commandment pertaining to eating leaven [and that there is] a positive and negative commandment pertaining to removing the leaven.

[S]   The positive commandment concerning eating the leavened bread is as follows: "Seven days you shall eat with it unleavened bread" (Deut. 16:3)—not leaven.

[T]   Any negative commandment which derives from the force of a positive one is deemed itself to be a positive one.

[U]   And the negative commandment concerning eating it is as follows:

[V]   "You shall eat no leavened bread with it" (Deut. 16:3).

[W]   The positive commandment having to do with removing leaven is as follows: "But on the first day you shall put away leaven out of your houses" (Ex. 12:15).

[X]   The negative commandment having to do with removing leaven is as follows: "For seven days no leaven shall be found in your houses" (Ex. 12:19).

[Y] Lo, R. Meir said, "From six hours and beyond, leaven is prohibited] by reason of the decrees of sages."

[Z] Thus the seventh hour is prohibited as a fence around the law. But why should the sixth also be forbidden?

[AA] It is because of building a fence as well.

[BB] And is a fence built around a fence?

[CC] But the sixth hour may be confused with the seventh.

[DD] R. Judah says, "From five hours and beyond, [leaven is prohibited] by reason of the decree of Sages. Thus the sixth hour is prohibited as a fence around the law. But why should the fifth also be forbidden. It is because of building a fence as well. And is there a fence built around a fence. But the fifth hour may be confused with the seventh."

[EE] The opinions assigned to R. Judah appear to be contradictory.

[FF] There he has said, "The fifth hour is not going to be confused with the seventh," and here he has said, "The fifth hour *may* be confused with the seventh." [The fifth hour is forbidden for eating leaven. It may be confused with the seventh—vs. M. San. 5:3G–H.]

[GG] Said R. Yosé, "There [at Passover] the matter is handed over to women, and they may be slovenly, while here the matter is handed over to the court, and they are punctilious."

[HH] Said R. Yosé b. R. Bun, "There it is the beginning of the fifth hour and the end of the seventh; there it is the end of the fifth hour and the beginning of the seventh. [In the case of testimony, one witness says the event was at the beginning of the fifth hour, the other, at the end of the seventh. There is ample evidence as to the difference between these two times, so the witnesses contradict one another. With regard to leaven and Passover, if people may eat leaven at the fifth hour, they may do so at the end of the hour. The difference between the end of the fifth hour and the beginning of the seventh is not so obvious and visible.]"

[II] And thus it is taught: The beginning of the fifth hour is when the sun is in the east, and the end of the seventh is when the sun is in the west. The sun never turns westward until the end of the seventh hour [cf. M. San. 5:3H].

Once more, we have a light gloss of the Mishnah, unit **I**, and then a protracted discussion, relevant to the Mishnah only tangentially. The point of contact of unit **II** comes at **II.DD–HH**, and, we see, that discussion (except for HH) is integral to its setting in the exegesis of M. Pes. 1:4. Consequently, apart from the opening lines, there is no Talmud for the present pericope.

5:4

[A]   *And afterward they bring in the second witness and examine him.*

[B]   *[If] their statements check out, they begin the argument in favor of acquittal.*

[C]   *[If] one of the witnesses said, "I have something to say in favor of acquittal,"*

[D]   *or [if] one of the disciples said, "I have something to say in favor of conviction,"*

[E]   *they shut him up.*

[F]   *[If] one of the disciples said, "I have something to say in favor of acquittal," they promote him and seat him among the [judges], and he did not go down from that position that entire day.*

[G]   *If there is substance in what he says, they pay attention to him.*

[H]   *And even if [the accused] said, "I have something to say in my own behalf," they pay attention to him,*

[I]   *so long as there is substance in what he has to say.*

[I.A]   It is taught: *[If] they found him innocent, they sent him away. If not, they postpone judging him until the next day [M. San. 5:5A].*

[B]   [23a] *They come together in pairs and would not eat very much or drink wine that entire day, and they would discuss the matter all that night [M. San. 5:5B].*

[C]   *And the next day they would get up and come [to court] [M. 5:5C].*

[D]   The court officers call on each one, "[Judge] So-and-so and [Judge] Such-and-such."

[E]   [If Judge So-and-so answers,] "I held him guilty, and now I hold him guilty," "I held him innocent, and now I hold him innocent," "I held him guilty, and now I hold him innocent," they accept that statement [cf. M. 5:5D].

[F]   "I held him innocent, and now I hold him guilty"—[Tosefta: they do not accept that statement] [cf. M. 5:5F].

[G]   ("I held him guilty, and now I hold him innocent"—they accept that statement [cf. MN. 5:5F].)

[H]   ("I held him guilty, and now I hold him guilty" [cf. M. 5:5E])—they said to him, "Explain your opinion first."

[I]   It is taught: [If] one of those who had held him innocent made a mistake in his opinion, the scribes of the court remind him [M. 5:5G].

[J]   If one of those who hold the accused guilty erred, the scribes of the judges do not remind him.

[K]   But they say to him, "Explain your opinion afresh" [T. San. 9:1].

[II.A]   [With reference to M. San. 5:5G] Said R. La, "On what account do they write down the words of the one who argues in favor of innocence? It is because of the one who argues in favor of guilt, lest [the former] become confused [and lose track of the reasons in favor of acquittal]."

[B]   Thus if he confuses something, the scribes remind him, "This is what you said, this is not what you said."

[C]   If so, the case should require two days [of hearings] [to make provision for fresh argument, as at B].

[D]   It will turn out that the case will grow stale, [and the accused will be subjected to unnecessary distress by the delay in the trial].

[E]   R. Yosé b. R. Bun said, [The scribes write down what is said in favor of innocence not on account of the one who argues in favor of guilt, but] because of the one who argues in favor of innocence [himself, to preserve the fresh arguments he has supplied].

The Talmud assigned to M. San. 5:4 in fact serves M. San.
5:5, as is self-evident. I assume it is only a printer's error
which has divided M. 5:4 from M. 5:5. Substantively, there is
no Talmud to M. 5:4.

5:5

[A]   *If they found him innocent, they sent him away. If not they
       postpone judging him till the next day.*

[B]   *They would go off in pairs and would not eat very much or
       drink wine that entire day, and they would discuss the matter
       all that night.*

[C]   *And the next day they would get up and come to court.*

[D]   *The one who favors acquittal says, "I declared him innocent
       [yesterday], and I stand my ground and declare him innocent
       today."*

[E]   *And the one who declares him guilty says, "I declared him
       guilty [yesterday], and I stand my ground and declare him
       guilty today."*

[F]   *The one who argues in favor of guilt may [now] argue in favor
       of acquittal, but the one who argues in favor of innocence may
       not now go and argue in favor of guilt.*

[G]   *[If] they made an error in some matter, the two judges' clerks
       remind them [of what had been said].*

[H]   *If they now found him innocent, they sent him off.*

[I]   *And if not, they arise for a vote.*

[J]   *[If] twelve vote for acquittal and eleven vote for conviction, he
       is acquitted.*

[K]   *[If] twelve vote for conviction and eleven vote for acquittal,*

[L]   *and even if eleven vote for acquittal and eleven vote for
       conviction,*

[M]   *but one says, "I have no opinion,'*

[N]   *and even if twenty-two vote for acquittal or vote for conviction,*

[O]   *but one says, "I have no opinion,"*

[P]   *they add to the number of the judges.*

[Q]   *How many do they add? Two by two, until there are seventy-one.*

[R]   *[If] thirty-six vote for acquittal and thirty-five vote for conviction, he is acquitted.*

[S]   *[If] thirty-six vote for conviction and thirty-five vote for acquittal, they debate the matter, until one of those who votes for conviction accepts the arguments of those who vote for acquittal.*

[I.A]   **[If one of the disciples said, "I have an argument to offer in favor of acquittal," they receive him in a friendly way,** *and promote him and seat him among the (judges) (M. San. 5:4D, T. San. 9:3).* **If the accused said,** *"I have something to say in behalf of my own innocence," they pay attention to him (M. 5:4F).* **If he said, "I have something to say in favor of my own conviction," they emphatically shut him up. A witness does not give an argument either for acquittal or for conviction (M. 5:4C). R. Yosé b. R. Judah says, "He may argue in favor of acquittal, but he may not argue in favor of conviction"** *(T. San. 9:4).]* [In connection with this passage,] it was taught: [In regard to the view of Yosé b. R. Judah that a witness may argue in favor of acquittal,] If one of the witnesses said, "I have an argument for acquittal," and his fellow came along and supported his argument, which of these do they appoint [to the court, as they do with disciples]?

[B]   Is it the first or the second or both of them?

[C]   Let us derive the answer from the following statement of R. Yohanan: "And he who was acquitted on the basis of his own arguments do they *not* seat on the court as a judge.

[D]   "For lo, if he was acquitted on the basis of his own arguments, he turns out to be both a witness and a judge, and a witness cannot be made into a judge in the same trial."

[E]   **In property cases they say, "The case is clear." In capital cases they do not say, "The case is clear." And the most prominent of the judges say, "The case is clear." [T. San. 7:6A–B].**

[II.A]   [Leiden MS and *editio princeps:* 5:6] It was taught: In what regard do they add judges to the court?

[B]   It is so that, if two of the first judges declare the accused to be innocent, and one of the second pair concurs that he is innocent, the decision may be reached by three judges [out of the five now on the court]. [The one who declares he has no opinion is treated as if he is not present. That is the case even if one of the two additional judges also declares that he has no opinion.]

[C]   R. La said, "[If one of the two additional judges also says he has no opinion, that is not acceptable,] since it appears that the decision ultimately has been reached with four judges. They do not reach a decision in the case with only three judges. [So they have to add two more judges (PM).]"

[D]   Said R. Yosé, "From the aforestated argument [B], we infer the following: If three judged a case and reached a decision, and one of them then died, they sign the court decree with the two surviving judge's names, and they write therein, 'Even though we have written up the decree with two judges, it was with three that we reached the decision.' "

[E]   Said R. Haggai, "The Mishnah itself has made the same point: '[This is the formula of the prozbul: 'I affirm to you . . . , the judges in such and such a locale, that, in regard to any debt due to me, I shall collect it whenever I wish.]' And the judges sign below, or the witnesses (M.Sheb. 10:4). [Thus even though the case came to the court of three, it is sufficient for two to sign the court decree.]"

[F]   Now do they truly derive the rule covering a court case from the one covering the prozbul [which is, after all, a special remedy for a special problem]?

[G]   [Indeed we do, for] it is taught, One does learn the rule covering an ordinary court case from the rule covering the prozbul.

[III.A]   [In regard to M. San. 5:5S: One of these two votes for conviction accepts the arguments of those who vote for acquittal, if [in the end] one did not accept [those arguments], [how do we decide the case and resolve it finally]?

[B]   R. Yohanan said, "The accused is dismissed as innocent."

[C]   R. Simeon b. Laqish said, "He is guilty,"

[D]   Said to him R. Yohanan, "Now is he not innocent?"

[E]   And why do the two parties argue back and forth [as specified
       in Mishnah]? It is so that the court procedure should not ap-
       pear to people to be in a state of confusion. [Consequently,
       they attempt to reach a decision. It is in hope that a final deci-
       sion in favor of innocence can be reached in an orderly way.
       But, lacking such a result, the accused is still deemed innocent
       until voted guilty.]

       Unit **I** takes up the matter of seating an apprentice on the court
       and raises the question of doing the same when a witness has
       testified in behalf of the defendant. It turns out that the reason-
       ing involved is faulty, for the consideration adduced by Yo-
       hanan, I.C–D; there is no such procedure in law. I do not
       know why I.E is appended. Important in unit **II** is Yosé's ob-
       servation, II.D, concerning the position of B. The decisive con-
       sideration is that three reach the decision, not that they appear
       to conclude the trial and sign the decree. Haggai then presents
       evidence that the decree need not be signed by all three judges.
       Unit **III** provides an important clarification of a matter left
       open at Mishnah, as indicated.

6:1

[A]   [23b] *[When] the trial is over, [and the felon is convicted], they take him out to stone him.*

[B]   *The place of stoning was well outside the court, as it is said, "Bring forth him who cursed to a place outside the camp" (Lev. 24:14).*

[C]   *One person stands at the door of the courthouse, with flags in his hand, and a horseman is some distance from him, so that he is able to see him.*

[D]   *[If] one of the judges said, "I have something to say in favor of acquittal," the one at the door waves the flags, and the horseman races off and stops [the execution].*

[E]   *And even if [the convicted party] says, "I have something to say in favor of my own acquittal," they bring him back,*

[F]   *even four or five times,*

[G]   *so long as there is substance in what he has to say.*

[I.A]   The Mishnah pericope accords with either Rabbi or sages in regard to the provision to be made in the case of a town populated by gentiles [when it states that the one who is stoned must be taken outside the court, including one who has committed idolatry]. [They stone him in the place in which he performed the act of worship. But if it was a gentile town, they stone him at the door of the Israelite court.]

[B]   For it has been taught: "[If there is found among you . . . a man or woman who . . . has gone and served other gods . . . , then you shall bring forth to] your gates [that man or woman

170

... and you shall stone that man or woman to death with stones . . .]"

[C]   Rabbi says, " 'Your gates' (Deut. 17:5) means in the gate of the city in which the man has been found.

[D]   "You say so. But perhaps it refers only to the gate by which he was judged [that is, in which the court was in session]?

[E]   "Here it is stated, 'In your gates,' and elsewhere it is stated, 'In your gates': 'If there is found among you in one of your gates a man or a woman who does what is evil in the sight of the Lord . . . and has gone and served other gods and worshipped them . . . then you shall bring forth to your gates that man or woman and you shall stone . . .' (Deut. 17:2ff.).

[F]   "Just as 'your gates' stated above [where the crime has been committed] speaks of the gate of the city in which the act of worship took place, so 'your gates' mentioned below (Deut. 17:5) refers to the gates of the city where the act has taken place."

[G]   And rabbis say, " 'In your gates' refers to the gate at which the person is judged.

[H]   "You say so. But perhaps it refers only to the gate at which the person was located when the act was done?

[I]   "Here 'your gates' is said, and later on, it is stated, 'Then you shall bring forth to your gates [that man or woman who has done this evil thing, and you shall stone that man or woman to death with stones]' (Deut. 17:5).

[J]   "Just as 'gates' stated later refers to the gate at which the man or woman was judged, so 'gates' which is stated here refers to the gate at which he is judged."

[II.A] [With regard to M. 6:1E–G,] said R. Yohanan, "At the beginning, whether **there is or is not substance in what the accused says, they pay attention to him.**

[B]   **"Later on, if there is substance in what he says, they pay attention to him, and if not, they do not pay attention to him"** [T. San. 9:4].

[C]   They say, "And that rule [of M. San. 6:1G] applies in a case in which, in his later statements, there is substance."

[D]   Hezekiah raised the question, "Lo, if he was going out to be put to death and was struck dumb, do we say that if he had not been struck dumb, if he had something to say in his own behalf, [he would have said it]?"

[E]   R. Yohanan heard this and stated, "Lo, that is the question of an ass.

[F]   "But thus is the question:

[G]   "Lo, if he was going forth to be put to death, and he said, 'I have something to say in my own behalf,' and *then* he was struck dumb, do we say that if he had not been struck dumb, if he had something to say in his own behalf, [he clearly would have said it]?"

[H]   He said, "That is truly a worthwhile question [but it is not answered]."

Unit I is a rather convoluted effort to link Mishnah to a totally unrelated passage, by pointing out, I.A, that all authorities in the other passage will find the present rule congruent with their own views. But it is surely stretching to find M. 6:1A pertinent to the exegetical dispute of I.C–J. Unit II does relate to the rule of Mishnah; D, E–G, raise a relevant question, even though here too it is a casuistic one.

6:2

[A]   *[If] they then found him innocent, they dismiss him.*

[B]   *And if not, he goes out to be stoned.*

[C]   *And a herald goes before him, crying out, "Mr. So-and-so, son of Mr. So-and-so, is going out to be stoned because he committed such-and-such a transgression, and Mr. So-and-so and Mr. So-and-so are the witnesses against him. Now anyone who knows grounds for acquittal—let him come and speak in his behalf!"*

[I.A]   It was taught:

[B]   An ox which was going forth to be stoned, and the witnesses against it turned out to be perjurers—

[C]   R. Yohanan said, "Whoever grabbed the ox first has acquired possession of it [since it is ownerless]."

[D]   R. Simeon b. Laqish said, "It is a case in which it has been declared ownerless in error, [and it remains the property of the original owner]."

[E]   And so in the case of a slave who was going forth to be stoned, and its owner declared him to be consecrated [to the Temple]—

[F]   R. Yohanan said, "[If he then was found to be innocent,] he has acquired ownership of himself."

[G]   R. Simeon b. Laqish said, "It is a case in which the owner has in error given up ownership out of despair, [and that is not a valid act on the part of the owner, who then retains possession of the slave]."

The sole point of contact with the Mishnah is the notion of reversing the ruling, implied at M. 6:2C.

6:3[1]

[A]   *[When] he is ten cubits from the place of stoning, they say to him, "Confess," for it is usual for those about to be put to death to confess.*

[B]   *For whoever confesses has a share in the world to come.*

[C]   *For so we find concerning Achan, to whom Joshua said, " 'My son, I pray you, give glory to the Lord, the God of Israel, and confess to him, [and tell me what you have done; hide it not from me].' And Achan answered Joshua and said, 'Truly have I sinned against the Lord, the God of Israel, and thus and thus I have done' (Josh. 7:19)." And how do we know that his confession achieved atonement for him? For it is said, "And Joshua*

---

1. Note the diverse order of pericope in Chapter 6:

Printed Edition	Leiden MS and *editio princeps*
6:3	6:3, 4, 5, 6
6:4	6:8
6:5	6:7
6:6	6:9
6:7	6:9 contd.
6:8	6:10

said, 'Why have you troubled us? The Lord will trouble you this day' (Josh. 7:25)"—This day the Lord will trouble you, but you will not be troubled in the world to come.

[D]   And if he does not know how to confess, they say to him, "Say as follows: 'Let my death be atonement for all of my transgressions.' "

[E]   R. Judah says, "If he knew that he had been subjected to perjury, he says, 'Let my death be atonement for all my sins, except for this particular sin [of which I have been convicted by false testimony]!' "

[F]   They said to him, "If so, then everyone is going to say that, so as to clear themselves."

[I.A] You find that: when Achan committed sacrilege, Joshua began to attempt to appease the Holy One, blessed be he, saying to him, "Lord of the world, 'Tell me who this man is [who committed sacrilege.' "

[B]   He said to him, "I am not going to inform on any creature, and not only so, but if I did so, I should turn out to commit an act of slander.

[C]   "But go and arrange the Israelites in their tribes, and cast lots on them.

[D]   "Forthwith, I shall produce him."

[E]   This is in line with that which is written, "So Joshua rose early in the morning and brought Israel near, tribe by tribe, and the tribe of Judah was taken; and he brought near the families of Judah, and the family of the Zerahites was taken; and he brought near the family of the Zerahites man by man, and Zabdi was taken; and he brought near his household man by man, and Achan the son of Carmi, son of Zabi, son of Zerah of the tribe of Judah, was taken" (Josh. 7:16–18).

[F]   Achan said to him, "Are you going to seize me by a mere lot? In this entire generation, there are only two who are truly faithful, you and Phineas. Cast lots between yourselves, and *one* of you will be trapped by the lot!

[G]   "Not only so, but your teacher, Moses, died only thirty or forty days ago. Now did not Moses, our rabbi, teach us, 'By the testimony of two witnesses [will the accused be put to death]' (Deut. 17:6)?

[H]   "Now have you already begun to err?"

[I]   At that moment Joshua foresaw through the Holy Spirit that he would eventually divide up the Land of Israel by lots.

[J]   That is in line with the following verse of Scripture: "Joshua cast lots for them in Shiloh before the Lord; and there Joshua apportioned the land to the people of Israel, to each his portion" (Josh. 18:10).

[K]   [So Joshua reasoned:] "Will you then say on this basis that we are giving a bad name by casting lots?

[L]   "And not only so, but if the lots now are confirmed, then all Israelites will say, 'The lots were confirmed in a capital case, all the more so in property cases [e.g., such as in the division of the Land].' But if the lots now are nullified, then all the Israelites will say, 'In a capital case the lots were nullified, all the more so in property cases!' "

[M]   At that moment Joshua began to try to mollify Achan.

[N]   So he imposed an oath on him by the God of Israel and said to him, " 'My son, give glory to the Lord God of Israel and render praise to him; and tell me now what you have done; do not hide it from me.' And Achan answered Joshua, 'Of a truth I have sinned against the Lord God of Israel, and this and that are what I did' (Josh. 17:19, 20)."

[O]   What is the meaning of "of a truth"? It means, "truthfully."

[P]   [Joshua] said to him, "Now note, I asked of you only one matter, but you answered me in two regards [saying, "This and that"].

[Q]   He said to him, "I was the one who committed sacrilege against the *herem* of Midian and against the *herem* of Jericho."

[R]   Said R. Tanhuma, "In the case of four *herems* did he commit sacrilege: in the case of the *herem* of Canaani, the King of Arad; in the case of the *herem* of Sihon and Og; in the case of the *herem* of Midian; and in the case of the *herem* of Jericho."

[S]   *And how do we know that his confession achieved atonement for him [M. San. 6:3C]?*

[T]   As it is said, "The sons of Zerah: Zimri, Ethan, Heman, Calcol, and Dara, five in all; the sons of Carmi: Achar, the troubler of Israel, who transgressed in the matter of the devoted thing; and Ethan's son was Azariah" (1 Chron. 2:6–7).

[U]   Said R. Joshua b. Levi, "Zimri really is Achan, but Achan did the deed of Zimri."

[V]   R. Samuel bar Nahman said, "Heman is Achan: In truth (*amanah*) I have sinned."

[W]   "All of them are five."

[X]   And do I not know that they are five?

[Y]   But it is meant to teach that also Achan has a share in the world to come.

[**II.**A]   [Leiden MS and *editio princeps:* 6:4]MᶜSH B: **A person was going out to be put to death. They said to him,** *"Say, 'May my death be atonement for all my sins.' "*

[B]   *He said, "May my death be atonement for all my sins, except for this particular sin,* **if I actually committed it, let it not be forgiven to me, and let the court of Israel be innocent.** [But I did not commit it, and they, not I, are guilty.]"

[C]   **Now when the matter came to sages, their eyes ran with tears. They gave thought to bringing him back. But if so, there is no end to the matter. "But lo, his blood is on the neck of the witnesses" [T. San. 9:5].**

[**III.**A]   [Leiden MS and *editio princeps:* 6:5] Said R. Judah b. Tabbai, "May I [not] see consolation if I did not put a false witness to death, for they would say that the false witness is not put to death until the accused is put to death, as it is said, 'A soul for a soul' (Ex. 21:23)."

[B]   Said to him Simeon b. Shatah, "May I not see consolation if it is not attributed to you as if you have shed innocent blood, [for behold, the Torah has said, 'At the testimony of two or three witnesses the accused will be put to death' (Deut. 17:6). Just as there must be two witnesses, so also the two false witnesses cannot be punished unless both of them are punished."

[C]   At that moment he undertook not to teach except upon the authority of Simeon b. Shatah (cf. T. San. 6:6].

[D]   The hands of Simeon b. Shatah were heated [he was severe in executing judgment]. A conspiracy of scoffers came, saying, "Take counsel. Let us testify against his son and kill him."

[E]   They gave testimony against him, and he was tried and condemned to death. When he went forth to be executed, they
said to him, "My lord, we lied." His father wanted to bring
him back. The son said to him, "Father if you seek to bring
salvation by your hand, make me as a threshhold."

[F]   [Leiden MS and *editio princeps:* 6:6] M^SH B: A certain saintly
man was walking along the way, and he saw two men having
sexual relations with a female dog [23c]. They said, "We know
that he is a saintly man, and he will go and testify against us
and our master, David, will put us to death.

[G]   "But let us move first and give testimony against him."

[H]   They testified against him and he was tried and condemned to
death.

[I]   That is the meaning of that which David said, "Deliver my
soul from the sword, my life from the power of the dog! (Ps.
22:20)."

[J]   "From the sword"—from the sword of Uriah.

[K]   "From a dog"—from the dog of the holy man.

[L]   R. Judah b. Pazzi went to go up to the schoolhouse, and he
saw two men having sexual relations with one another. They
said to him, "Rabbi, please take note that you are one and we
are two, [so your testimony against us will be null in any
event]."

Unit **I** expands on M. 6:3C. Unit **II** proceeds to M. 6:3D–F
and illustrates that saying with a story. The point of unit **III** is
secondary, namely, the matter of punishing false witnesses,
mentioned in unit **II**, only when the falsely accused person actually has been punished. Simeon b. Shatah's son understood
that his father's enemies could be put to death only if he himself was killed in a judicial error, and that accounts for **III.E**,
illustrative of the teaching of Simeon to Judah. The final two
stories, **III.F–K** and **L**, move still further away from the Mishnah's interests.

6:4 [In Leiden MS and *editio princeps:* 6:8]

[A]   *[When] he is four cubits from the place of stoning, they remove his clothes.*

[B]   *"In the case of a man, they cover him up in front, and in the case of a woman, they cover her up in front and behind," the words of R. Judah.*

[C]   *And sages say, "A man is stoned naked, but a woman is not stoned naked."*

[I.A] The opinions imputed to R. Judah are contradictory.

[B]   There [M. Sot. 1:5] he has said, *"If her hair is beautiful, one did not loosen it,"* and he here says this [that the woman is stoned naked, so he is not of one mind about allowing a prurient situation].

[C]   Here in any event the woman is going to die. But there [with regard to the accused wife] if she is found to be clean [and not an adulteress], the young priests will lust for her.

[D]   The opinion imputed to rabbis is confused. There they say, *"The man is stoned naked, but the woman is not stoned naked,"* and here [M. Sot. 1:5] they say this [that the woman's hair is loosed].

[E]   Thus: "And you will love your neighbor as yourself" (Lev. 19:18)—means , choose for your neighbor [who is convicted and sentenced to death] an easy mode of execution [so the woman is not needlessly ashamed].

[F]   But here [in the case of the accused wife]: ". . . that all the women may take warning and not commit lewdness as you have done" (Ez. 23:48).

The Talmud contrasts M. Sot. 1:5 and M. San. 6:4.

6:5 [In Leiden MS and *editio princeps:* 6:7]

[A]   *The place of stoning was twice the height of a man.*

[B]   *One of the witnesses pushes [the felon] over from the hips.*

[C]   *If he turned upward [in his fall], he turns him over on his hips again [to see whether he had died].*

[D]   *[If] he had died thereby, that sufficed.*

[E]   *If not, he takes a stone and puts in on his heart.*

[F]   *[If] he died thereby, it sufficed.*

[G]   *And if not, the second witness takes a stone and puts it on his heart.*

[H]   *If he died thereby, it sufficed.*

[I]   *And if not, stoning him is [the duty] of all Israelites, as it is said, "The hand of the witnesses shall be first upon him to put him to death, and afterward the hand of all the people" (Deut. 17:7).*

[I.A]   It was taught: **And the height of the one who falls—lo, three [T. San. 9:6].**

[B]   Lo, you say, "The height of the one who is falling, lo, three."

[C]   But in the case of the pit which causes injury, you say, "Up to ten handbreadths"? [*Just as a pit to be reckoned as causing death must be ten handbreadths deep, so must all others be of the same height (M. B.Q. 5:5).* Why so much more of a height in this case?]

[D]   The distance required to do damage is not the same for the one who falls knowingly and the one who falls unknowingly.

[II.A]   R. Jonathan b. Hali, R. Abudimi son of the daughter of R. Tabi in the name of R. Josiah: "Those who throw an ox down with full force [in the slaughterhouse]—in such a case, there is no consideration of the possibility of shattering the limbs, [and the animal is validly slaughtered]."

[B]   In the time of R. Pinhas they threw down an ox with force.

[C]   He said to them, "By your lives, release it [and see whether it has been injured by being thrown down]."

[D]   They let it up, and it got up and fled.

[E]   He said, "Blessed is he who chose the sages and their teachings.

[F]   "For it has been said, 'Those who throw down an ox with full force—there is no consideration of the possibility of shattering the limbs.' "

[III.A]   And how do we know that [a felon] requires stoning?

[B]   As it is said, "He will certainly be stoned [or shot]" (Ex. 19:13).

[C]   And how do we know that he must be pushed off [a height]?

[D]   As it is said, ". . . he will certainly be shot."

[E]   And how do we know that there must be two acts of pushing off?

[F]   As it is said, ". . . be shot . . ."

Units **I** and **III** complement Mishnah, and **II** pursues the matter of injury through a fall. The problem of unit **I** is set by a contrasting rule in M. B.Q. 5:5. Unit **II** deals with slaughter of a beast without prior injury. Unit **III** presents the requisite proof texts for the entire procedure.

6:6 [In Leiden MS and *editio princeps:* 6:9]

[A]   *"All those who are stoned are hung on a tree [afterward]," the words of R. Eliezer.*

[B]   *And sages say, "Only the blasphemer and the one who worships an idol are hung."*

[C]   *"As to a man, they hang him facing the people, and as to a woman, her face is toward the tree," the words of R. Eliezer.*

[D]   *And sages say, "The man is hung, but the woman is not hung."*

[E]   *Said to them R. Eliezer, "And did not Simeon b. Shatah hang women in Ashkelon?"*

[F]   *They said to him, "He hung eighty women, and they do not judge even two on a single day!"*

[I.A]   What is the reasoning of R. Eliezer [who holds that all who are stoned are afterward hung on a tree]?

[B]   Now just as the blasphemer, who is stoned, is hung (Deut. 21:23), so I encompass all others who are stoned, that they too are to be hung.

[C]   What is the reasoning of rabbis?

[D]   Just as the blasphemer, because he struck out at the fundamental principle, is hung, so I encompass all those who have struck out at the fundamental principle, that they too should be hung.

[**II**.A]   [With reference to Simeon b. Shatah, M. San. 6:6E,] there is a Tanna who teaches that Judah b. Tabbai was patriarch, and there is a Tanna who teaches that Simeon b. Shatah was patriarch.

[B]   He who says that Judah b. Tabbai was patriarch finds support in the following incident about Alexandria.

[C]   The men of Jerusalem wanted to appoint Judah b. Tabbai as patriarch in Jerusalem. He fled and went to Alexandria. The men of Jerusalem would write, "From Jerusalem, the great, to Alexandria, the small: 'How long will my betrothed dwell with you, while I am left a deserted wife on his account?' "

[D]   He departed, coming in a boat.

[E]   He who says Simeon b. Shatah was patriarch finds support in the following incident about Ashqelon.

[F]   There were two holy men in Ashqelon, who would eat together, drink together, and study Torah together. One of them died, and he was not properly mourned.

[G]   But when Bar Maayan, the village tax collector died, the whole town took time off to mourn him.

[H]   The surviving holy man began to weep saying, "Woe, for [the enemies of] Israel will have nothing."

[I]   [The deceased holy man] appeared to him in a dream, and said to him, "Do not despise the sons of your Lord. This one did one sin, and the other one did one good deed, and it went well for [the latter on earth, so while on earth I was punished for my one sin, he was rewarded for his one good deed]."

[J]   Now what was the culpable act which the holy man had done?

[K]   Heaven forefend! He committed no culpable act in his entire life. But one time he put on the phylactery of the head before that of the hand [which was in error].

[L]   Now what was the meritorious deed which Bar Maayan the village tax collector had done?

[M]   Heaven forefend! He never did a meritorious deed in his life. But one time he made a banquet for the councillors of his town but they did not come. He said, "Let the poor come and eat the food, so that it not go to waste."

[N]   There are, moreover, those who say that he was traveling along the road with a loaf of bread under his arm, and it fell. A poor man went and picked it up, and the tax collector said nothing to him so as not to embarrass him.

[O]   After a few days the holy man saw his fellow [in a dream] walking among gardens, orchards, and fountains of water. He saw Bar Maayan the village tax collector with his tongue hanging out by a river. He wanted to reach the river but he could not reach it.

[P]   He saw Miriam, the daughter of 'LY BSLYM [Jastrow: the leeklike sprouts of onions], hanging by the nipples of her breasts. Some say that the pin of the gate of Gehenna was fastened to her ear.

[Q]   He said to them, "How long will things be this way?"

[R]   They said to him, "Until Simeon b. Shatah will come, and we shall remove it from her ear and set it in his ear!"

[S]   He said to him, "And what is his crime?"

[T]   They said to him, "Because he vowed, 'If I am made patriarch, I shall kill off all the witches,' and lo, he has been made patriarch, but he has not killed off the witches. Lo, there are eighty witches in a cave of Ashqelon, doing destruction to the world, so go and tell him."

[U]   He said to him, "He is a great man, and he will not believe me."

[V]   He said to him, "He is humble, go and he will believe you. Now if he does not believe you, do this as your sign before him: Put your hand in your eye and remove [your eye], and hold it in your hand." He took out his eye and put it in his hand. They said to put it back, and he put it back next to the other.

[W]   He went and reported the incident to him. He wanted to do the sign for him, but he would not allow him to do so.

[X]   [Simeon] said to him, "I know you are a holy man. Furthermore, I did not say publicly [that I would uproot witchcraft], but I only thought about it [so I know that your knowledge comes from Heaven]."

[Y]   Now that day it was raining. Simeon b. Shetah took with him eighty young men and dressed them in eighty clean cloaks. He took with them eighty new pots. He said to them, "When I whistle once, put on your garments. When I whistle a second time, all of you come out at once."

[Z]   When he came to the mouth of the cave, he said, "Hello, hello! Open up for me. I am one of yours."

[AA]   When he came in, one of them said something and produced bread. One of them said something and produced cooked food. One of them said something and produced wine. They said to him, "And what can you do?"

[BB]   He said to them, "I can whistle twice and produce eighty handsome young men, dressed in clean clothes, who will have pleasure with you and give you pleasure too."

[CC]   They said to him, "We want them! We want them!"

[DD]   He whistled once, and they put on their clean clothes. He whistled a second time, and they all came out at once. He signaled to them, "Each of you pick a partner and lift her up off the ground."

[EE]   At that point what the witch could do would not work. He said to the one who produced bread, "Bring forth bread," but she produced none. He said, "Take her and crucify her."

[FF]   "Bring forth cooked food," but she could not produce, and he said, "Take her and crucify her."

[GG]   "Bring forth wine," and she could not do it, and he said, "Take her and crucify her."

[HH]   And so did he to all of them.

[II]   This is the background of that which we have learned: *Eighty women did Simeon b. Shatah hang in Ashqelon. They do not judge two capital cases on the same day,* but the times required it.

Unit **I** contrasts the reasoning of the Mishnah's authorities, M. 6:6A vs. B, and unit **II** expands M. 6:6E–F.

6:7

[A]   *How do they hang him?*

[B]   *They drive a post into the ground, and a beam juts out from it, and they tie together his two hands, and they hang him.*

[C]   *R. Yosé says, "The post leans against a wall, and then one suspends him the way butchers do it."*

[D]   *And they hang him and untie him forthwith.*

[E]   *And if he is left overnight, one transgresses a negative commandment on his account, as it is said, "His body shall not remain all night on the tree, but you will surely bury him on the same day, for he who is hanged is a curse against God" (Deut. 21:23).*

[F]   *That is to say, On what account has this one been hung? Because he cursed the Name, so the Name of Heaven came to be profaned.*

[I.A]   It was taught: R. Eliezer b. Jacob says, "The rule governing the one who disgraces the divine name is more strict than the one covering the one who blasphemes, and the rule governing the one who blasphemes is more strict than the one who disgraces the divine name.

[B]   "In regard to the one who blasphemes, it is written, 'His body shall not remain all night on the tree,' while in regard to the one who disgraces the divine name it is written, 'Then Rizpah, the daughter of Aiah, took sackcloth, and spread it for herself on the rock, from the beginning of harvest until rain fell upon them from the heavens [thus leaving out the bones of Saul and Jonathan]' (2 Sam. 21:10). [So a more strict rule covers the bones of the blasphemer.]

[C]   "This teaches that they were hung from the sixteenth of Nisan until the seventh of Marheshvan." [This truncated pericope resumes at **III**.YY–BBB.]

[**II**.A]   [The cited verse, 2 Sam. 21:10, is in the context of the complaint of the Gibeonites to David, because Saul had put them to death, despite the oath to spare them taken in the time of Joshua. Consequently, a repertoire of materials on the Gibeonites follows.] It is written, "But Joshua made them that day hewers of wood and drawers of water for the congregation and for the altar of the Lord" (Josh. 9:27).

[B]   There is no difficulty understanding why he made them serve the congregation. But as to the altar of the Lord—[what is the reason for such a reference, there being no such altar in Joshua's time]?

[C]   But Joshua kept them in a state of suspense. He said, "I shall neither drive them away nor bring them near. But he who is destined in time to come to build the chosen house—the one whom he wishes to draw near will he draw near, and the one whom [23d] he wishes to put far he will put far."

[D]   And David came along and put them away.

[E]   "Now the Gibeonites were not of the people of Israel" (2 Sam. 21:2).

[F]   Why did he put them afar off?

[G]   Because: "Now there was a famine in the days of David for three years; [and David sought the face of the Lord]" (2 Sam. 21:1).

[H]   Said David, "It is on account of three things that rain will be held back: idolatry, fornication, and murder.

[I]   "Idolatry, as it is written, 'Take heed lest your heart be deceived, and you turn aside and serve other gods and worship them' (Deut. 11:16), and adjacent to this verse: 'And the anger of the Lord be kindled against you, and he shut up the heavens, so that there be no rain' (Deut. 11:17).

[J]   "Fornication, as it is written, 'Therefore the showers have been withheld, and the spring rain has not come; yet you have a harlot's brow' (Jer. 3:3).

[K]   "Murder, as it is written, 'For blood pollutes the land' (Num. 35:33)."

[L]   And there are those who say, "Also one who publicly pledges to give to charity but fails to carry out his pledge, as it is written, 'Like clouds and wind without rain is a man who boasts of a gift he does not give' " (Prov. 25:14).

[M]   Now [in inquiring as to the reason for the drought and famine], David made inquiry into all his doings, and he did not find any reason. He addressed his question to the Urim and Thummim. This is in line with that which is written, "And David sought the face of the Lord" (2 Sam. 21:1).

[N]   Said R. Eleazar, "It is written, 'Seek the Lord, all you humble of the land, who do his commands' " (Zeph. 2:3).

[O]   "And the Lord said, 'There is bloodguilt on account of Saul and on his house, because he put the Gibeonites to death' " (2 Sam. 21:1).

[P]   "On account of Saul"—because you did not properly bury him.

[Q]   "And on account of the bloodguilt on his house, because he put the Gibeonites to death."

[R]   So David sent and called them and said to them, "What is between you and the house of Saul?"

[S]   They said to him, "It is because he killed seven of us, two hewers of wood, two drawers of water, a scribe, a teacher, and a beadle."

[T]   He said to them, "And what do you now want?"

[U]   They said to him, "Let seven of his sons be given to us, so that we may hang them up before the Lord at Gibeon on the mountain of the Lord" (2 Sam. 21:6).

[V]   He said to them, "Now what pleasure do you have if you kill them? Take silver and gold for yourselves."

[W]   They said to him, "We don't want anything to do with silver and gold from Saul and his house."

[X]   He said, "Perhaps some of them are ashamed before others to accept such a ransom."

[Y]   So he took each one of them and tried to win him over by himself, but none of them went along with him. This in line with the following verse of Scripture, "It is not a matter of silver and gold between us and Saul or his house" (1 Sam. 21:4). Between *me* [individually] . . ." is written.

[Z]   At that moment David said, "The Holy One, blessed be he, gave to Israel three good qualities: modesty, kindness, and caring.

[AA]   "Modesty, as it is said, 'And Moses said to the people, Do not fear; for God has come to prove you, and that the fear of Him may be before your eyes, that you may not sin' (Ex. 20:20).

[BB]   "Kindness, as it is written, '. . . so that He will show you mercy, and have compassion on you, and multiply you, as he swore to your fathers' (Deut. 13:17).

[CC]   "Caring, as it is said, 'Know therefore that the Lord your God is God, the faithful God who keeps covenant and steadfast love . . .' (Deut. 7:9).

[DD]   "Now these, by contrast, do not exhibit any one of these traits."

[EE]   So he set them afar from the Israelites: "Now the Gibeonites were not of the people of Israel" (2 Sam. 21:2).

[FF]   Furthermore, Ezra came along and put them away: "But the temple servants [Nethinim] lived in Ophel; and Ziha and Gishpa were in charge of the temple servants" (Neh. 11:21).

[GG]   And furthermore in the age to come the Holy One, blessed be he, will set them apart, as it is written, "And the workers of the city, from all the tribes of Israel, shall till ('BD) it" (Ez. 48:19).

[HH]   They will perish ('BD) from among all the tribes of Israel.

[II]   "And the king said, 'I will give them' " (2 Sam. 21:6).

[JJ]   "The king took the two sons of Rizpah the daughter of Aiah, whom she bore to Saul, Armoni and Mephibosheth; and the five sons of Merab the daughter of Saul, whom she bore to Adriel the son of Barzillai the Meholathite; and he gave them into the hands of the Gibeonites, and they hanged them" (2 Sam. 21:8–9).

[KK]   "And Michal the daughter of Saul had no child to the day of her death' (2 Sam. 6:23).

[LL]   So she had no child, and how can you say this?

[MM]   On the basis you must say that they were really the children of Merab, and Michal raised them, so they bore her name.

[NN]   "And he gave them into the hands of the Gibeonites, and they hanged them on the mountain before the Lord, and the seven of them perished together" (2 Sam. 21:9).

[OO]   "It is written, 'Seven times'—lacking one."

[PP]   This is Mephibosheth, for whom David prayed, and the altar afforded him protection.

[QQ]   He said to [the Gibeonites], "Lo, I shall make them pass before the altar. Anyone of them to whom the altar affords protection—lo, that one belongs to [the altar, and not to you]."

[RR]   It was because Mephibosheth was great in learning in the Torah before the altar, so it afforded him protection.

[SS]   Said R. Abin, " 'I cry to God Most High, to God who fulfills his purpose for me. He will send from heaven and save me, he will put to shame those who trample me' (Ps. 57:2–3).

[TT]   " '. . . for me,' because the Holy One, blessed be he, concurred with David."

[UU]   "They were put to death in the first days of harvest, at the beginning of barley harvest" (2 Sam. 21:9).

[VV]   "Then Rizpah the daughter of Aiah took sackcloth, and spread it for herself on the rock, from the beginning of harvest until rain fell upon them from the heavens" (2 Sam. 21:10).

[WW]   What is the meaning of "on the rock"?

[XX]   Said R. Oshaiah, "For she recited the verse: 'The Rock, his work is perfect; for all his ways are justice' " (Deut. 32:4).

[YY]   R. Ba bar Zamina in the name of R. Hoshaiah: "Greater is the sanctification of the divine name than the profanation of the divine name.

[ZZ]   "In regard to the profanation of the divine name, it is written, 'His body shall not remain all night on the tree' (Deut. 21:23).

[AAA]   "In regard to the sanctification of the divine name, it is written, "And they hung until rain fell upon them . . .' " (2 Sam.
21:10).

[BBB]   This teaches that they were hung from the sixteenth of Nisan
to the seventeenth of Marheshvan, and passersby would say
"What sort of sin did these men do, that the attribute of divine
justice should be so egregiously enforced against them?"

[CCC]   And people said to them, "It is because they did harm to proselytes who are subject to the protection of a curse."

[DDD]   Now it is a matter of an argument *a fortiori:* If these [Gibeon-
ites], who did not convert with a proper motive [for the sake of
Heaven], the Holy One, blessed be he, exacted vengeance for
their death, those who convert out of purity of motive, how
much the more so [will the Holy One, blessed be he, avenge
their blood, if it is wrongfully spilled].

[EEE]   Many were converted on that day, as it is said, "Then Solomon
took a census of all the aliens who were in the land of Israel,
after the census of them which David his father had taken; and
there were found a hundred and fifty-three thousand six
hundred. Seventy thousand of them he assigned to bear bur-
dens, eighty thousand to quarry in the hill country, and three
thousand six hundred as overseers to make the people work" (2
Chron. 2:17–18).

As noted, the rule on hanging the body of the deceased triggers
this protracted discourse on a biblical tale about doing just
that.

6:8 [In Leiden MS and *editio princeps:* 6:10]

[A]   *Said R. Meir, "When a person is distressed, what words does
the Presence of God say? As it were: 'My head is too heavy for
me, my arm is too heavy for me.'*

[B]   *"If thus is the Omnipresent distressed on account of the blood
of the wicked when it is shed, how much the more so on account of the blood of the righteous!"*

[**I**.A]   We have learned, "[My head is too heavy . . . .]" [qlyny]

[B]   And there are Tammaim who teach the tradition in the language, "It is too heavy for me" [ql'ny; a slight variation in language, not in meaning (PM)].

[C]   He who said, "It is too heavy for me" reads only, "It is weighty."

[D]   He who said, "It is too heavy for me" reads only, "I am burdened."

[E]   R. Meir is not in accord with the Mishnah (6:7E–F) which [interprets "a curse against God" of Deut. 21:23 as referring to a blasphemer and that, therefore,] if the blasphemer [is left overnight on the tree] one transgresses a negative commandment. [R. Meir must be in disagreement with this, since he interprets "a curse" of Deut. 21:23 to mean "It is too heavy for me."]

I follow PM in interpreting this (to me) obscure passage.

6:9 [In Leiden MS and *editio princeps:* 6:11]

[A]   *And not this only [constitute a transgression of Deut. 21:23], but whoever allows his deceased to lie unburied overnight transgresses a negative commandment.*

[B]   *But [if] one kept [a corpse] overnight for its own honor, [e.g.,] to bring a bier for it and shrouds, he does not transgress on its account.*

[C]   *And they did not bury [the felons] in the burial grounds of their ancestors.*

[D]   *But there were two graveyards made ready for the use of the court, one for those who were beheaded or strangled, and one for those who were stoned or burned.*

[I.A]   It was taught: He who moves a bier from place to place is not subject to [the rite of mourning required when] one gathers bones [of an ancestor for secondary burial]. [Merely moving the bier is not part of the reburial process. So new fresh rites of mourning are not required, e.g., for that day only.]

[B]   Said R. Aha, "That statement which you have laid down applies to a bier made of marble. But as to one made of wood [in which case there will have been putrefaction of the bier itself], the person is subject to [carry out rites of mourning involved when] one gathers bones [of an ancestor for secondary burial]."

[C]   Said R. Yosé, "Even in the case of a bier made of wood, [there is no consideration of the rite of mourning required when one] gathers bones [of an ancestor for secondary burial]."

[D]   What constitutes the act of gathering bones [for secondary burial]?

[E]   They carry the skeleton, wrapped in sheets, from one place to another.

[F]   And so it has been taught: Gathering up the bones means that one collects the bones once the flesh has putrefied.

[G]   It was taught, Merely hearing about the secondary collection and burial of the bones of an ancestor does not impose [upon a relative] the obligation of mourning on that day.

[H]   Said R. Haggai, "That is so if one heard a day later. But if one heard on the same day that the bones were collected, then merely hearing about the collection of the bones of an ancestor does impose the obligation to carry out the rites of mourning on that day."

[I]   Nichomachi taught before R. Zeira, "There is no lower limit [to the number of bones which must be collected in a case of] the gathering of bones [for secondary burial, so that even if only a few bones have been collected, the rites of mourning are invoked]."

[J]   R. Mani instructed R. La of Kapra to make a tear in his garments and to go into mourning, in line with the view of R. Aha [above, B],

[K]   but not to undergo cultic uncleanness [if he was a priest, that is, he is not to become unclean to collect his father's bones], in accord with the view of R. Yosé [above, C].

[L]   It was taught: [The rite of mourning applies] in a case of gathering the bones [even when one has merely] heard [about the secondary burial].

[M]   What is the gathering of bones? He who collects bone by bone, once the flesh has putrefied [thus carries out the rite of gathering of bones for secondary burial].

[N]   It was taught: As to a case of gathering of the bones, one does not say in that connection lamentations of obsequies, nor does one state the blessing due to mourners, nor does one express the consolation due to mourners.

[O]   What is the blessing due to mourners?

[P]   It is that said in the synagogue.

[Q]   What is the consolation due to mourners?

[R]   It is that which is said when passing in line before the mourners.

[S]   It was taught: A mourner says something to them.

[T]   What does one say?

[U]   Rabbis of Caesarea say, "One expresses praises [of the deceased]."

The entire passage of the Talmud serves M. 6:10A, and, once more, I assume that it is a mere printer's error which has separated M. 6:9 from M. 6:10.

6:10 [In Leiden MS and *editio princeps:* 6:12]

[A]   When the flesh had rotted, they [then] collect the bones and bury them in their appropriate place.

[B]   And the relatives [of the felon] come and inquire after the welfare of the judges and of the witnesses,

[C]   as if to say, "We have nothing against you, for you judged honestly."

[D]   And they did not go into mourning.

[E]   But they observe a private grief, for grief is only in the heart.

[I.A]   It was taught: At first they would collect the bones and bury them in mounds [as in a pauper's grave]. When the flesh had putrefied, they would collect the bones and bury them in cedar chests.

[B]   On that day the mourner would engage in the rite of mourning. The next day he would rejoice, saying that his ancestors would free him from the rigors of judgment.

[II.A]   Not only so [with regard to M. 6:9D, there were two graveyards, one for those beheaded or strangled, the other for those stoned or burned], but they would bury them by themselves: the ones stoned with the ones burned to death, the ones beheaded with the ones strangled.

[B]   That is in line with that which David says, "Sweep me not away with sinners, nor my life with bloodthirsty men" (Ps. 26:9).

[C]   "With sinners" [refers to] those stoned and burned to death.

[D]   "With bloodthirsty men" [refers to] those who are beheaded and strangled.

[III.A]   R. Abbahu was bereaved. One of his children had passed away from him. R. Jonah and R. Yasi went up [to comfort him]. When they called on him, out of reverence for him, they did not express to him a word of Torah. He said to them, "May the rabbis express a word of Torah?"

[B]   They said to him, "Let our master teach us."

[C]   He said to them, "Now if in regard to the government below, in which there is no reliability, [but only] lying, deceit, favoritism, and bribe-taking—

[D]   "which is here today and gone tomorrow—

[E]   "if concerning that government, it is said, *And the relatives* [24a] *of the felon come and inquire after the welfare of the judges and of the witnesses, as if to say, 'We have nothing against you, for you judged honestly,'*

[F]   "in regard to the government above, in which there is reliability, no lying, deceit, favoritism, or bribe taking—

[G]   "and which endures forever and for all eternity—

[H]   "all the more so are we obligated to accept upon ourselves the just decree [of that heavenly government]."

[I]   And it says, "That the Lord . . . may show you mercy, and have compassion on you . . ." (Deut. 13:17).

Unit **I** serves M. 6:10A, unit **II**, M. 6:9D, and unit **III**, M. 6:10B–C. Unit **II** provides a proof text for its stated distinction.

7:1

[A] [24b] *Four modes of execution were given over to the court [in order of severity]:*

[B] *(1) stoning, (2) burning, (3) decapitation, and (4) strangulation.*

[C] *R. Simeon says, "(2) Burning, (1) stoning, (4) strangulation and (3) decapitation."*

[D] *This [considered in Chapter 6] is how the religious requirement of stoning is carried out.*

[I.A] **But to the civil regime was given over only death by the sword alone [T. San. 9:10B].**

[B] How do we know that stoning [is a mode of execution]?

[C] "And you shall stone that man or woman to death with stones" (Deut. 17:5).

[D] Burning?

[E] As it is said, "[If a man takes a wife and her mother also, it is wickedness;] they shall be burned with fire, both he and they" (Lev. 20:14).

[F] Decapitation?

[G] Here it is said, ". . . he will be punished . . ." (Ex. 21:20), and there it is said, "And I shall bring a punishing sword upon you, that shall execute punishment . . ." (Lev. 26:25).

[H] Just as punishment stated in the latter verse involves use of the sword, so punishment stated in the former one involves use of the sword.

[I]   As to strangling, it is not found [in Scripture].

[J]   You may state matters as follows: As to any reference to the death penalty which is required in the Torah without further specification, you are not permitted to impose a severe mode of execution, but only to impose a lenient mode of execution, and sages have designated strangulation as that lenient mode of execution.

[**II**.A]   R. Simeon says, "Burning is more severe than stoning," and sages teach that stoning is more severe than burning.

[B]   R. Simeon says, "Strangulation is more severe than decapitation," and rabbis teach that decapitation is more severe than strangling [M. San. 7:1B, C].

[C]   [What follows takes for granted knowledge of these verses: "And the daughter of any priest, if she profanes herself by playing the harlot, profanes her father; she shall be put to death" (Lev. 21:9); "But if the thing is true, that the tokens of virginity were not found in the young woman, then they shall bring out the young woman to the door of her father's house, and the men of her city shall stone her to death with stones, because she has wrought folly in Israel by playing the harlot in her father's house" (Deut. 22:20–21); "If there is a betrothed virgin, and a man meets her in the city and lies with her, then you shall bring them both out to the gate . . . and stone them to death with stones . . ." (Deut. 22:23–24.] R. Simeon points to the fact that whoever is subject to the death penalty as the daughter of a priest [who has committed adultery, whether betrothed or married] is subject to the death penalty through burning. [Since the betrothed daughter of a priest who has committed adultery is subjected to burning and not to stoning, as is a betrothed daughter of an Israelite who has committed adultery, it follows that burning is the more severe punishment. For the priest is subject to more severe rules.]

[D]   But rabbis point out that whoever is subject to the death penalty as a *betrothed* daughter of an Israelite or a priest is subject to stoning. [The daughter of a priest who commits adultery when she is married, alone is subject to the penalty of burning. It is only the married daughter of a priest who has committed adultery who is subjected to burning, while the betrothed one is stoned. Since that is the case, stoning is more severe, for it is specified in a special most grave case. In normal cases, then,

burning is the penalty. What is treated as special is more severe, as indicated.]

[E] [Proceeding to nos. B, C, 3, 4:] R. Simeon argues as follows:
Note that in the case of the daughter of a priest, the Torah has
imposed a strict ruling in the case of a betrothed daughter of a
priest [who has committed adultery], for she is put to death
through burning. The Scripture nonetheless has imposed a lenient rule in the case of a married daughter of a priest [who
commits adultery], for she is put to death through stoning. By
contrast, upon the daughter of an Israelite to begin with the
Torah has imposed a lenient form of death, namely, through
stoning. Then is it not logical that we should impose a lenient
rule in her case if she is a married woman and has committed
adultery: she should be put to death through decapitation?

[F] And rabbis argue in this wise: Note that upon the betrothed
daughter of an Israelite [convicted of adultery] the Torah has
imposed a more strict ruling, for she is put to death through
stoning. Yet in the case of a married woman, daughter of an
Israelite, [who has committed adultery] the Torah has imposed
the more lenient rule that she is put to death through burning.
Then to the daughter of a priest [convicted of adultery] the Torah has applied a lenient rule, for she is put to death through
burning. It is not reasonable that we should impose upon her
an easy form of death if she is married [and commits adultery],
that she should be put to death through strangulation?

[III.A] R. Abbahu in the name of R. Yosé b. Haninah: "In any case
in which [a woman who has committed adultery is put to death
in a way] more lenient than her father would be put to death
[for incest with his daughter, that is, in the case of an Israelite's daughter, who is married and commits adultery], her punishment is burning,

[B] "then [in the case of a priest's daughter], her punishment is the
same as that of her father, which is burning;

[C] "and [if she should commit incest] with her father-in-law, the
punishment is execution through stoning."

[D] ["And the daughter of any priest, if she profanes herself by
playing the harlot,] profanes her father; she shall be burned
with fire" (Lev. 21:9).

[E]   R. Eliezer says, "If she committed incest with her father, she is put to death through burning; if she did so with her father-in-law, she is put to death through stoning" [as at B–C].

[F]   She [of D] is put to death through burning, but her lover is not put to death through burning.

[G]   She is put to death through burning, but those who falsely conspire to put her to death and turn out to be perjured witnesses are not put to death through burning [as at M. 11:6H].

[H]   **[All perjurers and illicit lovers go and suffer the form of death which they had brought on their victim; if it was for stoning, they are stoned; if it was for burning, they were burned. Under what circumstances? When they are in the same status as the victim, so as to be subject to that same mode of execution:]** if the death penalty attached to the crime is stoning, the accused is stoned, and the witnesses are stoned; if it was to burning, the victim is burned, and they are burned; if it was to be strangulation, the victim is strangled, they are burned, but she is strangled. But here [M. 11:6H], he is subject to the death penalty through burning, while the perjurers are killed through strangulation [T. San. 14:17].

[IV.A]   R. Abbahu in the name of R. Yosé b. Haninah, Rabbis point to the following argument [that strangulation is more severe:]

[B]   The men of the town which is to be destroyed for collective idolatry originally were in the generality of idolaters, and so were to be subject to stoning [as at Deut. 13:9–10: "You shall kill him . . . you shall stone him to death with stones . . ."]

[C]   But they were made an exception and subjected to a more lenient form of the death penalty, which is burning [Deut. 13:16: "You shall gather all its spoil . . . and burn the city and all its spoil . . ."].

[D]   It is not sufficient for you that you treat them as an exception and impose judgment in accord with the easiest of forms of the death penalty, which is burning.

[E]   But you should then treat the inhabitants as still more of an exception and subject them to the easiest form of the death penalty, which is strangulation.

[F]   R. Simeon points to the following argument:

[G]   A false prophet in fact should subject to the general rule governing all idolaters, that is, to be put to death with burning.

[H]   He was treated as an exception and subjected to the death penalty through the most lenient of modes of death penalty, through stoning.

[I]   It should not be sufficient for you that you treat him as an exception and impose upon him the death penalty through stoning.

[J]   But you should treat him as still more of an exception and impose upon them the most lenient of the death penalties, which is decapitation.

[K]   R. Samuel bar Suseretai in the name of R. Abbahu shifts the grounds of argument:

[L]   Rabbis point to the following argument: The false prophet was in the general category of idolatry, to be put to death through stoning.

[M]   He was treated as an exception and so judged in accord with the most lenient of the forms of execution, which is through burning.

[N]   It is not sufficient for you that you treat him as an exception and impose the death penalty of burning, but you treat him as still more of an exception and impose upon him the most lenient of the modes of execution, which is strangulation.

[O]   R. Simeon points to the following argument:

[P]   The inhabitants of a city which is collectively guilty of idolatry were in the generality of idolatry and so to be put to death through burning.

[Q]   They were treated as an exception so as to impose upon them the death penalty which is most lenient among them all, which is stoning.

[R]   It is not enough for you to do so, but you treat them as still more of an exception and impose upon them the most lenient mode of execution of all, which is decapitation.

At issue in M. 7:1B–C is the relative order of severity, with the differences as signified, 1, 2, 3, 4 vs. 2, 1, 4, 3. The position of

M. 7:1A–C is dictated by the character of Chapter 6, which, for its part, wishes to carry forward without interruption the narrative of trial and execution begun in Chapter 5. Unit **I** presents the anticipated exegesis, providing a Scriptural basis for the facts of Mishnah. Unit **II** states the disagreements indicated by Mishnah, **II**.A, B, and supplies arguments to each party. These differences of opinion in regard to our pericope's law turn out to flow from prior differences over facts governing the priest's daughter, with special reference to whether she is subjected to the same death penalty when convicted of adultery as a betrothed and as a married woman. If that is so, then one set of conclusions follows, and if there is a different penalty for adultery by a priest's betrothed daughter from that applying to the same crime by a priest's married daughter, then another set of conclusions will be reached. This is spelled out at **II**.C–F. Unit **III**.A–C are not clear to me; the parallel version in B provides no help. **III**.D–H serve M. 11:6H. For an account of their relevance here, see PM. Unit **IV** then presents another set of arguments for the position of both Simeon and sages of the Mishnah. A measure of irony seems to be involved at **IV**. D, E, and its parallels in the matched argument given to Simeon, and there is yet a second version of the same exchange of reasoning, **IV.K–R.**

7:2

[A]   *The religious requirement of burning [is carried out as follows]:*

[B]   *They would bury him in manure up to his knees, and put a towel of hard material inside one of soft material, and wrap it around his neck.*

[C]   *This [witness] pulls it to him from one side, and that witness pulls it to him from the other side, until he opens up his mouth.*

[D]   *And one kindles a wick and throws it into his mouth, and it goes down into his bowels and burns his intestines.*

[E]   *R. Judah says, "Also this one: if he died at their hands [through strangulation], they will not have carried out the religious requirement of burning [in the proper manner].*

[F] *"But: They open his mouth with tongs, against his will, kindle a wick, and throw it into his mouth, and it goes down into his bowels and burns his intestines."*

[G] Said R. Eleazar b. Sadoq, *"MᶜSH B: The daughter of a priest committed adultery.*

[H] *"And they put bundles of twigs around her and burned her."*

[I] They said to him, *"It was because the court of that time was not expert [in the law]."*

[I.A] And [why not] put a towel of hard material [around his neck] all by itself [instead of wrapping it in soft cloth]?

[B] They say: So that the man may not die [when the towel is tightened to force his mouth open].

[C] For so we find that when Hezekiah stopped up the outlet of the water of Upper Gihon, he did so with soft materials [so as to absorb the water].

[II.A] Said R. Qerispai in the name of R. Yohanan, "The Mishnah [at M. 7:2C, regarding the wick] speaks of a wick of tin."

[B] What is a wick of tin?

[C] Rabbis of Caesarea say, "A mixture of lead and cassiterum."

[D] Said R. Yosé b. R. Bun, "This is in accord with the one who said that *one kindles the wick and throws it into the mouth* [of the criminal] [M. 7:2D]. But in accord with the one who says that it flows down into his intestines *and burns the intestines* [M. 7:2D], the Mishnah speaks of a wick soaked in oil."

[III.A] It is taught: Forty years before the Temple was destroyed, the right to judge capital cases was taken away from Israelite courts.

[B] In the time of R. Simeon b. Shatah, the right to judge property cases was taken away from Israelite courts.

[C] Said R. Simeon b. Yohai, "Blessed is the All Merciful, for I am not sufficiently wise to make such decisions [in any event]."

[IV.A] Said R. Eleazar b. Sadoq, "I was a child and riding on my father's shoulders, and I saw a *priest's daughter who had committed adultery, and they put bundles of twigs around her and burned her* [M. 7:2H]."

[B]   **They said to him, "You were a child, and children don't give
testimony" [T. San. 9:11].**

[C]   When he saw that affair, he was not less than ten years old.

[D]   When he [left home and] went with his master, he was no less
than thirty years old.

[E]   For it is not the way of a great man to go with someone less
than thirty years old.

[F]   It is taught thus: Said Rabbi, "There is the precedent for I
came with R. Eleazar b. R. Sadoq from Bet Sirion, and we
nibbled at dates and grapes outside of the *sukkah*."

Units **I** and **II** gloss Mishnah, as indicated. **II**.D suggests that
the language chosen by the Mishnah is an amalgam of two different theories and accords with both (hence: neither). Unit **III**
is relevant in a general way. Unit **IV** presents a somewhat revised and amplified version of Eleazar's statement, **IV**.A–B,
and then, at C–D, adds some facts about the stages of a disciple's education. E then explains D, and F presents a further
fact about Eleazar's education.

7:3

[A]   *A religious requirement of decapitation [is carried out as
follows]:*

[B]   *They would cut off his head with a sword,*

[C]   *just as the government does.*

[D]   *R. Judah says, "This is disgusting.*

[E]   *"But they put his head on a block and chop it off with a
hatchet."*

[F]   *They said to him, "There is no form of execution more disgusting than this one."*

[I.A]   R. Judah concedes that *there is no more disgusting form of execution than this one.*

[B]   Nonetheless, the Torah has said, "You shall not walk in their statutes" (Lev. 18:3) [in consequence of which one must do the killing in a way opposite that of M. 7:3B–C].

[II.A]   Said R. Yohanan, "And thus is it too taught:

[B]   " 'The murderer shall be put to death' (Num. 35:17)—with that which he put the victim to death.

[C]   "Is it possible that, if he put him to death with a sword, the murderer should be put to death with a sword, or if with a staff, with a staff?

[D]   "It is stated here, '. . . here he will be punished . . .' (Ex. 21:20), and there it is said, 'And I shall bring a punishing sword upon you, that shall execute punishment . . .' (Lev. 26:25). Just as punishment stated in the latter context involves use of the sword, so punishment stated in the former one involves use of the sword [only].

[E]   "Is it possible that one should remove [the head] from between the shoulders?

[F]   "Here it is stated, 'And you will wipe out evil from your midst' (Deut. 17:7), and later on it is stated, 'You will wipe out innocent blood from your midst' (Deut. 21:9).

[G]   "We thus have reference to both removal and to breaking the neck.

[H]   "Just as removal stated below involves a blow at the base of the neck, so too a blow at the base of the neck is required here.

[I]   "Just as breaking the neck stated later involves actually severing the head from the neck, so here too it involves severing the head from the neck."

Unit I amplifies M. 7:3B–F, and unit II presents pertinent materials.

7:4

[A]   *The religious requirement of strangulation [is carried out as follows]:*

[B]   *They would bury him in manure up to his knees, and put a towel of hard material inside one of soft material, and wrap it around his neck.*

[C]   *This [witness] pulls it to him from one side, and that witness pulls it to him at the other side,*

[D]   *until he perishes.*

[I.A]   As to strangling, it is not found [in Scripture].

[B]   "You may state matters as follows: As to any reference without further specification to the death penalty which is required in the Torah, you are not permitted to draw it out, to impose a severe mode of execution, but only to impose a lenient mode of execution, and sages have designated strangulation as that lenient mode of execution," [24c] the words of R. Josiah.

[C]   Said to him R. Jonathan, "It is not because it is a more lenient mode of execution, but it is stated without further specification, and in the case of any form of death which is stated without further specification you are not permitted to impose a more severe mode of execution but only a more lenient one. They designated strangulation as that lenient mode of execution."

[II.A]   Thus do you state the mode of strangulation:

[B]   *This witness pulls it to him from one side, and that witness pulls it to him at the other side [M. 7:4I].*

[C]   Kahana raised the question before Rab: "There you say, 'This one pulls it to him from one side, and that one pulls it to him from the other side' [M. Zabim 3:2].

[D]   "and here you say, 'This one pulls it to him, and that one pulls it to him . . .' [M. 7:4I]?"

[E]   He said to him, "There, this one stands in front of him and that one behind him, while here, this one stands on the one side and that one stands at the other side."

For a simpler version of unit I see M. 7:1, I.I–J. Unit II contrasts the slightly different wording between M. San. 7:4, I and M. Zabim 3:2.

7:5

[A]   *These are [the felons] who are put to death by stoning:*

[B]   *He who has sexual relations with his mother, with the wife of his father, with his daughter-in-law, with a male, and with an animal;*

[C]   *and the woman who brings an animal on top of herself;*

[D]   *and he who blasphemes, he who performs an act of worship for an idol, he who gives of his seed to Molech, he who has a medium, and he who is a soothsayer;*

[E]   *he who profanes the Sabbath,*

[F]   *he who curses his father or his mother,*

[G]   *he who has sexual relations with a betrothed maiden,*

[H]   *he who incites [an individual] or beguiles [a whole town, to idolatry],*

[I]   *a sorcerer,*

[J]   *and a stubborn and incorrigible son.*

[I.A]   [The materials which follow are relevant to M. Ker. 1:1, which is as follows: *Thirty-six transgressions subject to extirpation are in the Torah: He who has sexual relations with his mother, his father's wife, and his daughter-in-law; he who has sexual relations with a male or a beast, and the woman who has sexual relations with a beast . . . he who blasphemes, he who performs an act of blasphemous worship, he who gives his seed to Molech, he who has a familiar spirit, he who profanes the Sabbath . . .*] Now it was necessary to specify [that there are thirty-six such transgressions] to indicate that if one carried all of them out in a single spell of inadvertence, he is liable on each and every count.

[B]   But if one carried them out in two spells of inadvertence, [what is the law]?

[C]   For even if one had intercourse with a [forbidden] woman and went and did so a second time, [in two spells of inadvertence,] he is liable for each act of sexual relations.

[D]   R. Simeon son of R. Hillel b. Pazzi raised the question before R. Hillel b. Pazzi: "The Mishnah pericope speaks of violation

of the law with a single woman who is prohibited on a number
of different counts.

[E]   "But if there were many women [prohibited on a single count
or one woman and many spells of inadvertence, do we consider
the man's multiple transgressions as a single spell of inadvertence?" (PM).

[F]   He said to him, "That is why it was necessary [to specify the
thirty-six counts of M. Ker. 1:1, so to indicate that even if it
was] in a single spell of inadvertence, [one is liable on each and
every count]."

[G]   [And we derive the same basic conception from] the dispute
which follows:

[H]   [If the male partner committed many acts of forbidden intercourse, e.g., with a menstruating woman or a close relative,] in
a single spell of inadvertence, but the female partner [did so] in
many distinct spells of inadvertence [because she knew and
then forgot that she was menstruating or was related],

[I]   R. Yohanan said, "He is liable to bring a single offering, but
she is liable to bring five [offerings covering the five distinct
spells of inadvertence]."

[J]   R. Simeon b. Laqish said, "Just as he brings only a single offering, so she brings only a single offering." [It follows that
both Yohanan and Simeon concur that we do make distinctions
among spells of inadvertence, if there is call to do so, in line
with F.]

[K]   [Continuing the line of F, it was indeed necessary to specify
the thirty-six counts under which one may be liable,] so that
you may not say that they treat cases of transgression with
many different women or [one woman] and many different
spells of inadvertence, as if they were subject to a single spell
of inadvertence [with the false result] that one will be liable on
only a single count. On this account it is necessary to state that
one is liable on each and every count.

[II.A]   R. Bun bar Hiyya said, "R. Ishmael taught as follows:

[B]   " 'You shall not practice augury or witchcraft' (Lev. 19:26).

[C]   "Now are not augury and witchcraft subject to the same general prohibition [of magic]? They have been treated as distinct

[and requiring specification] so as to make distinctions therein, [and so to indicate that one is punishable on each count]."

[D]   [In a case where [the general rule] is stated with the punishment of] extirpation and a specific instance [is also stated with the punishment of] extirpation, in the view of R. Yohanan, we deal with a generalization followed by a specification [so that whatever is stated in the specification limits what is implied by the generalization, a conception which will now be spelled out. This conception is spelled out as follows:]

[E]   For R. Abbahu stated in the name of R. Yohanan: " 'For whoever shall do any of these abominations, the persons that do them shall be cut off from among their people' (Lev. 18:29) [with reference to the prohibited sexual unions, e.g., son and mother or stepmother].

[F]   "Now was the man's sister not within the general principle [by which consanguineous marriages are prohibited]? [And why was the union of brother and sister specified, at Lev. 18:9?] It was treated as a specific item in order to effect a differentiation among the various categories of prohibited unions contained within the generalization [and so to indicate that one is punishable on each count]. [This then indicates that if one has violated the entire range of rules against consanguineous marriages in a single spell of inadvertence, he is liable on each count.]"

[G]   R. Eliezer objected, "And it is not written, 'You shall not uncover the nakedness of your mother's sister . . . you shall not uncover the nakedness of your father's sister . . .' (Lev. 18:12, 13)? [Why should these items be treated specifically, since they are covered by the same general principle? What rule—by the same mode of exegesis—does Yohanan impute here?]"

[H]   He said to him, "They were specified explicitly for a specific purpose. It is to make the rule that one is liable for reaching even the first stage of sexual connection [and not fully consummating the sexual act]."

[I]   [He replied, "But that same rule, H, is available elsewhere.] For is it not written, 'If a man lies with a woman having her menstrual period and uncovers her nakedness, he has made naked her fountain, and she has uncovered the fountain of her blood; both of them shall be cut off from among their people' (Lev. 20:18)? [Now this would seem superfluous in the light of H.]"

[J]   He said to him, "They were specified explicitly for a specific purpose. It is to make the rule that one is liable for reaching even the first stage of sexual connection.

[K]   "[It was to make a very specific point, specifically, so that] you should not maintain that position that, since one is liable in the case of a menstruating woman only on the count of the uncleanness involved, even in the primary sexual connection, in such a case one should *not* treat the one who begins the sexual relationship as equivalent in guilt to the one who fully consummates it. On this account it was necessary to make the entire matter specific." [So Yohanan's exegetical principle stands.]

[L]   And is it not written: "If a man lies with his uncle's wife, he has uncovered his uncle's nakedness" (Lev. 20:20)? [Does this not repeat Lev. 18:14: "You shall not uncover the nakedness of your father's brother . . ."?]

[M]   He said to him, "They were specified explicitly for a specific purpose. It is to indicate the punishment of dying childless."

[N]   This is in line with that which R. Yudan said, "In any place in which it is said, 'They shall be childless' [as at Lev. 20:21: "If a man takes his brother's wife, it is impurity; he has uncovered his brother's nakedness, they shall die childless"], they shall live without children.

[O]   "And in any place in which it is said, 'They shall die childless' [as at, "If a man lies with his uncle's wife . . . they shall die childless" (Lev. 20:20)], it means that they shall bury their children."

[P]   Said R. Yosé, "Reference to his aunt was necessary. It is stated explicitly rather than as part of a general rule in order to exclude the wife of his brother on his mother's side [whom one may marry]."

[Q]   What is the Scriptural basis for that statement?

[R]   Here "his aunt" is stated [Lev. 20:20], and there, "Either his uncle or the son of his uncle will redeem him" (Lev. 25:49).

[S]   Just as "his uncle" to which reference is made later on refers specifically to the brother of his father on his father's side [and not in the female line], so "his aunt" to which reference is made in this context refers to his father's brother's wife, on his father's side [and not on his mother's side]. [Consanguinity in the female line is limited, as at P.]

[T]   Also the prohibition of the wife of his brother is to be derived by analogy to the prohibition of his aunt.

[U]   Now just as the case of the aunt to which reference is made later means specifically the wife of the father's brother on the father's side, so the matter of the wife of his brother to which reference is made here refers to the wife of his brother on his father's side.

[V]   Up to now [the interpretation of the several verses has accorded with the exegetical theory] of R. Aqiba [who derives (1) the law concerning the aunt by analogy, and (2) the law covering the wife of his brother by analogy from the law covering his aunt].

[W]   But what is to be said from the viewpoint of R. Ishmael?

[X]   R. Ishmael taught: "Here reference is made to the wife of his brother, and below, reference is made as follows: 'If a man takes his brother's wife, it is [menstrual] impurity' (Lev. 20:21).

[Y]   "Just as, in the case of such an impurity, there is a point at which one is permitted [to have sexual relations] after the woman has been prohibited from having sexual relations, so also with regard to the wife of one's brother there may be a period in which one may have sexual relations [after the time at which one may not, e.g., if the husband dies without children].

[Z]   "Excluded from the rule then is the wife of his brother on his mother's side, in which there is no point at which one is permitted to have sexual relations after the woman has been prohibited to him by reason of her marriage to his brother [for even if the husband dies childless in this case, there is no levirate marriage]."

[AA]   [Reverting to II.F, Yohanan says that the sister is specified for the stated reason, we now ask:] And lo, R. Yohanan must confront this same question himself, and how does he bring evidence for the stated proposition [that there are distinct counts on which one is liable? For, after all, there has been solid objection to his original proof for that proposition in context].

[BB]   R. Abbahu in the name of R. Eleazar in the name of R. Hoshaiah: "In a case in which we have two negative commandments and a single penalty of extirpation [stated in context], the specification of the negative commandments serves the purpose of treating the penalty of extirpation as divided and so applicable to each of the negative commandments [and thus, as above, there will be liability on a number of distinct counts]."

[CC]   What is the Scriptural basis for this position?

[DD]   "It shall not be poured upon the bodies of ordinary men, and you shall make no other like it in composition" (Ex. 30:32).

[EE]   And it is written, "Whoever compounds any like it or whoever puts any of it on an outsider shall be cut off from his people" (Ex. 30:33).

[FF]   Thus we have two negative commandments [DD and EE] but only a single statement regarding extirpation [EE]. The function of the two explicit negative statements is to effect a differentiation within the penalty of extirpation and so to apply the penalty of extirpation to one who violates either one of the two negative rules.

[GG]   [(Restoring the text for GG and HH from Y. Shab. 7:2:) Now since that fact is to be derived from the above proof,] why does Yohanan have [to derive the same proposition from the verses with which he has dealt earlier]?

[HH]   How does R. Yohanan deal with this matter? Scripture (Lev. 18:29) speaks of men and the reference to "his sister" serves the purpose of applying that same general principle to all cases involving women.
        And doesn't R. Eleazar hold this rule too?
        He derives it from "None of you shall approach [anyone near of kin to him" (Lev. 18:6)] which implies both male and female.
        And how does R. Yohanan treat this verse?
        He explained it, but it isn't clear.

[II]   Now further did Samuel b. Abba raise the question before R. Zeira, "[With reference to the following verses the question is raised. Lev. 7:20: 'But the person who eats of the flesh of the sacrifice of the Lord's peace offerings while an uncleanness is on him—that person shall be cut off from his people.' Now the prohibition of eating peace offerings in a state of uncleanness is part of the general principle of preserving the cleanness of all offerings. It is treated explicitly here. But at Lev. 22:3 it is

part of the following general rule: 'If any one of all your descendants throughout your generations approaches the Holy
Things, which the people of Israel dedicate to the Lord, while
he has an uncleanness, that person shall be cut off from my
presence. Thus we have two verses which prohibit eating Holy
Things while in a state of uncleanness. So the reference to
peace offerings has a specific purpose. It would then—by the
stated reasoning—be the purpose of indicating that if inadvertently one ate a variety of Holy Things in a single spell of inadvertence, he will be liable on the count of each distinct sort of
Holy Things. This is the proposition now to be stated:] Now
peace offerings have been specified explicitly and is the purpose
to impose a distinction on all varieties of Holy Things eaten in
a state of uncleanness, [and so impose liability on each count,
as stated above]?"

[JJ]   He said to him, "It was made explicit for a distinctive purpose.
[Holy Things in the form of peace offerings] are mentioned explicitly in order to exclude [from the stated rule] Holy Things
given for the upkeep of the Lord's house,

[KK]   "and to make the point that people are not liable in the case of
Holy Things given for the upkeep of the house on the count of
violating the rule of refuse, remnant, and uncleanness, [so that
if one should keep those Holy Things too long or eat them in a
state of uncleanness, he is not liable]."

[LL]   "[Continuing Zeira's statement:] Now is that rule not stated explicitly in the Mishnah, as follows: *Things consecrated for the
altar join together with one another [for making up the requisite quantity to be subject to] the law of sacrilege, and to impose liability on their account for transgression of the laws of
refuse, remnant, and uncleanness [M. Me. 4:1A–B]*,

[MM]   "which is not the case of things consecrated for the upkeep of
the house.

[NN]   "Since they do join together, they are not subject to the distinctions made above, [but one is liable on a single count for
the whole lot of them]."

[OO]   Said R. Haninah, "[What sort of proof derives from the cited
Mishnah? It itself poses problems.] For it was necessary to derive the stated proof. For otherwise why should they not be
deemed distinct from one another and *not* to be joined
together?"

[**III**.A]   Where we have a general rule stated affirmatively, and a specific instance of the rule expressed negatively [how do we interpret the matter, and for what purpose]?

[B]   In the opinion of R. Eleazar, you have a case of a general rule followed by a specific explication of the general rule [which limits the general rule], [as illustrated in the following dispute]:

[C]   R. Eleazar says, "People receive a flogging on the count of ploughing in the Sabbatical Year."

[D]   R. Yohanan said, "People receive a flogging on the count of ploughing in the Sabbatical Year."

[E]   What is the Scriptural basis for the position of R. Eleazar?

[F]   "In the seventh year there shall be a Sabbath of solemn rest for the Land, a Sabbath to the Lord" (Lev. 25:4).

[G]   "You shall not sow your field or prune your vineyard" (Lev. 25:4).

[H]   The former represents a general statement, the latter a specific explication of the general statement.

[I]   Sowing and pruning were part of the general rule, and why are they explicitly stated? It is to build an analogy on them and to rule as follows: Just as sowing and pruning are distinctive in that they represent work on the land and on trees, so I prohibit only acts of labor which represent work on the land or on trees. [Now this would encompass ploughing.]

[J]   How does R. Yohanan treat the verses?

[K]   You have two distinct acts of labor, and they are two matters which have been treated as distinctive as apart from the general rule which covers them. It is for the purpose of making a distinction [and indicating that, if one does both of them in a single act of inadvertence, he is liable on the count of each]. [The purpose then is not to encompass ploughing as a forbidden act of labor in the Sabbatical Year.]

[L]   In the opinion of R. Eleazar, are they not treated as distinct acts of labor [so one would not be liable on the count of each, as explained]?

[N]   But surely he should treat them as distinct actions, for on the count of each of which one should be liable.

[O]   They are not treated as distinct acts, but they do serve to provide a lesson [as specified above, covering other actions which are going to be prohibited, e.g., ploughing].

[P]   [Now we turn to R. Yohanan and ask,] In the view of R. Yohanan do they not serve to provide further lessons [about other acts of labor which, like them and sharing their traits, will be forbidden]?

[Q]   The rule is different here [on which case we cannot derive further lessons], for we have a case in which the general rule is expressed in affirmative language, while the specification illustrative of the rule is expressed in negative language,

[R]   and a commandment stated in affirmative language does not serve to impart lessons concerning a commandment stated in negative language, nor does a commandment stated in negative language teach lessons concerning a commandment stated in affirmative language.

[S]   In the opinion of R. Eleazar, a commandment stated in affirmative language does teach lessons concerning commandments stated in negative language,

[T]   but a commandment stated in negative language does not teach lessons concerning a commandment stated in affirmative language.

[U]   Now in accord with the position of R. Yohanan, we have no problem. It is permitted in the Sabbatical Year to dig wells, caves, and caverns [for this is not a prohibited act of agricultural labor in the Sabbatical Year].

[V]   But in the opinion of R. Eleazar, what is the law as to digging wells, caves, and caverns [given that ploughing is prohibited]?

[W]   Just as the [cited verses] do not teach lessons for one another for matters subject to a prohibition, so they do not provide lessons concerning matters which are permitted [so far as Yohanan is concerned]. [But so far as Eleazar is concerned, it will be permitted to dig.]

[X]   Said R. Ba Qartegenah: "The Scriptural basis for the position of R. Yohanan [that ploughing is permitted in the Sabbatical Year] is as follows:

[Y]   " 'Six years you shall sow your field' (Lev. 25:3)—not in the Seventh Year.

[Z]   " 'Six years you shall prune your vineyard and gather in its fruits' (Lev. 25:3)—not in the Seventh Year.

[AA]   "Any negative commandment which is derived from an affirmative statement is deemed itself to be an affirmative statement, and [one who violates it] has violated an affirmative statement. [But it is permitted to plough.]"

[BB]   R. Jeremiah said, "One thereby violates an affirmative statement."

[CC]   R. Yosé says, "Even the consideration of an affirmative commandment is not present in such a case, [and the prohibition of ploughing does not derive from the Torah]."

[DD]   And is it not fully spelled out: "There shall be a Sabbath of solemn rest for the Land, a Sabbath to the Lord" (Lev. 25:4)?

[EE]   This serves the purpose [of imposing the penalty of flogging] on those who violate the negative rules of the Sabbatical Year during the additional period [added on to the Sabbatical Year, in which time the negative rules also apply]. [That is, during a number of months prior to the advent of the Sabbath Year, certain acts of agricultural labor may not be carried out because the benefit therefrom will be felt in the Sabbatical Year itself.]

[EE]   [There is a tannaitic teaching as follows:] "Is it possible they should be flogged on account of the addition?" [Of course not.]

[FF]   R. Yohanan explains the teaching as follows:

[GG]   Is it possible that people should be flogged on the count of ploughing in the Seventh Year [which is in "addition" to the sowing and pruning mentioned in the verse]? [Surely not.]

[HH]   (Lo,) R. Eleazar explains the teaching as follows: [24d] Is it possible that people should be flogged for violating the prohibitions stated in the first two chapters [of Tractate Shebiit which deal with the additional period added on to the Sabbatical Year]? [Surely not.]

[II]   There is a Tanna who teaches, "And six years you should sow your field, and six years you should prune your vineyard," and there is a Tanna who repeats the tradition, "You should not sow . . . you should not prune . . ."

[JJ] The one who said, "Six years . . ." supports the position of R. Yohanan, and the one who said ". . . your field you should not sow" supports the position of R. Eleazar.

[KK] The following pericope differs from the position of R. Eleazar:

[LL] ["Take heed lest you offer your burnt offerings at every place that you see; but at the place which the Lord will choose in one of your tribes, there you shall offer your burnt offerings, and there you shall do all that I am commanding you" (Deut. 12:13–14).] "Take heed"—stated as a negative commandment.

[MM] "Lest"—stated as a negative commandment.

[NN] And it is written, "There you shall offer your burnt offerings . . ."

[OO] "There you shall offer up"—this refers to the offering up.

[PP] "And there you shall do"—this refers to the act of slaughtering the beast and sprinkling the blood.

[QQ] Just as the act of offering up is stated in affirmative language, and lo, it also is subject to a negative commandment, so the acts of slaughtering the beast and sprinkling the blood, which are stated in affirmative language, should be subject to a negative commandment as well. [So we have a negative commandment deriving from one phrased in affirmative language. The net result is contrary to Eleazar's exegetical position at S–T.]

[RR] Since it is written, "There you shall offer up . . . and there you shall do . . . ," lo, if it were not written, "There you shall offer up and there you shall do . . . ,"

[SS] you would *not* have a case in which a religious commandment stated in affirmative language teaches concerning one stated in negative language,

[TT] and one stated in negative language does not teach any rules governing one expressed in affirmative language [as is Yohanan's view at Q–R]. [The affirmative and negative rules do not have a bearing on one another, exactly as Yohanan maintains.]

[UU] Now how does R. Yohanan [*sic!* Better: Eleazar] deal with this same matter?

[VV] So that you should not interpret the matter as you do in regard to the Sabbath law:

[WW]   If one has dug a hole, ploughed a furrow, and dug a ditch, he should be liable on only a single count [treating all as part of a single category of labor].

[XX]   And similarly if one has slaughtered a beast and offered it up he should be liable on only a single count.

[YY]   Accordingly it was necessary to state matters as they are stated, so that one will be liable on each count by itself [as Scripture specifies].

[IV.A]   R. Zeira, R. Hiyya bar Ashi in the name of Kahana: "He who plants in the Sabbatical Year is liable on the count of sowing."

[B]   R. Zeira says, "He who prunes is equivalent to him who sows."

[C]   If one sowed and pruned on the Sabbath—

[D]   In the opinion of Kahana, he is liable on two counts [that is, for planting, and pruning is a distinct act of labor from sowing].

[E]   In the opinion of R. Zeira, he is liable on only one count.

[F]   Has not R. Zeira stated that he who prunes is like him who sows? And did he not say that he who sows is like him who prunes?

[G]   All acts were subject to the same general rule prohibiting sowing, and pruning was treated as a special case and made explicit [at Lev. 25:4], to impose a strict rule on pruning.

[H]   And since pruning has been treated as a special case and a more strict rule has been applied to it, do you then exempt the man on the count of sowing? [Obviously not.]

[I]   It must follow that there is no difference between planting and pruning on the Sabbath whether in the opinion of R. Kahana, or of Zeira: One is liable on two distinct counts.

The elegant Talmud before us serves other tractates. That is most striking at unit I, which goes over, from the perspective of M. Ker. 1:1, the items on the list before us. (Presumably if there were a Palestinian Talmud to the Division of Holy Things, the bulk of the present Talmud would be located there as well as here.) Unit II takes up the analysis of a basic exegetical exercise. The basic theory is that, if a subcategory of a given category is covered by a rule stated for that larger category of which it is a part, there is no need to specify said subcategory. If then Scripture does make an explicit reference to that subcategory, it is to make some point over and above that which governs the subcategory as part of the principal category of which it is part. This is amply clear at the simple statement at **II**.A–C. What unit **II** proceeds to present is a full account of the position outlined at **II**.A–C, testing the general principle of exegesis against a variety of examples. Unit **III** carries forward this same interest in general rules of exegesis, involving Yohanan and Eleazar. The point of contact with the foregoing is at **III**.K. But unit **III** should be seen, along with its supplement at unit **IV**, as distinct from what has preceded. The issue is joined at the difference between I and K. Once that is set forth, the position of each must be amplified and tested. The critical point is reached at Q–R vs. S–T. U–W represent a fresh initiative, X–AA, yet another. KK–TT revert to the position of Yohanan and show how his exegetical principle applies to a separate matter. UU cannot possibly ask Yohanan to counter a proof of his own position. Unit **IV**, as we see, is simply a supplement to the matter of the Sabbatical Year's law.

7:6 [In Leiden MS and *editio princeps*: 7:6–7:7]

[A]   He who [inadvertently] has sexual relations with his mother is liable on her account because of her being his mother and because of her being his father's wife [Lev. 18:6–7, 20:11].

[B]   R. Judah says, "He is liable only on account of her being his mother alone."

[C]   He who has sexual relations with his father's wife is liable on her account because of her being his father's wife and because of her being a married woman,

[D]   whether this is in the lifetime of his father or after the death of his father,

[E]   whether she is only betrothed or already married [to the father].

[F]   He who has sexual relations with his daughter-in-law is liable on her account because of her being his daughter-in-law and because of her being another man's wife,

[G]   *whether this is in the lifetime of his son or after the death of his*
       son [Lev. 20:12],

[H]   *whether she is only betrothed or already married [to the son].*

[I.A] Whence in Scripture do we derive a warning against having
       sexual relations with one's mother?

[B]   "You shall not uncover . . . the nakedness of your mother"
       (Lev. 18:7).

[C]   Whence in Scripture do we derive that the penalty is
       extirpation?

[D]   "For whoever shall do any of these abominations—the persons
       that do them shall be cut off from among their people" (Lev.
       18:29).

[E]   Whence in Scripture do we derive a warning against having
       sexual relations with one's father's wife?

[F]   "You shall not uncover the nakedness of your father's wife"
       (Lev. 18:8).
       Whence in Scripture do we derive that the penalty is
       extirpation?
       "For whoever shall do any of these abominations . . ." (Lev.
       18:29).

[G]   Whence in Scripture do we derive a [court-administered]
       penalty?

[H]   "The man who lies with his father's wife has uncovered his
       father's nakedness; both of them shall be put to death, their
       blood is upon them" (Lev. 20:11).

[I]   [Leiden MS and *editio princeps:* 7:8] Whence in Scripture do we
       derive a warning against having sexual relations with one's
       daughter-in-law?

[J]   "You shall not uncover the nakedness of your daughter-in-law"
       (Lev. 18:15).

[K]   Whence in Scripture do we derive that the penalty is
       extirpation?

[L]   "For whoever shall do any of these abominations—the persons
       that do them shall be cut off from among their people" (Lev.
       18:29).

[M]   Whence in Scripture do we derive a [court-administered] penalty?

[N]   "If a man lies with his daughter-in-law, both of them shall be put to death; they have committed incest, their blood is upon them" (Lev. 20:12).

[II.A]   [The consideration that one is liable on two counts, expressed at M. San. 7:6A, C, F] is stated here, and it also is stated in tractate Keritot [in connection with the obligation to bring a sin offering for inadvertently committing such an act].

[B]   It makes sense to state matters in that way in tractate Keritot, for one may bring a sin offering and go and bring yet another sin offering.

[C]   But in the context of Sanhedrin [which deals with the death penalty], do you have the option of stating that one is stoned and goes and is stoned yet a second time?!

[D]   Said R. Yudan father of R. Mattenaiah, "It is for the purpose of effecting a warning that the matter is taught.

[E]   "That is to say, if others warned the man on the count of having sexual relations with a married woman, he will be flogged [if he disregards their warning], and if it was on the count of her being his mother, he will be flogged on that count. [So the principal consideration here has to do with appropriate warning.]"

[F]   And let them warn him on the count of a married woman [and why should he not be liable also, if it is his mother, on the count of another man's wife]?

[G]   Said R. Abin, "Interpret the Mishnah pericope to speak of an unmarried woman."

[III.A]   There we have learned the following:

[B]   R. Judah says, "If his mother was not a suitable wife to his father [by reason of a genealogical impairment], he is liable on only one count [for the marriage is null by reason of said impairment]."

[C]   Lo, if she was a suitable wife for his father, he is liable on two counts [contrary to M. 7:6B]!

[D]   R. Abbahu in the name of R. Yohanan: "There is no difference [from Judah's viewpoint] whether his mother was a suitable wife to his father or not. He is liable on only one count."

[E]   What is the Scriptural basis for R. Yohanan's view [of Judah's
opinion]?

[F]   "She is your mother" (Lev. 18:7)—on account of his mother
you impose liability on him. The entire passage is directed to
the mother, [so there is no difference whether it was a legitimate marriage or otherwise].

[G]   R. Bun bar Hiyya raised the question before R. Zeira: "Why
did R. Yohanan [F] seize upon the count of the mother and
ignore the count of the married woman?"

[H]   He said to him, "The reason is that he concurs with R. Ishmael, for R. Ishmael interpreted the passage as follows:

[I]   " 'The nakedness of your father . . . ,' (Lev. 18:7)—Scripture
speaks of the male [in prohibiting having sexual relations with
the father].

[J]   Now is not the father in the category of the male? [That is,
why is he made a specific subject of the law? The prohibition is
general.]

[K]   But it is to impose upon the malefactor liability on two counts,
as it is taught:

[L]   He who has sexual relations with his father is liable on two
counts; [first, because he is the father; second, because he is
male].

[M]   Then why should we not learn [at the opening line of tractate
Keritot 1:1]: Thirty-*seven* [rather than thirty-six] counts of extirpation are listed in the Torah [thus encompassing the one
just now stated]?

[N]   R. Mana said, "Whatever comes under the count of [sexual relations with a] male is included in a single count."

[IV.A]   "You shall not uncover the nakedness of your father's wife"
(Lev. 18:8).

[B]   Scripture speaks of the father's wife.

[C]   ". . . the nakedness of your mother" (Lev. 18:7)—this is the
mother married to his father.

[D]   What about his mother not married to his father? [That is, if the father has raped a woman, how do we know that the son may not marry her?]

[E]   "She is your mother, you shall not uncover her nakedness" (Lev. 18:7).

[F]   How does R. Aqiba deal with this matter [since, as we shall see, he interprets the verse differently, below, J–K]?

[G]   He interprets it to speak of the situation prevailing after death [that is, after the father dies, one still may not have sexual relations with the woman].

[H]   And does R. Ishmael not maintain the same view?

[I]   "It is your father's nakedness" (Lev. 18:8)—and that is the case whether he is alive or after his death.

[J]   [As noted at F,] R. Aqiba interprets ["You shall not uncover] the nakedness of your father, [which is the nakedness of your mother; she is your mother, you shall not uncover her nakedness" (Lev. 18:7)] to mean that Scripture speaks of the wife of the father [who is not the son's mother].

[K]   ". . . the nakedness of your mother . . ."—this refers to his mother who *is* the wife of the father.

[L]   How do we know that it is prohibited to have relationships with his mother who is not the wife of his father?

[M]   "She is your mother, you shall not uncover her nakedness." [So differing from Ishmael, Aqiba holds that Scripture does not speak of not having sexual relations with the father, but rather of not having sexual relations with his wife.]

[N]   How does R. Ishmael interpret these same passages, [since he too must make sense of the reference to "she is your mother . . . ," for which Aqiba satisfactorily accounts]? [How does Ishmael prove that there is a prohibition of sexual relations with his mother, wife of his father, and his mother, not the wife of his father?]

[O]   He interprets the Scripture to speak of the situation prevailing after the father's death, [and he interprets the passage to mean that even after the father's death, the son may not marry the father's wife].

[P]   And does not R. Aqiba maintain the same view [in which case how does he demonstrate that one may not have sexual relations with the woman the father has raped]?

[Q]   [Indeed, that is the case:] ". . . the nakedness of your father . . . ," ". . . the nakedness of your mother . . ."

[R]   Now just as "your father" encompasses anyone who is your father, whether for the purposes of inflicting punishment or of giving a warning against the contemplated union, so reference to "your mother" encompasses all cases of "your mother," whether it is for purposes of punishment, or of giving a warning against the contemplated union. [Thus, anyone in the status of one's mother is covered in the same Scriptural statements, by analogy as specified.]

[S]   [As to **III**.Gff., Zeira's statement that Judah concurs with Ishmael in the interpretation of Lev. 18:7, indicating that one is liable on a distinct count for having sexual relations with one's father,] it is likely that only R. Judah interprets these verses [as stated], for he does not maintain that if it is his mother who is his father's wife, a verse must be available for exegetical purposes to prove that proposition [since in any case there is no guilt on that count, apart from her being a married woman].

[T]   For he requires the verses for the following exegesis: ". . . the nakedness of your father . . . ," ". . . the nakedness of your mother . . ."

[U]   Now just as your father encompasses anyone who is your father, whether for the purposes of inflicting punishment or of giving a warning against the contemplated union, so reference to "your mother" encompasses all cases of "your mother," whether it is for purposes of punishment or of giving a warning against the contemplated union. [That is, Judah does not require the verse to demonstrate that one is liable on the count of one's mother, in addition to being liable on the count of a married woman, since he does not deem one guilty on two counts, as the Mishnah has stated. But he does have to provide an exegetical basis for the stated positions, just as does Aqiba.]

[V]   Said R. Zeira, "That is to say that they derive a lesson from an argument by analogy, even when the verse utilized for the proposed analogy is available for that purpose in only one aspect, [because it serves some other exegetical purpose in some other aspect]. [The cited verse is required to prove that the Scripture speaks of marital relations, and not, as Ishmael maintains, relations between males. Nonetheless, as we see, the cited verse is further utilized for the proposed purpose.]"

[W]   Said to him R. Yudan, "Is that not self-evident to R. Aqiba? For R. Aqiba said, 'One may construct an argument by analogy, even though the verses used for that purpose are not free [at all] but are used for some other exegetical proof in addition.' "

[V.A]   R. Jeremiah raised the question: "He who has sexual relations with his mother—what is the law as to his being liable on her account on the count [in addition] of having relations with a married woman?"

[B]   Now look here: If someone else had sexual relations with her, he would be liable on the count of having relations with a married woman. In the case of her son, is it not an argument *a fortiori?*

[C]   R. Yosé objected, "No indeed! An outsider—lo, he is liable on her account on the count of having sexual relations with a married woman. But her son is not [specified in Mishnah as] liable on her account on the count of having sexual relations with a married woman [but with his father's wife]."

[D]   Indeed it has been taught: Also in the case of other relationships prohibited by reason of consanguinity the law is the same:

[E]   [If a woman is one's] mother-in-law and also a married woman, you hold him accountable on the count of her being his mother-in-law.

[F]   [If a woman is] his daughter-in-law and a married woman, you hold him accountable on the count of her being his daughter-in-law.

[G]   [If a woman is] his sister and a married woman, you hold him accountable on the count of her being his sister.

[H]   To allow the man to avoid liability on the more severe count and to hold him accountable on the less severe one is something you cannot do,

[I]   for it has been taught: **He who has sexual relations with his sister is liable on the count of her being his sister and on the count of her being his father's wife's daughter.**

[J]   R. Yosé b. R. Judah says, "He who has sexual relations with his sister is liable only on one count [her being his sister] alone,

[K]   "and so he who has sexual relations with his daughter-in-law" [T. San. 10:2].

[L]   R. Jeremiah, R. Abbahu in the name of R. Yohanan: The position of R. Yosé b. R. Judah accords with the theory of R. Judah his father [at M. 7:6B].

[M]   "Just as R. Judah holds one accountable on one count, so R. Yosé b. R. Judah holds one accountable on one count."

[N]   R. Jeremiah, R. Abbahu in the name of R. Yohanan rejected their earlier theory: "R. Yosé b. R. Judah does *not* accord with the theory of R. Judah his father."

[O]   [R. Yosé b. R. Judah may concur with the rabbis of the Mishnah pericope, for] there [in the Mishnah] one will be guilty of having sexual relations with his mother, even when she is not also the wife of his father, or one may be guilty of having sexual relations with the wife of his father, even though it is not also his mother. [So he may concur with the Mishnah's sages.]

[P]   "But here we find a case in which one is the daughter of the wife of his father, without her also being his sister, and he would be permitted to marry her. [So in the Mishnah each one is prohibited on a distinct count. In such cases Yosé may concur that one is liable on two distinct counts. But here we do not find a case in which the daughter of the wife of the father would be prohibited at all, if she is not his sister *in addition*. So here there is a single count of liability.]"

Once more the Talmud's interest is to locate the exegetical foundations of Mishnah, and this further leads to an interest in the exegetical methods by which conclusions are reached in general. Unit **I** is a straightforward repertoire of proofs for Mishnah's fundamental facts. Unit **II** raises a further, entirely relevant question of Mishnah exegesis. Unit **III** is the point at which the explication of exegetical methods comes to the fore. The reference to Ishmael's interpretation of relevant verses in unit **III**, moreover, provokes further interest in Aqiba's approach to these same, entirely pertinent verses. The comparison of Ishmael's and Aqiba's approaches is then spelled out in

detail. Unit **IV** ends with the issue of whether the verse used
for one exegesis—an argument by analogy—must be "free" for
that purpose, that is, may be used for that purpose and no
other. Aqiba does not maintain that view. He is given a less
mechanistic conception of the uses of Scripture. Unit **V** goes
over familiar ground once more, namely, the interpretation of
Judah's position in the Mishnah. What is interesting here is the
analysis of traditions about his son's opinions, and whether one
must concur with Judah if one takes up the positions assigned
to the son.

7:7 [In Leiden MS and *editio princeps:* 7:9]

[A]   *He who has sexual relations with a male [Lev. 20:13, 15–16],
or a beast, and the woman who brings an animal on top of
herself—*

[B]   *if the human being has committed a sin, what sin has the beast
committed?*

[C]   *But because a human being has offended through it, therefore
the Scripture has said that it is to be stoned.*

[D]   *Another matter: So that the beast should not amble through the
marketplace and people say, "This is the one on account of
which Mr. So-and-so got himself stoned."*

[I.A]   [25a] Whence do we derive a [Scriptural] warning against having sexual relations with a male?

[B]   "You shall not lie with a male as with a woman; it is an abomination" (Lev. 18:22).

[C]   How do we derive [from Scripture] that the penalty is
extirpation?

[D]   "For whoever shall do any of these abominations, the persons
that do them shall be cut off from among their people" (Lev.
18:29).

[E]   How do we derive a [court-administered] penalty [for such a
deed]?

[F]   "If a man lies with a male as with a woman, both of them have
committed an abomination; they shall be put to death, their
blood is upon them" (Lev. 20:13).

[G]   You derive the penalty that "their blood is upon them" from the statement that "their blood is upon them" [stated with regard to the one who turns to mediums and wizards]. [Just as stoning applies to the latter, so it applies to those under discussion here.]

[H]   Up to this point proof has been adduced for the one who effects the act of intercourse. How do we know that the one upon whom it is committed also is covered by the law?

[I]   "You shall not lie with a man as with a woman" (Lev. 18:22)—read "you shall not be lain with . . . ," [thus reading the verb in the passive].

[J]   Up to this point proof has been adduced in accord with the exegetical principles of R. Aqiba [who derives from the cited verse a warning against being the one upon whom sexual relations are practiced].

[K]   As to R. Ishmael [how does he derive the same lesson]?

[L]   "There shall be no cult prostitute of the sons of Israel" (Deut. 23:17).

[M]   How, in accord with R. Ishmael, do we derive from the Torah the penalty of extirpation applying to the one with whom sexual relations are practiced?

[N]   R. Jeremiah in the name of R. Abbahu: " 'Cult prostitute' is stated here [as indicated], and further on it says, "And there also were male cult prostitutes in the land. They did according to all the abominations of the nations which the Lord drove out before the people of Israel' (1 Kings 14:24). One then derives the rule governing cult prostitutes from cult prostitutes, and the rule for abominations from the rule [at Lev. 18:27] for abominations [thus invoking Lev. 18:29, as above]."

[O]   R. Hiyya bar Ada in the name of R. Haninah: "One derives the rule governing an abomination from that covering an abomination."

[P]   Said R. Yosé b. R. Bun, "The following Tannaitic tradition makes the same point:

[Q]   " 'If a man lies with a male as with a woman, both of them have committed an abomination; they shall be put to death, their blood is upon them' (Lev. 20:13).

[R]   "Both of them are subject to the death penalty through stoning, both of them are subject to a warning, both of them are
subject to the penalty of extirpation."

[S]   Whence in the Torah do we derive warning against having sexual relations with a beast?

[T]   "And you shall not lie with any beast and defile yourself with
it" (Lev. 18:23).

[U]   The penalty of extirpation—whence do we derive it?

[V]   "For whoever shall do any of these abominations, the persons
that do them shall be cut off from among their people" (Lev.
18:29).

[W]   A [court-administered] penalty—whence do we derive it?

[X]   "If a man lies with a beast, he shall be put to death; and you
shall kill the beast. [If a woman approaches any beast and lies
with it, you shall kill the woman and the beast; they shall be
put to death, their blood is upon them]" (Lev. 20:15–16).

[Y]   You derive the penalty that [their blood is upon them] from
the statement that "their blood is upon them" [as at G].

[Z]   Up to this point proof has been adduced in accord with the exegetical principles of R. Aqiba.

[AA]   As to R. Ishmael?

[BB]   R. Ishmael derives the rule from its appropriate source [at
Deut. 23:17, cited above], and R. Aqiba from its appropriate
source.

[CC]   As to the penalty of extirpation applying to the one with whom
the beast has sexual relations in the view of R. Ishmael, we
find no proof [for that proposition from the Torah].

[DD]   As to a [court-administered] penalty applying to the one who is
victim of an act of beastiality, in the opinion of R. Ishmael and
in that of R. Aqiba, there is no proof from Scripture. [For in
the earlier instance the construction is based on the recurrence
of the word "abomination," but that is not available here. An
effort now will be made to provide such a proof.]

[EE]   [Ishmael's proof is now given:] Now it is written, "[Whoever lies with a beast shall be put to death]. Whoever sacrifices to any god, save to the Lord only, shall be utterly destroyed" (Ex. 22:19–20).

[FF]   Just as this one [who sacrifices to any god] is put to death through stoning and is subject to extirpation, so this other one [mentioned in the immediately preceding verse about lying with a beast] is put to death through stoning and is subject to the penalty of extirpation. [This is the proof besought at DD.]

[GG]   What is the difference between these two [modes of exegesis, S–Z vs. AA, EE–FF]?

[HH]   The one who performs an act of sexual relations with a male and is subjected to an act of sexual relations by the male—

[II]   in the opinion of R. Ishmael, he is liable on two counts, and in the opinion of R. Aqiba, he is liable on only one count.

[JJ]   He who had sexual relations with a beast and who was the object of sexual relations from a beast, in the opinion of both R. Aqiba and R. Ishmael, is liable on two counts.

[KK]   He who has sexual relations with a male and with a beast is liable on two counts.

[LL]   He who is the object of sexual relations by a male and by a beast is liable on two counts.

[MM]   He who has sexual relations with two males at the same time— since they are liable on his account on two counts, so he is liable on two counts.

[NN]   If one is the object of sexual relations by two males at one time, since they are subject to liability on his account for two counts, so he is liable on two counts.

[II.A]   It was taught: In the case of sexual relations between males, the law has not treated the minor as equivalent to an adult [so if the one upon whom the act is committed is younger than three years and one day old, it is null]. In the case of a beast, the law has treated the minor as equivalent to the fully grown beast.

[B]   Said R. Eleazar, "One is not liable in the case of sexual relations between males unless the one upon whom the act is committed is three years and one day old or older" (PM).

[**III**.A]   [Reverting to the proof texts of unit **I**,] R. Bun bar Hiyya raised the question of R. Zeira, "Why did R. Ishmael and R. Aqiba make distinctions in regard to sexual relations with a male and with a beast, while in regard to all other forms of illicit sexual relations they made no such distinctions, [but derived the law from a single set of verses]? [So in the present instances we do not maintain that the one who has sexual relations and the one upon whom the sexual act is committed are subject to a single general rule, such as applies to all other cases of sexual misdeed.]"

[B]   He said to him, "[The reason is] that in regard to all other forms of illicit sexual relations there is a general and inclusive reference to '*anyone* near of kin' (Lev. 18:6) [which is taken to be a general and encompassing rule], while in the present cases there is no such reference to 'anyone.' [The reference, 'None of you shall approach anyone near of kin to him to uncover nakedness' does not cover the acts under discussion, and that is why distinct proofs are required for the items under discussion.]"

[C]   They objected: "Lo, there is the case of the menstruating woman, concerning whom, 'anyone near of kin' [of Lev. 18:6] does not apply, and have they provided distinct proofs for that matter as well? [Obviously not. The one who has sexual relations with a menstruating woman and the woman herself are subject to the same law, and there is no distinct proof for that adduced by either Ishmael or Aqiba.]"

[D]   R. Jeremiah in the name of R. Abbahu: "Since 'drawing near' is stated in both contexts ['You shall not draw near a woman to uncover her nakedness while she is in her menstrual uncleanness' (Lev. 18:19), and, 'None of you shall draw near anyone near of kin to him to uncover nakedness' (Lev. 18:6)], it is as if all of the rules pertaining here apply there, and all of the rules pertaining there apply here."

[E]   R. Hiyya bar Ada in the name of R. Hanina: " 'You shall not approach a woman to uncover her nakedness while she is in her menstrual uncleanness' (Lev. 18:19)—[which applies to the male]. [But how do we know that the female also is subject to the same warning?]"

[F]   Said R. Yosé b. R. Bun, "She is subject to the warning not to draw near, she is subject to the warning not to be made naked."

[IV.A] Whence do we derive from Scripture a warning that a woman should not have sexual relations with a beast?

[B]   "Neither shall any woman give herself to a beast to lie with it; it is perversion" (Lev. 18:23).

[C]   Whence do we derive from Scripture the punishment of extirpation?

[D]   "For whoever shall do any of these abominations, the persons that do them shall be cut off from among their people" (Lev. 18:29).

[E]   Whence do we derive a [court-administered] punishment?

[F]   "If a woman approaches any beast and lies with it, you shall kill the woman and the beast; they shall be put to death, their blood is upon them" (Lev. 20:16).

[G]   You derive the penalty of death from the penalty of death, the mode of execution through stoning from the mode of execution through stoning specified elsewhere, and "their blood is upon them" from "their blood is upon them" [as above, I.G].

[V.A]   [With reference to M. 7:7C–D,] R. Ba bar Mamel raised the question: "Take note. If a man had sexual relations with a beast in a spell of inadvertence, lo, the beast is stoned on the man's account, but the man is exempt from stoning, [and this indicates that the principal consideration in this matter is M. 7:7D's reasoning, namely, avoiding unnecessary embarrassment to the man]."

[B]   R. Simeon raised the question: "Take note. If a man ploughed with a beast on the Sabbath, lo, he is stoned to death on account of the beast, but the beast is exempt [in consequence of which the principal consideration in this matter is M. 7:7C's reasoning]."

[C]   [In fact, the principal consideration is disgrace to man, and] you have only the saying of R. Samuel bar R. Isaac: " 'With their silver and gold they made idols, for his destruction' (Hos. 8:4). It is not written, '. . . for their destruction,' but '. . . for his destruction.'

[D]   "This is exemplified in one's saying, 'May the bones of Mr. So-and-so be crushed, who has enticed his son to evil conduct.' [And this applies only in a case of deliberate misdeed. Here too we speak of deliberate misdeed, in which case the beast is stoned, and the matter of ploughing with the beast on the Sabbath is irrelevant, for there is no shame brought to man in that case by the deed of the beast.]"

Once again the Talmud's principal activity is to show the exegetical foundations for the Mishnah's statements. These are not general, but particular to Aqiba and Ishmael. The repeated pattern indicates what is to be expected. Perhaps the clearest and least-adorned version is at unit **IV**. Unit **I**, for its part, systematically goes through a number of the Mishnah's items, not even bothering to spell matters out when it is not necessary, as at **I.BB**. The exposition is thorough and leads to a sequence of important conclusions, **I.GGff**. Unit **II** appears interpolated with no good reason, a piece of information, but unrelated to what has gone before and what follows. Unit **III** then completes the discourse undertaken so fully at unit **I**. Unit **IV**, as we noticed, simply repeats a familiar procedure with fresh materials, and unit **V** takes up the exegesis of the remainder of the Mishnah's statements, thus a thorough and convincing exercise.

7:8 [In Leiden MS and *editio princeps*: 7:10]

[A]   *"He who blasphemes" [Lev. 24:11] is liable only when he will have fully pronounced the divine Name.*

[B]   *Said R. Joshua b. Qorha, "On every day of a trial they examine the witnesses with a substituted name [such as,] "May Yose smite Yose.'*

[C]   *"[Once] the trial is over, they would not put him to death [on the basis of evidence given] with the euphemism, but they put everyone out and ask the most important of the witnesses, saying to him, "Say, what exactly did you hear [in detail]?'*

[D]   *"And he says what he heard.*

[E]   *"And the judges stand on their feet and tear their clothing, and never sew it back up.*

[F]   *"And the second witness says, 'Also I [heard] what he heard.'*

[G]   *"And the third witness says, 'Also I [heard] what he heard.' "*

[I.A]   Whence in Scripture do we find a warning against blaspheming?

[B]   "You shall not revile God [nor curse a ruler of your people]" (Ex. 22:28).

[C]   Whence in Scripture do we find that the penalty is extirpation?

[D]   "Whoever curses his God shall bear his sin. [He who blasphemes the name of the Lord shall be put to death; all the congregation shall stone him; the sojourner as well as the native, when he blasphemes the Name, shall be put to death]" (Lev. 24:15–16).

[E]   Whence do we find a [court-administered] penalty?

[F]   "He who blasphemes the name of the Lord shall be put to death."

[G]   And how are these same propositions adduced in accord with the exegetical methods of R. Ishmael?

[H]   For R. Ishmael said, "The Scripture speaks of the judges [who are not to be cursed or blasphemed].

[I]   "If Scripture warns against cursing the judges, is it not an argument *a fortiori* that there should be a warning against cursing God with euphemisms.

[J]   "If for cursing God with euphemisms one suffers the penalty of extirpation, if one does so with the fully expressed Name of God, is it not an argument *a fortiori* [that the penalty should be extirpation]?"

[II.A]   There are Tannaim who teach that there is a warning and extirpation because of cursing God with euphemisms, and for cursing with the fully expressed Name of God one is subject to the death penalty.

[B]   And there are Tannaim who teach that, on account of cursing with euphemisms, one is subject to a warning, and for cursing with the fully expressed name of God, one is subject to the death penalty and extirpation.

[C]   He who said that on account of using euphemisms there is a warning and penalty of extirpation [adduces in evidence]: "You will not revile God," and further: "Whoever curses his God shall bear his sin," [meaning that he is subject] to extirpation.

[D]   And in regard to making use in a curse of the fully expressed Name, that one is subject to the death penalty: "He who blasphemes the name of God shall be put to death."

[E]   And he who teaches that on account of making use of euphemisms one is subject to a warning adduces in evidence: "You will not revile God." And as to not using the fully expressed divine name, one is liable for the death penalty and for extirpation: "Whoever curses his God shall bear his sin," and "He who blasphemes the name of God shall be put to death."

[III.A]   [Since Joshua b. Qorha says that they make use of a substituted name, M. 7:8B,] R. Jeremiah in the name of R. Samuel bar R. Isaac [said], "That is to say that they judge a case on the basis of doubt."

[B]   What would be a practical case?

[C]   If so-and-so killed someone, let him be put on trial before the witnesses against him come to court.

[D]   R. Yosé said to him, "Now do they seize someone in the marketplace and disgrace him?"

[E]   But thus it is: "So-and-so killed someone, and lo, there are witnesses against him that he killed someone. Let him then be arrested even before the witnesses against him come."

[IV.A]   [With reference to M. 7:8C, "Say what exactly did you hear in detail"]. Do they say to him, "Curse God"?

[B]   But: "That name which I said in your presence, that is the one which he cursed, and with that one did he curse."

[C]   And the witnesses do not have to tear their garments, for they already did so at the moment at which they heard the man express the curse in the first place.

[V.A]   [With reference to M. 7:8E, the judges stand on their feet,] R. Simeon b. Laqish said, "On the basis of this rule, we learn that judges who have accepted testimony stand, for their decision now is final."

[B]   You derive from the Mishnah pericope six rules:

[C]   You derive from it that rule which R. Samuel bar R. Isaac stated [**III**.A].

[D]   And you derive from it that rule which R. Simeon b. Laqish has stated [**V**.A].

[E]   And you derive from it: He who hears from one who hears [a profanation of God's name] is liable to tear his garments.

[F]   And you derive from this pericope of Mishnah the rule that if a witness gave his testimony, the second, corroborating witness, may say, "Also I testify as does he," and the third says, "Also I testify as does he."

[G]   And you derive from this pericope of the Mishnah the rule that this is one of the tears which they do not sew up.

[H]   And you derive from the Mishnah pericope the rule that since they knew in the first place that it would be the fully expressed divine name, one has to tear his garments [when he hears it expressed].

[I]   R. Hiyya said, "R. Yasa raised the question [regarding E]: 'We have learned: *And a herald goes before him, crying out, "Mr. So-and-so, son of Mr. So-and-so, is going out to be stoned, because he committed such-and-such a transgression, and Mr. So-and-so and Mr. So-and-so are the witnesses against him. He who knows grounds for acquittal—let him come and testify in his behalf!"* '" [M. San. 6:2C]. [So will everyone in town make a tear?!]

[J]   We have heard that one who hears from the one who hears also has to tear his garment [but not third-hand].

[K]   We have heard, He who hears from the one who hears, and the one who hears from the one who hears, also has to tear his garment [but not fourth hand].

[**VI**.A]   What is the law as to tearing one's garment because he has heard the name of God cursed by a Gentile?

[B]   Let us derive the law from the following:

[C]   "When King Hezekiah heard the words of Rabshakeh, he tore his clothes and covered himself with sackcloth" (2 Kings 19:1).

[D]   What is the law as to tearing one's clothes on hearing the curse of an [25b] idolater [of the name of God]?

[E]   He who says that Rabshakeh was an idolater holds that they do tear their clothes at the blasphemy of an idolater.

[F]   One who said that he was an Israelite holds that they do not tear their clothes when an idolater curses God.

[G]   R. Hoshaiah taught: "All the same is the law for one who hears the cursing of the divine name on the part of an Israelite and one who hears the cursing of the divine name on the part of an idolater: one is liable to tear one's clothes."

[H]   What is the Scriptural basis for that statement?

[I]   "The word of the Lord came to Jeremiah: 'Behold, I am the Lord, the God of all flesh; is anything too hard for me?' " (Jer. 32:27).

[VII.A]   What is the law as to tearing one's garments in this time?

[B]   R. Yosé, R. Jeremiah in the name of R. Hiyya bar Ba, R. Hezekiah, R. Jeremiah in the name of R. Yohanan: "Once blasphemers became many, they have ceased from tearing their garments upon hearing blasphemy."

[C]   What is the law as to tearing one's garments at this time upon hearing God cursed through euphemisms?

[D]   Let us derive the answer to that question from the following:

[E]   R. Simeon b. Laqish was riding along on the road. A Samaritan crossed his path, and was cursing, and [Simeon] tore his clothes, and again the Samaritan cursed, and again [Simeon] tore his clothes.

[F]   Simeon got off his ass and gave the Samaritan a punch in the chest.

[G]   He said to him, "Son of Samaria—does your mother have enough new clothes to give me [for your causing me to tear mine]?"

[H]   From this story it is clear that they do tear their clothing when they hear God cursed through euphemisms, and they also do tear their clothing at this time [after the destruction of the Temple].

First, units I and II go over familiar ground, the former following a recurrent pattern. Second, units III, IV, and V then take up the exegesis of other statements of the Mishnah, fully working out the implications of the law of Mishnah and augmenting it. Third, unit **VI** then asks a relevant, but secondary, question and unit **VII** yet another. So, in all, the Talmud to this pericope systematically and thoroughly explains and augments the Mishnah.

7:9 [In Leiden MS and *editio princeps:* 7:11]

[A]   *"He who performs an act of worship for an idol"—*

[B]   *all the same is the one who performs an act of service, who actually sacrifices, who offers up incense, who pours out a libation offering, who bows down,*

[C]   *and the one who accepts it upon himself as a god, saying to it, "You are my god."*

[D]   *But the one who hugs it, kisses it, sweeps before it, sprinkles before it, and washes it,*

[E]   *anoints it, puts clothing on it, and puts shoes on it, [merely] transgresses a negative commandment [Ex. 20:5].*

[F]   *He who takes a vow in its name and he who carries out a vow made in its name transgress a negative commandment [Ex 23:13].*

[G]   *He who uncovers himself to Baal Peor—[he is stoned, for] this is how one performs an act of service to it.*

[H]   *He who tosses a pebble at Merkolis [Hermes] [is stoned, for] this is how one performs an act of service to it.*

[I.A]   Whence in Scripture do we find a warning against worshipping idols?

[B]   "You shall not make for yourself a graven image . . . ; you shall not bow down to them or serve them" (Ex. 20:4–5).

[C]   Whence do we derive that the penalty is extirpation?

[D]   "But the person who does anything with a high hand . . . reviles the Lord, and that person shall be cut off . . ." (Num. 15:30).

[E]   Now does the cited verses of Scripture not refer to one who blasphemes, [and not to an idolater]?

[F]   [Blasphemers and idolaters are equivalent to one another,] like a man who says to his fellow, "You have scraped out the whole plate and left nothing on it," [likewise the idolater completes what the blasphemer starts].

[G]   There is a parable [illustrating this same point]. R. Simeon b. Eleazar says, "It is comparable to two people sitting with a plate of beans between them. One of them stuck out his hand and scraped off the whole plate and left nothing on it. So are the blasphemer and the idolater: he leaves not a single religious duty after him."

[H]   Whence do we derive a [court-administered] punishment?

[I]   "If there is found . . . a man or woman . . . who has gone and served other gods . . . , then you shall bring forth to your gates that man or woman who has done this evil thing, and you shall stone that man or woman to death with stones" (Deut. 17:2–5).

[J]   ". . . you shall not serve them . . ." (Ex. 20:4)—[since the commandment refers to *them*,] I might have supposed that one is liable only once he has served all of the idols in the world.

[K]   On this account, Scripture states, "You shall not bow down to them" (Ex. 20:5).

[L]   "Bow[ing] down" was part of the general prohibition, and why was it explicitly specified? It was to draw an analogy to it, as follows:

[M]   Just as bowing down is distinctive in that it is done as a single action [before an idol at a time], and people are liable on its account for that action alone, so I encompass every individual deed, on which account people are liable for a single action alone.

[N]   Even though R. Simeon b. Eleazar has said, "[If] one sacrificed, offered incense, and poured out a libation offering, in a single spell of inadvertence, he is liable on only one count," he concedes that if one has worshipped an idol in the correct way in which it is worshipped, in the way in which the Most High is worshipped, for example, through an act of worshipful prostration, he is liable on each count. [This is because Scripture specifies worship and prostration as distinct, forbidden acts, so each is culpable by itself.]

[**II**.A]   [With reference to M. 7:9G, H, liability for a normal act of service,] when R. Samuel said in the name of R. Zeira, " 'So they
shall no more slay their sacrifices for satyrs, after whom they
play the harlot' (Lev. 17:7). '[This indicates that one is liable
even for an act of worship of an idol which is not normal,]' he
said to him, 'You have come to a verse applicable to Holy
Things [and not applicable to the purpose for which you have
cited it]. [So proof for Mishnah's view is not in that verse.]' "

[B]   R. Yasa in the name of R. Yohanan: "[If] one has sacrificed to
an idol a blemished lamb, he is liable."

[C]   On what basis [does he rule as he does]?

[D]   It is in accord with that which R. Hela said: "['You shall hew
down the graven images of their gods and destroy their name
out of that place.'] You shall not do so to the Lord your God"
(Deut. 12:3–4). Whatever you may not do for the Lord your
God [and you may not slaughter a blemished beast to the Lord,
so that would constitute an act of service to an idol].

[E]   [Delete through F:] R. Bun bar Hiyya raised the question before R. Zeira: " 'You shall not serve them . . .' (Ex. 20:5) is a
general rule. 'You shall not bow down to them . . .' (Ex. 20:5)
is a particular example of the general rule. 'You shall not bow
down to any other god' (Ex. 34:14)—Scripture has gone and
stated yet a further general rule.

[F]   "Thus we have a general rule, a particular example of the general rule, and yet a further general rule. Nothing is encompassed by the general rule except for what is specified by the
particular example of the general rule. [In consequence only
bowing down to an idol is punishable.]" [This passage is cor-
rupt (cf. PM).]

[G]   R. Bun bar Kahana raised the following question before R.
Hela: " 'You shall not serve them' (Ex. 20:5) is a general rule.
'Whoever sacrifices to any god, [save to the Lord only,] shall
be utterly destroyed' (Ex. 22:20) is a specific example of what
is covered by the general rule. 'Save to the Lord only'—Scripture has gone and stated a further general rule, [meaning one
may not worship an idol in any manner whatsoever].

[H]   "Thus we have a general rule, a particular example of the general rule, and yet a further, general rule.

[I]   "All sorts of actions were covered by the general rule. Thus Scripture has gone and encompassed [under the general prohibition even one who merely] hugs and kisses [an idol] [M. San. 7:9D]."

[J]   He said to him, "In what regard was bowing down specified? Is it not to indicate as to itself that it is a concrete deed? [In fact] hugging and bowing down are not concrete deeds [and bowing down is made explicit to indicate that it is prohibited, even though it is not a concrete deed]. [But other merely symbolic actions are not culpable, contrary to the view of G–I.]" [This pericope is carried forward at unit IV.]

[III.A]   How do we know from Scripture that he who says to it, "You are my god," [is culpable]?

[B]   R. Abun in the name of rabbis from over there [in Babylonia]: "They have made for themselves a molten calf and have worshipped it and sacrificed to it and said, 'These are your gods, O Israel, who brought you up out of the land of Egypt' " (Ex. 32:8).

[C]   If that verse is cited as evidence, then one should not be liable unless he *also* worships and sacrifices to the idol and offers up incense to it, as well as making the prohibited statement.

[D]   Said R. Yosé, "[In mentioning these other actions, apart from the statement, 'These are your gods . . . ,'] the intent of Scripture was merely to record the whole of Israel's degradation before the calf."

[E]   "And they have bowed down to it"—not to the Most High.

[F]   "And they have sacrificed to it"—not to the Most High.

[G]   "And they have said to it . . . ,"—not to the Most High.

[H]   In the end, what is [the evidence that this verse of Scripture indicates that merely saying, "You are my god" is culpable without a confirming deed]?

[I]   Here an act of speech is mentioned, and an act of speech is mentioned in the case of the one who merely incites the people to idolatry.

[J]   Just as an act of speech stated with reference to one who incites the people to idolatry is treated as a concrete deed [and so culpable], so an act of speech noted here likewise is treated as a concrete deed [and culpable].

[**IV**.A]   It is written, "If there is found . . . a man or woman who does what is evil in the sight of the Lord . . . and has gone and served other gods and worshipped them, *and* the sun or the moon or any of the host of heaven which I have forbidden . . ." (Deut. 17:2–3).

[B]   Said R. Zeira, " '. . . the sun . . . ,' is not written here, but rather, '. . . *and* the sun . . .' What we have therefore is not a generalization followed by a particularization, but rather a sequence of encompassing clauses. [So the meaning is not that we have a general rule limited by the example following, hence, as suggested at unit **II**.E–F, above, including bowing down but excluding other actions. What we have is an encompassing clause, meaning that all modes of worship are subject to a prohibition. That is, whether or not one does an act of worship appropriate to a given idol, he will be liable.]"

[C]   R. Aba bar Zimna objected before R. Zeira: "And lo, it is written, 'These you may eat of all that are in the waters. Everything in the waters that has fins and scales, . . . you may eat. And anything in the seas or rivers that has not fins and scales . . . is an abomination to you' (Lev. 11:9–10). In this context, too, shall we say that we have *not* a generalization followed by an exemplification in the particular of what is general, but rather an encompassing clause [as above]? [The meaning, if we lay emphasis on the presence of the word, *and*, would be to encompass.]"

[D]   "But because *and* is written [at Deut. 17:3ff., I encompass diverse acts of worship, whether appropriate or otherwise, as culpable]. [But in the argument that we have, an encompassing clause is not operable and invalid.]"

[E]   Said R. Yohanan b. Maria, "Then in any place in which I find an *and*, am I to wipe it out?"

[F]   Said R. Samuel bar Abudema, "I might have said, 'What is in the oceans [and does not have fins and scales] indeed is forbidden, but what is in ponds and barrels [lacking fins and scales will be permitted.' Scripture accordingly says, 'And everything which is in water . . . ,' [without regard to the sort of water,] which serves to encompass [any kind of water]. [The meaning then is that any kind of fish, wherever it flourishes, must have fins and scales to be edible by Israelites.]"

[V.A] R. Samuel bar Nahmani in the name of R. Hoshaiah: "[The culpability of] one who says to an idol, 'You are my god,' is subject to a dispute between Rabbi and sages. [That is, whether or not such a person is obligated to bring an offering has yet to be worked out.]"

[B] If one has bowed down to it, what is the law?

[C] R. Yohanan said, "All concur in the case of one who bows down by bending over, that he is liable. [In this case we have a concrete deed.]"

[D] [If so, then why is saying something also not a deed, for what is the difference between raising and lowering one's body and raising and lowering one's lips? [Is this too not a deed?]

[E] R. Yohanan said, "It is subject to a dispute [whether there is such an analogy to be drawn as is stated at D]."

[F] R. Simeon b. Laqish said, "It is subject to a dispute [whether bowing down itself is a deed and culpable]."

[G] Said R. Zeira, "The following verse of Scripture supports the view of R. Simeon b. Laqish: 'You shall have one law for him who does anything unwittingly, for him who is native among the people of Israel, and for a stranger who sojourns among them' (Num. 19:29). [This indicates that we require a concrete deed, and bowing down does not constitute a concrete deed.]

[H] "I thus know only that something which is a concrete deed is culpable. Hugging and bowing down, which are not concrete deeds—whence shall we derive proof that they are liable?" [cf. **II.J**].

What captures the Talmud's attention are two problems: first, culpability for what is not a normal act of service (for, logically, one in general would not be culpable for what does not represent a prohibited action); and, second, culpability for what is not a concrete deed at all but rather a mere statement. In both of these cases the usual theory of the law, which takes seriously what is normal but not what is abnormal, and which, further, deals with deeds but not with mere words, is set aside.

The reason, of course, is the unusual seriousness of an act of idolatry. At the outset we have the predictable exercise of finding Scriptural foundations for the Mishnah's rules, at unit **I**. The unfolding of unit **I** poses no problems. Unit **II**, by contrast, awaits lower criticism of some sort, since **II**.E–F do not belong, and, further, **II**.G–J, on the contrasting modes of exegesis (general, particular, general, as against encompassing clauses), continues at unit **IV**. Exactly how the materials should be reconstructed is not easy to say. PM struggles to explain each item in its present location, solving all problems in sequence. Perhaps matters are less clear than he suggests, but I cannot make progress in the present context, apart from joining **II**.E–F to **IV**. A–B. Unit **III**, for its part, is smooth and elegant, proving in a persuasive way precisely what it sets out to prove. Unit **IV** continues the difficulties of unit **II**, as I said. **V**.A–G likewise flow fairly fluently, but I cannot account for the addition of **V**.H.

7:10 [In Leiden MS and *editio princeps:* 7:13]

[A]   *"He who gives of his seed to Molech" [Lev. 20:2] is liable only when he will both have given him to Molech and have passed him through fire.*

[B]   *[If] he gave him to Molech but did not pass him through fire,*

[C]   *passed him through fire but did not give him to Molech,*

[D]   *he is not liable—*

[E]   *until he will both have given him to Molech and have passed him through fire.*

[F]   *"He who has a medium" [Lev. 20:27]—this is one who has a Python and causes the dead to speak from his armpits;*

[G]   *"and he who is a soothsayer"—this is one whose [spirit] speaks through his mouth—*

[H]   *lo, these are put to death by stoning.*

[I]   *And the one who makes inquiry of them is subject to a warning [Lev. 19:31; Deut. 18:10–11].*

[I.A]   Whence in Scripture do we find a warning against giving one of one's children to Molech?'

[B]   "You shall not give any of your children to devote them by fire to Molech, and so profane the name of your God" (Lev. 18:21).

[C]   Whence in Scripture do we find that extirpation applies?

[D]   "[I myself will set my face against that man, and] will cut him off from among his people, because he has given one of his children to Molech" (Lev. 20:3).

[E]   [Whence in Scripture do we find that] the [court-administered] punishment [is through stoning]?

[F]   "Any man of the people of Israel, or of the strangers that so-journ in Israel, who gives any of his children to Molech shall be put to death; the people of the land shall stone him with stones" (Lev. 20:2).

[II.A]   "And any of your children you shall not give . . ."—

[B]   Is it possible to suppose that *if one gave him to Molech but did not pass him through fire* [M. San. 7:10B], should he be liable?

[C]   Scripture says, ". . . give . . . to pass them through fire . . ." [thus specifying both stages].

[D]   Is it possible to suppose that if one gave them and passed them by fire not to Molech [but to some other god], he should be liable?

[E]   Scripture says, "And any of your children you shall not give to devote them by fire to Molech" [in particular].

[F]   Is it possible to suppose that if one gave them and passed them to Molech, but not by fire, he should be liable?

[G]   Scripture states, "There shall not be found among you anyone who makes his son or his daughter pass through the fire" (Deut. 18:10).

[H]   "Passing through" stated in both [Lev. 20:3 and Deut. 18:10] serves to establish an analogy between the two passages.

[I]   Just as "passing through" stated below refers specifically to doing so through fire, so passing through stated here refers specifically to one who does so through fire.

[J]   You turn out therefore to state the rule as follows: One is liable only if he gives his son over and passes him through fire to Molech.

[**III**.A] R. Nissah in the name of R. Eleazar: "Under no circumstances is one liable unless he hands him over to priests, and they take him and pass him through."

[B] If he passed him through in his normal way of walking [by foot], what is the law? [Is this the usual way with Molech?]

[C] It was taught [that one drew him through, as follows:]

[D] One would draw him along and so pass him through.

[E] **And he is liable only when he will have passed him through fire in the usual way.**

[F] **[If] he passed him through fire by foot, he is exempt.**

[G] **[And he is liable, moreover, only on account of those who are his natural children [T. San. 10:4]. He who passes his father, mother, or sister through fire [for Molech] is exempt. He who passes himself through is exempt.**

[H] **R. Eleazar b. R. Simeon declares him liable.**

[I] **All the same in doing so for Molech and for any other idol: one is liable.**

[J] **And R. Eleazar b. R. Simeon says, "He is liable only on account of Molech alone" [T. San. 10:5].**

[K] Said R. Yohanan, "The Scriptural basis for the ruling of R. Eleazar b. R. Simeon is from the following verse: 'There shall not be found among you (BK) . . . ,' (Deut. 18:10)—in regard to your body, there should not be found any who passes to Molech [thus one is liable for himself]."

[L] "And I will cut him off from among his people" (Lev. 20:3)— [this statement serves] to encompass other forms of idolatry, [which also are subject to the penalty] of extirpation.

[M] And how do we find in Scripture the appropriate penalty?

[N] "He who gives any of his children to Molech shall be put to death" (Lev. 20:2).

[O] And this law applies in the case of one who himself passed the child through the fire, not with his foot. He transgresses because he has passed him through, he is liable [as above, **III**.B, C].

[P]   Truly, if he dragged him through [25c] and so passed him through, he is liable [as above].

[Q]   What is the meaning of that which R. Eleazar b. R. Simeon said, "If he passed him through with his foot, he is exempt"? [Compare **III.F.**]

[R]   That is a case in which he passed him through by jumping from one side of the fire to the other.

[**IV**.A]   R. Bun bar Hiyya raised the following question before R. Zeira: "If one handed over the son but did not cause him to pass through [but an agent did so], we have a parallel in the dispute between Hezekiah and R. Yohanan, for they differ as follows:

[B]   "If one slaughtered the beast but did not sell it [in the case of a thief who stole a beast, in line with Ex. 21:37 = Ex. 22:1],

[C]   "R. Hezekiah said, 'He is liable.'

[D]   "R. Yohanan said, 'He is exempt.' [That is, do we not have a parallel? In the cited case, one stole the beast but handed it over to an agent to slaughter it. Hezekiah holds the thief liable for the actions of the agent, and Yohanan maintains that he is exempt. Likewise, if one handed over the son to a third party to pass him through fire, if one holds that in the case of slaughter by another, one is liable, so here too he would be liable, and so with the contrary position.]"

[**V**.A]   R. Ba, R. Hiyya in the name of R. Yohanan: "Note the language the Torah has taught you.

[B]   " 'Molech' refers to anyone whom you treat as a king over you, even a chip of wood or a pebble."

[C]   "And I shall cut off that man from the midst of his people" serves to encompass every form of idolatry under the penalty of extirpation. [Passing one's children in fire is an act of idolatry, even not before Molech.]

[D]   R. Nisa in the name of R. Eleazar, "It serves to encompass other forms of idolatry, so far as devoting one's sons and daughters is concerned.

[E]   "For thus has it been taught:

[F]   "All the same are Molech and all other idols; whether one has served an idol with his sons and daughters or whether one has served the idol through his fathers and mothers, he is liable."

[G]   Said R. Zeira, "That is so when it is not normally worshipped in such a way.

[H]   "But if that is the normal mode of worship of such an idol, one is exempt [if he passes his mother or his father through the fire, since liability on that count is imposed only if one passes his son or his daughter, as the Torah itself has made explicit]."

[I]   Said R. Hela, "Even if the normal mode of service is in that way, one will be liable—[indeed,] on two counts [for Molech's manner of service and for its own as well]."

[J]   The following Tannaitic teaching supports the position of R. Hela:

[K]   [Said R. Simeon], "Molech was subsumed in the general rule against worshipping idols, and why was it treated as an exceptional case?

[L]   "To impose a more lenient qualification in that regard, that one should be liable only on account of handing over and passing through his own children [but not if he passes his parents through the fire, for example]."

[M]   [As to R. Eleazar b. R. Simeon's statement that one is liable only for the service of Molech alone, in the stated context,] said R. Tanhum bar Jeremiah, "The statement of R. Eleazar b. R. Simeon accords with the theory of R. Simeon his father.

[N]   "For thus did R. Simeon state, 'Molech was subsumed in the general rule against worshipping idols, and why was it treated as an exceptional case? To impose a more lenient qualification in that regard, that one should be liable only on account of handing over and passing through his own children [but not if he passes his parents through the fire, for example].'

[O]   "So did R. Eleazar b. R. Simeon state, 'It was subsumed in the general rule against worshipping idols, and why was it treated as an exceptional case? To impose a more lenient qualification in that regard, that one should be liable only on account of handing over and passing through his own children [as above].' " [Cf. III.I–J.]

[VI.A] Said R. Tanhum bar Yudan, "Even though R. Eleazar b. R. Simeon said, 'If one sacrificed, offered incense, and made a libation offering, in a single spell of inadvertence, he is liable on only one count,' still he concurs that, if one has worshipped an idol in the correct way in which it is worshipped, in the way in which the Most High is worshipped, for example, through an act of worshipful prostration, he is liable on each count."

[B] How do we know that if one has worshipped an idol in the correct way in which it is worshipped, in the way in which the Most High is worshipped, and also through an act of worshipful prostration, that he is liable on each count?

[C] R. Samuel in the name of R. Zeira, " 'So they shall no more slay sacrifices for satyrs, after whom they play the harlot' " (Lev. 17:7).

[D] He said to him, "You have come to a verse applicable to Holy Things."

[E] R. Yasa in the name of R. Yohanan said, "If one has sacrificed to an idol a blemished lamb, he is liable."

[F] On what basis does he rule as he does?

[G] It is in accord with that which R. Hela said, "['You shall hew down the graven images of their gods, and destroy their name out of that place.] You shall not do so to the Lord your God' (Deut. 12:3–4). Whatever you may not do for the Lord your God, and since you may not slaughter a blemished beast to the Lord, that would then constitute an act of service to an idol."

[VII.A] Said R. Pinhas in the presence of R. Yosé in the name of R. Hisda, "If its correct mode of service was through sons and daughters, and one worshipped it through [passing through] fathers and mothers, he is liable on two counts."

[B] And R. Zeira was happy to hear this statement.

[C] He considered saying that in accord with the theory of R. Hela his master was this statement made [= V.I], and according to the view of R. Eleazar b. R. Simeon was this statement made [= V.D–F].

[D] [Pinhas] said to him, "And what do you have in your hand [to please you]? And this statement was made according to the view of the rabbis. [Hisda's saying is in the context of the rabbis' view that one is liable even in regard to doing so for other idols than Molech. One is liable on two counts: one because one serves it by passing through fire, and the other because we encompass other idols than Molech. Eleazar b. R. Simeon holds there is no liability at all.]"

[E]   He said to him, "For this purpose was it required at all? [That is self-evident that rabbis hold the view you have attributed to them. If what you said pertains to rabbis' view, it is no contribution.]"

[VIII.A]   Whence in Scripture do we derive a warning against a medium?

[B]   "Do not turn to mediums or wizards; do not seek them out, to be defiled by them" (Lev. 19:31).

[C]   Whence in Scripture do we derive that the penalty is extirpation?

[D]   "If a person turns to mediums and wizards, playing the harlot after them, I will set my face against that person, and will cut him off from among his people" (Lev. 20:6).

[E]   Whence in Scripture do we derive the mode of punishment?

[F]   "And a man or a woman who is a medium or a wizard shall be put to death; they shall be stoned with stones, their blood shall be upon them" (Lev. 20:27).

[G]   Then why do we not learn, "one who is a soothsayer" [in the list of those subject to extirpation at M. Ker. 1:1]?

[H]   R. Hezekiah in the name of R. Simeon, "It is because all of them are covered under the generalization of a single negative commandment: 'Do not turn to mediums or wizards.' "

[I]   R. Yasa in the name of R. Simeon b. Laqish: "It is because it is subject to a negative commandment which is derived from an affirmatively stated religious requirement. [For 'do not turn' addresses mediums, so wizard (= soothsayer) is not subject to a negative formulation.]"

[J]   Said R. Zeira before R. Yasa, "Thus not a single authority comes to teach the medium among those to be listed in tractate Keritot except for you? [That is, this reason at I is worthless. "Do not turn" addresses soothsaying too.]"

[K]   He said to him, "Just as the Scripture treats the matter, so the Mishnah treats the matter, [that is, in both cases, they are deemed alternatives]. [One cannot be guilty of both.]"

[IX.A]   *He who has a medium—this is one who has a Python which speaks from his armpits; and he who is a soothsayer—this is one whose spirit speaks through his mouth—lo, these are put to death by stoning, and the one who makes inquiry of them is subject to a warning [M. San. 7:10G–I].*

[B]   ". . . or a necromancer . . ." (Deut. 18:11)—

[C]   There is a Tanna who teaches "This is one who asks questions of a skull."

[D]   There is a Tanna who teaches "This is one who asks questions of the penis [of a corpse] [raising the corpse thereby]."

[E]   What is the difference between one who asks questions of the skull and one who raises the dead by the penis? [Cf. T. San. 10:7.] For in the case of one who asks questions of the skull, [the deceased] goes up in the normal way, he goes up on the Sabbath, and an ordinary person brings up a king [to ask questions of him].

[F]   But the one who brings up the deceased through the penis does not bring him up in his normal way, does not bring him up on the Sabbath, and an ordinary person does not call up a king.

[G]   Said R. Huna, "Scripture supports the position of the one who says that a medium is one who brings up the deceased through his penis.

[H]   "What is the Scriptural basis?

[I]   "And he said, 'Divine for me by a spirit, and bring up for me whomever I shall name to you' " (1 Sam. 28:8).

[J]   What do you derive from this verse?

[K]   Said R. Mana, "On this basis, we may prove that the woman knew a great many things."

[L]   What is the proof [of G–I]?

[M]   "Your voice shall come from the ground like the voice of a ghost, and your speech shall whisper out of the dust" (Is. 29:4).

[**X**.A]   The opinion of rabbis supports the view of R. Yasa, for R. Yasa said in the name of rabbis: "It is because they offer incense to shades."

[B]   R. Hela in the name of R. Yasa, "It is because all of them are subsumed in a single deed [that the two are not numbered separately at M. Ker. 1:1 (cf. **VIII**.G–K)]."

Unit **I** goes through a familiar procedure. Unit **II** then takes up the analysis of the relevant verses within a different rhetorical pattern. Unit **III** takes up the analysis of Eleazar b. R. Simeon's position, expressed both in Tosefta and otherwise cited. There are some textual problems toward the end of the unit; PM provides a sequence of alternative explanations, which indicates that all is not smooth. Unit **IV** proceeds in its own direction. The comparison between the two cases is clear as spelled out. Unit **V** reverts to the familiar problem of whether or not an act of service not usual for a given idol is deemed culpable. This is the position of Nisa in Eleazar's name, **V**.D–F. Zeira maintains that Scripture specifies the culpable act of worship for Molech; it involves sons and daughters, but not parents. In that instance, therefore, there is an exception to the general rule stated by Nisa. The introduction of Simeon's saying in support of Hela's position, **V**.J–L, once more raises the question of a Tanna's opinions in relationship to those of his father—now Eleazar and his father Simeon. Unit **VI** goes over the ground of M. 7:9, **I**.N, **II**.A–D. I see no better place for the passage here than there, and its appearance here also does not help solve the problem of **II**.E–F and its strange location. Pinhas's statement, **VII**.A, returns us then to the issues of **V**.G–I's dispute. The relevance to the foregoing is clear as explained. Unit **VIII** then moves on to the next items, M. 7:10F and G. The anticipated pattern is reviewed. At the end, **VIII**.Gff., we compare the formulation of our passage with its counterpart at M. Ker. 1:1. Unit **IX** cites and then augments the Mishnah, as indicated. Unit **X** then reverts to the discussion of unit **VIII**, interrupted by the interpolation of unit **IX**.

7:11 [In Leiden MS and *editio princeps:* 7:14]

[A]   *"He who profanes the Sabbath"*—in regard to a matter, on account of the deliberate doing of which they are liable to extirpation, and on account of the inadvertent doing of which they are liable to a sin offering.

[B]   *"He who curses his father and his mother" is liable only when he will have cursed them by the divine Name.*

[C]   *[If] he cursed them with a euphemism,*

[D]   *R. Meir declares him liable.*

[E]   *And sages declare him exempt.*

[F]   *"He who has sexual relations with a betrothed maiden" [Deut. 22:23–24] is liable only if she is a virgin maiden, betrothed, while she is yet in her father's house.*

[G]   *[If] two different men had sexual relations with her, the first one is put to death by stoning, and the second by strangulation.*

[I.A]   Whence do we derive a warning against profaning the Sabbath?

[B]   "You shall not do any work on it" (Ex. 20:10).

[C]   Whence do we derive that the penalty of extirpation applies?

[D]   "Whoever does any work on it—that soul shall be cut off from among his people" (Ex. 31:14).

[E]   Whence do we derive a [court-administered] punishment?

[F]   "Everyone who profanes it shall be put to death" (Ex. 31:14).

[G]   [Now, inclusive of violating the Sabbath,] there should be thirty-seven occasions for extirpation [and not thirty-six] taught in the Torah [at M. Ker. 1:1].

[H]   Said R. Yosé b. R. Bun, "The reason is that if one has performed all of the actions deliberately, knowing that it is the Sabbath."

[I]   [And is there a case of violations of the law] deliberately knowing that it was a form of labor which is prohibited? One is then liable on each count. [That is, there is only the possibility of a single liability.]

[II.A]   Whence do we find a warning against cursing one's father and mother?

[B]   "Every one of you shall revere his mother and his father" (Lev. 19:3).

[C]   Whence do we derive both the [court-administered] penalty and extirpation?

[D]   "Whoever curses his father or his mother shall be put to death" (Ex. 21:17), [so the death penalty].

[E]   And it says, "For whoever shall do any of these abominations, the persons that do them shall be cut off from among their people" (Lev. 18:29), [so extirpation].

[III.A]   *He who has sexual relations with a betrothed maiden—*

[B]   R. Yasa in the name of R. Yohanan, R. Hiyya in the name of R. Eleazar, [maintained, "In insisting that it is a maiden, the Mishnah expresses the opinion] of R. Meir.

[C]   "But so far as rabbis are concerned, even if she is a minor [less than three years and one day], one is liable."

[D]   What is the Scriptural basis of the position of R. Meir?

[E]   The word "maiden" is spelled without its full complement of letters [which is taken to mean that Scripture wishes to exclude a category of young girls, namely, those less than the specified age].

[F]   And how do rabbis interpret the same deficient spelling of the word for "maiden"?

[G]   R. Abbahu in the name of R. Simeon b. Laqish: "The word for 'maiden' is fully spelled out one time in the passage, and it imparts its meaning on the entire passage, meaning that the maiden spoken of therein must be of the requisite age."

[H]   Objected R. Meir to rabbis, "Lo, he who brings forth an evil name—lo, only 'maiden' in not fully spelled out form is written in that connection, and yet she is invariably deemed to be an adult!

[I]   "The reason is that [if this girl is found guilty, she is put to death by stoning], but a minor is not put to death by stoning."

[J]   How do rabbis deal with this passage?

[K]   Said R. Abin, "Interpret the passage [in which 'maiden' is not fully spelled out] to speak of a case in which the man had sexual relations through the anus." [That is, the husband who brings forth slander against the bride is liable, even if he had sexual relations in an unnatural manner.] [That is, the particular spelling introduces a distinct consideration into the law.]"

[IV.A]   R. Jacob bar Aba raised the question before Rab: "He who has sexual relations with a betrothed minor—what is the law?"

[B]   He said to him, "He is put to death through stoning [as he would if she were an adult virgin, just as rabbis hold at **III**.C]."

[C]   He who has sexual relations with a pubescent girl—what is the law [from rabbis' viewpoint]? [Is the penalty the same?]"

[D]   He said to him, "I read in the Bible: 'a maiden' and not a pubescent girl," [and the penalty is not stoning but strangulation]. [He replied,] "They read [Scripture also to mean] 'maiden' and not a minor [as rabbis hold]."

[E]   "And do you not agree with me that the man is subject to a fine: ['Then the man who lay with her shall give to the father of the young woman fifty shekels of silver, and she shall be his wife . . .' (Deut. 22:29)]?" [Rab points out that the rabbis' position is supported by the view that even if the man has sexual relations with a minor, he still is liable to the fine. This would then support the view of rabbis as against Meir.]

[F]   He said to him, " '. . . because he has violated her . . .' (Deut. 22:29)—this serves to encompass even a minor girl within the law of the fine.

[G]   "And read, '. . . because he has violated her . . .' to encompass a pubescent girl to be under the law of the fine."

[H]   Said Rab, "Even though R. Jacob bar Abba won over me in the discussion of the law, in fact the final decision is this: 'He who has sexual relations with a minor is put to death through stoning, but she is exempt from punishment.' "

[I]   R. Abin in the name of R. Samuel, "And why did he not interpret the matter along the lines of the following [to prove that he who has intercourse with a minor is stoned to death]?—

[J]   " '[But if in the open country a man meets a young woman who is betrothed, and the man seizes her and lies with her,] then only the man who lay with her shall die. [But to the young woman you shall do nothing; in the young woman there is no offense punishable by death, for this case is like that of a man attacking and murdering his neighbor; because he came upon her in the open country, and though the betrothed young woman cried for help there was no one to rescue her]' (Deut. 22:25–27).

[K]   "Now do we not know that 'in the young woman there is no offense punishable by death'?

[L]   "And why does Scripture tell us, 'But to the young woman you shall do nothing; in the young woman there is no offense punishable by death'?

[M]   "But on the basis of this needless statement, we conclude the following:

[N]   "He who has sexual relations with a minor is punished by stoning, and she is exempt from all punishment."

The Mishnah's three items are systematically expounded at units **I**, **II**, and **III–IV**. The pattern at units **I** and **II** require no comment. Unit **III**, drawing in its wake the secondary one at **IV**, introduces the dispute of Meir and sages on the status of a minor, a girl less than three years and a day old. Meir's position, including such a girl under the law, is spelled out. A secondary debate on the same matter, at unit **IV**, yields a solid proof for Meir's basic point at **IV.I–N**.

7:12 [In Leiden MS and *editio princeps:* 7:16]

[A]   *"He who beguiles others to idolatry—this [refers to] an ordinary fellow who beguiles some other ordinary fellow.*

[B]   *[If] he said to him, "There is a god in such a place, who eats thus, drinks thus, does good in one way, and harm in another"—*

[C]   *against all those who are liable to the death penalty in the Torah they do not hide witnesses [for the purposes of entrapment] except for this one.*

[D]   *[If] he spoke [in such a way] to two, and they serve as witnesses against him,*

[E]   *they bring him to court and stone him.*

[F]   *[If] he spoke [in such a way] to [only] one person, [the latter then] says to him, "I have some friends who will want the same thing."*

[G]   *If he was clever and not prepared to speak in [the friend's] presence,*

[H]   *they hide witnesses on the other side of a partition,*

[I]   *and he says to him, "Tell me what you were saying to me, now that we are by ourselves."*

[J]   *And the other party says to him [what he had said], and then this party says, "Now how are we going to abandon our God who is in Heaven and go and worship sticks and stones?"*

[K]   *If he repents, well and good.*

[L]   *But if he said, "This is what we are obligated to do, and this is what is good for us to do,"*

[M]   *those who stand on the other side of the partition bring him to court and stone him.*

[N]   *["He who beguiles others" is] he who says, "I am going to worship," "I shall go and worship," "Let's go and worship," "I shall make an offering," "I shall go and make an offering," "Let's go and make an offering," "I shall offer incense," "I shall go and offer incense," "Let's go and offer incense," "I shall make a libation," "I shall go and make a libation," "Let's go and make a libation," "I shall bow down," "I shall go and bow down," "Let's go and bow down."*

[O]   *"He who beguiles [and leads a whole town astray]" is one who says, "Let's go and perform an act of service to an idol."*

[I.A]   [When M. 7:12A refers to an ordinary fellow, does it mean to say,] "Lo, a sage is not [subject to the law]?"

[B]   [The meaning is this:] Since the person incites someone to idolatry, this is no sage.

[C]   Since one is incited to idolatry, this is no sage.

[II.A]   How do they get testimony against him?

[B]   **They conceal against him two witnesses [Tosefta: disciples of sages], [who are put] in an inside room, and he sits [25d] in an outside room.**

[C]   **And they light a candle near him, so that they can see him.**

[D]   **And they listen to what he says.**

[E]   **And so did they do to Ben Stada [Sutra] in Lydda.**

[F]   **They appointed against him two disciples of sages, and [in consequence of what they heard and saw], they stoned him [T. San. 10:11].**

[**III**.A]   [In the light of M. Yeb. 16:6: *They permit a woman to marry again on the evidence of an echo that her husband has died,*] do you say this [that it is necessary to light a lamp so that the witnesses should see him while they hear him]. [It should be sufficient merely to hear him.]

[B]   It is different in the present case [of M. Yeb. 16:6], because he has said, "I . . ." [That is, the man is heard to speak of himself, so it is not necessary to identify him further.]

[C]   And if he said, also here, "I"? [That is, let the inciter also identify himself.]

[D]   It is so that he will not practice deception [and flee].

[E]   And let him practice deception [and flee]?

[F]   It is so that he will not go and entice himself and entice others with him [so he must be caught].

[**IV**.A]   He who entices others speaks in elevated language, and he who beguiles [a whole town] speaks in earthy language.

[B]   If the one who entices spoke in earthy language, he falls into the category of one who beguiles [a whole town].

[C]   And if one who beguiles [a whole town] spoke in elevated language, he falls into the category of one who entices [an individual].

[D]   The one who entices speaks in the Holy Language, while the one who beguiles [a whole town] speaks in ordinary language.

[E]   If the one who entices spoke in ordinary language, he falls into the category of one who beguiles.

[F]   And if one who beguiles speaks in the Holy Language, he falls into the category of one who entices.

Unit **I** presents a minor clarification of Mishnah's law, and unit **II** restates the procedure outlined in Mishnah. Unit **III** compares the present law's procedure with the acceptability of the statement of an unseen witness in another context, namely, receiving evidence that a man has died so that his wife may remarry. A less stringent rule of evidence applies in that other context. Unit **IV**, finally, differentiates the two different sorts of dangerous leadership of which Mishnah speaks.

7:13 [In Leiden MS and *editio princeps:* 7:19]

[A]   *"The sorcerer"—he who does a deed is liable,*

[B]   *but not the one who merely creates an illusion.*

[C]   *R. Aqiba says in the name of R. Joshua, "Two may gather cucumbers. One gatherer may be exempt, and one gatherer may be liable.*

[D]   *"[Likewise:] He who does a deed is liable, but he who merely creates an illusion is exempt."*

[I.A]   "You shall not permit a sorceress to live" (Ex. 22:18).

[B]   All the same are a sorcerer and a sorceress [that is, both are to be put to death].

[C]   But [in referring to a sorceress] the Torah has taught you how things really are, for the vast majority who practice sorcery are women.

[II.A]   Said R. Eleazar, "A sorcerer is subject to the death penalty through stoning."

[B]   What is the Scriptural basis for the opinion of R. Eleazar?

[C]   Here it is written, "You shall not permit a sorceress to live" (Ex. 22:18), and further it is stated, "[Take heed that you do not go up into the mountain or touch the border of it; whoever touches the mountain shall be put to death; no hand shall touch him, but he shall be stoned or shot;] whether beast or man, he shall not live" (Ex. 19:12–13).

[D]   Just as the language, "He shall not live," stated in the latter passage means that the malefactor is put to death by stoning, so the language, ". . . shall not live," stated in the former passage means that the malefactor is put to death by stoning.

[E]   And what is the Scriptural basis for the view of rabbis [who call for decapitation]?

[F]   Here it is stated, "You shall not permit a sorceress to live" (Ex. 22:18), and further it is stated, "You shall save alive nothing that breathes" (Deut. 20:16).

[G]   Just as the language, "You shall save alive nothing that breathes" in the latter context means death by the sword, so the language, "You shall not permit . . . to live . . . ," in the former context means death by the sword.

[H]   Said R. Aqiba, "I shall then settle the matter. It is better to derive the appropriate lesson from the language, 'You shall not permit to live . . . ,' for another usage of that same language, but let not the variant formulation, '*He* shall not live . . . ,' [used at Ex. 19:13] prove the matter [since it does not apply, as does the usage which is precisely the same in both contexts]. [Hence rabbis are to be favored.]"

[I]   What is the Scriptural basis for the position of R. Judah?

[J]   Here it is stated, "You shall not permit a sorceress to live" (Ex. 22:18), and later on it is stated, "Whoever lies with a beast shall be put to death" (Ex. 22:19).

[K]   Just as the death penalty executed against the beast is through stoning, so here too stoning is the preferred mode of execution.

[III.A]   When R. Eleazar, R. Joshua, and R. Aqiba went in to bathe in the baths of Tiberias, a *min* saw them. He said what he said, and the arched chamber in the bath [where idolatrous statues were put up] held them fast, [so that they could not move].

[B]   Said R. Eleazar to R. Joshua, "Now Joshua b. Haninah, see what you can do."

[C]   When that *min* tried to leave, R. Joshua said what he said, and the doorway of the bath seized and held the *min* firm, so that whoever went in had to give him a knock [to push by], and whoever went out had to give him a knock [to push by].

[D]   He said to them, "Undo whatever you have done [to let me go]."

[E]   They said to him, "Release us, and we shall release you."

[F]   They released one another.

[G]   Once they got outside, said R. Joshua to that *min*, "Lo, is that all you know?" (PM).

[H]   He said, "Let's go down to the sea."

[I]   When they got down to the sea, that *min* said whatever it was that he said, and the sea split open.

[J]   He said to them, "Now is this not what Moses, your rabbi, did at the sea?"

[K]   They said to him, "Do you not concede to us that Moses, our rabbi, walked through it?"

[L]   He said to them, "Yes."

[M]   They said to him, "Then walk through it."

[N]   He walked through it.

[O]   R. Joshua instructed the ruler of the sea, who swallowed him up.

[IV.A]   When R. Eliezer, R. Joshua, and Rabban Gamaliel went up to Rome, they came to a certain place and found children making little piles [of dirt]. They said, "Children of the land of Israel make this sort of thing, and they say, 'This is heave offering,' and 'That is tithe.' It's likely that there are Jews here."

[B]   They came into one place and were received there.

[C]   When they sat down to eat, [they noticed] that each dish which they brought in to them would first be brought into a small room, and then would be brought to them, and they wondered whether they might be eating sacrifices offered to the dead. [That is, before the food was brought to them, it was brought into a small chamber, in which, they suspected, sacrifices were taken from each dish and offered to an idol.]

[D]   They said to [the host], "What is your purpose, in the fact that, as to every dish which you bring before us, if you do not bring it first into a small room, you do not bring it in to us?"

[E]   He said to them, "I have a very old father, and he has made a decree for himself that he will never go out of that small room until he will see the sages of Israel."

[F]   They said to him, "Go and tell him, 'Come out here to them, for they are here.' "

[G]   He came out to them.

[H]   They said to him, "Why do you do this?"

[I]   He said to them, "Pray for my son, for he has not produced a child."

[J]   Said R. Eliezer to R. Joshua, "Now, Joshua b. Hananiah, let us see what you will do."

[K]   He said to them, "Bring me flax seeds," and they brought him flax seeds.

[L]   He appeared to sow the seed on the table; he appeared to scatter the seed; he appeared to bring the seed up; he appeared to take hold of it, until he drew up a woman, holding on to her tresses.

[M]   He said to her, "Release whatever [magic] you have done [to this man]."

[N]   She said to him, "I am not going to release [my spell]."

[O]   He said to her, "If you don't do it, I shall publicize your [magical secrets]."

[P]   She said to him, "I cannot do it, for [the magical materials] have been cast into the sea."

[Q]   R. Joshua made a decree that the sea release [the magical materials] and they came up.

[R]   They prayed for [the host], and he had the merit of producing a son, R. Judah b. Bathera.

[S]   They said, "If we came up here only for the purpose of producing that righteous man, it would have been enough for us."

[T]   Said R. Joshua b. Hananiah, "I can take cucumbers and pumpkins and turn them into rams and hosts of rams, and they will produce still more."

[V.A] Said R. Yannai, "I was going along in the road in Sepphoris, and I saw a *min*, who took a pebble and threw it up into the sky, and it came down and was turned into a calf."

[B]   And did not R. Eleazar say in the name of R. Yosé bar Zimra, "If everyone in the world got together, they could not create a single mosquito and put breath into it."

[C]   But we must say that that *min* did not take a pebble and throw it up into the air, so when it came down it was turned into a calf.

[D]   But he ordered his servant to steal a calf from the herd and bring it to him.

[VI.A]   Said R. Hinena b. R. Hananiah, "I was walking in the turf [?] of Sepphoris, and I saw a *min* take a skull and throw it up into the air, and when it came down, it had turned into a calf.

[B]   "And I came and I told father, and he said to me, 'If you actually ate of the calf meat, it really happened, and if not, it was a mere illusion.' "

[VII.A]   **Said R. Joshua, "Three hundred laws did R. Eliezer expound concerning the verse, 'You shall not allow a witch to live' (Ex. 22:18),**

[B]   **"and of all of them I have heard only two things:**

[C]   **" 'Two may gather cucumbers. One gatherer may be exempt, and one gatherer may be liable. He who does a deed is liable, but he who merely creates an illusion is exempt' "** [T. San. 11:5].

[D]   Said R. Derosa, "They were nine hundred pericopae: three hundred leading to a decision of guilt, three hundred leading to a decision of innocence, and three hundred leading to a decision of guilt which was innocence. [That is, one is prohibited but not punished if he should do the deed.]"

After unit **I**'s exegetical exercise, we have a series of stories about rabbinical magic. **II**.H clearly presupposes a text we do not have, or Judah and Eleazar concur.

9 Yerushalmi Sanhedrin
Chapter Eight

8:1

[A] [26a] "A rebellious and incorrigible son"—

[B] At what point [does a child] become liable to be declared a rebellious and incorrigible son?

[C] From the point at which he will produce two pubic hairs, until the "beard" is full—

[D] (the lower [pubic], not the upper [facial] beard, but the sages used euphemisms)—

[E] as it is said, "If a man has a son" (Deut. 21:18)—a son, not a daughter; a son, not an adult man.

[F] And a minor is exempt, since he has not yet entered the scope of the commandments.

[I.A] R. Zeira, R. Abbahu, R. Yosé b. Haninah in the name of R. Simeon b. Laqish: "It is written, 'If a man willfully attacks another to kill him treacherously . . .' (Ex. 21:14)—

[B] "From what point is he treated as a man?

[C] "From the point at which he may act willfully.

[D] "From what point does he act willfully?

[E] "When the crest of the genitals begins to flatten."

[F] A comparison: When the seed is cooking inside, the pot grows black outside.

[G] Said R. Zeira, "R. Shila bar Bina taught, 'If a man has a son'—(Deut. 21:18)—not when the son is himself a father.

[H] "Once the boy can have sexual relations with a woman and make her pregnant, he is in the status of a father and not of a son.

[I] "The Torah thus has said, 'A son and not a father.' "

[J] This saying accords with that which R. Yasa said in the name of R. Sabbetai, "The entire period during which a boy is eligible to be declared a rebellious and incorrigible son is not more than six months alone."

[II.A] Said R. Yasa, "All these rules are not [merely] reasonable, for the opposite is the case."

[B] It was taught [along these same lines]: You should know that that is the case [that the law runs contrary to reason].

[C] For whom was it more likely to declare liable, a son or a daughter? You admit that it is the daughter.

[D] Yet the Torah has declared the daughter to be exempt, but has declared the son to be liable.

[E] Who was the more likely to be declared liable, the minor or the adult?

[F] You must say that it is the adult.

[G] Yet the Torah has declared the adult to be exempt and has made the minor liable.

[H] Who was the more likely to be declared liable: he who steals from others, or he who steals from his father and his mother?

[I] You must say that it is he who steals from others.

[J] Yet the Torah has declared exempt the one who steals from others, and has declared liable him who steals from his father and his mother.

[K] This teaches you that all these rules derive solely from the decree of the King [and not from reason].

The two units present no surprises. Unit I provides relevant facts, and unit II presents reflections on them.

8:2

[A]   *At what point is he liable?*

[B]   *Once he has eaten a "tartemar" of meat and drunk a half-"log" of Italian wine.*

[C]   *R. Yosé says, "A 'mina' of meat and a 'log' of wine."*

[D]   *[If] he ate in an association formed for a religious duty,*

[E]   *[if] he ate on the occasion of the intercalation of the month,*

[F]   *[if] he ate food in the status of second tithe in Jerusalem,*

[G]   *[if] he ate carrion and "terefah" meat, forbidden things or creeping things,*

[H]   *[if] he ate untithed produce, first tithe, the heave offering of which had not been removed, second tithe or consecrated food which had not been redeemed [by money],*

[I]   *[if] he ate something which fulfilled a religious duty or committed a transgression,*

[J]   *[if] he ate any sort of food except meat, drank any sort of liquid except wine—*

[K]   *he is not declared a rebellious and incorrigible son—*

[L]   *unless he eats meat and drinks wine,*

[M]   *since it is said, "a glutton and a drunkard" (Deut. 21:20).*

[N]   *And even though there is no clear proof for the proposition, there is at least a hint for it,*

[O]   *for it is said, "Do not be among the wine drinkers, among gluttonous meat eaters" (Prov. 23:20).*

[I.A]   Said R. Yosé, "A *tartemar* is a half-*litra*."

[II.A]   He is not liable unless he eats meat lightly roasted.

[B]   If one eats it raw, he is a dog.

[C]   If he eats it cooked, he is a man.

[D]   If he ate the cartilages forming the ear, what is the law?

[E]   If he ate the soft veins, what is the law [for in both cases they will harden]?

[F]   R. Yohanan said, "They are counted for it [as meat of the pas-
      chal lamb, and it is meat for fulfilling the obligation]."

[G]   R. Simeon b. Laqish said, "They are not counted for it. [It is
      not meat.]"

[H]   R. Jacob bar Aha in the name of R. Zeira: "R. Yohanan and
      R. Simeon b. Laqish differ," as we have learned there:

[I]   In the case of these, *their skin is in the status of their flesh* [M.
      Hul. 9:2A]. [Now for what purpose is the skin deemed equiva-
      lent to meat?]

[J]   Said R. Yohanan, "As to this flesh, they have made mention of
      it solely to impose a prohibition on it and to declare it unclean,
      but as to inflicting a flogging for eating it, they did not impose
      such a flogging [because it ultimately hardens]."

[K]   R. Simeon b. Laqish said, "Rabbi has taught a complete and
      perfect Mishnah: whether for purposes of prohibiting it or for a
      flogging or for purposes of declaring it unclean."

[L]   The theory attributed to R. Simeon b. Laqish has been
      reversed.

[M]   There he treated it as meat [even though it ultimately hardens],
      and here he has not treated it as meat [since he says it is not
      meat, G].

[N]   Said R. Judah b. bar Pazzi, "There the case is different, be-
      cause it is skin, and [only] in the end will it get hard."

[O]   All the more so then has the opinion assigned to R. Simeon b.
      Laqish proved reversed: Now if there, in which case it will end
      up getting hard, he has treated it as meat, here, in which it is
      not going to end up hard, all the more so should he treat it as
      meat!

[P]   Said R. Abbahu, "The Scriptural basis for the position of R.
      Simeon b. Laqish is as follows: 'They shall eat the flesh' (Ex.
      12:8)—not the sinews."

[III.A] *If he ate in an association formed for a religious duty, if he ate
      on the occasion of the intercalation of the month, if he ate food
      in the status of second tithe in Jerusalem* [M. San. 8:2D–F]—

[B]   "And though they chastise him [26b], he will not give heed to
      them" (Deut. 21:18)—this excludes this one [described in the

cited passage of Mishnah], who assuredly does heed the voice of his Father who is in heaven.

[**IV**.A]   Said R. Yohanan, "If your name is mentioned for service on the council, let the Jordan be your border."

[B]   Said R. Yohanan, "People appeal to the government to be rid of the duty of serving on the council."

[C]   Said R. Yohanan, "People may lend on interest to an association formed for a religious duty and for sanctifying the new moon."

[D]   R. Yohanan would go up to the synagogue in the morning, and he would gather crumbs and eat them, and he said, "Let my lot be with him who sanctifies the month here evenings [because they have such a fine meal]."

[**V**.A]   *If he ate carrion and terefah meat, forbidden things or creeping things [M. San. 8:2G]—*

[B]   "And though they chastise him, he will not give heed to them"—

[C]   this excludes this one [described in the cited passage], for even the voice of his Father in heaven does he not heed.

Unit **I** lightly glosses the Mishnah. Unit **II** raises the quesiton of whether soft veins count as meat. It is relevant to Mishnah because the wayward son is a glutton for meat and wine. Will sinews count against him as meat? But its correct place, of course, is in regard to the Passover, and the issue is phrased in terms of whether or not eating such a part of the paschal lamb fulfills one's obligation to eat of the lamb's meat, as required at Ex. 12:8. Units **III** and **V** are carefully balanced. The insertion of a set of Yohanan's sayings presumably is because of **IV**.C, but why the rule should be as Yohanan says I do not know.

8:3

[A]   *[If] he stole something belonging to his father but ate it in his father's domain,*

[B]   *or something belonging to others but ate it in the domain of those others,*

[C]   *or something belonging to others but ate it in his father's domain,*

[D]   *he is not declared a rebellious and incorrigible son—*

[E]   *until he steals something of his father's and eats it in the domain of others.*

[F]   *R. Yosé b. R. Judah says, ". . . until he steals something belonging to his father and his mother."*

[I.A]   Whence do we locate the first warning against stealing [kidnapping]?

[B]   "You shall not steal" (Ex. 20:15).

[C]   Whence do we locate the second warning against stealing [property]?

[D]   "You [pl.] shall not steal" (Lev. 19:11).

[E]   "You shall not steal" for spite [returning the object later on].

[F]   "You shall not steal" planning then to pay double compensation or fourfold or fivefold damages.

[G]   Ben Bag Bag says, "You shall not steal from the thief [even] what belongs to you, so that you will not appear to be a thief."

[II.A]   R. Ba, R. Yohanan in the name of R. Hoshaiah: "[The accused] son is liable only if he will steal money [to buy meat for his gluttony]."

[B]   R. Zeira in the name of R. Hoshaiah: "He is liable only if he will waste money."

[C]   What do we mean by "wasting money"?

[D]   If it is a case in which he says to the butcher, "Here are five and give me meat worth three," he is a mere idiot.

[E]   "Here are three and give me [meat worth] five," he is an ordinary person.

[F]   But thus do we interpret the matter: "Here are five, and give me meat worth five"; [in this case, having failed to effect a bargain, he has wasted money].

[III.A]   What is a thief, and what is a robber?

[B]   Said R. Hela, "[If] one stole before witnesses, he is a thief, and if he did so before the owner, he is a robber [so the criterion is the presence of the owner, which turns a thief into a robber]."

[C]   R. Zeira raised the question: "If so, even if he intended to commit a robbery against the owner, this one is not a robber [if the deed is not done before others]. [That is to say, by Hela's definition, the presence of the witness or the owner is decisive, and without committing the theft in the presence of the witness or the owner, one is no robber.]"

[D]   Then what is meant by a robber in the view of R. Zeira?

[E]   R. Samuel bar Sosetra in the name of R. Abbahu: "Only if one steals an object in the presence of ten men.

[F]   "The principal source dealing with the matter is as follows: 'The Egyptian had a spear in his hand, but Benaiah went down to him with a staff and robbed the spear out of the Egyptian's hand' (2 Sam. 23:21) [in front of many people]."

Units **I** and **III** ignore our pericope of Mishnah. Unit **II** is generally relevant in interpreting the sort of thievery for which the son may be declared incorrigible.

8:4

[A]   *[If] his father wanted [to put him to judgment as a rebellious and incorrigible son] but his mother did not want to do so,*

[B]   *[if] his father did not want and his mother did want [to put him to judgment],*

[C]   *he is not declared a rebellious and incorrigible son—*

[D]   *until both of them want [to put him to judgment].*

[E]   *R. Judah says, "If his mother was unworthy of his father, he is not declared to be a rebellious and incorrigible son."*

[I.A]   Said R. Yohanan [in regard to M. 8:4E], "And even if his mother was not worthy of his father, [he may be declared incorrigible]."

[II.A]   [With regard to M. 8:3F:] For is not everything which belongs to his mother in fact within the domain of his father?

[B]   Said R. Yosé b. R. Bun, "Interpret the rule to speak of a case in which the mother took a pot [belonging to her] and prepared meat from an ox [belonging to the husband], and so the son stole meat from the two of them."

Yohanan, **I**, differs from Judah. Unit **II** refers back to M. 8:3, as indicated, and provides an instance relevant to the question raised at **II.**A.

8:5

[A]   *[If] one of the [parents] was maimed in the hand, lame, dumb, blind, or deaf,*

[B]   *he is not declared a rebellious and incorrigible son,*

[C]   *since it is said, "Then his father and his mother will lay hold of him" (Deut. 21:19)—so they are not (1) maimed in their hands;*

[D]   *"and bring him out"—(2) so they are not lame;*

[E]   *"and they shall say"—(3) so they are not dumb;*

[F]   *"This is our son"—(4) so they are not blind;*

[G]   *"He will not obey our voice"—(5) so they are not deaf.*

[H]   *They warn him before three judges and flog him.*

[I]   *[If] he went and misbehaved again, he is judged before twenty-three judges.*

[J]   *He is stoned only if there will be present the first three judges, since it is said, "This our son"—this one who was flogged before you.*

[**I.**A]   Just as you interpret the verse pertaining to the parents, so you must interpret the matter to apply also to the elders of the court [who likewise must be unblemished in the specified ways].

[B]   This is in line with the following [interpretation of Deut. 21:2, 6–7: "Then your elders and your judges shall come forth . . . and they shall wash their hands . . . and shall say, 'Our hands did not shed this blood, neither did our eyes see it shed . . .' "]:

[C]   "They shall come forth"—thus excluding the lame.

[D]   "And they shall say"—thus excluding the dumb.

[E]   "Our hands have not shed this blood"—thus excluding those maimed in the hand.

[F]   "And our eyes did not see"—thus excluding the blind.

[G]   Scripture thereby teaches us that, just as the elders of the court must be whole in righteousness, so they must be whole in their limbs.

[II.A]   Said R. Yohanan [with reference to M. 8:5J], "If one of the first three judges who judged the boy should die, [the boy] is not stoned to death."

[B]   Now is this not precisely what the Mishnah states: *He is stoned only if there will be present the first three judges*?

[C]   Said R. Hoshaiah, "[Yohanan's saying] is so that you should not treat the second case [in which the son should steal] as if it were the first, [so that if he should then go and repeat the deed, he should be stoned]. [Yohanan thus points out that, if one of the judges of the original trial, at which the son was flogged, should die, then that entire process is null. Then, if the son should do the act a second time, that is not treated as if it were the first violation. And if there should be a further violation, he will not be stoned.]"

Unit I extends the conception of Mishnah, and unit II clarifies Yohanan's comment on Mishnah, as indicated.

8:6

[A]   *[If] he fled before his trial was over, and afterward [while he was a fugitive,] the lower "beard" became full, he is exempt.*

[B]   *If after his trial was done he fled, and afterward the lower beard became full, he is liable.*

[I.A]   Said R. Josiah, "Zeira told me in the name of the men of Jerusalem, 'There are three whom, if [the injured parties] seek to forgive, they may forgive, and these are they:

[B]   " 'A wife accused of adultery, a rebellious and incorrigible son, and an elder who rebels against the decision of a court.' "

[C]   And in regard to the wife accused of adultery, this not clearly stated in the Mishnah itself, [when it says that] if the husband does not wish to administer the bitter water to her, [she is let go]?

[D]   One might have supposed that the rule applied only prior to the writing of the scroll [with the divine name]. What the cited saying comes to state is that even after the scroll is written out, [the husband still may refrain from administering the bitter water to his wife].

[E]   Now that is so before the scroll is blotted out. But once it has been blotted out, it is not in such a case that the husband any longer has the power to forgive.

[F]   In regard to the rebellious and incorrigible son, is this not clearly stated in the Mishnah itself, [when it says:] *If his father wanted but his mother did not, if his father did not want and his mother did [to put him on trial], he is not declared a rebellious and incorrigible son [M. San. 8:4A–C]*?

[G]   One might have supposed that this rule applied only prior to the son's coming to court. What the cited saying comes to state is that even after the son has come to court, [the trial still may be canceled].

[H]   Now that is so before the court process is completed. But once the court process has been completed, it is not in such a case [that the trial is then canceled].

[I]   As to the rebellious elder: That is to say that one may decide not to put him to death.

[J]   But as to returning him to his town, they would not return him to his town.

[K]   [Continuing Josiah's statement, A–B above:] "Now when I came to R. Judah b. Beterah in Nisibis [and told him the saying cited at B], on two of them he agreed with me, but on one of them he did not agree with me.

[L]   "[Specifically] concerning the rebellious elder he did not agree with me.

[M]   "This was so as not to create dissension in Israel."

[**II**.A]   [The citation of the law of the wife accused of adultery provokes insertion of further materials relevant to that topic. Under discussion now is M. Sot. 4:2G–I: *If their husbands died
before the wives drank the bitter water—the House of Shammai
say, "They receive their marriage-settlement but do not
undergo the ordeal of drinking the bitter water." And the
House of Hillel say, "They do not undergo the ordeal of drinking the bitter water and do not receive the marriage settlement."*] What is the reason behind the position of the House of
Shammai [who allow the woman to collect her marriage
settlement]?

[B]   [She may claim,] "Bring me my husbasnd, and I shall drink
the water [and so prove my innocence]. [The fault is then not
mine.]"

[C]   What is the reason behind the position of the House of Hillel
[who will not permit the woman to collect]?

[D]   Since there is no husband here to administer the water to her,
the Torah puts her back in the status of one subject to doubt,
and she is subject therefore to a double doubt [since, further,
we do not know whether or not she should collect her marriage
settlement].

[E]   And the matter of doubt affecting her stands by itself, [that is,
by reason of doubt she may not collect money].

[F]   There we have learned: *She who impairs her marriage settlement [by admitting that she has received part, but not all, of
the funds which are due it] collects the remainder only through
an oath* [M. Ket. 9:7A, 9:8A–C, M. Shebu. 7:7].

[G]   It was taught: That rule applies to the one who impairs the
marriage settlement, but not to the one who claims less [in her
marriage settlement than is imputed to the document, e.g., saying it was worth only one hundred *zuz*, when the other party
claimed to have paid two hundred]. [In such a case, the wife
collects the settlement of one hundred without taking an oath]
[cf. T. Ket. 9:4].

[H]   She who claims less [than the full value of her marriage contract collects it without an oath:] How so?

[I]   If her marriage settlement was for two hundred *zuz*, and she
says, "It was only a *maneh* [a hundred *zuz*]," she collects it
without taking an oath.

[J]   What then is the difference between one who impairs and one who diminishes her marriage contract?

[K]   Said R. Haninah, "In the case of one who impairs the settlement, there has been give and take in-between times. [Since the woman admits to having received part of the settlement, we have a case in which there is partial admission of the claim, so there are grounds for an oath.]

[L]   "In the case of one who claims less, there has been no give and take in-between times."

[M]   R. Jeremiah proposed: "Just as you rule there [in connection with oaths], *'If a single witness gives testimony in her regard that the marriage settlement has been collected, she may then collect the contract only by taking an oath'* [M. Ket. 9:7B, M. Shebu. 7:7], so here too: 'If a single witness gives testimony in her connection that the sum of the marriage contract is less [than contemplated, in which case her admission of the fact is null], she may collect her marriage settlement only by taking an oath.' [The matters are parallel, since, in both instances, the presence of a single witness suffices to deny the wife the claim that she might be demand a more substantial sum, and so is believed when she claims less than is within her power.]"

[N]   Said R. Yosé, "[The cases are different]. When a single witness testifies that the marriage settlement has been collected, he does not contradict the testimony of two witnesses [so he may be believed]. But when he testifies that the amount of the marriage settlement is less, he contradicts two witnesses, [namely, those listed in the marriage settlement's document, who have signed their names to the document and so testified that the amount of money covered therein is what is represented by the document]."

[O]   It was taught: *She who collects her marriage settlement not in the husband's presence collects only by taking an oath* [M. Ket. 9:7, M. Shebu. 7:7D].

[P]   But do they exact payment from a person in his absence?

[Q]   Said R. Jeremiah, "Interpret the rule to apply to a document in which the interest payments are eating up [the man's property, in which case it is to his advantage to pay off]."

[R]   Now will a court exact payment for interest?

[S]   Interpret the rule to apply to a case in which a gentile serves as pledge, [and he can collect interest from the Israelite].

[T]   Has it not been taught: **An heir, the father of whom has impaired his bond, may collect without taking an oath. In this case the power of the heir is stronger than the power of the father [T. Shebu. 6:5E–F],** for the father collects only by taking an oath.

[U]   Said R. Eleazar, "But [the heir] does take the oath applying to an heir [in any event]: *'We swear that father gave us no instructions [in this matter], father said nothing to us about it, and we did not find among his bonds evidence that this bond had been paid off' [M. Shebu. 7:7F].* This means, does it not, that if a bond *were* found, it would be assumed to have been paid off [on which account one must take an oath that, 'I have not found . . .']." [The relevance of this item will now be clarified.]

[V]   R. Hoshaiah raised the question: "Does the Mishnah [just now cited] then follow the opinion of the House of Shammai, for *the House of Shammai say, 'She collects her marriage contract and does not drink the bitter water'?* [The basic reasoning of the House of Shammai is that the wife enjoys the presumption of having collected her settlement and so of owning the property she now claims as her settlement. The heirs of the deceased must then prove that that is *not* the case, if they wish to retrieve the property from her. This they cannot do. Here, too, if the bond is in hand, it is assumed to have been collected, and that is why the heir must swear that it is not in existence at all, so 'we did not find . . .']."

[W]   Said R. Yosé, "[The cases are not really comparable]. The reason of the House of Shammai [is that the wife may claim,] 'Bring me my husband, and I shall drink the water [and prove my innocence].' But here, in law and logic, even the father should not have been required to take an oath at all. But sages ordained in this case that the father should take an oath. So for the father such an oath has been ordained. But for the son, no such oath has been ordained. [That is, if the bond has been impaired, there must be an oath from the father.] Since the father has died, the position of the son is defined through the requirement of the law of the Torah, [and not the law as sages have revised it]. [So the son then may collect without an oath.]"

[X]   If the father was obligated in court to take an oath and then died, his son may not collect what is owing, for, if that is not the case, then shall we end up saying that a man may leave to his son the requirement to take an oath? [That is absurd.]

[Y]   Said R. Ba, "Thus is the matter to be stated [applying to the case before us]: If the father impaired his bond in court and then died, [the son] may not collect."

[Z]   [Rejecting this thesis,] R. Hisda raised the question: "Because this one has gone two steps [to court], should the other one lose out?

[AA]   "Had he impaired the bond outside of court, you rule that the son may collect the bond. Because he has impaired it in court, do you then rule that he may *not* collect it? [The rule that the obligation to take an oath is not handed on as an inheritance applies only when the oath is imposed by law. But in the case of an impaired bond, the father himself is subject to an oath only by sages' ordinance, not by Torah law, and there is no reason here to invoke the notion that an oath is not handed on as an inheritance. The heir collects by the usual oath taken by heirs, as specified at U, above.]"

The sole point of relevance to Mishnah comes at unit **I**, with its comparison of the three sorts who may be forgiven. Because of **I.B**, the remainder of the materials before us are tacked on.

8:7

[A]   *A rebellious and incorrigible son is tried on account of [what he may] end up to be.*

[B]   *Let him die while yet innocent, and let him not die when he is guilty.*

[C]   *For when the evil folk die, it is a benefit to them and a benefit to the world.*

[D]   *But [when the] righteous folk [die], it is bad for them and bad for the world.*

[E]   *Wine and sleep for the wicked are a benefit for them and a benefit for the world.*

[F]   *But for the righteous, they are bad for them and bad for the world.*

[G]   *Dispersion for the evil is a benefit for them and a benefit for the world.*

[H]   *But for the righteous, it is bad for them and bad for the world.*

[I]   *Gathering together for the evil is bad for them and bad for the world.*

[J]   *But for the righteous, it is a benefit for them and a benefit for the world.*

[K]   *Tranquillity for the evil is bad for them and bad for the world.*

[L]   *But for the righteous, it is a benefit for them and a benefit for the world.*

[I.A]   The Holy One, blessed be he, foresaw that in the end this one will use up the property of his father and the property of his mother,

[B]   and he will then set himself at the crossroads and bother, and finally kill, people.

[C]   So in the end he will forget his learning in the Torah.

[D]   [26c] So the Torah has said, *"Let him die while yet innocent, and let him not die when he is guilty, for when the evil folk die, it is a benefit to them and a benefit to the world, but when the righteous folk die, it is bad for them and bad for the world"* [M. 8:7B–D]

[II.A]   *Wine and sleep for the wicked are a benefit for them, and a benefit for the world. But for the righteous, they are bad for them and bad for the world* [M. 8:7E–F].

[B]   Said R. Abbahu, "That is so only in the case when there is a lot of drinking of wine and [then] sleep."

[C]   Said R. Jonathan, "[The righteous] sleep a little at a time, so that their minds may be serene."

The Talmud at I.A–C fills in the space between M. 8:7A and M. 8:7B, and at II.B, C, lightly glosses the cited clause of M. 8:7E–F.

8:8

[A]   *He who breaks in [Ex. 22:2] is judged on account of what he may end up to be.*

[B]   *[If] he broke in and broke a jug, if bloodguilt applies to him, he is liable.*

[C]   *If bloodguilt does not apply, he is exempt.*

[I.A]   It was taught: R. Ishmael says, "This is one of three verses used in the Torah in the sense of a parable:

[B]   " 'When men quarrel and one strikes the other . . . and the man does not die but keeps his bed, then, if the man rises again and walks abroad with his staff, he that struck him shall be clear' (Ex. 21:18–19).

[C]   " 'If a thief is found breaking in, and is struck so that he dies, there shall be no bloodguilt for him' (Ex. 22:2).

[D]   " 'But if the sun has risen upon him, there shall be bloodguilt for him' (Ex. 22:3).

[E]   "Now does the sun rise on him alone? And does it not rise upon everyone in the world?

[F]   "But just as sunshine is special in that it is at peace with the entire world, so, as long as you know that you are at peace with the intruder, whether by day or by night, he who kills him is put to death."

[G]   There are times that he comes to steal, and there are times that he comes to kill.

[H]   Thus must you state matters therefore: If he comes solely to steal, and this is a matter of certainty, and he is killed, then the one who kills him is put to death.

[I]   There are times that he comes to kill, in which case he is to be killed.

[J]   On this basis [that in doubt, Ex. 22:2, one kills the intruder] you must reason in the matter of danger to life in general, and so you must say the rule:

[K]   Idolatry is distinctive in that it imparts uncleanness to the land, involves a profanation of Name, drives the Presence of God out of the world, and in its case they set aside every sort of doubt,

[L]   all the more so in the case of a matter involving danger to life, that they ignore every doubt [and act decisively].

[II.A] It is written, "If in breaking in a thief is found, and is struck so that he dies, there shall be no bloodguilt for him" (Ex. 22:2).

[B]   R. Hiyya taught: "When he is breaking in, he is not subject to bloodguilt. If he is smitten outside of a break-in, he is subject to bloodguilt. [That is, once he has left the house, if the householder kills him, he is subject to bloodguilt.]"

[C]   R. Simeon b. Yohai taught, "[Even if he is smitten] outside of the break-in, [the householder] is not subject to bloodguilt; [if the owner kills the thief, the owner is exempt from penalty], because a person's property is as valuable to him as his life."

[D]   If he sees him going along and wants to take his money from him and goes and kills him, [the victim is exempt from bloodguilt].

[III.A] R. Huna said, "If he took the purse and turns to leave and goes along, and the victim goes and kills him, the one who kills him is not put to death."

[B]   What is the Scriptural basis for the statement of R. Huna?

[C]   "Lest the avenger of blood in hot anger pursue the manslayer" (Deut. 19:6) [and the householder is angry about the theft].

[D]   Rab said, "Whoever comes against me shall I kill, except for Hananiah b. Shila, because I know that he comes only to take my property from me [but would not harm me otherwise]."

[E]   Said R. Isaac, "Since his heart was so bold to do such a thing to him, this is not someone of the sort of Hananiah b. Shila [anyhow]."

The Talmud concentrates on the rather secondary matter of the liability for the death of the thief. Unit I contains two viewpoints, A–F and G–L. The former holds the householder liable under some circumstances, and the latter maintains that, in a case of doubt, one kills the intruder without liability. Unit II contains a parallel dispute, A–B vs. C, and unit III goes over the same ground.

8:9

[A]   *And these are those who are to be saved [from doing evil] even at the cost of their lives:*

[B]   *he who pursues after (1) his fellow in order to kill him—*

[C]   *after (2) a male, or after (3) a betrothed girl;*

[D]   *but he (1) who pursues a beast, he (2) who profanes the Sabbath, he (3) who does an act of service to an idol—they do not save them even at the cost of their lives.*

[I.A]   **He who pursues after his fellow to kill him [M. 8:9B] whether at home or in the field—they save him at the cost of his life.**

[B]   **All the same are he who pursues his fellow to kill him and all the other prohibited relationships which are listed in the Torah—they save [the one who pursues them] at the cost of his life.**

[C]   **But if it was a widow pursued by a high priest, or a divorcée or a woman who had performed the rite of removing the shoe pursued by an ordinary priest,** or a *mamzeret* girl or a *Nethinah* girl pursued by an Israelite, or an Israelite girl pursued by a *Nethin* or a *mamzer*, **they do not save him at the cost of his life.**

[D]   If the deed already was done, they do not save him at the cost of his life.

[E]   If there are present people able to save [the prospective victim], they do not save him at the cost of his life.

[F]   R. Judah says, "If she herself had said, 'Let him be,' they do not save him at the cost of his life,

[G]   **"even though [by] leaving him, he gets involved with a capital crime" [T. San. 11:11].**

[II.A]   The following proposition is self-evident: A murderer who [after the act of murder] broke utensils or did bodily injury is liable to pay restitution [because the culpability for murder and that for property damage are not simultaneous] [cf. M. 8:8B–C].

[B]   But if he broke a utensil before he reached the city [that is, when the man was being pursued while he was escaping to the city],

[C]   R. Zeira and R. Hoshaiah—

[D]   one of them said, "He must pay compensation."

[E]   And the other one said, "He does not pay compensation."

[III.A]   A pursuer who became one of the pursued [if one was pursuing his fellow to kill him, and the pursued caught the pursuer and began to run after him]—what is the law as to saving the pursuer [who was the pursued] at the cost of the life of the one who had been pursued? [Since the one now being pursued originally was the pursuer, one cannot intervene and save the one who is now in pursuit at the cost of his own life. Or perhaps we maintain that the original pursuer never intended to murder the other party—now in pursuit—and consequently the present pursuer in fact is in danger of committing murder and must be saved at the cost of his own life.]

[B]   A stronger party who turned out to be the weaker party—what is the law as to saving the [originally]stronger party at the cost of the life of the [then]weaker party [just as at A]?

[C]   R. Jeremiah responded: "Now have we not learned the following: *The woman who is in hard labor—they chop up the child in her womb and they remove it limb by limb, because her life takes precedence over his life. If its greater part has gone forth, they do not touch him, for they do not set aside one life on account of another life [M. Oh. 7:6].* [This would indicate that they certainly do *not* save the [originally]stronger party at the cost of the life of the [then]weaker party.]"

[D]   R. Yosé b. R. Bun in the name of R. Hisda: "[The case cited regarding childbirth is] different from the one before us, for it is not known who will cause the death of whom [the mother, the child]. [Here we know who is the aggressor.]"

[IV.A]   It was taught: R. Eleazar b. R. Simeon says, "He who is going to worship an idol—they save him at the cost of his life [vs. M. 8:9D(3)].

[B]   "For if on account of the honor owing to mortal man they save him at the cost of his life, is it not a matter *a fortiori* that they should save him on account of what is owing to the Eternal?"

Unit **I** presents supplementary materials to the Mishnah. Unit **II** reverts to M. 8:8B–C; it is curiously undeveloped. Unit **III** presents a secondary expansion of Mishnah's law, and unit **IV** provides an opinion contrary to that in Mishnah.

10 Yerushalmi Sanhedrin
Chapter Nine

9:1

[A]   [26d] *And these are those who are put to death through burning:*

[B]   *(1) he who has sexual relations with both a woman and her daughter [Lev. 18:17, 20:14], and (2) a priest's daughter [Talmud omits: who committed adultery] [Lev. 21:9].*

[C]   *In the same category as a woman and her daughter are [the following]: (1) his daughter, (2) his daughter's daughter, (3) his son's daughter, (4) his wife's daughter, (5) the daughter of her daughter, (6) the daughter of her son, [Talmud omits: (7) his mother-in-law, (8) the mother of his mother-in-law, and (9) the mother of his father-in-law].*

[I.A]   There we have learned: *They marry in regard to the kinswomen of a woman whom one has raped or seduced [M. Yeb. 11:1].*

[B]   This is the meaning of the Mishnah pericope: They marry one related to one whom one has raped or seduced.

[C]   [Thus, if] one has raped a woman, he is permitted to marry her mother.

[D]   [If] one has seduced a woman, he is permitted to marry her daughter.

[E]   He who rapes or seduces a married woman is liable.

[F]   Said R. Yohanan, "The law taught here applies via marriage.

[G]   "[That is to say, if] one has married a woman and afterward raped her mother, he is liable.

"[And if] one has married a woman and afterward seduced her daughter [by another marriage], he is liable."

[II.A]   Said R. Eleazar, "Sumkhos and R. Yohanan b. Nuri said the same thing.

[B]   "For we have learned there: *If he slaughtered a beast and its granddaughter and afterward slaughtered its daughter, he incurs forty stripes. Sumkhos says in the name of R. Meir, 'He incurs eighty stripes'* [M. Hul. 5:3O–P].

[C]   "There we have learned: *R. Yohanan b. Nuri says, 'He who has sexual relations with his mother-in-law is liable on her account because of the prohibition against having sexual relations with (1) his mother-in-law, and (2) the mother of his mother-in-law, and (3) the mother of his father-in-law.' They said to him, 'All three in fact fall into a single prohibition'* [M. Ker. 3:6C–D]. [In Sumkhos's view, a single warning and a single negative commandment suffice to impose liability on two counts. In Yohanan b. Nuri's, under the stated condition, in which the woman stands in multiple relationships to the man, the man is culpable on all counts of all relationships. So both say the same thing, that is, that for a single deed, one may bear multiple liabilities.]"

[D]   R. Judah bar Pazzi in the name of R. Yohanan: "Sumkhos agrees in the first instance [in which it is stated: If one slaughtered a cow and afterward its two offspring, he incurs eighty stripes. If he slaughtered the two offspring and then slaughtered it, he incurs forty (M. Hul. 5:3M)]. [In that case the violation is on a single count. Now why does Sumkhos not differ in the first case?]"

[E]   In fact, there is a teaching which states, "The matter indeed is still subject to dispute." [So he does differ on both counts.]

[F]   What is the reasoning behind the position of R. Yohanan b. Nuri [cited above]? [For in the case of the mother-in-law, we have a woman in the following situation: the man had been married to his mother-in-law's daughter's daughter and her son's daughter, so she is his mother-in-law's mother and his father-in-law's mother. But all of these relationships are in a single person, so why should he maintain that there are multiple counts of liability?]

[G]   Just as a woman and her daughter and the daughter of her daughter are subject to two distinct negative commandments, so a woman, the daughter of her son, and the daughter of her daughter, are subject to two negative commandments.

[H]   What is the reasoning behind the position of rabbis [who maintain that all are under a single count]?

[I]   Just as the daughter of her son and the daughter of her daughter are covered by a single negative commandment, so a woman, the daughter of her daughter, and the daughter of her son are all covered by a single negative commandment.

[III.A]   It is written, "You shall not uncover the nakedness of a woman and of her daughter, and you shall not take her son's daughter or her daughter's daughter to uncover her nakedness; they are your near kinswomen; it is wickedness" (Lev. 18:17). ["Taking" is understood to refer to marrying.]

[B]   And it is written, "If a man takes a wife and her mother also, it is wickedness; they shall be burned with fire, both he and they, that there may be no wickedness among you" (Lev. 20:14).

[C]   Now in the rest of these passages, "lying with" is written, while here, "taking" is the language used.

[D]   This is to teach you that he is not liable for the latter until the former is taken by him; [so only if he is married to the one is there liability for the other].

[E]   Or perhaps it is that he is not liable on her account unless it is through an actual marriage [and not merely through rape or seduction without actual marriage]. [That is, if he is married to the one, then he is liable on the count of the other. The alternative view is that he must be married to them both for liability to be incurred on account of either one.]

[F]   This latter possibility is null, for we have learned that the sanctification effected by marriage does not apply in the case of prohibited consanguineous unions.

[G]   For has it not been written, "A man shall not take his father's wife, nor shall he uncover her who is his father's" (Deut. 22:30)? [This would indicate that the prohibition applies only to marriage, but that one who merely seduces or rapes his father's wife should not be culpable, since the language, "take," suggests marriage.]

[H] The Scripture comes to inform you that the son was permitted with regard to this woman before she was married to his father. [If the father merely had seduced her, the son could have married her.]

[I] And is it not written, "The man who lies with his brother's wife, it is impurity; he has uncovered his brother's nakedness" (Lev. 20:21)?

[J] What does this verse come to inform you?

[K] It is that he was at one point permitted to marry this woman, before she was [actually] married to his brother [as at H].

[L] And know that this is so, for lo, in Levirate marriage she becomes permitted to him [which indicates that only so long as the woman is taken as a wife by the brother is he prohibited to marry her].

[M] And is it not written, "And you shall not take a woman as a rival wife to her sister, uncovering her nakedness while her sister is yet alive" (Lev. 18:18)?

[N] This verse in Scripture comes to inform you that he was permitted to marry her before he had married her sister.

[O] And you should know that that is so, for after the death of her sister [he may marry her].

[P] And is it not written, "If a man takes his sister, a daughter of his father or a daughter of his mother, and sees her nakedness, and she sees his nakedness, it is a shameful thing (hesed), and they shall be cut off in the sight of the children of their people; he has uncovered his sister's nakedness, he shall bear his iniquity" (Lev. 20:17)? [Does this apply solely to marriage, but that rape would then not be subject to the present prohibition.]

[Q] [The purpose of the reference to "taking" in the sense of marriage is for the purpose of a lesson to be learned, namely,] so that you should not say that Cain married his sister, Abel married his sister, [so marrying sisters is all right]. Thus I have done a kindness with the early generations, through whom the world would be built up, [but that does not apply later on].

[R]   "I have said, The world will be built up on the basis of mercy (hesed)" (Ps. 89:3).

[S]   And is it not written, "A widow, or one divorced, or a woman who has been defiled, or a harlot, these he shall not marry" (Lev. 21:14)? [Here too shall we say that rape or seduction are not culpable within the present count?]

[T]   The cited verse comes to teach you that if a priest sanctified such a woman as his wife, the act of sanctification is effective.

[**IV**.A]   Rab Huna said, "Up to this point we have dealt with the daughter of his daughter as to marriage.

[B]   "What about the daughter of his daughter as to rape? [That is, we have shown that there is liability for marrying a woman and her daughter. But what about raping the woman and her daughter?]"

[C]   It is written, "You shall not uncover the nakedness of your son's daughter or of your daughter's daughter, for their nakedness is your own nakedness" (Lev. 18:10).

[D]   Now how shall we interpret that statement?

[E]   If it makes reference to [prohibiting] marriage, lo, that matter already has been stated [in the prohibition against marrying a woman and her daughter (Lev. 18:17)].

[F]   So if it does not apply to marriage, treat the statement as referring to rape.

[G]   Up to now we have dealt with the daughter of his daughter.

[H]   How shall we demonstrate that the same law applies to his daughter?

[I]   Rab said, "If a man is warned against marrying the daughter of his daughter, is it not an argument *a fortiori* to apply the same rule to his own daughter?

[J]   "If on account of marrying the daughter of his daughter, he will suffer the penalty of extirpation, is it not an argument *a fortiori* that that penalty should apply if he marries his daughter?"

[K]   And from the viewpoint of R. Ishmael, who says that we derive a warning from an argument *a fortiori*, but we do not derive [Scriptural warrant for] a punishment applicable to a felon from an argument *a fortiori*, how do we prove this same proposition?

[L]   The following is available: Hezekiah taught, " 'And the daughter of a priestly man, if she profanes herself by playing the harlot, profanes her father; she shall be burned with fire' (Lev. 21:9).

[M]   "Why does Scripture say, 'A priestly man'?

[N]   "It is to encompass him who has sexual relations with his daughter [even in a case of rape], to indicate that he is subject to the death penalty through burning."

[V.A] R. Huna derived all of them [mother's mother, father's mother] from the following verse: "You shall not uncover the nakedness of a woman and of her daughter . . . they are your near kinswomen; it is wickedness" (Lev. 18:17).

[B]   And it is written, "If a man takes a wife and her mother also, it is wickedness; they shall be burned with fire, both he and they, that there may be no wickedness among you" (Lev. 20:14).

[C]   "Wickedness" is stated in both verses, so establishing grounds for an exegesis by analogy.

[D]   Just as three generations below [grandchildren] are encompassed, so three generations above [grandparents] are encompassed.

[E]   Just as below [in the case of a man and daughter], there is the violation of a negative commandment, so above [in the case of a man with the mother], there is the violation of a negative commandment.

[F]   Just as below [in the case of the generations following] the prohibited relationship is via marriage, so above [in the prior generations] what is prohibited is marriage.

[G]   Just as below [in the case of the coming generations], the penalty is execution by burning, so above [in the case of marriage with the prior generations], the form of execution is burning.

[H]   Just as below [in the case of the later generations], the law treats the daughter of the male as equivalent to the daughter of the female, so above [in the prior generations], the law treats the mother of the male as the mother of the female.

[I]   And [how about interpreting the matter] in accord with R. Meir? For R. Meir said, "An analogy [serves only to apply the law] to the place from which [the analogy to begin with] derives," how do we know that the third generation later [that is, the daughter's daughter] is prohibited by a negative commandment?

[J]   And in accord with the rabbis, who hold that an analogy is in accord with that which is stated therein, the third generation above [that is, the mother's mother], how do we know that the man is put to death by burning?

[K]   And whether from the viewpoint of rabbis or from that of R. Meir, as to the third generation below, how do we know that it is subject to a negative commandment?

[L]   Said R. Yosé, "Since it is written, 'Wickedness . . .' 'wickedness . . . ,' it is as if all of them are now present [subject to a single rule]."

[VI.A] [Reverting to IV.N,] said R. Yosé b. R. Bun, "[We do not derive a warning from the logical argument either]. Rather, there is a verse of Scripture which supplies a warning, as follows: 'Do not profane your daughter by making her a harlot' " (Lev. 19:29).

[VII.A] They raised the question before R. Abbahu, "He who had sexual relations with a woman, and she produced a daughter, and he went and had sexual relations with her and she produced a daughter, and he went and had sexual relations with her [that is, his granddaughter, in sequence],—[in this third case, that is, of relations with the granddaughter,] is he liable on her account on these counts: having sexual relations with a woman, her daughter, and her granddaughter? [In the sexual relations with the granddaughter, is he liable for having relations with a woman and her daughter, and also on the count of the granddaughter?]"

[B]   He said to them, " 'They are your near kinswomen; it is wickedness' (Lev. 18:17). All of them produce liability on the count of wickedness. [So he is liable on a single count, that of wickedness, and not on several distinct counts.]"

[C]   [Following PM, we now introduce the materials moved from above, following VI.A:] R. Haggai asked before R. Yosé, "Why do I require this verse? Do we read, 'Your daughter you should not uncover,' 'the daughter of your daughter you should not uncover'? [Scripture does not specify these as distinct counts. No other is needed.]"

[D]   He said to him, "And let Scripture state, 'The nakedness of a woman and the daughter of her daughter you should not uncover,' and then we should argue, 'Your daughter you should not uncover, your daughter's daughter you should not uncover,' so in this case we have two rules in a negative formulation covered by a single statement that the penalty is extirpation, and the two negatively formulated rules are both covered by the penalty of extirpation."

[E]   What is the Scriptural basis for this position?

[F]   [27a] "This shall be my holy anointing oil throughout your generations. It shall not be poured upon the bodies of ordinary men, and you shall make no other like it in composition; it is holy. . . . Whoever compounds any like it or whoever puts any of it on an outsider shall be cut off from his people" (Ex. 30:31–33).

[G]   Thus you have two negatively formulated rules, with a single statement of extirpation.

[H]   The two negative rules share the stated penalty of extirpation [which then applies to both of them] [cf. Y. San. 7:5].

[VIII.A]   [Referring back to M. Yeb. 11:1: They marry the kinswomen of a woman whom one has raped or seduced. R. Judah prohibits in the case of one raped by his father or seduced by his father. So that prohibition applies not only when the father has actually married or betrothed the woman. We now ask why Judah rejects the proof texts adduced above for the contrary view.] What is the Scriptural basis behind the position of R. Judah?

[B]   "A man shall not take the wife of his father and shall not uncover the garment of his father" (Deut. 22:30).

[C]   This ["garment"] refers to a woman whom his father has raped.

[D]   How do rabbis interpret the reference to "garment"?

[E]   There [in Babylonia] they say [that "garment" of the Scripture accords with the position of rabbis, but] we do not know whether this report is accurate.

[F]   [The stated report is as follows:] "Garment"—this refers to a woman who is subject to the father [in a Levirate connection], [and the meaning is that one may not have sexual relations with a woman who is awaiting Levirate marriage with his father].

[G]   But that is not so: Is one not liable on her account on the count of her being his father's wife? [The stated passage need not indicate that that liability is by reason of her being subject to the father, for in any event it is established that a candidate for Levirate marriage is tantamount to being the father's wife. So why does it make reference to "garment"?]

[H]   Said R. Hela, "It is for the purpose of effecting a warning, namely, if they warned him on the count of her being his father's wife, he is flogged, and if it was on the count of 'garment' [meaning one raped by the father], he also is flogged."

[I]   [Judah's position is not what it appeared to be.] [In fact,] R. Judah concurs in the matter of flogging. R. Judah concurs in the matter of an offering. [He holds that one indeed is prohibited from marrying a woman the father has raped. But the text cited above does not prove that position. It merely sustains it.]

[J]   R. Judah concurs in the case of all other women that they have been raped, that in such a case the man will be exempt [from punishment if he marries such a woman].

[K]   R. Judah concurs that if he has betrothed such a woman, the betrothal is valid. [That is, if one has betrothed a woman the father has raped, the betrothal is valid.]

[L]   R. Haggai raised the question before R. Yosé, "What is the law as to the offspring of such a marriage's being deemed a mamzer in the view of R. Judah?" [This question is raised in ignorance of the antecedent concessions of Judah.]

[M]   He said to him, " 'He whose testicles are crushed or whose male member is cut off shall not enter the assembly of the Lord' (Deut. 23:1), immediately follows (Deut. 22:30): 'A man shall not take his father's wife nor shall he uncover her who is his father's' Then follows (Deut. 23:2): 'No mamzer shall enter the assembly of the Lord.'] Thus the discourse is deliberately cut off [to indicate that if he marries a woman raped by his father, the offspring of such a marriage is not a mamzer]."

[N]   [He replied,] "If so, let the construction of the verses serve to cut off the matter in regard to the father's wife [and so indicate that if he marries his father's wife and produces offspring, they too are not deemed *mamzerim*]."

[O] "That is not possible, for the matter of the father's wife is part of the general prohibition against all consanguineous marriages, and it was singled out from the general rule to indicate that violation of the prohibition in the case of *all* forms of consanguineous marriage produces a *mamzer*."

[P] "By the same argument, let the one raped by the father be treated as a special case in order to provide the rule governing all matters of rape [and to indicate that one may not marry the woman raped by his brother and various male relatives, besides the father]."

[Q] "The matter of the wife of the father was part of the generality of the prohibition of consanguineous marriages, and it was singled out from the generality to teach the rule that in the case of violating any of the prohibitions against consanguineous marriage, the offspring will be a *mamzer*.

[R] "But do you have the possibility in the present matter, dealing with the woman raped by the father, to maintain that such a woman was part of the generality but was singled out to teach concerning all women raped by a male relative, that they are prohibited?"

[S] "Then let the wife of the father be treated as a special case to teach concerning a woman that was raped by the father [that she indeed is prohibited, even though the father has not married her]."

[T] He said to him, "Now if she is the wife of the father, she cannot be deemed a woman raped by the father, and if she was merely raped by the father, she cannot be deemed a wife of the father, [so that argument is simply not possible]."

The opening unit, **I**, serves M. Yeb. 11:1 more directly than it does our pericope of Mishnah. But the importance here is self-evident. If one has had sexual relations, without betrothal or marriage, that does not constitute a violation of the law punishable by burning. The prohibition pertains to one subject to betrothal. The main point of unit **II** is clear as stated. The relevance to Mishnah is difficult to discern. Unit **III** returns to the theme announced at unit **I**, the notion that mere sexual relations do not constitute a violation of the law of consanguinity, which is concerned with institutional and permanent ties among relatives, not with illicit sex. This matter is amply spelled out. The basic thesis is tested against various verses which refer to "taking" in the sense of marriage. Throughout, the main point is that, if the one party had merely seduced the woman but not married her, the other, close relative might then have married her. But if the former had actually married the woman, the latter then would be prohibited from doing so and burned if he did. The relevance to Mishnah, of course, is to indicate which sorts of relationships are to be punished by burning; the exclusions then are substantial. The question of unit **IV** is clearly stated at the outset. In unit **III** we prove that, if one has married a woman and her daughter, he is culpable. But what is the law as to rape? That is what is now to be proved. Further, since ample discussion deals with the prohibition of betrothing or marrying a granddaughter, how shall we prove that the same prohibition applies to the daughter? This too is dealt with. Unit **V** relates to M. Yeb. 2:4, and is carried along here because of the other references to Huna's proofs (PM), thus unit **V** in fact is inserted between unit **IV** and its continuation at unit **VI**. For a full account of its meaning and problems, see PM. In the present context we need not deal with the matter, for it is fully worked out at Y. Yeb. *ad loc.* Unit **VI**, as noted, continues the problem dealt with at unit **IV**. What follows **VI**.A in the printed text in fact belongs below, as indicated in my translation, following PM. The main point of the rather obscure exegetical discussion is to explain why Ab-bahu answers the question as he does, rather than resorting to a different exegetical argument. Unit **VIII** reverts to M. Yeb. 11:1, as indicated. The argument focuses upon Judah's position and its exegetical basis. As we see, the entire construction is hardly focused upon the Mishnah pericope before us.

9:2

[A]   *And these are those who are put to death through decapitation:*

[B]   *the murderer, and the townsfolk of an apostate town.*

[C]   *A person who committed murder because he hit his neighbor with a stone or a piece of iron [Ex. 21:18],*

[D]   or who pushed him under the water or into the fire, and [the other party] cannot get out of there and so perished—

[E]   he is liable.

[F]   [If] he pushed him into the water or into the fire, and he can get out of there but [nonetheless] he died, he is exempt.

[G]   [If] he sicked a dog on him, or sicked a snake on him, he is exempt.

[H]   [If] he made a snake bite him,

[I]   R. Judah declares him liable.

[J]   And sages declare him exempt.

[I.A]   It is written, "But if he struck him down with a stone in the hand, by which a man may die, so that he died, he is a murderer; the murderer shall be put to death" (Num. 35:17).

[B]   "Or if he struck him down with a weapon of wood in the hand, by which a man may die, and he died, he is a murderer; the murderer shall be put to death" (Num. 35:18).

[C]   Now when Scripture treats a weapon of iron [at Num. 35:16], it does not say either "by which a man may die" or "by which a man may not die." [So in this case we do not take account of the size of the weapon at all.]

[D]   Even if it is a small chip of metal [one is liable], for it can cut through the gullet and kill the man.

[E]   [But in the case of an object of wood or stone, the rule applies] when the stone is sufficiently sizable to kill the man, or the wood is sufficiently sizable to kill the man.

[II.A]   If one pushed a man in front of a horse, or if he pushed him in front of an arrow, or if he pushed him in front of a spear,

[B]   if he put him out in the cold, if he gave him polluted water to drink,

[C]   if he removed the roof covering from over him so that it rained on him,

[D]   and in one of these ways he died,

[E]   if he directed a watercourse over him and the water came along and drowned him, [all of these constitute acts of murder].

[**III**.A]   What is the reasoning behind the position of R. Judah [M. San. 9:2K–L]?

[B]   It is because of the venom which is between the snake's fangs.

[C]   What is the reasoning of the rabbis?

[D]   The venom is to be found at the fangs only when he rears back and spits it, [so it is the snake, not the man, that ejects the venom, and the man is only indirectly responsible].

Unit **I** makes an important point on the relevant verses of Scripture. Unit **II** expands on the reasoning of M. 9:2G–H, as against **I**, and I assume that what the Talmud wishes to do is to provide more examples parallel to the former. Then unit **III** provides a clear exegesis for the dispute at M. 9:2K–M.

9:3

[A]   *He who hits his fellow, whether with a stone or with his fist,*

[B]   *and they diagnosed him as likely to die,*

[C]   *[but] he got better than he was,*

[D]   *and afterward he got worse, and died—*

[E]   *he is liable.*

[F]   *R. Nehemiah says, "He is exempt,*

[G]   *"for there is a basis to the matter [of thinking that he did not die from the original injury]."*

[**I**.A]   Thus the Mishnah pericope [should read at M. 9:3F–G]:

[B]   "R. Nehemiah declares exempt,

[C]   "and sages declare liable, for there is a basis to the matter [of thinking that he did die from the original injury, since, after all, there was a diagnosis to that effect].

[D]   "[The reason that rabbis hold him liable] is that two estimates [of the victim's condition, the one at the outset, the one at the end after which he died] are of greater weight than one [in the middle, at which he appeared to have gotten somewhat better]."

[E]   R. Nehemiah says, "The estimate of the man's condition in the middle is greater than the one fore or aft."

[II.A]   What is the Scriptural basis for R. Nehemiah's opinion?

[B]   "[When men quarrel and one strikes the other with a stone or with his fist and the man does not die but keeps his bed,] then if the man rises again and walks abroad with his staff, he that struck him shall be clear" (Ex. 21:18–19).

[C]   Now would it have entered your mind that this one should be walking about in the marketplace while the other is put to death on his account? [Obviously not, and so the purpose of Scripture's statement is as follows:] Even though the victim should die after he was originally examined and diagnosed as dying, the other party is exempt [should the man's condition improve in the meantime].

[D]   What is the Scriptural basis for rabbis' opinion?

[E]   "And the man does not die but keeps his bed"—

[F]   Now do we not know that "if he does not die but keep his bed"—[why does Scripture specify both his not dying and also his going to bed]?

[G]   It is to speak of a case in which they did not make prognosis that he would die. [That is, Scripture is to be interpreted to mean, "if he does not die," that is, they did not reach a prognosis that he would die, but that he would not die.]

[H]   In this case it is written, "Then if the man rises again and walks abroad with his staff, then the one who struck him shall be clear" (Ex. 21:19).

[I]   [This then means that] lo, if then he does not get up, the one who struck him is liable.

[J]   Rather, the case is one in which the prognosis was made that he would die.

[K]   If then they reached the prognosis that he would die, in such a case it is written, "Only he shall pay for the loss of his time, and shall have him thoroughly healed" (Ex. 21:19). [That is, if he was not expected to die, the one who hit him nonetheless must pay the costs of his recovery.]

[III.A]   [But why should that be the case? There has been no prognosis that healing would be required.] R. Hela in the name of R. Simeon b. Laqish: "It is Scripture's innovation, saying that he must pay the costs of his recovery [despite the absence of a prognosis to that effect]."

[B]   R. Abbahu in the name of R. Yosé b. Haninah: "It was an erroneous prognosis. [That is, one must pay financial compensation because retrospectively we see that the original prognosis was an error. Then the physicians thought the man would die. So, retrospectively, we reinterpret the prognosis and say that it was that the one who hit the man would have to pay financial compensation.]"

[C]   What is the difference between these two positions [the one maintaining that the Scripture has made a decree that one must pay, the other maintaining that the point is that the original prognosis was erroneous, and so the aggressor must pay]?

[D]   It would be a case in which *he got better than he was, and then he got worse, and died*—

[E]   *he is liable.*

[F]   *R. Nehemiah declares him exempt, for there is a basis to the matter of thinking that he did not die from the original injury.*

[G]   The one who said that the reason is that it is Scripture's innovative decree that the aggressor pay for recovery maintains that if he paid funds for recovery, he has paid them over.

[H]   [His problem is this:] If he did not pay them out, what is the law as to his paying them out?

[I]   The one who said that the original prognosis was in error maintains that if the aggressor did not pay over the funds for recovery [before the victim in fact died], they do not say to him to pay that money over.

[J]   [His problem is this:] If he did pay out the money, what is the law as to the [victim's] accepting the funds?

[K]   There is a Tannaite pericope which supports the position of this party, and there is one which supports the position of that party.

[L]   The Mishnah pericope which supports the position of R. Yosé bar Haninah [B] is as follows:

[M]   If they reached the prognosis that he would die, but the man lived, at what point do they pay him the costs of his recovery?

From the moment at which he began to improve. [That is, the man got better and then got worse and died. At what point do we say that they have to pay out the costs of his medical treatment? It is from the time that he got better. But if he did not pay out the funds until the time that he got worse, he does not have to pay out at all.] [It follows that it is not Scripture's decree, but because] the original prognosis was in error.

[N]   For if you say it is Scripture's decree that he pay, he should pay from the very outset.

[O]   The Tannaite pericope which supports the position of R. Simeon b. Laqish [A] is as follows:

[P]   If they reached the prognosis that he would live, and he died, at what point does he pay out the funds? From the moment at which he got worse. [That is to say, even though he paid out nothing earlier, he pays from the time that the man got worse. The reason is not that the original prognosis had been in error, because if that were the case we should require payment at the opposite time. For once the man got worse, there should be no payment, since, it is clear, the original prognosis was in error. Thus the reason for the payment is that it is Scripture's decree, and the aggressor has to pay under all circumstances—this by Scriptural decree—even if the man got worse.]

[Q]   Said R. Yosé, "[Rejecting the proof in favor of R. Simeon b. Laqish,] There is no consideration here of paying [merely] when the man starts failing. But he has to pay from the beginning of the transaction.

[R]   "One must then say that it is Scripture's own decree that the man must pay.

[S]   "And if you say it was originally a false prognosis, one must then pay the man's cost until he actually dies."

[IV.A]   If one hit him on his hand, and it was smashed and the physician said, "If I cut off his hand, he will live," what is the law as to his having to pay compensation for the cost of the hand? [Is he liable, for having hit him, or exempt, for not having intended to injure the hand?]

[B]   Let us derive the answer to that question from the following:

[C]   "When men strive together [and hurt a woman with child, so that there is a miscarriage, and yet no harm follows, the one who hurt her shall be fined . . .]" (Ex. 21:22).

[D]   "When men quarrel [and one strikes the other with a stone . . . and the man does not die . . .]" (Ex. 21:18)—

[E]   "Striving together" and "quarreling" are one and the same thing. Why does Scripture then use the language, "When men *strive together*" and "When men *quarrel*"?

[F]   But it is to apply the law covering the one who deliberately does bodily injury upon the one who does not deliberately do so, and to apply the law covering the one who does not deliberately do so upon the one who does deliberately do so. [That is, at Ex. 21:18, one man deliberately injures the other, while at Ex. 21:22, the two men do not deliberately injure the pregnant woman. Accordingly, A, one has to pay compensation.]

[G]   It is easy to see why it was necessary to explicitly apply the law governing the one who deliberately does bodily injury to the one who does not deliberately do so.

[H]   But as to applying the law for the one who does not deliberately do bodily injury on the one who does deliberately do so, [why was this made explicit]?

[I]   For if for not deliberately doing bodily injury, one is liable, is it not an argument *a fortiori* that the one who deliberately does bodily injury should also be liable!

[J]   But thus is the purpose of Scripture in so stating the law:

[K]   If one hit the other on his hand and it was smashed, if the physician said, "If one cuts off his hand, he will live," what is the law as to paying compensation for the hand?

[L]   Just as that which you have stated there, "It is a decree of Scripture that one must pay compensation for the hand," here likewise it is a decree of Scripture that one must pay compensation for the hand.

[V.A]   [Leiden MS and *editio princeps:* 9:4] R. Isaac raised the question: "If they reached a prognosis that he would live, but he died,—surely it is natural for the living to die. [Why should he pay healing?]

[B]   "Since it is written, 'Only he that shall pay for the loss of his time, and shall have him thoroughly healed' (Ex. 21:19), the law is that he is liable to compensate him for lost time and for medical care."

[C]   R. Isaac raised the question, "If they reached a prognosis that he would die, but he lived—it is surely not usual for the dead to live [so there was a miracle]. [Why should he pay healing?]

[D]   "Since it is written, 'Only he shall pay for the loss of his time, and shall have him thoroughly healed' (Ex. 21:19), the law is that he is liable to pay compensation for lost time and for medical care."

The Talmud provides a sustained inquiry into Mishnah's rule, and, in particular, its Scriptural foundations. Unit I lays out the basic thesis of the Mishnah, revising the reasoning to show that the logic of the case supports rabbis as much as sages. Consequently, only Scriptural evidence is now suitable. Unit II, continuous with unit I, then sets forth the proofs for the two positions. Continuing this matter, unit III then analyzes the character of the stated proofs, a rich and fully articulated discussion and certainly the high point of the entire Talmud for this pericope. Unit IV then raises a secondary problem, essentially going over familiar materials from an unfamiliar perspective, and unit V is a distinct treatment of essentially the same issues. In all, the discourse is consistent and pointed.

9:4 [In Leiden MS and *editio princeps:* 9:6]

[A]   *[If] he intended to kill a beast and killed a man,*

[B]   *a gentile and killed an Israelite,*

[C]   *an untimely birth and killed an offspring that was viable,*

[D]   *he is exempt.*

[E]   *[If] he intended to hit him on his loins with a blow that was not sufficient to kill him when it struck his loins, but it went and hit his heart, and there was sufficient force in that blow to kill him when it struck his heart, and he died,*

[F]   *he is exempt.*

[G]   *[If] he intended to hit him on his heart, and there was in that blow sufficient force to kill when it struck his heart, and it went and hit him on his loins, and there was not sufficient force in that blow to kill him when it struck his loins, but he died,*

[H]   *he is exempt.*

[I]   *[If] he intended to hit a large person, and there was not sufficient force in that blow to kill a large person, but it went and hit a small person, and there was sufficient force in that blow to kill a small person, and he died,*

[J]   *he is exempt.*

[K]   *[If] he intended to hit a small person, and there was in that blow sufficient force to kill a small person, and it went and struck the large person, and there was not sufficient force in that blow to kill the large person, but he died,*

[L]   *he is exempt.*

[M]   *But: [if] he intended to hit him on the loins, and there was sufficient force in the blow to kill him when it struck his loins, and it went and hit him on his heart and he died,*

[N]   *he is liable.*

[O]   *[If] he intended to hit a large person, and there was in that blow sufficient force to kill the large person, and it went and hit a small person and he died,*

[P]   *he is liable.*

[Q]   *R. Simeon says, "Even if he intended to kill this party, and he actually killed some other party, he is exempt."*

[I.A]   Hezekiah raised the question: "If one threw a stone, and it was sufficient to kill, and it killed one person, and [also] broke the pots of someone else—

[B]   "[in this case, what is the law]? [Do we say that] in this case Scripture made the decree [that one is exempt from paying compensation, if he is liable to the death penalty, only when the compensation is owing to the same person whom one has murdered? But if one owes compensation to one party and has murdered another in the same action, he still will owe compensation for the one and pay the death penalty on account of the other].

[C]   "[Or do we say that] in this case [in which the death penalty is on one person's account, the compensation on another's,] Scripture made no such decree?"

[D]   Hezekiah raised the question: "If one threw a stone, and it was not sufficient in size to kill someone, but it killed this one, and it also broke the pots belonging to another—

[E]   "[as above,'] do we say that in this case Scripture made the decree [that one is exempt, as stated], but in that case, Scripture did not make such a decree?"

[II.A]   [With reference to M. 9:4Q, Simeon's statement,] said R. Simeon, "Members of the household of Rabbi taught as follows: *Even if he intended to kill this party, and he actually killed some other party, he is exempt" [as at M. 9:4Q].*

[B]   And the view of the members of Rabbi's household accords with that which R. Nathan said, for it was taught in the name of R. Nathan, "If one was standing at the side of a group of people [27b] and said, 'One of them I plan to kill,' even if he intended to kill this party, and he actually killed some other party, he is exempt."

Hezekiah's questions, **I**, are not answered. What is accomplished is to link the present discourse with the one at M. 9:3, that is, the basic theory that Scripture has made a rule which logic would not have produced is tested once more. Unit **II** provides others who take the view of Mishnah's Simeon.

9:5 [In Leiden MS and *editio princeps*: 9:7]

[A]   *A murderer who was mixed up with others—all of them are exempt.*

[B]   *R. Judah says, "They put them all in prison."*

[C]   *All those who are liable to death who were mixed up with one another are judged [to be punished] by the more lenient mode of execution.*

[D]   *[If] those to be stoned were confused with those to be burned—*

[E]   *R. Simeon says, "They are judged [to be executed] by stoning, for burning is the more severe of the two modes of execution."*

[F]   *And sages say, "They are adjudged [to be executed] by burn-*
       ing, for stoning is the more severe mode of execution of the
       two."

[G]   *Said to them R. Simeon, "If burning were not the more severe,*
       it would not have been assigned to the daughter of a priest who
       committed adultery."

[H]   *They said to him, "If stoning were not the more severe of the*
       two, it would not have been assigned to the blasphemer and to
       the one who performs an act of service for idolatry."

[I]   *Those who are to be decapitated who were confused with those*
       who are to be strangled—

[J]   *R. Simeon says, "They are killed with the sword."*

[K]   *And sages say, "They are killed by strangling."*

[I.A] Said R. Yohanan, "The Mishnah [at M. 9:5A speaks of a case
       in which] a murderer was mixed up with blameless people."

[B]   R. Simeon b. Laqish said, "The Mishnah [at M. 9:5A] speaks
       of a case in which a person accused of murder whose trial was
       not finished was confused with a murderer who had been con-
       victed. [That accounts for Judah's view, M. 9:5B, J.]"

[C]   Samuel said, "The Mishnah speaks of a case in which an ox
       sentenced to be stoned was confused with other oxen."

[D]   If the Mishnah speaks of a case in which an ox sentenced to be
       stoned was confused with other oxen, in such a case do we say,
       They put them all in prison?

[II.A] R. Simeon says, "Burning is a more severe mode of execution
       than stoning."

[B]   And rabbis say, "Stoning is a more severe mode of execution
       than burning" [M. 9:5E–F].

[C]   R. Simeon says, "Strangulation is a more severe mode of exe-
       cution than decapitation."

[D]   And rabbis say, "Decapitation is a more severe mode of execu-
       tion than strangulation" [M. 9:5I–K].

Unit **I** interprets M. 9:5A–B, and unit **II** simply restates what
is clear at M. 9:5E–K.

9:6 [In Leiden MS and *editio princeps:* 9:9]

[A]   *He who is declared liable to be put to death through two differ-*
ent modes of execution at the hands of a court is judged [to be
executed] by the more severe.

[B]   *[If] he committed a transgression which is subject to the death*
penalty on two separate counts, he is judged on account of the
more severe.

[C]   *R. Yosé says, "He is judged by the penalty which first applies*
to what he has done."

[D]   *He who was flogged [and did the same deed] and was flogged*
again—

[E]   *[if he did it yet a third time] the court puts him in prison and*
feeds him barley until his belly explodes.

[F]   *He who kills someone not before witnesses—they put him in*
prison and feed him "the bread of adversity and the water of
affliction" (Is. 30:20).

[I.A]   There we have learned: *R. Yosé says, "He is judged by the*
penalty which first applies to what he has done [M. 9:6C].

[B]   **"How so?**

[C]   **"He who has sexual relations with his mother-in-law, and**
she was married,

[D]   **"[or] she was his mother-in-law and she got married—**

[E]   **"he is put to death through burning.**

[F]   **"[If] she had been married and afterward became his**
mother-in-law, he is put to death through strangulation" [T.
San. 12:5].

[II.A]   [With reference to M. Ker. 3:6C: *R. Yohanan b. Nuri says,*
"He who has sexual relations with his mother-in-law may be li-
able on her account because of the prohibition against having
sexual relations with his mother-in-law, and the mother of his
mother-in-law, and the mother of his father-in-law,] if one is
both his mother-in-law and his daughter-in-law, in Yosé's view,
would he be liable on both counts? [That is, if a man marries a
woman's daughter, and his son marries the woman herself, so
the mother of the daughter is both mother-in-law—by reason of
the man's wife, the daughter—and also daughter-in-law—by

reason of the man's son's wife, the mother, will the man be liable on both counts for having sexual relations with that woman? Now we have a concrete example of the problem.]

[B]   What would be a concrete illustration?

[C]   A man married a woman, and the daughter of the brother of his wife, [= the daughter of the son of his mother-in-law], and the daughter of the sister of his wife [thus the daughter of the daughter of his mother-in-law].

[D]   Then, when he has sexual relations with the old woman [his mother-in-law], he is liable on her account for having sexual relations with his mother-in-law [the mother of his mother-in-law and the mother of his father-in-law].

[E]   Now [reverting to A,] as to his mother-in-law being also his daughter-in-law at one and the same time, what did R. Yosé say in such a case? [Did R. Yosé say that it is in particular in the case of a married woman to which the prohibition against having sexual relations with his mother-in-law applies, but as to his daughter-in-law, subject to a more severe mode of execution, namely, stoning, he concurs that the prohibition of his mother-in-law applies, and he would be subject to stoning?]

[F]   That is, where there is a more severe mode of punishment in a less strict case, what did R. Yosé say?

[G]   If there are two prohibitions applicable at the same time, what did R. Yosé say? [Is the more severe mode of execution applicable here?] [The question is not answered.]

[H]   They say: Just as the question is raised in regard to R. Yosé, so the question is to be raised in regard to R. Ishmael.

[I]   For it has been taught in the name of R. Ishmael: "If a woman was widowed and divorced, rendered profane, acted as a prostitute, and afterward, [a high priest] had sexual relations, he is liable on all counts.

[J]   "If she acted as a prostitute, was profaned, divorced, widowed, and afterward he had sexual relations, he is liable on only one count." [A + I: the high priest is liable for her being a widow, first, then, an added prohibition, her being a divorcée, and so on down. At J she was prohibited at the outset, so was never eligible on the other counts.]

[K]   Now, if she was widowed and divorced at the same time, how
        does R. Ishmael rule in such a case?

[L]   As to a more strict prohibition and a less strict one, what does
        R. Ishmael say in such a case?

[M]   In the case of two prohibitions applicable at the same time,
        how does R. Ishmael rule in such a case? [The question again
        is not answered.]

[III.A] Rab said, "The Mishnah [at M. 9:6F] speaks of a case in
        which the witnesses against the man were inside."

[B]   R. Yosé b. Hanina said, "It speaks of a case in which the man
        is not able to accept the warning."

There may be two counts of culpability on the basis of a single
transgression. M. 9:6A's point is that if one has intercourse
with a married woman and is liable for strangulation, and afterward he has sexual relations with his mother-in-law and is liable for burning, he is judged on the count of burning. If his
mother-in-law had been married, we should have the problem
of B. He then would be tried on the count of the mother-in-
law, which produces the execution by burning, rather than on
the count of the married woman, which produces the penalty
of strangulation. Yosé's clarification requires that the woman
should have passed through several relationships to the lover.
First she was a widow whose daughter he had married, and so
she was his mother-in-law. Afterward she was married. He had
sexual relations with her. He is tried for having sexual relations
with his mother-in-law, thus for burning, since that was the
first aspect in which the woman was prohibited to him. If the
story were reversed, he would be tried under the count of
strangulation for his sexual relations with a married woman.
This brings us to the Talmud. Unit I instances Yosé's position.
What unit II does is raise questions made possible by Yosé's
position. That is, how will Yosé deal with a case of simultane-
ity? Here his stated condition does not apply. The case is
spelled out at A, E–G, and it is repeated, that is, E, F, G. The
same rhetorical pattern is applied to Ishmael. First we have a
case of sequential prohibitions, in which, in the former, the
prohibitions become increasingly severe, so that the woman remains available on one count after being prohibited on the former, and, in the latter, the prohibition at the outset is so severe

that the woman is not available on any other count. Then come the repeated questions, again, with no answer. Why **II**.C–D are inserted I do not know. Unit **III** brings us to the clarification of a case in which there is not adequate testimony against the accused.

9:7 [In Leiden MS and *editio princeps:* 9:11]

[A]   *He who stole a sacred vessel [of the cult (Num. 4:7)], he who curses using the name of an idol, and he who has sexual relations with an Aramaean woman—*

[B]   *zealots beat him up [on the spot (Num. 25:8, 11)].*

[C]   *A priest who performed the rite in a state of uncleanness—*

[D]   *his brothers, the priests, do not bring him to court.*

[E]   *But the young priests take him outside the courtyard and break his head with clubs.*

[F]   *A nonpriest who served in the Temple—*

[G]   *R. Aqiba says, "[He is put to death] by strangling (Num. 18:7)."*

[H]   *And sages say, "[He is put to death] at the hands of Heaven."*

[I.A]   *A sacred vessel* [M. 9:7A] is a flagon.

[B]   R. Judah said, "It is a utensil belonging to the Temple, as you read: '. . . and the flagons for the drink offering' " (Num. 4:7).

[II.A]   *He who curses using the name of an idol,* for example, these Nabataeans, who curse, "May the charm slay you, your master, your provider" [cf. B. San. 81b, Rabbah b. Mari].

[III.A]   *He who has sexual relations with an Aramaean woman—*

[B]   R. Ishmael taught, "This is one who marries a gentile woman and produces children.

[C]   "He thereby brings up from her enemies of the Omnipresent."

[D]   It is written, "When Phinehas the son of Eleazar, son of Aaron the priest, saw" (Num. 25:7).

[E]   What did he see?

[F]   He saw the incident and he remembered the law: *He who has sexual relations with an Aramaean woman—zealots beat him up.*

[G]   It was taught: This is not with the approval of sages.

[H]   Is it possible that Phinehas acted without the approval of sages?

[I]   Said R. Judah bar Pazzi, "They wanted to declare him excommunicated, were it not that the Holy Spirit rested upon him and stated, 'And it shall be to him, and to his descendants after him, the covenant of a perpetual priesthood, because he was jealous for his God, and made atonement for the people of Israel' " (Num. 25:13).

[IV.A]   What is the Scriptural basis for the opinion of rabbis (R. Aqiba) [at M. 9:7H]?

[B]   It is said here [in regard to a false prophet], "He will surely die" (Deut. 13:5).

[C]   And it is said in another context, "Everyone who comes near to the tabernacle of the Lord shall die" (Num.17:13). [Derive the rule governing an ordinary person from Num. 17:13, not from Deut. 13:5, which speaks of a prophet.]

[D]   What is the Scriptural basis for the position of R. Aqiba?

[E]   Here it is said, "He will surely die," and in another context it is said, "The stranger who comes near shall be put to death" (Num. 18:7).

[F]   It is better that the language, "he will die," should impute meaning to the same usage, namely, "he shall die," but let not, "he shall die," impart meaning to the language, "shall be put to death."

The Talmud at units **I**, **II**, and **III** cites and lightly glosses Mishnah. Unit **III** bears a further supplement, illustrating the application of the law. Unit **IV** then takes up the Scriptural foundations for the positions of Mishnah's authorities. In the printed version, **IV**.A–C serve Aqiba, D–F, sages, but these have to be reassigned, as I have done.

11 Yerushalmi Sanhedrin
Chapter Ten

10:1

[A]   [27c] *All Israelites have a share in the world to come,*

[B]   *as it is said, "Your people also shall be all righteous; they shall inherit the land forever, the branch of my planting, the work of my hands, that I may be glorified" (Is. 60:21).*

[C]   *And these are the ones who have no portion in the world to come:*

[D]   *(1) He who says, the resurrection of the dead is a teaching which does not derive from the Torah, (2) and the Torah does not come from Heaven; and (3) an Epicurean.*

[E]   *R. Aqiba says, "Also: He who reads in heretical books,*

[F]   *"and he who whispers over a wound and says, 'I will put none of the diseases upon you which I have put on the Egyptians; for I am the Lord who heals you' " (Ex. 15:26).*

[G]   *Abba Saul says, "Also: He who pronounces the divine Name as it is spelled out."*

[I.A]   **They added to the list of those [who have no portion in the world to come (M. San. 10:1)]:**

[B]   **he who breaks the yoke, violates the covenant, deals arrogantly with the Torah,** *pronounces the Divine Name as it is spelled out (M. 10:1G)—*

[C]   **they have no portion in the world to come [T. San. 12:9].**

[D]   "He who breaks the yoke"—this is he who says, "There is a Torah, but I do not bear it [on me]."

[E] "He who violates the covenant" is he who extends the foreskin [to hide the mark of circumcision].

[F] "He who deals arrogantly with the Torah" is he who says, "The Torah does not come from Heaven."

[G] Now have you not already learned this item: "... and the Torah does not come from Heaven" [M. San. 10:1D(2)]?

[H] R. Haninah of Antonia (*'ntwny*) taught before R. Mana, "This is one who violates the rules of the Torah in public,

[I] "for example, Jehoiakim son of Josiah, king of Judah, and his followers."

[II.A] As to idolatry and fornication,

[B] R. Jonah and R. Yosah—

[C] One of them said, "These are among the lesser violations of the law [which are punished in this world only]."

[D] The other of them said, "They are among the greater violations of the law [which are punished in the world to come]." [This is clarified shortly.]

[E] How shall we interpret this matter?

[F] If it concerns repentance, nothing stands before those who repent.

[G] But this is how we must interpret the matter: concerning one who did not repent and died through extirpation.

[H] If the greater part of his record consisted of honorable deeds, and the smaller part, transgressions, they exact punishment from him [in this world, as at C].

[I] If the smaller part of the transgressions which he has done are of the lesser character, [he is punished] in this world so as to pay him his full and complete reward in the world to come.

[J] If the greater part of his record consisted of transgressions and the lesser part of honorable deeds, they pay him off with the reward of the religious deeds which he has done entirely in this world, so as to exact punishment from him in a whole and complete way in the world to come.

[K]   If the greater part of his record consisted of honorable deeds, he will inherit the Garden of Eden. If the greater part consisted of transgressions, he will inherit Gehenna.

[L]   [If the record] was evenly balanced—

[M]   Said R. Yosé b. Haninah, " '. . . forgives sins . . . ,' is not written here, but rather, '. . . forgives [a] sin' (Num 14:18). That is to say, the Holy One, blessed be he, tears up one bond [recorded] among the transgressions, so that the honorable deeds then will outweigh the others."

[N]   Said R. Eleazar, " 'And that to thee, O Lord, belongs steadfast love. For thou dost requite a man according to his work' (Ps. 62:13). 'His deed' is not written here, but '*like* his deed'—if he has none, you give him one of yours."

[O]   That is the view of R. Eleazar. R. Eleazar said, " '[The Lord passed before him, and proclaimed, The Lord, the Lord, a God merciful and gracious, slow to anger,] and abounding in steadfast love [and faithfulness]' (Ex. 34:6). He tips the scale in favor of mercy."

[P]   R. Jeremiah said R. Samuel bar R. Isaac asked about the following: " 'Righteousness guards him whose way is upright, but sin overthrows the wicked' (Prov. 3:6). 'Misfortune pursues sinners, but prosperity rewards the righteous' (Prov. 13:21). 'Toward the scorner he is scornful, but to the humble he shows favor' (Prov. 3:34). 'He will guard the feet of his faithful ones; but the wicked shall be cut off in darkness; [for not by might shall a man prevail]' (1 Sam. 2:9). 'The wise will inherit honor, but fools get disgrace' (Prov. 3:35).

[Q]   "Now do they build a fence and lock the doors? And thus indeed is the way, that they do build a fence and lock the doors, [as we shall now see that God makes it possible for the righteous to do righteous deeds and confirms the wicked in their way too]."

[R]   R. Jeremiah in the name of R. Samuel bar R. Isaac: "[If] a man keeps himself from transgression once, twice, and three times, from that time forth, the Holy One, blessed be he, keeps him from it."

[S]   What is the Scriptural basis for this statement?

[T]   " 'Behold, God does all these things, twice, three times, with a man' " (Job 33:29).

[U]   Said R. Zeira, "And that is on condition that the man not revert [to his evil deeds]."

[V]   What is the Scriptural basis for this statement?

[W]   " 'A threefold cord is *never* broken' is not written, but rather:

[X]   " '[And though a man might prevail against one who is alone, two will withstand him.] A three fold cord is not quickly broken' " (Qoh. 4:12).

[Y]   For if one lays stress on it, indeed it will snap.

[Z]   R. Huna in the name of R. Abbahu: "The Holy One, blessed be he—before him there is no forgetting, as it were.

[AA] "But in behalf of Israel he turns absentminded."

[BB] What is the Scriptural basis for this statement?

[CC] "[Who is a God like thee,] pardoning iniquity [and passing over transgression for the remnant of his inheritance]?" (Mic. 7:18).

[DD] And so did David say, "Thou didst forgive the iniquity of thy people; thou didst pardon all their sin" (Ps. 85:2).

[III.A] R. Mattia b. Heresh raised the question in session before R. Eleazar b. Azariah, saying to him, "Have you heard the four distinctions among kinds of atonement which R. Ishmael expounded?"

[B]   He said to him, "They are three, outside of repentance."

[C]   One verse in Scripture says, "Return, O faithless children, [says the Lord; for I am your master; I will take you, one from a city and two from a family, and I will bring you to Zion]" (Jer. 3:14).

[D]   And another verse in Scripture says, "For on this day shall atonement be made for you, to cleanse you; [from all your sins you shall be clean before the Lord]" (Lev. 16:30).

[E]   And one verse in Scripture says, "Then I will punish their transgression with the rod and their iniquity with scourges" (Ps. 89:33).

[F] And another verse in Scripture says, "[The Lord of hosts has revealed himself in my ears:] 'Surely this iniquity will not be forgiven you till you die,' [says the Lord God of Hosts]" (Is. 22:14).

[G] [Supply: **R. Ishmael says,**] **"There are four kinds of atonement.**

[H] **"[If] one has violated a positive commandment but repented, he hardly moves from his place before the Holy One, blessed be he, forgives him.**

[I] **"And in this case it is said, 'Return backsliding children. I will heal your backsliding' (Jer. 3:22) [T. Yoma 4:6].**

[J] **"[If] he has violated a negative commandment but repented, repentance suspends the punishment, and the Day of Atonement effects atonement.**

[K] **"And in this case it is said, 'For that day will effect atonement for you' (Lev. 16:30) [T. Yoma 4:7].**

[L] **"[If] he has deliberately violated [a rule for which the punishment is] extirpation or death at the hands of an earthly court, but repented, repentance and the Day of Atonement atone for half [of the punishment], and suffering on other days of the year wipes away the other half.**

[M] **"And in this case it says, 'Then will I visit their transgression with a rod' (Ps. 89:32).**

[N] **"But he through whom the Name of Heaven is profaned deliberately (but who repented)—repentance does not have power to suspend [the punishment], nor the Day of Atonement to atone.**

[O] **"But repentance and the Day of Atonement atone for a third, suffering atones for a third, and death wipes away the sin [27d], with suffering.**

[P] **"And in this case it is said, 'Surely this iniquity shall not be purged from you until you die' " (Is. 22:14) [T. Yoma 4:8].**

[Q] "Thus we learn that death wipes away sin."

[R] Said R. Yohanan, "This is the opinion of R. Eleazar b. Azariah, R. Ishmael, and R. Aqiba.

[S] "But in the view of sages, the scapegoat effects atonement."

[T]   How does it effect atonement?

[U]   R. Zeira said, "Step by step."

[V]   R. Haninah said, "At the end [only]."

[W]   What is the difference between these two views?

[X]   If one died suddenly.

[Y]   In the opinion of R. Zeira, the scapegoat already has effected atonement for him.

[Z]   In the opinion of R. Haninah, the scapegoat has not effected atonement for him.

[AA]   Said R. Hanina, "A Tannaitic teaching supports the position of R. Zeira."

[BB]   **R. Eleazar b. R. Simeon says, "A strict rule applies to the goat which does not apply to the Day of Atonement,**

[CC]   **"and to the Day of Atonement which does not apply to the goat:**

[DD]   **"for the Day of Atonement effects atonement [even if] no goat [is offered].**

[EE]   **"But the goat effects atonement only along with the Day of Atonement [T. Yoma 4:16].**

[FF]   **"A more strict rule applies to the goat:**

[GG]   **"For the goat['s sacrifice takes effect] immediately,**

[HH]   **"but the Day of Atonement [takes effect only] at dusk" [T. Yoma 4:17].**

[II]   Said R. Huna, "I was sitting before R. Jeremiah, and he said, 'Interpret the saying to apply to a case in which they intended to bring yet another goat but did not bring it.' "

[JJ]   Said R. Yosah b. Yosah, "But does the Holy One, blessed be he, not see what is to happen? Let the goat then effect atonement forthwith."

[IV.A] It is written, "Because he has despised the word of the Lord, [and has broken his commandment, that person shall be utterly cut off; his iniquity shall be upon him]" (Num. 15:31).

[B]   I know that this applies only when he despised the teaching of Torah [entirely].

[C]   How do I know that [this applies] if he denied even a single word of Scripture, a single verse of Targum, a single argument *a fortiori?*

[D]   Scripture says, "[Because he has despised the word of the Lord,] and has broken his commandment, [that person shall be utterly cut off; his iniquity shall be upon him]" (Num. 15:31).

[E]   As to a single verse of Scripture: "[The sons of Lotan were Hori and Heman;] and Lotan's sister was Timna" (Gen. 36:22).

[F]   As to a single verse of Targum: "Laban called it Jegarsahadutha: [but Jacob called it Galeed]" (Gen. 31:47).

[G]   As to a single argument *a fortiori:* "If Cain is avenged sevenfold, [truly Lamech seventy-sevenfold]" (Gen. 4:24).

[H]   Another interpretation: "For he has despised the word of the Lord" (Num. 15:31)—this refers to one who makes mention of teachings of Torah in a filthy place.

[I]   This teaching is illustrated in the following: R. Ila and the associates were sitting before an inn at evening [so not realizing where they were]. They said, "What is the law as to expressing a teaching of Torah?"

[J]   They said, "Now, since if it were day, we should see what is before us, but under these conditions, it is forbidden."

[V.A]   Bar Kappara said, "Ahaz and all of the evil kings of Israel have no portion in the world to come."

[B]   What is the Scriptural basis for this statement?

[C]   "[All of them are hot as an oven, and they devour their rulers.] All their kings have fallen; and none of them calls upon me" (Hos. 7:7).

[D]   They objected to him, "And lo, he is numbered in the era of the kings:

[E]   " '[The vision of Isaiah the son of Amoz, which he saw concerning Judah and Jerusalem] in the days of Uzziah, Jotham, Ahaz and Hezekiah, kings of Judah' " (Is. 1:1).

[F]   He said to them, "Because he was subject to shame."

[G]   What sort of shame applied to him?

[H] R. Aha in the name of R. Eleazar, R. Yosé in the name of R. Joshua b. Levi: "You find that when the prophet came to indict him, he fled to an unclean place and hid his face in an unclean place, as if to say that the Presence of God does not dwell in an unclean place."

[I] This is in line with that which is written: "And the Lord said to Isaiah, 'Go forth to meet Ahaz, you and Shear-jashub your son, at the end of the conduit of the upper pool on the highway to the Fuller's Field' " (Is. 7:3).

[J] Do not read "The Fuller's (KWBS) Field" but "The Field of the one who hides (KWBŠ) his face," for he hid his face and fled from him.

[K] Lo, how is this so?

[L] When the prophet came to indict him, he fled to an unclean place and hid his face in an unclean place.

[M] R. Judah says, "It was because he was punished through the suffering of his firstborn son."

[N] What is the Scriptural basis for this statement?

[O] "And Zichri, a mighty man of Ephraim, slew [Maaseiah the king's son and Azrikam the commander of the palace and Elkanah the next in authority to the king]" (2 Chron. 28:7).

[P] R. Hoshaiah the Great said, "It was because his father [Jotham b. Uzziah] was a righteous man."

[Q] As to Manassah, was his father not a righteous man?

[R] Manassah's father was a righteous man, but his son was evil.

[S] And Hezekiah—his father was an evil man, and his son was evil.

[T] For Hezekiah says, " 'Lo, it was for my welfare that I had great bitterness; [but thou hast held back my life from the pit of destruction, for thou hast cast all my sins behind my back]' " (Is. 38:17).

[U] "It was bitter for me on the count of my predecessor, Ahaz, and it was bitter for me on the count of my successor, Manassah."

[V] As to Ahaz, his father was a righteous man and his son was a righteous man.

[W]   This is in line with the following verse of Scripture:

[X]   "Be assured, an evil man will not go unpunished, but those who are righteous will be delivered" (Prov. 11:21).

[Y]   "He who is righteous" is not written, but rather, "Those who are righteous will be delivered."

[Z]   "He who is located between two righteous men [Jotham and Hezekiah] will be delivered."

[AA] Another interpretation as to, "Be assured, an evil man will not go unpunished."

[BB] Said R. Phineas, "This refers to him who does a righteous deed and wants to take the reward for it right away."

[CC] Said R. Simon, "It is like a man who says, 'Here is the sack, here is the *sela*, here is the *seah* measure—get up and measure out [wheat].' "

[DD] And you should know that that is the case, for lo, the fathers of the world, if they had wanted to take the reward for the commandments which they did in this world—how would the merit of their deeds have remained for their children after them?

[EE] That is the meaning of that which Moses said to Israel, "Then I will remember my covenant with Jacob, [and I will remember my covenant with Isaac and my covenant with Abraham, and I will remember the land]" (Lev. 26:42).

[VI.A] How long did the merit of the patriarchs endure [to protect Israel]?

[B]   R. Tanhuma said in the name of R. Hiyya the Great, Bar Nahman stated in the name of R. Berekiah, R. Helbo in the name of R. Ba bar Zabeda: "Down to Joahaz."

[C]   "But the Lord was gracious to them and had compassion on them, [because of his covenant with Abraham, Isaac, and Jacob, and would not destroy them; nor has he cast them from his presence] until now" (2 Kings 13:23).

[D]   "Up to that time the merit of the patriarchs endured."

[E]   Samuel said, "Down to Hosea."

[F]   "*Now* I will uncover her lewdness in the sight of her lovers, and no man shall rescue her out of my hand" (Hos. 2:12).

[G]   "Now 'man' can refer only to Abraham, as you say, 'Now then
restore the man's wife; for he is a prophet, [and he will pray
for you, and you shall live. But if you do not restore her, know
that you will surely die, you, and all that are yours]' (Gen.
20:7).

[H]   "And 'man' can refer only to Isaac, as you say, '[Rebekah said
to the servant,] "Who is the man yonder, walking in the field
to meet us?" [The servant said, "It is my master." So she took
her veil and covered herself]' (Gen. 24:65).

[I]   "And 'man' can refer only to Jacob, as you say, '[When the
boys grew up, Esau was a skilful hunter, a man of the field,]
while Jacob was a quiet man, [dwelling in tents]' " (Gen.
25:27).

[J]   R. Joshua b. Levi said, "It was down to Elijah."

[K]   "And at the time of the offering of the oblation, Elijah the
prophet came near and said, 'O Lord, God of Abraham, Isaac,
and Israel, let it be known this day that thou art God in Israel,
and that I am thy servant, [and that I have done all these
things at thy word]' " (1 Kings 18:36).

[L]   R. Yudan said, "It was down to Hezekiah."

[M]   "Of the increase of his government and of peace there will be
no end, [upon the throne of David, and over his kingdom, to
establish it, and to uphold it with justice and with righteousness from this time forth and for evermore. The zeal of the
Lord of hosts will do this]" (Is. 9:6).

[N]   Said R. Aha, "The merit of the patriarchs endures forever [to
protect Israel]."

[O]   "For the Lord your God is a merciful God; [he will not fail
you or destroy you or forget the covenant with your fathers
which he swore to them]" (Deut. 4:31).

[P]   This teaches that the covenant is made with the tribes.

[Q]   R. Yudan bar Hanan in the name of R. Berekiah: "Said the
Holy One, blessed be he, to Israel, "My children, if you see
the merit of the patriarchs declining, and the merit of the matriarchs growing feeble, go and cleave unto the trait of steadfast
love.' "

[R]   What is the Scriptural basis for this statement?

[S]   "For the mountains may depart and the hills be removed, [but my steadfast love shall not depart from you, and my covenant of peace shall not be removed, says the Lord, who has compassion on you]" (Is. 54:10).

[T]   "For the mountains may depart"—this refers to the merit of the patriarchs.

[U]   "And the hills be removed"—this refers to the merit of the matriarchs.

[V]   Henceforth: "But my steadfast love shall not depart from you, and my covenant of peace shall not be removed, says the Lord, who has compassion on you."

[VII.A]   *An Epicurean [M. San. 10:1D(3)].*

[B]   R. Yohanan and R. Eleazar—

[C]   One said, "It is a priest who said, 'Now is *that* a scribe?!' "

[D]   The other said, "It is a priest who said, 'Now are *those* rabbis?!' "

[E]   R. Eleazar and R. Samuel bar Nahman—

[F]   One said, "It [unbelief] is comparable to a pile of stones. Once one of them shifts, all of them tumble down."

[G]   And the other said, "It is comparable to a storehouse full of straw. Even though you take out all of the straw which is in the storehouse, there still is straw which eventually will weaken the walls."

[H]   Rab said, "Korach was very rich. [The location of] Pharaoh's treasures was revealed to him, between Migdol and the sea." [This item breaks off here.]

[I]   Rab said, "Korach was an Epicurean. What did he do? He went and made a prayer shawl which was entirely purple [although the law is that only the fringe was to be purple]."

[J]   He went to Moses, saying to him, "Moses, our rabbi: A prayer shawl which is entirely purple, what is the law as to its being liable to show fringes?"

[K]   He said to him, "It is liable, for it is written, 'You shall make yourself tassels [on the four corners of your cloak with which you cover yourself]' " (Deut. 22:12).

[L]   [Korach continued,] "A house which is entirely filled with holy books, what is the law as to its being liable for a *mezuzah* [containing sacred scripture, on the doorpost]?"

[M]   He said to him, "It is liable for a *mezuzah*, for it is written, 'And you shall write them on the doorposts of your house [and upon your gates]' " (Deut. 6:9).

[N]   He said to him, "A bright spot the size of a bean—what is the law [as to whether it is a sign of uncleanness in line with Lev. 13:2ff.]?"

[O]   He said to him, "It is a sign of uncleanness."

[P]   "And if it spread over the whole of the man's body?"

[Q]   He said to him, "It is a sign of cleanness."

[R]   [28a] At that moment Korach said, "The Torah does not come from Heaven, Moses is no prophet, and Aaron is not a high priest."

[S]   Then did Moses say, "Lord of all worlds, if from creation the earth was formed with a mouth, well and good, and if not, then make it now!"

[T]   "But if the Lord creates [something new, and the ground opens its mouth, and swallows them up, with all that belongs to them, and they go down alive to Sheol, then you shall know that these men have despised the Lord]" (Num. 16:30).

[U]   Said R. Simeon b. Laqish, "Three denied their prophetic gift on account of the baseness [with which they were treated].

[V]   "And these are they: Moses, Elijah, and Micha."

[W]   Moses said, "If these men die the common death of all men, [or if they are visited by the fate of all men, then the Lord has not sent me]" (Num. 16:29).

[X]   Elijah said, "Answer me, O Lord, answer me, [that this people may know that thou, O Lord, art God, and that thou hast turned their hearts back]" (1 Kings 18:37).

[Y]   Micah said, "[And Micaiah said,] 'If you return in peace, the Lord has not spoken by me.' [And he said, 'Hear, all you peoples!']" (1 Kings 22:28).

[Z] "So they and all that belonged to them went down alive into Sheol; [and the earth closed over them, and they perished from the midst of the assembly]" (Num. 16:33).

[AA] R. Berekiah in the name of R. Helbo: "Even the mention of their names flew off the pages of the record books [of bonds and documents] containing them."

[BB] Said R. Yosé bar Haninah, "Even a needle belonging to them which had been lent to an Israelite by them was swallowed up with them,

[CC] "as it is written, 'So they and all that belonged to them went down alive into Sheol' " (Num. 16:33).

[DD] And who prayed in their behalf?

[EE] R. Samuel bar Nahman said, "Moses prayed in their behalf: 'Let Reuben live and not die, [nor let his men be few]' " (Deut. 33:6).

[FF] R. Joshua b. Levi said, "Hannah prayed in their behalf."

[GG] That indeed is the view of R. Joshua b. Levi, for R. Joshua b. Levi said in the name of R. Yosé, "So did the band of Korach sink and fall, until Hannah went and prayed for them.

[HH] "She said, 'The Lord kills and brings to life; he brings down to Sheol and raises up' " (1 Sam. 2:6).

[VIII.A] *R. Aqiba says, "Also: He who reads in heretical books" [M. San. 10:1E].*

[B] These are, for example, the books of Ben Sira and the books of Ben Laanah.

[C] But as to the books of Homer and all books written henceforward—he who reads in them is tantamount to one who [merely] reads a letter.

[D] What is the Scriptural basis for that statement?

[E] "My son beware of anything beyond these. [Of making many books there is no end, and much study is weariness of the flesh]" (Qoh. 12:12).

[F] They are permitted for speculation, they are not permitted for serious work.

[G]   "The sayings of the wise are like goads, [and like nails firmly fixed are the collected sayings which are given by one Shepherd]" (Qoh. 12:11).

[H]   R. Huna said, "Like lovely pearls."

[I]   There they call a pearl "dirah."

[J]   "Like goads" (KDRBNWT)—

[K]   That is, like this ball for little girls (KDR BNWT).

[L]   Just as this ball falls from hand to hand, but in the end comes out in yet some other hand, so *did Moses receive Torah from Sinai and hand it on to Joshua, Joshua to elders, elders to prophets, and prophets handed it on to the men of the Great Assembly [M. Abot. 1:1].*

[M]   Another interpretation: "Like goads"—the same object bears three names, staff, goad, and lead.

[N]   Staff (*marde^ca*), because it shows the way for a cow.

[O]   Goad—because it imparts knowledge to a cow.

[P]   Lead—for it leads the cow to plough so as to give life to its owner.

[Q]   Said R. Hama bar Haninah, "Now if for a cow a man makes a goad, for his impulse to do evil, which leads him from the life of this world and from the life of the world to come, how much the more so [should he make a goad]!"

[R]   "[The sayings of the wise are like goads,] and like nails firmly fixed [are the collected sayings which are given by one Shepherd]" (Qoh. 12:11).

[S]   Now why did he not say, "And like nails permanently knocked in," and "like trees firmly fixed"?

[T]   They chose [to compare] them to iron, and [also] praised them as the [pole] which is planted firmly.

[U]   Another matter: "And like nails firmly fixed"—Now just as in the case of a nail, if you fix it firmly, then, even if fire should come and take the nail away from its place, the place in which it had been located still is to be discerned,

[V]   so against whomever the sages have stretched forth their hands [for the purpose of excommunication], even though they went and drew him near again, in the end he will take what is his from their hands [that is to say, he will ultimately be punished].

[W]   Another matter: "Like nails firmly fixed"—nails is written not with an S but with an Ś *[sin]*. This represents an allusion to the twenty-four [nails used in a sandal], and so to the twenty-four cohorts watches [of the Temple].

[X]   And how many nails may there be in a sandal [for a person to be permitted to go about in it on the Sabbath without violating the law of M. Shab. 6:2: *A man may not go out with a nail-studded sandal*]?

[Y]   Yohanan said, "Five, for the five books of the Torah."

[Z]   Hanina said, "In seven, '[Your bars shall be iron and bronze;] and as your days, so shall your strength be' " (Deut. 33:25).

[AA]   R. Aha expounded in the name of R. Haninah, "Nine."

[BB]   Rabbi would put eleven on this one and thirteen on the other, that is, the number of priestly cohorts.

[CC]   R. Yosé b. Haninah said, "The shoemaker's pegging is not counted as one of the nails."

[DD]   R. Ba bar Zabeda raised the question before R. Zeira: "What is the law as to putting all of them on one shoe?"

[EE]   He said to him, "It is permitted."

[FF]   He said to him, "What is the law as to putting all of them on one sandal?"

[GG]   He said to him, "It is permitted."

[HH]   It was taught: They do not scrape off sandals and old shoes, but they do anoint and wash them off [to make them fit for wear on the Sabbath].

[II]   R. Qerispai in the name of R. Yohanan, a disciple of R. Hiyya the Elder says, "The former authorities would say, 'They do scrape them off.' The later authorities would say, 'They do not scrape them off.' "

[JJ]   They asked Rabbi, who said to them, "They do not scrape them off."

[KK] Said R. Zeira, "[Rabbi was one of the earlier authorities, yet he said they do not scrape them off]. Thus is to be discounted one of the disciples of R. Hiyya the Elder.

[LL] "R. Hiyya bar Ashi said, 'We would be accustomed to sit before Rab and annoint and rinse off [our shoes], but we did not scrape them.' "

[MM] It was taught: A person should not put on new shoes or sandals unless he walked about in them while it was still day [prior to the Sabbath].

[NN] And how much should he have walked about in them?

[OO] The members of the household of Bar Qappara say, "From the schoolhouse of Bar Qappara to the schoolhouse of R. Hoshaiah."

[PP] The men of Sepphoris say, "From the synagogue of the Babylonians to the courtyard of R. Hama bar Haninah."

[QQ] The men of Tiberias say, "From the great school to the shop of R. Hoshaiah."

[RR] It was taught: A person should not anoint shoes and new sandals [on the Sabbath]. A person should not anoint his foot with oil while it is in a shoe, or his foot when it is in a sandal. But he may anoint his foot with oil and then put it into a shoe, or his foot with oil and put it into a sandal. A man may anoint his body with oil and roll about on new leather [on the Sabbath] and need not scruple on that account. **But he should not put [oil] on a marble table in order to roll about it on it [T. Shab. 16:14].** Rabban Simeon b. Gamaliel permits doing so.

[SS] Another interpretation: "And like nails firmly fixed"—when teachings of Torah go forth in a proper way from the mouth of the one who presents them, they are a pleasure to the ones who hear them, like nails firmly fixed.

[TT] And when they go forth in a garbled way, they are as bitter to the ones who hear them as nails.

[IX.A] "Collected sayings"—the reference to "collections" refers only to the *Sanhedrin,*

[B] as you say, "[And the Lord said to Moses,] collect for me seventy men of the elders of Israel, [whom you know to be the elders of the people and officers over them; and bring them to the tent of meeting, and let them take their stand there with you]" (Num. 11:16).

[C]   Another interpretation: "Collected sayings"—sayings which are stated at an assembly.

[D]   Said R. Simeon b. Laqish, "If someone should tell me that [there are traditions concerning] the Book of Chronicles in Babylonia, lo, I should make the trip and bring [them] back from there. And now, if all of our rabbis should gather together, they will be unable to bring them back from there [because they are so numerous and weighty]."

[E]   "Given by one shepherd"—

[F]   Said the Holy One, blessed be he, "If you hear a teaching from an Israelite minor, and it gave pleasure to you, let it not be in your sight as if one has heard it from a minor, but as if one has heard it from an adult,

[G]   "and let it not be as if one has heard it from an adult, but as if one has heard it from a sage,

[H]   "and let it not be as if one has heard it from a sage, but as if one has heard it from a prophet,

[I]   "and let it not be as if one has heard it from a prophet, but as if one has heard it from the shepherd,

[J]   "and there is as a shepherd only Moses, in line with the following passage: 'Then he remembered the days of old, of Moses his servant. Where is he who brought out of the sea the shepherds of his flock? Where is he who put in the midst of them his holy Spirit?' (Is. 63:11).

[K]   "It is not as if one has heard it from the shepherd but as if one has heard it from the Almighty."

[L]   "Given by one Shepherd"—and there is only One who is the Holy One, blessed be he, in line with that which you read in Scripture: "Hear, O Israel: the Lord our God is one Lord" (Deut. 6:4).

[X.A]   *He who whispers over a wound and says, "I will put none of the diseases upon you which [28b] I have put on the Egyptians; for I am the Lord who heals you" (Ex. 15:26).*

[B]   Rab said, "But this [statement is prohibited] only if the one who says it then spits."

[C]   R. Joshua b. Levi said, "Even if one has said, 'When a man has on the skin of his body a swelling or an eruption or a spot, and it turns into a leprous disease on the skin of his body' (Lev. 13:2), and then has spat—he has no portion in the world to come."

[**XI**.A]   *Abba Saul says, "Also: he who pronounces the divine Name as it is spelled out" [M. San. 10:1G].*

[B]   R. Mana said, "For example, the Cutheans, who take an oath thereby."

[C]   R. Jacob bar Aha said, "It is written YH[WH] and pronounced AD[onai]."

Unit **I** takes up the exposition of materials closely relevant to Mishnah. The absence of the items at **II**.A requires comment, since, in general, one would have expected those items to be on the list at M. 10:1D. That discussion draws in its wake the matter of atonement and repentance, on which basis, I assume, unit **III** is inserted, nearly whole, and, in its wake, the remainder of unit **III**'s materials. Unit **IV** carries forward the same concern, namely, atonement for sin; but this is in general relevant to M. 10:1D, namely, dishonoring the Torah. Unit **V** is entirely out of the range of M. 10:1, and perhaps would be more appropriately located in the repertoire of materials thematically relevant to M. 10:2. Unit **VI** carries forward a minor theme of unit **V**. Unit **VII** provides a rich repertoire of materials to define the Epicurean, or nonbeliever, using Korach as the example. There are some inserted materials, **VII**.U–Z, but on the whole unit **VII** is unitary and well put together. The same cannot be said of unit **VIII**, because of the elaborate insertion, whole and complete, of **VIII**.W–QQ. Without that insertion, we have a systematic account of the exegesis of Qoh. 12:11–12. None of this has very much to do with the cited lemma of Mishnah. Unit **IX** contains the exegesis of the same verses, but moves on to different elements thereof. Units **X** and **XI**, finally, briefly complement Mishnah as cited. In all we have a vastly expanded anthology, only partly relevant to Mishnah.

10:2

[A] *Three kings and four ordinary folk have no portion in the world to come.*

[B] *Three kings: Jeroboam, Ahab, and Manasseh.*

[C] *R. Judah says, "Manasseh has a portion in the world to come,*

[D] *"since it is said, 'And he prayed to him and he was entreated of him and heard his supplication and brought him again to Jerusalem into his kingdom' " (2 Chron. 33:13).*

[E] *They said to him, "To his kingdom he brought him back, but to the life of the world to come he did not bring him back."*

[F] *Four ordinary folk: Balaam, Doeg, Ahitophel, and Gahazi.*

[I.A] And all of [the three kings] invented new kinds of transgression.

[B] Now what did Jeroboam do?

[C] It was because he made two golden calves.

[D] And is it not so that the Israelites had made any number of golden calves [so what was new about this]?

[E] R. Simeon b. Yohai taught, "Thirteen golden calves did the Israelites make, and there was one which was common property for all of them."

[F] What is the Scriptural basis for this statement?

[G] "[And he received the gold at their hand, and fashioned it with a graving tool, and made a molten calf; and they said,] 'These are your gods, O Israel, [who brought you up out of the land of Egypt]' " (Ex. 32:4).

[H] Lo, they were for the twelve tribes.

[I] "[Even when they had made for themselves a molten calf and said,] 'This is your God [who brought you up out of Egypt,' and had committed great blasphemies]" (Neh. 9:18).

[J] [The reference to "this is your god"] indicates the one which was common property for all.

[II.A] Now what did Ahab do?

[B]   It is written, "And as if it had been a light thing for him to walk in the sins of Jeroboam the son of Nebat, [he took for wife Jezebel the daughter of Ethbaal king of the Sidonians, and went and served Baal, and worshipped him]" (1 Kings 16:31).

[C]   And is it not so that the minor peccadilloes of Ahab are like the major crimes of Jeroboam?

[D]   So why was Jeroboam listed first of all?

[E]   It is because he is the one who began first the process of the ruin [of Israel].

[F]   What did Ahab do?

[G]   He would adorn himself every day and get up before Hiel, commander of his army (1 Kings 16:34], and he would say to him, "How much am I worth today?" And he would say to him, "Thus and so." Then he would take the amount [that he was said to be worth] and set it apart for an idol.

[H]   That is in line with the following:

[I]   [Ahab said to Elijah, "Have you found me, O my enemy?" He answered, "I have found you,] because you have sold yourself to do what is evil in the sight of the Lord" (1 Kings 21:20).

[J]   For six months R. Levi would interpret the following verse of Scripture in a negative sense:

[K]   "There was none who sold himself to do what was evil in the sight of the Lord like Ahab, [whom Jezebel his wife incited]" (1 Kings 21:25).

[L]   Then [Ahab] came to him by night and said to him, "What made you take this view, and how have I sinned in your sight? You take account of the beginning of the verse, but you ignore the end of it: 'whom Jezebel his wife incited'!"

[M]   So for six months Levi went and interpreted the matter in a positive way, "There was none who sold himself to do what was evil in the sight of the Lord like Ahab, whom Jezebel his wife incited" (1 Kings 21:25).

[III.A]   It is written, "In his days Hiel of Bethel built Jericho; he laid its foundation at the cost of Abiram his firstborn, and set up its gates at the cost of his youngest son, Segub, [according to the word of the Lord, which he spoke by Joshua the son of Nun]" (1 Kings 16:34).

[B]   Hiel came from Jehoshaphat. Jericho is in the territory of Benjamin.

[C]   But they assign more credit to the one who is creditable, and they assign more blame to the one who is blameworthy.

[D]   And that is in line with the following: "He laid its foundation at the cost of Abiram, his firstborn, and set up its gates at the cost of his youngest son, Segub."

[E]   Now in the case of Abiram, the firstborn, he had none whence to learn, but in the case of Segub, the youngest son, that evil man surely had whence to learn.

[F]   [They did as they did] because they wanted to make money, so the curse fell upon them, and they [the walls and gates] went and trembled, in line with the following verse: "[In his days Hiel of Bethel built Jericho; he laid its foundation at the cost of Abiram his firstborn, and set up its gates at the cost of his youngest son, Segub,] according to the word of the Lord, which he spoke by Joshua the son of Nun" (1 Kings 16:34). [T. San. 14:7–9].

[G]   It is written, "Now Elijah the Tishbite, of Tishbe in Gilead, said to Ahab, 'As the Lord the God of Israel lives, before whom I stand, there shall be neither dew nor rain these years, except by my word' " (1 Kings 17:1).

[H]   Now what has one thing to do with the other [that the matter of Hiel is joined to the matter of the drought]?

[I]   But the Holy One, blessed be he, said to Elijah, "This Hiel is a great man. Go and see him [because his sons have died]."

[J]   He said to him, "I am not going to see him."

[K]   He said to him, "Why?"

[L]   He said to him, "For if I go and they say things which will outrage you, I shall not be able to bear it."

[M]   He said to him, "Then if they say things which outrage me, then whatever you decree against them I shall carry out."

[N]   He came and found them occupied with the following verse: "Joshua laid an oath upon them at that time, saying, 'Cursed before the Lord be the man that rises up and rebuilds this city, Jericho. At the cost of his firstborn shall he lay its foundation,

and at the cost of his youngest son shall he set up its gates' "
(Josh. 6:26).

[O]   He said, "Blessed be the God of the righteous, for he carries
out the words of righteous men."

[P]   Now Ahab was there. Ahab said to him, "Now who is greater
than whom—Moses or Joshua?"

[Q]   They said to him, "Moses."

[R]   He said to him, "In the Torah of Moses it is written, 'Take
heed lest your heart be deceived, and you turn aside and serve
other gods and worship them' (Deut. 11:16).

[S]   "Now what is written thereafter? 'And he will be angry with
you and shut up the heaven that there be no rain' (Deut.
11:16f.).

[T]   "Now I have not left a single idol in the world, which I have
not worshipped. And yet every sort of good and consolation
which there are in the world have come in my generation.

[U]   "Thus what Moses taught has not come about, while what
Joshua taught did come about [in the death of the two sons]."

[V]   Elijah then said to him, "As the Lord God of Israel lives, before whom I stand, there shall not be dew or rain these years,
but according to my word" (1 Kings 17:1).

[W]   When he heard this, he began to cry.

[X]   That is in line with the following verse of Scripture: "And
when Ahab heard those words, he rent his clothes, and put
sackcloth upon his flesh, and lay in sackcloth, and went about
dejectedly" (1 Kings 21:27).

[Y]   How long did he afflict himself? It was in periods of three
hours. [That is to say,] if he was accustomed to eat at three
hours, he ate at six. If it was at six, he ate at nine.

[Z]   "And he went about dejectedly"?

[AA]   What is the meaning of "dejectedly"?

[BB]   R. Joshua b. Levi said, "That he went about barefooted."

[CC]   It is written, "And the word of the Lord came to Elijah the
Tishbite, saying, 'Have you seen how Ahab has humbled himself before me, [I will not bring the evil in his days; but in his

son's days I will bring the evil upon his house]' " (1 Kings 21:28–29).

[DD]   Said the Holy One, blessed be he, to Elijah, "Now see the good lot which I have given in my world. If a man sins before me in much but repents, I accept him back."

[EE]   This is in line with the following verse of Scripture: "Have you seen how Ahab has humbled himself before me" (1 Kings 21:28).

[FF]   Do you see how Ahab has repented?

[GG]   "Because he has humbled himself before me, 'I shall not bring the evil in his days; but in his son's days, I will bring the evil upon his house' " (1 Kings 21:29).

[IV.A]   Now what did Ahaz do?

[B]   It was because he built a throne in the courtyard of the Temple.

[C]   This is in line with the following verse of Scripture: "And on the eighth day of the month they came to the vestibule of the Lord" (2 Chron. 29:17, cited following PM).

[D]   R. Honiah in the name of R. Eleazar: "Why is he called 'Ahaz' [seize]?"

[E]   "Because he seized the synagogues and schools."

[F]   To what is Ahaz to be compared?

[G]   To a king who had a son, who handed him over to a governor. He wanted to kill him. He said, "If I kill him, I shall be declared liable to death. But lo, I'll take his wet-nurse from him, and he'll die on his own."

[H]   So did Ahaz say, "If there are no lambs, there will be no sheep; if there are no sheep, there will be no flock; if there is no flock, there will be no shepherd; if there is no shepherd, there will be no world, if there is no world—as it were. . . ."

[I]   So did Ahaz reckon, saying, "If there are no children, there will be no adults; if there are no adults, there will be no sages; if there are no sages, there will be no prophets; if there are no prophets, there will be no Holy Spirit; if there is no Holy Spirit, there will be no synagogues or schoolhouses—as it were.

... In that case, as it were, the Holy One, blessed be he, will not let his Presence rest upon Israel."

[J]   R. Jacob bar Abayye in the name of R. Aha brings proof of the same proposition from the following verse of Scripture: "I will wait for the Lord, who is hiding his face from the house of Jacob, and I will hope in him" (Is. 8:17).

[K]   There was never a more difficult hour for the world than that hour at which the Holy One, blessed be he, said to Moses, "And I will surely hide my face in that day [on account of all the evil which they have done, because they have turned to other gods]" (Deut. 31:18).

[L]   At that hour: "I will wait for the Lord," for thus did he say to him at Sinai, "[And when many evils and troubles have come upon them, this song shall comfort them as a witness,] for it will live unforgotten in the months of their descendants; [for I know the purposes which they are already forming, before I have brought them into the land that I swore to give]" (Deut. 31:21).

[M]   And to what end?

[N]   "Behold, I and the children whom the Lord has given me [are the signs and the portents in Israel from the Lord of hosts, who dwells on Mount Sinai]" (Is. 8:18).

[O]   Now were they really his children? And were they not his disciples?

[P]   But it teaches that they were as precious to him as his children, so he called them, "My children."

[V.A]   Now what did Manasseh do?

[B]   It is written, "In those days Hezekiah became sick and was at the point of death. [And Isaiah the prophet and son of Amoz came to him, and said to him, 'Thus says the Lord: Set your house in order; for you shall die, you shall not recover]' " (Is. 38:1).

[C]   "For [28c] you shall die, and you shall not recover"—

[D]   "You shall die" in this world, "And you shall not recover" in the world to come.

[E]   He said to him, "Why?"

[F]   He said to him, "Because you did not want to raise up children."

[G]   He said to him, "And why did you not want to raise up children?"

[H]   He said to him, "Because I saw that I would produce an evil son. On that account, I did not want to raise up children."

[I]   He said to him, "Take my daughter. Perhaps on my account and on your account she will produce a good man."

[J]   Even so, only a bad person came forth.

[K]   That is in line with the following verse of Scripture: "The knaveries of the knave are evil; [he devises wicked devices to ruin the poor with lying words, even when the plea of the needy is right]" (Is. 32:7).

[L]   He said to him, "I am not going to listen to you. I am going to follow only that which my elder said to me, 'If you see bad dreams or bad visions, seek three things and you will be saved, and these are they: prayer, charity, and repentance.' "

[M]   And three of them are to be derived from a single verse of Scripture:

[N]   "If my people who are called by my name humble themselves, and pray and seek my face, and turn from their wicked ways, then I will hear from heaven, and will forgive their sin and heal their land" (2 Chron. 7:14).

[O]   "Pray"—this refers to prayer.

[P]   "And seek my face"—this refers to charity,

[Q]   as you say, "As for me, I shall behold thy face in righteousness; when I awake, I shall be satisfied with beholding thy form" (Ps. 17:15).

[R]   "And turn from their wicked ways"—this refers to repentance.

[S]   Now if they do these things, what is written concerning them?

[T]   "Then I will hear from heaven and will forgive their sin and heal their land."

[U]   Forthwith, "And he turned . . . ," as it is written, "Then Hezekiah turned his face to the wall, and prayed to the Lord" (Is. 38:2).

[**VI**.A]   To which wall did he turn?

[B]   R. Joshua b. Levi, "It was to the wall of Rahab that he turned: '[Then she let them down by a rope through the window,] for her house was built into the city wall, so that she dwelt in the wall' " (Josh. 2:15).

[C]   He said to him, "Lord of all worlds, Rahab saved two souls for you, and see how many souls you saved for her!"

[D]   That is in line with the following verse which is written: "So the young men who had been spies went in, and brought out Rahab, and her father and mother and brothers and all who belonged to her; and they brought all her kindred, and set them outside the camp of Israel" (Josh. 6:23).

[E]   R. Simeon b. Yohai taught, "Even if there were in her families two hundred men, who went and married into two hundred families, all the two hundred families were saved on her account.

[F]   "Now my forefathers, who brought near to you all these proselytes, how much the more so should you give me back my life!"

[G]   R. Samuel b. Nahman said, "He looked toward the wall of the Shunamite: 'Let us make a small roof chamber with walls, and put there for him a bed, a table, a chair, and a lamp, [so that whenever he comes to us, he can go in there]' " (2 Kings 4:10).

[H]   He said to him, "Lord of all worlds, the Shunamite made a single wall for Elisha, and you saved the life of her son. My forefathers, who made all this glory for you—how much the more so that you should give me back my life?"

[I]   R. Hinnena bar Papa said, "It was to the walls of the Temple that he turned."

[J]   "By setting their threshold against my threshold and their doorpost against my doorpost, with only a wall between me and them. [They have defiled my holy name by their abominations which they have committed, so I have consumed them in my anger]" (Ez. 43:8).

[K]   "They were great men and could not go up and pray whenever at any time, and they would pray in their houses. The Holy One, blessed be he, credited it to them as if they had prayed in

the Temple. Now my fathers, who gave such glory to you—
how much the more so that you should give me back my life."

[L]   And rabbis say, "It was to the walls of his heart that he
turned."

[M]   "My anguish, my anguish! I writhe in pain! Oh, the walls of
my heart! My heart is beating wildly; I cannot keep silent; [for
I hear the sound of the trumpet, the alarm of war]" (Jer. 4:19).

[N]   He said before him, "Lord of all worlds, I have gone over the
two hundred and forty-eight limbs which you have given me,
and I have not found that I ever angered you in any one of
them. How much the more so, then, that my life should be
given back to me?"

[O]   It is written, "Then the word of the Lord came to Isaiah: 'Go
and say to Hezekiah, Thus says the Lord, the God of David
your father: I have heard your prayer, I have seen your tears;
behold I will add fifteen years to your life' " (Is. 38:4–5).

[P]   [Isaiah] said to him, "Thus I've already told him, and how
thus do I say to him?

[Q]   "He is a man occupied with great affairs, and he will not believe me."

[R]   [God] said to him, "He is a very humble man, and he will believe you. And not only so, but as yet the rumor has not yet
gone forth in the city."

[S]   "And before Isaiah had gone out of the middle court, [the
word of the Lord came to him]" (2 Kings 20:4).

[T]   When Manasseh arose, he pursued Isaiah, wanting to kill him.
[Isaiah] fled from before him. He fled to a cedar, which swallowed him up, except for the show fringes [of his cloak], which
revealed where he was.

[U]   They came and told him. He said to them, "Go and cut the
cedar down." They cut the cedar down, and blood showed [in-
dicating that Isaiah had been sawed too].

[V]   "[And also for the innocent blood that he had shed; for he
filled Jerusalem with innocent blood,] and the Lord would not
pardon" (2 Kings 24:4).

[W]   It is on this basis that he has no portion in the world to come.

[VII.A]   [Challenging the view of Judah, M. 10:2C,] And lo, it is written, "[Surely this came upon Judah at the command of the Lord, to remove them out of his sight,] for the sins of Manasseh, [according to all that he had done]" (2 Kings 24:3).

[B]   Shall we say that this was before he repented [so he did inherit the world to come after all]?

[C]   "On account of all the wrath whereby Manasseh had caused him to be wrathful"—

[D]   Shall we say that this was before he repented?

[E]   And lo, it is written, "[And he did not humble himself before the Lord, as Manasseh his father had humbled himself,] but this Amon incurred guilt more and more" (2 Chron. 33:23).

[F]   He did not add [to the sins], he made entirely new [and unprecedented ones].

[G]   And is it not written, "Moreover Manasseh shed very much innocent blood, till he had filled Jerusalem from one end to another, [besides the sin which he made Judah to sin so that they did what was evil in the sight of the Lord]" (2 Kings 21:16).

[H]   Now is it possible for human beings to fill up the whole of Jerusalem with innocent blood from one end to the other?

[I]   But he killed Isaiah, who was equal to Moses, as it is written concerning him, "With him I speak mouth to mouth, [clearly, and not in dark speech; and he beholds the form of the Lord]. [Why then were you not afraid to speak against my servant Moses?]" (Num. 12:8).

[J]   And it is written, "The Lord spoke to Manasseh and his people, but they gave no heed. Therefore the Lord brought upon them the commanders of the army of the king [of Assyria], who took Manasseh with hooks [and bound him with fetters of bronze and brought him to Babylon]" (2 Chron. 33:10–11).

[K]   What is "with hooks"?

[L]   [They took him] with handcuffs.

[M]   Said R. Levi, "They made him a mule of bronze, and they put him in it, and they made a fire under it. When he began to feel pain, he left not a single idol in the world, on the name of which he did not call.

[O]   "When he realized that it did him no good, he said, 'I remember that my father would read to me this verse in the synagogue: "When you are in tribulation, and all these things come upon you in the latter days, you will return to the Lord your God and obey his voice, for the Lord your God is a merciful God; he will not fail you or destroy you or forget the covenant with your fathers which he swore to them" ' (Deut. 4:30–31).

[P]   "Lo, I shall call upon him. If he answers me, well and good, and if not, lo, all ways are the same [and no good]."

[Q]   Now all the ministering angels went and closed the windows, so that the prayer of Manasseh should not reach upward to the Holy One, blessed be he.

[R]   The ministering angels were saying before the Holy One, blessed be he, "Lord of the world, a man who worshipped idols and put up an image in the Temple—are you going to accept him back as a penitent?"

[S]   He said to them, "If I do not accept him back as a penitent, lo, I shall lock the door before all penitents."

[T]   What did the Holy One, blessed be he, do? He made an opening [through the heavens] under his throne of glory and listened to his supplication.

[U]   That is in line with the following verse of Scripture: "He prayed to him, and God received his entreaty ('TR) and heard his supplication and brought him again [to Jerusalem into his kingdom]. [Then Manasseh knew that the Lord was God]" (2 Chron. 33:13).

[V]   Said R. Eleazar b. R. Simeon, "In Arabia that they call 'breaking through (ḤTRTH) 'supplication' ('TRTH)."

[W]   "And they brought him again to Jerusalem into his kingdom" (2 Chron. 33:13).

[X]   With what did they bring him back?

[Y]   Samuel bar Buna in the name of R. Aha: "They brought him back with the wind."

[Z]   This is in line with that which you say, "He brings back the wind."

[AA]   "And Manasseh knew that the Lord [28d] was God" (2 Chron. 33:13).

[BB]   At that moment Manasseh said, "There is justice and there is a judge."

[VIII.A]   Now what did the evil Balaam do [to warrant losing his portion in the world to come]?

[B]   It was because he gave advice to Balak son of Zippor on how to cause Israel's downfall by the sword.

[C]   He said to him, "The God of this nation hates fornication. So put up your daughters for fornication, and you will rule over them."

[D]   He said to him, "And will [the Moabites] listen to me [when I tell them to turn their daughters into whores]?"

[E]   He said to him, "Put up your own daughter first, and they will see and then accept what you say to them."

[F]   That is in line with the following verse of Scripture: "[And the name of the Midianite woman who was slain was Cozbi the daughter of Zur,] who was the head of the people of a father's house in Midian" (Num. 25:15).

[G]   What did they do? They built for themselves temples from Beth HaJeshimmon to the Snowy Mountain, and they set in them women selling various kinds of sweets. They put the old lady outside, and the young girl inside.

[H]   Now the Israelites would then eat and drink, and one of them would go out to walk in the marketplace, and he would buy something from a stallkeeper. The old lady then would sell him the thing for whatever it was worth, and the young girl would say, "Come on in and take it for still less." So it was on the first day, the second day, and the third day. And then, she would say to him, "From now on, you belong here. Come on in and choose whatever you like."

[I]   When he came in, [he found there] a flagon of wine, Ammonite wine, which is very strong. And it serves as an aphrodisiac to the body, and its scent was enticing. (Now up to this time the wine of gentiles had not been prohibited for Israelite use by reason of its being libation wine.)

[J]   Now the girl would say to him, "Do you want to drink a cup of wine," and he would reply to her, "Yes." So she gave him a cup of wine, and he drank it.

[K]   When he drank it, the wine would burn in him like the venom of a snake. Then he would say to her, "Surrender yourself [sexually] to me." She would say to him, "Do you want me to 'surrender' myself to you?" And he would say "Yes." Then she took out an image of Peor from her bosom, and she said to him, "Bow down to this, and I'll surrender myself to you." And he would say to her, "Now am I going to bow down to an idol?" And she would say to him, "You don't really bow down to it, but you expose yourself to it."

[L]   This is in line with that which sages have said, "He who exposes himself to Baal Peor—this is the appropriate manner of worshipping it; and he who tosses a stone at Merkolis—this is the appropriate manner of worshipping it."

[M]   [When he came in, he found] there a flagon full of wine, Ammonite wine, which is very strong. And it serves as an aphrodisiac to incite the body to passion, and its scent was enticing. (Now up to this time the wine of gentiles had not been prohibited for Israelite use by reason of its being libation wine.) Now the girl would say to him, "Do you want to drink a cup of wine," and he would reply to her, "Yes." So she gave him a cup of wine, and he drank it. When he drank it, the wine would burn in him like the venom of a snake. Then he would say to her, "Surrender yourself to me."

[N]   And she would say to him, "Separate yourself from the Torah of Moses, and I shall 'surrender' myself to you."

[O]   That is in line with the following verse of Scripture: "[Like grapes in the wilderness, I found Israel. Like the first fruits on the fig tree, in its first season, I saw your fathers.] But they came to Baal Peor, and consecrated themselves to Baal, and became detestable like the thing they loved" (Hos. 9:10).

[P]   They became detested until they became detestable to their Father who is in Heaven.

[Q]   Said R. Eleazar, "Just as this nail—one cannot separate it from the door without a piece of wood, so it is not possible to separate from Peor without [the loss of] souls."

[R]   M'SH B: Subetah from Ulam hired out his ass to a gentile
       woman, [to take her] to bow down to Peor. When they got to
       Peor's house, she said to him, "Wait for me here, while I go in
       and worship to Peor." Shen she came out, he said to her,
       "Wait for me here, until I go in and do just what you did."
       What did he do? He went in and took a shit, and he wiped his
       ass on the nose of Peor. Everyone present praised him, and
       said to him, "No one ever did it the way this one did it!"

[S]   M'SH B: Menahem of Gypta Arye was moving jugs. The chief
       of Peor came to him by night. What did he do? He took the
       spit and stood up against him, and [the chief] fled from him.
       He came to him the next night. Menahem said to him, "How
       are you going to curse me? You are afraid of me!" And he said
       to him, "I'm not going to curse you anymore."

[T]   M'SH B: An officer came from overseas to bow down to Peor.
       He said to them, "Bring me an ox, a ram, a sheep, to worship
       Peor." They said to him, "You don't have to go to all that
       trouble. All you have to do is expose yourself to it." What did
       he do? He called up his troops, who beat them and broke their
       skulls with staves, and he said to them, "Woe for you and for
       this big 'mistake' of yours!"

[U]   It is written: "And the Lord was angry at Israel, and the Lord
       said to Moses, 'Take all the chiefs of the people, and hang
       them in the sun before the Lord, [that the fierce anger of the
       Lord may turn away from Israel]' " (Num. 25:4).

[V]   He said to him, "Appoint their heads as judges over them, and
       let them put the sinners to death toward the sun."

[W]   This is in line with the following verse of Scripture: "And
       Moses said to the judges of Israel, 'Everyone of you slay his
       men who have yoked themselves to Baal Peor' " (Num. 25:5).

[X]   And how many are the judges of Israel? They are 78,600 [cal-
       culation as follows:]

[Y]   Heads of thousands are six hundred.

[Z]   Heads of hundreds are six thousand.

[AA]   Heads of troops of fifty are twelve thousand.

[BB]   Heads of troops of ten are sixty thousand.

[CC]   It thus turns out that the judges of Israel [heads of all units] are 78,600.

[DD]   He said to them, "Each one of you kill two. So 157,200 turned out to be put to death.

[EE]   "And behold, one of the people of Israel came and brought a Midianite woman to his family, in the sight of Moses [and in the sight of the whole congregation of the people of Israel, while they were weeping at the door of the tent of meeting]" (Num. 25:6).

[FF]   What is the meaning of, "In the sight of Moses"?

[GG]   It was like someone who says, "Here—right in your eye!"

[HH]   He said [to Moses] "Is your Zipporah not Midianite, and are not her feet cloven? [Is she not clean for you, fit to be your wife?] This one [Zipporah] is clean but that one [my woman] is unclean?!"

[II]   Now Phineas was there. He said, "Is there no man here who will kill him even at the expense of his life?"

[JJ]   "Where are the lions?"

[KK]   "Judah is a lion's whelp; [from the prey, my son, you have gone up. He stooped down, he couched as a lion, and as a lioness who dares to rouse him?]" (Gen. 49:9).

[LL]   "[And of Dan he said,] 'Dan is a lion's whelp, [that leaps forth from Bashan]' " (Deut. 33:22).

[MM]   "Benjamin is a ravenous wolf, [in the morning devouring the prey, and at even dividing the spoil]" (Gen. 49:27).

[NN]   When he [Phineas] saw that no Israelite did a thing, forthwith, Phineas stood up from his Sanhedrin seat and took a spear in his hand and put the iron head of it under his *fascia*. He leaned on the wood [of the spear so concealing its purpose] until he reached his door. When he came to his door, [the occupant] said to him, "Whence and whither, Phineas?"

[OO]   He said to them, "Do you not agree with me that the tribe of Levi is near the tribe of Simeon under all circumstances?"

[PP]   They said to him, "Leave him [me] alone. Maybe the separatists have permitted this matter [after all]!"

[QQ]   When he got in, the Holy One, blessed be he, did six miracles.

[RR] The first miracle: It is the usual way [after intercourse] to separate from one another, but the angel of the Lord kept them stuck together.

[SS] The second miracle: He aimed the spear directly into the belly of the woman, so that the man's penis would stick out of her belly.

[TT] And this was on account of the nitpickers, so that they should not go around saying, "He too shouldered his way in and did what came naturally."

[UU] The third miracle: The angel sealed their lips, so that they could not cry out.

[VV] The fourth miracle: They did not slip off the spear but remained in place. [Phineas lifted them up on the spear.]

[WW] The fifth miracle: The angel raised the lintel [so that he could carry the two of them on the spear], so that both of them could go out on his shoulders.

[XX] The sixth miracle: When he went out and saw the plague [29a] afflicting the people, what did he do? He threw them down to the ground and stood and prayed.

[YY] This is in line with the following verse of Scripture: "Then Phinehas stood up and interposed, and the plague was stayed" (Ps. 106:30).

[ZZ] Now when the Israelites came to take vengeance against Midian, they found Balaam ben Beor there.

[AAA] Now what had he come to do?

[BBB] He had come to collect his salary for the twenty-four thousand Israelites who had died in Shittim on his account.

[CCC] Phineas said to him, "You did not do what you said, and you also did not do Balak's bidding.

[DDD] "You did not do what you said, for He said to you, 'You shall not go with the messengers of Balak,' but you went along with them.

[EEE] "And you did not do what Balak said, for he said to you, 'Go and curse Israel,' but you blessed them.

[FFF] "So, for my part, I'm not going to withhold your salary!"

[GGG] That is in line with that which is written in Scripture: "Balaam also, the son of Beor, the soothsayer, the people of Israel killed with the sword among the rest of their slain" (Josh. 13:22).

[HHH] What is the meaning of "among the rest of their slain"?

[III] That he was equal to all the other slain put together.

[JJJ] Another interpretation: "Among the rest of their slain"—Just as their slain no longer have substance, so he was of no substance.

[KKK] Another interpretation: "Among the rest of their slain"—for he hovered [in the air] over their slain, and Phineas showed him the [priestly] frontlet, and he fell down [to earth].

[LLL] Another interpretation: "Among the rest of their slain"—this teaches that the Israelites paid him his salary in full and did not hold it back.

[IX.A] Doeg was a great man in learning of Torah.

[B] The Israelites came and asked David, "In regard to the show-bread, what is the law as to its overriding the restrictions of the Sabbath?"

[C] He said to them, "Arranging it overrides the restrictions of the Sabbath, but kneading the dough and cutting it out do not override the restrictions of the Sabbath."

[D] Now Doeg was there, and he said, "Who is this one who comes to teach in my presence?"

[E] They told him, "It is David, son of Jesse."

[F] Forthwith, he went and gave advice to Saul, king of Israel, to kill Nob, the city of the priests.

[G] This is in line with the following statement of Scripture: "And the king said to the guard who stood about him, 'Turn and kill the priests of the Lord; because their hand is also with David, [and they knew that he had fled, and did not disclose it to me].' [But the servants of the king would not put forth their hand to fall upon the priests of the Lord]" (1 Sam. 22:17). Who were they.

[H] Said R. Samuel bar R. Isaac, "They were Abner and Amasa."

[I]   They said to him, "Now do you have any claim against us except for this belt and this cloak? Lo, they are thrown down before you!"

[J]   "[And the king said to the guard who stood about him, 'Turn and kill the priests of the Lord; because their hand is also with David, and they knew that he had fled, and did not disclose it to me.'] But the servants of the king would not put forth their hands to fall upon the priests of the Lord" (1 Sam. 22:17).

[K]   "And the king said to Doeg . . ."

[L]   Said R. Judah bar Pazzi, "It is written, 'to Du-eg' (DWYYG)."

[M]   He said to him, "You are trapped like a fish, you have done a great thing.

[N]   "[Then the king said to Doeg], 'You turn and fall upon the priests.' And Doeg the Edomite turned and fell upon the priests, [and he killed that day eighty-five persons who wore the linen ephod]" (1 Sam. 22:18).

[O]   Now did not R. Hiyya teach, "They do not appoint two high priests at the same time"? [How could there be many?]

[P]   But this teaches that all of them were worthy of the high priests.

[Q]   How was he [shown to be ultimately] set apart?

[R]   R. Haninah and R. Joshua b. Levi—

[S]   One of them said, "Fire burst forth from the house of the Holy of Holies and licked round about him."

[T]   And the other one said, "His old students got together with him, and they were studying, but he forgot [his learning].

[U]   "[This fulfills the verse which says, 'He swallows down riches and vomits them up again; God casts them out of his belly' (Job 20:25). [That was a sign of his excommunication; and the students killed him.]"

[X.A]   Ahithophel was a man mighty in Torah learning.

[B]   It is written, "David again gathered all the chosen men of Israel, thirty thousand. [And David arose and went with all the people who were with him . . . to bring up from there the ark of the Lord]" (2 Sam. 6:1–2).

[C]   R. Berekiah in the name of R. Abba bar Kahana: "Ninety
       thousand elders did David appoint on a single day, but he did
       not appoint Ahithophel among them."

[D]   This is in line with that which is written in Scripture: "David
       again gathered all the chosen men of Israel, thirty thousand.
       . . ." That is, "And he added" means "thirty." And "again"
       means "thirty." The Scripture explicitly speaks of thirty. Lo,
       there are then ninety in all.

[E]   You find that when David came to bear the ark of the covenant
       of the Lord, he did not bear it in accord with the Torah:

[F]   "And they carried the Ark of God on a new cart, [and brought
       it out of the house of Abinadab which was on the hill; and Uz-
       zah and Ahio, the sons of Abinadab, were driving the new
       cart]" (2 Sam. 6:3). [That is, the Torah requires that the
       priests carry it, but they carried it in a cart instead.]

[G]   Now the ark carried the priests on high, but let them fall
       down; the ark carried the priests on high, but let them fall
       down to the ground.

[H]   David sent and brought Ahithophel. He said to him, "Will you
       not tell me what is with this ark, which raises the priests up
       high and casts them down to the ground, raises the priests on
       high and casts them down to the ground?"

[I]   He said to him, "Send and ask those wise men whom you
       appointed!"

[J]   Said David, "One who knows how to make the ark stop and
       does not do so in the end is going to be put to death through
       strangulation."

[K]   He said to him, "Make a sacrifice before [the ark], and it will
       stop."

[L]   This is in line with the following verse which is written in
       Scripture: "And when those who bore the ark of the Lord had
       gone six paces, he sacrificed an ox and a fatling" (2 Sam. 6:13).

[M]   R. Haninah and R. Mana—

[N]   One of them said, "At every step an ox and a fatling, and at
       the end, seven oxen and seven rams."

[O]   And the other said, "At every step seven oxen and seven rams,
       and at the end, an ox and a fatling."

[P]   Said the Holy One, blessed be he, to Ahithophel, "A teaching which children say every day in the school you did not report to him!

[Q]   " 'But to the sons of Kohath he gave none, because they were charged with the care of the holy things *which had to be carried on the shoulder*' (Num. 7:9).

[R]   "And this [to sacrifice] you told him!"

[S]   And so you find that when David came to dig the foundations of the Temple, he dug fifteen hundred cubits and did not reach the nethermost void. In the end he found one clay pot, and he wanted to remove it.

[T]   It said to him, "You cannot do so."

[U]   He said to it, "Why not?"

[V]   It said to him, "For I here am the cover over the great deep."

[W]   He said to it, "And how long have you been here?"

[X]   It said to him, "From the time that I heard the voice of the All-Merciful at Sinai: 'I am the Lord your God, [who brought you out of the land of Egypt, out of the house of bondage]' (Ex. 20:2), the earth shook and trembled.

[Y]   "And I am set here to seal the great deep."

[Z]   Even so, [David] did not listen to it.

[AA]   When he removed the clay pot, the great deep surged upward to flood the world.

[BB]   And Ahithophel was standing there. He said, "Thus will David be strangled [in the flood] and I shall become king."

[CC]   Said David, "He who is a sage, knowing how to stop up the matter, and does not stop it, will in the end be put to death through strangulation."

[DD]   [Ahithophel] said what he said and stopped up [the flood].

[EE]   David began to say a Psalm, "A song of ascents. [In my distress I cry to the Lord, that he may answer me]" (Ps. 120:1).

[FF]   "A song of ascents" (*ma'alot*) is a song for a hundred (*meah*) ascents (*olot*).

[GG]   At every hundred cubits he would say a psalm.

[HH]   Even so, in the end [Ahithophel] was strangled to death.

[II]   Said R. Yosé, "This is in line with what the proverb says: A person has to scruple about a curse of a great master, even if it was for nought."

[JJ]   R. Jeremiah in the name of R. Samuel bar Isaac, "A scroll which Samuel handed over to David did Ahithophel recite by means of the Holy Spirit."

[KK]   What did Ahithophel do?

[LL]   When someone came to him for advice, he would say to him, "Go and do thus and so, and if you don't believe me, then go and ask the Urim and Thummim."

[MM]   And the man would go and ask and find out that indeed that was how matters were.

[NN]   This is in line with that which is written in Scripture: "Now in those days the counsel which Ahithophel gave was as if one consulted [the oracle of God; so was the counsel of Ahithophel esteemed, both by David and by Absalom]" (2 Sam. 16:23).

[OO]   You read "Man"; it is not written thus, for the Scripture could not call him a [mere] man.

[PP]   How was he set apart?

[QQ]   "When Ahithophel saw that his counsel was not followed, he saddled his ass [and went off home to his own city]. [And he set his house in order, and hanged himself; and he died, and was buried in the tomb of his father]" (2 Sam. 17:23).

[RR]   Three things did Ahithophel command his sons, saying to them:

[SS]   "Do not rebel against the royal house of David, for we shall find that the Holy One, blessed be he, shows favor to them even in public.

[TT]   "And do not have business [29b] dealings with someone on whom the hour smiles.

[UU]   "And if the day of Pentecost is bright, sow the best quality of wheat."

[VV]   But they did not know whether it meant "bright" in dew or "bright" in dry heat.

[**XI**.A]   Gehazi was a man powerful in learning of Torah.

[B]   But he had three bad traits: niggardliness, womanizing, and denying the resurrection of the dead.

[C]   Niggardliness: When Elisha was sitting in his learning session, Gehazi would be in session at the door, and his disciples looked to him, and they said, "Gehazi did not enter, so shall we enter?"

[D]   So [Elisha] would be repeating his traditions, but no one derived any benefits from them.

[E]   Once [Gehazi] was separated, what is written there?

[F]   "Now the sons of the prophets said to Elisha, 'See, [the place where we dwell under your charge is too small for us]' " (2 Kings 6:1).

[G]   "It cannot contain the crowd of disciples who are there."

[H]   And he was licentious: for lo, the Shunamite said to her husband, "[And she said to her husband,] 'Behold now, I perceive that this is a holy man of God, who is continuously passing our way' " (2 Kings 4:9).

[I]   Said R. Jonah, "*He* was a holy man—but his disciple was no saint."

[J]   Said R. Abin, "The fact was that [Elisha] never in his life laid eyes on her."

[K]   And rabbis of Caesarea say, "The reason was that he never produced a drop of semen on his garments in his entire life."

[L]   The serving girl of R. Samuel bar R. Isaac said, "I would wash the clothing of my master. In my whole life I never saw any sort of bad thing on the garments of my master."

[M]   It is written, "[And when she came to the mountain to the man of God, she caught hold of his feet.] And Gehazi came to thrust her away. [But the man of God said, 'Let her alone, for she is in bitter distress; and the Lord has hidden it from me, and has not told me]' " (2 Kings 4:27).

[N]   What is the meaning of "to thrust her away"?

[O]   Said R. Yosé b. Hanina, "He put his hand on the cleavage between her breasts."

[P]   Nor did he believe in the resurrection of the dead:

[Q]   You find that when Elisha came to resurrect the son of the Shunamite, he said to him, "[He said to Gehazi,] 'Gird up your loins, and take my staff in your hand, and go. If you meet anyone, do not salute him; and if anyone salutes you, do not reply; [and lay my staff on the face of the child]' " (2 Kings 4:29).

[R]   But he did not do so. Rather, when someone met him, he said to him, "Whence and whither, Gehazi?"

[S]   And he said to him, "*I am going to raise the dead.*"

[T]   And he said to him, "There is none who raises the dead except for the Holy One, blessed be he, as it is written in Scripture concerning him, 'The Lord kills and brings to life; he brings down to Sheol and raises up' " (1 Sam. 2:6).

[U]   He went his way and did nothing whatsoever.

[V]   He returned to [Elisha], who said to him, "I know that if he was asleep, he would not be awakened through you [because you did not carry out my instructions]."

[W]   You find that when Naaman the general of the army of the king of Aram came to Elisha, he came to him on his horse and with his chariot [2 Kings 5:9].

[X]   Said R. Yohanan, " 'With his *horse*' [singular] is written."

[Y]   He wanted to give to him gold and silver, robes and garments, precious jewels and pearls, but he would not accept them from him.

[Z]   This is in line with the following verse of Scripture: "[But he said, 'As the Lord lives, whom I serve, I will receive none.'] And he urged him to take it, but he refused" (2 Kings 5:16).

[AA]   Gehazi came along and said, "[Gehazi, the servant of Elisha the man of God, said, 'See, my master has spared Naaman the Syrian, in not accepting from his hand what he brought.] As the Lord lives, I will run after him, and get something from him' " (2 Kings 5:20).

[BB]   For "something (M'WMH)" "blemish" (MWMH) is written.

[CC]   He went and found him and took what he took and put it in his upper room.

[DD] He came to Elisha who said to him, "Whence and wither, Gehazi?

[EE] "You have refused to give the reward which is owing to the righteous."

[FF] He said to him, "[He went in, and stood before his master, and Elisha said to him, 'Where have you been, Gehazi?' And he said,] 'Your servant went nowhere' " (2 Kings 5:25).

[GG] And he said to him, "Did I not go with you in spirit when the man turned from his chariot to meet you? Was it a time to accept money and garments, olive orchards and vineyards, sheep and oxen, menservants and maidservants?" (2 Kings 5:26).

[HH] "Therefore the leprosy of Naaman shall cleave to you and to your descendants forever. So he went out from his presence a leper, as white as snow" (2 Kings 5:27).

[II] And it is written in Scripture: "Now there were four men who were lepers at the entrance to the gate; [and they said to one another, 'Why do we sit here till we die?]' " (2 Kings 7:3).

[JJ] Who were they?

[KK] R. Judah in the name of Rab: "They were Gehazi and his three sons."

[LL] It is written, "Now Elisha came to Damascus. Benhadad the king of Syria was sick; [and when it was told him, 'The man of God has come here,' the king said to Hazael, 'Take a present with you and meet the man of God, and inquire of the Lord through him, saying, "Shall I recover from this sickness?"]' " (2 Kings 8:7-8).

[MM] Why did [Elisha] go there? He wanted to do something there. He went, hoping to bring Gehazi back. He found him a certified [leper].

[NN] On this basis we learn that they push away [a sinner] with the left hand, but draw him near with the right hand.

[OO] R. Yohanan said, " 'The sojourner has not lodged in the street; I have opened my doors to the wayfarer' (Job 31:32). On the basis of this verse [we learn] that they push away with the left hand and draw near with the right."

[PP] And this is not as did Elisha, who drove away Gehazi with both hands.

[QQ]   There were two ailments which Elisha suffered: one from normal causes, the other in regard to his driving away Gehazi.

[**XII**.A]   R. Hananiah and R. Joshua b. Levi: "When they voted and decided, *Three kings and four ordinary folk have no portion in the world to come [M. San. 10:2A]*, an echo came forth and said, 'Will he then make requital to suit you, because you reject it? For you must choose and not I; therefore declare what you know' (Job 34:33).

[B]   "They proposed to include Solomon with them.

[C]   "David came along and prostrated himself before them,

[D]   "and there is he who says that a fire went forth from the house of the Holy of Holies and licked round about them.

[E]   "Hadar-Ila was learned in praying and fasting. When Solomon was counted with them, [Hadar-Ila] prayed but was not answered."

[F]   Those who interpret signs said, "All of them have a portion in the world to come."

[G]   What is the Scriptural basis for this position?

[H]   "Gilead is mine; Manasseh is mine; Ephraim is my helmet; Judah is my scepter. Moab is my washbasin; upon Edom I cast my shoe; over Philistia I shout in triumph [HTRW"Y]" (Ps. 60:7–8).

[I]   "Gilead is mine;—this refers to Ahab, king of Israel, who fell on the heights of Gilead.

[J]   "Manasseh is mine" means what it says.

[K]   "Ephraim is my helmet"—this is Jeroboam ben Nabat of Ephraim.

[L]   "Judah is my scepter" refers to Ahithophel.

[M]   "Moab is my washbasin"—this refers to Gehazi.

[N]   "Upon Edom I cast my shoe"—this refers to Doeg the Edomite.

[O]   The Israelites said before the Holy One, blessed be he, "Lord of all worlds, what shall we do when David, king of Israel, is cursing them?

[P] " 'Men of blood and treachery shall not live out half their days' " (Ps. 55:23).

[Q] He said to them, "It is my task to make them friends (RY⁣ʿYM) again with one another:

[R] " 'Over Philistia I shout in triumph' ('TRWᶜᶜ) (Ps. 108:9).

[S] " 'Over Philistia I shout in triumph' (HTRWᶜᶜY) (Ps. 60:8).

[T] "It is my task to seek out (PLŠ) for them good deeds, to make them friends (RY⁣ʿYM) once more with one another."

The first seven units deal with the materials of M. San. 10:2A–E. The Talmud unfolds fairly systematically, with Jeroboam, unit **I**, Ahab, units **II–III**, and Manasseh, units **V–VII**, with Judah's view, M. San. 10:2C, dealt with at **VII**. I am not sure why Ahaz is included at unit **IV**. The introduction, **IV**.A is consistent with **I**.A, **II**.A, and **V**.A, as if to indicate that Ahaz is in the same list as the others. I separate unit **VI** from unit **V** because it seems to me an essentially independent unit, but, of course, the opposite view is reasonable. The ordinary folk begin at unit **VIII** and run to the end. We notice that units **IX**, **X**, and **XI** open with the same theme, that the villain was the master of Torah and nonetheless so grievously sinned that he lost the world to come. But I see no important patterns in the formation of the subsequent constructions, which exhibit the expected character of an anthology. Unit **VIII** bears a number of inserted tales about the worship of Peor, **VIII**.R, S, T, and it also has some minor literary problems, e.g., of repetition. But in the main the story unfolds smoothly and makes its points clearly.

10:3

[A] *The generation of the flood has no share in the world to come,*

[B] *and they shall not stand in the judgment,*

[C] *since it is written, "My spirit shall not judge with man forever" (Gen. 6:3)—*

[D] *[neither judgment nor spirit].*

[E]   *The generation of the dispersion has no share in the world to come,*

[F]   *since it is said, "So the Lord scattered them abroad from there upon the face of the whole earth" (Gen. 11:8).*

[G]   *"So the Lord scattered them abroad"—in this world,*

[H]   *"and the Lord scattered them from there"—in the world to come.*

[I]   *The men of Sodom have no portion in the world to come,*

[J]   *since it is said, "Now the men of Sodom were wicked and sinners against the Lord exceedingly (Gen. 13:13)—*

[K]   *"Wicked"—in this world.*

[L]   *"And sinners"—in the world to come.*

[M]   *But they will stand in judgment.*

[N]   *R. Nehemiah says, "Both these and those will not stand in judgment,*

[O]   *"for it is said, 'Therefore the wicked shall not stand in judgment, nor sinners in the congregation of the righteous' (Ps. 1:5)—*

[P]   *" 'Therefore the wicked shall not stand in judgment'—this refers to the generation of the flood.*

[Q]   *" 'Nor sinners in the congregation of the righteous'—this refers to the men of Sodom."*

[R]   *They said to him, "They will not stand in the congregation of the righteous, but they will stand in the congregation of the sinners."*

[S]   *[The spies have no portion in the world to come,*

[T]   *as it is said, "Even those men who brought up an evil report of the land died by the plague before the Lord" (Num. 14:37)—*

[U]   *"Died"—in this world.*

[V]   *"By the plague"—in the world to come].*

[I.A]   [The generation of the flood (M. San. 10:3A)] will not live in the world to come.

[B]   What is the Scriptural basis for this statement?

[C]   "He blotted out every living thing that was on the face of the ground [man and animals and creeping things and birds of the air; they were blotted out of the earth]" (Gen. 7:23).

[D]   "[He blotted out every living thing that was on the face of the ground, man and animals and creeping things and birds of the air;] they were blotted out of the earth" (Gen. 7:23).

[E]   **"And he blotted out every living thing"—in this world.**

[F]   **"And they were blotted out of the earth"—in the world to come [T. San. 13:6].**

[G]   It was taught: R. Nehemiah says, "It is implied by the following verse of Scripture: '[Then the Lord said,] "My spirit shall not abide in man for ever, [for he is flesh, but his days shall be a hundred and twenty years"]' " (Gen. 6:3).

[H]   R. Judah says, "My spirit will not abide with him, for I shall not place my spirit on them when I place my spirit on mankind."

[I]   R. Simeon says, "My spirit will not abide with them, for I shall not put my spirit in them when I pay the reward which is coming to the righteous."

[J]   Others say, "My spirit will not abide with them, for I shall not bring back their souls to their cases [bodies]."

[K]   R. Joshua b. Levi said, "Their destruction by scalding water was final [so there is no resurrection for them]."

[L]   What is the Scriptural basis for this statement?

[M]   "In time of heat they disappear; when it is hot they vanish from their place" (Job 6:17).

[N]   What is the meaning of "when it is hot"?

[O]   "When they are scalded."

[P]   Said R. Yohanan, "Every single drop which the Holy One, blessed be he, brought down on them, did he boil in Gehenna, and then he brought it down on them."

[Q]   This is in line with the following verse of Scripture:

[R]   "When it is hot they vanish from their place" (Job 6:17).

[S]   Judah b. R. Hezekiah and Rabbi say, "The Holy One, blessed be he, judges the wicked in Gehenna for twelve months. At the outset he puts a hook into them, and then he hangs them in fire, and they say, 'Woe, woe!' Then he hangs them into snow, and they say, 'Oh, oh!' "

[T]   What is the Scriptural basis for this statement?

[U]   "He drew me up from the desolate pit, out of the miry bog, and set my feet upon a rock, making my steps secure]" (Ps. 40:3).

[V]   What is the meaning of "the miry bog (HYWN)"?

[W]   A place in which they say, "Oh (HWY)!"

[X]   And let them receive their punishment [29c] and then receive a portion in the world to come?

[Y]   [That is not possible,] in line with the following verse of Scripture: "[A wise son hears his father's instruction,] but a scoffer does not listen to rebuke" (Prov. 13:1).

[II.A]   *The men of Sodom have no portion in the world to come (M. San. 10:31),*

[B]   and they will not live in the world to come.

[C]   What is the Scriptural basis for that statement?

[D]   "Now the men of Sodom were wicked, great sinners against the Lord" (Gen. 13:13).

[E]   **"Wicked and sinners"—in this world.**

[F]   **"Against the Lord exceedingly"—in the world to come.**

[G]   **Another interpretation: "Evil"—to one another.**

[H]   **"And sinning"—in fornication.**

[I]   **"Against the Lord"—in idolatry.**

[J]   **"Exceedingly"—in murder [T. San. 13:8].**

The Talmud treats the generation of the flood at unit **I**, the men of Sodom at unit **II**. No materials on the other topics are included.

10:4

[A]   *"The generation of the wilderness has no portion in the world to come and will not stand in judgment,*

[B]   *"for it is written, 'In this wilderness they shall be consumed and there they shall die' (Num. 14:35)," the words of R. Aqiba.*

[C]   *R. Eliezer says, "Concerning them it says, 'Gather my saints together to me, those that have made a covenant with me by sacrifice' " (Ps. 50:5).*

[D]   *"The party of Korah is not destined to rise up,*

[E]   *"for it is written, 'And the earth closed upon them' (Num. 16:33) [—in this world].*

[F]   *" 'And they perished from among the assembly' [—in the world to come]," the words of R. Aqiba.*

[G]   *And R. Eliezer says, "Concerning them it says, 'The Lord kills and resurrects, brings down to Sheol and brings up again' " (1 Sam. 2:6).*

[I.A]   **"The generation of the wilderness has no portion in the world to come and will not live in the world to come,**

[B]   **"as it is said, 'In this wilderness they shall be consumed, and there they shall die.'**

[C]   **" 'They shall be consumed'—in this world.**

[D]   **" 'And there they will die'—in the world to come.**

[E]   **"And so it says, 'Therefore I swore in my anger that they should not enter my rest' " (Ps. 95:11), the words of R. Aqiba.**

[F]   **R. Eliezer says, "Concerning them it is said, 'Gather my saints together to me, those that have made a covenant with me by sacrifice' " (Ps. 50:5) [T. San. 13:10].**

[G]   **R. Joshua says, " 'I have sworn an oath and confirmed it' (Ps. 119:106).**

[H]   **Hananiah nephew of R. Joshua says, "It is written, 'Therefore I swore in my anger . . .' (Ps. 95:11)—**

[I]   **"In my anger did I swear, but I retract it" [T. San. 13:11].**

[J]   It was taught, **R. Simeon b. Menassia says, "Concerning them does Scripture state, 'Gather to me my faithful ones, who made a covenant with me by sacrifice!' (Ps. 50:5).**

[K]   " **'My faithful ones'—who acted faithfully with me.**

[L]   " **'Who have made a covenant with me'—who are cut in my behalf.**

[M]   " **'With me by sacrifice'—who exalted me and are sacrificed in my name"**

[N]   It was taught: **R. Joshua b. Qorha says, "Concerning these generations, Scripture states, 'And then the ransomed of the Lord shall return, [and come singing to Zion]' " (Is. 35:10) [T. San. 13:11].**

[O]   Rabbi says, "Both these and those do have a portion in the world to come."

[P]   What is the Scriptural basis for this viewpoint?

[Q]   "And in that day a great trumpet will be blown, and those who were lost in the land of Assyria [and those who were driven out to the land of Egypt will come and worship the Lord on the holy mountain at Jerusalem]" (Is. 27:13).

[R]   "In the land of Assyria"—these are the ten tribes.

[S]   "And those who were driven out to the land of Egypt"—this is the generation of the wilderness.

[T]   These and those "will come and worship the Lord on the holy mountain at Jerusalem."

[**II.A**]   *The party of Korach has no portion in the world to come and will not live in the world to come.*

[B]   What is the Scriptural basis for this view?

[C]   "[So they and all that belonged to them went down alive into Sheol;] and the earth closed over them, and they perished from the midst of the assembly" (Num. 16:33).

[D]   *"The earth closed over them"—in this world.*

[E]   *"And they perished from the midst of the assembly"—in the world to come [M. San. 10:4D–F].*

[F]   It was taught: **R. Judah b. Batera says, "[The contrary view] is to be derived from the implication of the following verse:**

[G]   " 'I have gone astray like a lost sheep; seek thy servant [and do not forget thy commandments]' (Ps. 119:176).

[H]   "Just as the lost object which is mentioned later on in the end is going to be searched for, so the lost object which is stated herein is destined to be searched for" [T. San. 13:9].

[I]   Who will pray for them?

[J]   R. Samuel bar Nahman said, "Moses will pray for them."

[K]   "Let Reuben live, and not die, [nor let his men be few]" (Deut. 33:6).

[L]   R. Joshua b. Levi said, "Hannah will pray for them."

[M]   This is the view of R. Joshua b. Levi, for R. Joshua b. Levi said, "Thus did the party of Korach sink ever downward, until Hannah went and prayed for them and said, 'The Lord kills and brings to life; he brings down to Sheol and raises up' " (1 Sam. 2:6).

The Talmud presents no surprises, once more drawing on To-sefta's materials and lightly augmenting them.

10:5 [In Leiden MS and *editio princeps:* 10:6]

[A]   *"The ten tribes are not destined to return,*

[B]   *"since it is said, 'And he cast them into another land, as on this day' (Deut. 29:28). Just as the day passes and does not return, so they have gone their way and will not return," the words of R. Aqiba.*

[C]   *R. Eliezer says, "Just as this day is dark and then grows light, so the ten tribes for whom it now is dark—thus in the future it is destined to grow light for them."*

[I.A]   "The ten tribes have no portion in the world to come and will not live in the world to come, *since it is said, 'And he cast them into another land, as on this day' (Deut. 29:28). Just as the day passes and does not return, so they have gone their way and will not return,"* the words of R. Aqiba [M. San. 10:5A–B].

[B] **R. Simeon b. Judah of Kefar Akkum says in the name of R. Simeon, "[Scripture said, 'As at this day']—**

[C] **"if their deeds remain as they are this day, they will [not] return, and if not, they will (not) return" [T. San. 13:12].**

[II.A] R. Hezekiah, R. Abbahu in the name of R. Eleazar, "If the righteous proselytes come to the world to come, Antolinus will come at the head of all of them."

[B] There are those who maintain that Antolinus did not convert, and there are those who maintain that Antolinus did convert.

[C] What implication do you derive from that statement?

[D] They saw him going out in a damaged shoe on the Day of Atonement.

[E] So you derive from that fact that even those who fear heaven go out in such wise.

[F] Antolinus came to Rabbi. He said to him, "Do you foresee that I shall eat from Leviathan in the world to come?"

[G] He said to him, "Yes."

[H] He said to him, "Now you did not let me eat from the Passover lamb in this world, and yet will you give me Leviathan's flesh to eat in the coming world?"

[I] He said to him, "And what can we do for you? Concerning the Passover lamb it is written, '[And when a stranger shall sojourn with you and would keep the passover to the Lord, let all his males be circumcised, then he shall come near and keep it; he shall be as a native of the land.] But no uncircumcised person shall eat of it' " (Ex. 12:48).

[J] (That is to say, Antolinus did not convert.)

[K] When he heard this, he went and converted. He came to Rabbi, saying to him, "Now look at the mark of my circumcision!"

[L] He said to him, "In my whole life I never looked at mine! Am I supposed to look at yours!"

[M] (That is to say that Antolinus did convert.)

[N]   Now why was he called, "Our Holy Rabbi"? Because in his entire life he never looked at the mark of circumcision on his penis.

[O]   And why is Nahum called, "The Most Holy Man"? Because he never in his entire life looked at the face of a coin [on which a human figure was incised].

[P]   Antolinus came to Rabbi. He said to him, "Pray for me."

[Q]   He said to him, "May He protect you from cold, as it is written, '[He casts forth ice like morsels,] who can stand before his cold?' " (Ps. 147:17).

[R]   He said to him, "Rabbi, this prayer is not much. If you cover yourself, lo, the cold goes away."

[S]   He said to him, "May he spare you from the hot winds which blow through the world."

[T]   He said to him, "Now that is a fitting prayer. May your prayer be heard,

[U]   "for it is written, '[Its rising is from the end of the heavens, and its circuit to the end of them.] And there is nothing hid from its heat' " (Ps. 19:7).

[III.A]   R. Yohanan said, "The party of Yohanan b. Korach has no portion in the world to come."

[B]   What is the Scriptural basis for this view?

[C]   "They have dealt faithlessly with the Lord; for they have borne alien children. Now the new moon shall devour them with their fields" (Hos. 5:7).

[IV.A]   R. Eleazar and R. Judah—

[B]   One said, "They did not go into exile until they had become uncircumcised."

[C]   And the other said, "They did not go into exile until they had become mamzerim."

[D]   The one who said, "Uncircumcised," refers the verse to circumcision and practice of religious duties, and the one who said, "mamzerim" refers the verse to the doings of their fathers [which caused the calamity].

[E]   Said R. Yohanan, "Israel did not go into exile until it had turned into twenty-four parties of heretics."

[F]   What is the Scriptural basis for that statement?

[G]   "[And he said to me,] 'Son of man, I send you to the people of Israel, to a nation of rebels, who have rebelled against me; [and I heard him speaking to me]' " (Ez. 2:3).

[H]   "To a nation which rebels" is not written here but, rather, "to rebellious nations which have rebelled against me."

[I]   They and their fathers have transgressed against me until this very day.

[J]   R. Berekiah and R. Helbo in the name of R. Samuel bar Nahman: "The Israelites went into three different lands of exile, one beyond the Sambatyon River, one to Daphne at Antioch, and one on which the cloud descended, and which the cloud covered."

[K]   Just as they went into three different exiles, so the tribe of Reuben, Gad, and the half tribe of Manasseh went into three different exiles.

[L]   What is the Scriptural basis for that statement?

[M]   "You have gone the way of your sister; therefore I will give her cup into your hand" (Ez. 23:31).

[N]   And when they come back, they will come back from all three exiles.

[O]   What is the Scriptural basis for that statement?

[P]   "Saying to the prisoners, 'Come forth' to those who appear in darkness, 'Appear.' They shall feed along the ways, on all bare heights shall be their pasture" (Is. 49:9).

[Q]   "Saying to the prisoners, 'Come forth' "—this refers to those who went into exile on the other side of the Sambatyon River.

[R]   "To those who appear in darkness, 'Appear' "—these are those on whom the cloud descended and whom it covered.

[S]   "They shall feed along the ways, on all the bare heights shall be their pastures"—these are those who went into exile in Daphne at Antioch.

Only unit **I** follows the pattern established earlier. Reference to the redemption presumably accounts for the topic of unit **II**. Unit **III** serves M. 10:4. Unit **IV** deals with the Israelite exile and answers the question of whether the exile was because of the deeds of that generation or the accumulation of wickedness of the fathers.

10:6 [In Leiden MS and *editio princeps:* 10:7]

[A]   *The townsfolk of an apostate town [have no portion in the world to come,*

[B]   *as it is said,] "Certain base fellows have come out from the midst of thee and have drawn away the inhabitants of their city" (Deut. 13:14).*

[C]   *Lo, they are not put to death unless those who misled the [town] come from that same town and from that same tribe,*

[D]   *and unless the majority is misled,*

[E]   *and unless men did the misleading.*

[F]   *[If] women or children misled them,*

[G]   *or if a minority of the town was misled,*

[H]   *or if those who misled the town came from outside of it,*

[I]   *lo, they are treated as individuals [and not as a whole town],*

[J]   *[and they thus] require [testimony against them] by two witnesses, and a statement of warning, for each and every one of the [residents].*

[K]   *This rule is more strict for individuals than for the community:*

[L]   *for individuals are put to death by stoning.*

[M]   *Therefore their property is saved.*

[N]   *But the community is put to death by the sword.*

[O]   *Therefore their property is lost.*

[**I.**A]   "A town" (Deut. 13:14)—not a village.

[B]   "A town"—not a city.

[C]   "And that is to say there should be from five to ten [men]," the words of R. Meir.

[D]   R. Judah says, "From a hundred to as much as the majority of the whole tribe."

[II.A]   Two who misled two [that is, those who misled the apostate city are two in number; in this case, they misled only two, while the others in the town were misled by outsiders]—

[B]   those two who misled two—what is the law as to applying to them the rule governing those who misled [or] the rule governing those who are misled? [Are those who misled the town treated as guilty and culpable by stoning? Or are they deemed part of the ones who are misled, others being involved? They misled only two people, and so along with the rest are subject to the law of punishment through decapitation.]

[C]   If there were in the apostate town proselytes and resident aliens—what is the law as to their completing the number to make the required a majority?

[D]   If there were in the town vivaria for wild beasts and birds [29d] and fish—

[E]   a bird flying above the town by more than ten cubits—

[F]   what is the law [governing their falling into the category of the possessions to be put to death]?

[III.A]   R. Simeon says, "The mode of execution through burning is more severe than the mode of execution through stoning."

[B]   And rabbis say, "The mode of execution through stoning is more severe than the mode of execution through burning."

[C]   R. Simeon says, "The mode of execution through strangulation is more severe than the mode of execution through decapitation."

[D]   And rabbis say, "The mode of execution through decapitation is more severe than the mode of execution through strangulation."

What is interesting are the several questions, not answered, in unit **II**. The rest is standard. Why unit **III** is appended I cannot say.

10:7 [In Leiden MS and *editio princeps:* 10:8]

[A] *"And you shall surely smite the inhabitants of the city with the edge of the sword" (Deut. 13:15)—*

[B] *A caravan of ass drivers or camel drivers passing from place to place—lo, these have the power to save it.*

[C] *"Destroying it utterly and all that is therein and the cattle thereof, with the edge of the sword" (Deut. 13:17)—*

[D] *On this basis they said, The property of righteous folk which happens to be located in it is lost. But that which is outside of it is saved.*

[E] *And as to that of evil folk, whether it is in the town or outside of it, lo, it is lost.*

[I.A] **R. Simeon says, " 'Its cattle,'—excluding firstlings and tithe of cattle in it.**

[B] **" 'And its spoil'—excluding money which has been consecrated, and money which has taken on the status of second tithe in it"** [T. San. 14:5].

[C] R. Yose b. Haninah raised the question: "The hair [wigs] belonging to the righteous women which are in the town—what is the law? [Is this deemed in the status of the property of the righteous, which is lost, or in the status of their clothing, which is saved, in line with M. 10:7D?]

[D] Let us derive the rule from the following: **R. Simeon says, " 'Its cattle'—excluding firstlings and tithe of cattle in it. 'And its spoil'—excluding money which has been consecrated and money which has taken on the status of second tithe in it."** [Similarly, the wigs of righteous women are not in the same status as ordinary property, just as firstlings are not in the same status as ordinary cattle.]

[II.A] As to the consecrated beasts located in an apostate city—

[B] R. Yohanan says, "The laws of sacrilege do not apply to them."

[C] And R. Simeon b. Laqish said, "The laws of sacrilege do apply to them."

[D] R. Yohanan raised the following objection to R. Simeon b. Laqish: "In your opinion, in holding that the laws of sacrilege do apply to them, we should also speak of *six* animals consecrated as sin offerings which are left to die, rather than merely five [as we find at M. Tem. 4:1, since these beasts too will retain the status of consecration and are left to die]."

[E]   He said to him, "But in fact even an animal consecrated as a whole offering in the apostate city is left to die."

[F]   R. Hela in the name of R. Simeon b. Laqish: "The laws of sacrilege apply to them, because the animals are in the status of beasts declared consecrated by an apostate to idolatry, [and the laws of sacrilege do apply to such beasts, since the apostate retains the power of sanctification inherent in the Israelite]."

[G]   [And why should they be left to die?] Let them be offered on the altar.

[H]   [This is not done, by reason of] the following verse: "The sacrifice of the wicked is an abomination" (Prov. 21:27).

[I]   Said R. Uqba, "Also in the following do they differ:

[J]   " 'An ox which is going forth to be stoned when the witnesses against it are proved to be perjurers'—

[K]   "R. Yohanan said, 'Whoever seizes possession of it first wins out.'

[L]   "And R. Simeon b. Laqish said, 'It is a case of the owner's having given up ownership by reason of despair [but having done so only] in error [and the owner retains ownership].'

[M]   "And so in the case of a slave being taken forth to be executed, when the witnesses against him are proved to be perjurers,

[N]   "R. Yohanan said, 'He acquires ownership of himself.'

[O]   "And R. Simeon b. Laqish said, 'It is a case of the owner's having given up ownership by reason of despair, [but having done so] only in error [so the original owner retains possession].' ' '

Unit I augments Mishnah's interest in the disposition of the property, M. 10:7C. Unit II then carries forward the same theme, namely, consecrated property. In place of II.I–O in the argument's construction is not clear to me; it appears tacked on.

10:8 [In Leiden MS and *editio princeps:* 10:9]

[A] *"And you shall gather all the spoil of it into the midst of the wide place thereof" (Deut. 13:16).*

[B] *If it has no wide place, they make a wide place for it.*

[C] *[If] its wide place is outside of it, they bring it inside, as it is said, ". . . into the midst of the wide place thereof."*

[D] *"And you will burn with fire the city and all the spoil thereof, every whit, unto the Lord your God" (Deut. 13:16).*

[E] *"The spoil thereof"—but not the spoil which belongs to heaven.*

[F] *On this basis they have said:*

[G] *Things which had been consecrated which are in it are to be redeemed; heave offering left therein is allowed to rot; second tithe and sacred scrolls are hidden away.*

[H] *"Every whit unto the Lord your God"—*

[I] *Said R. Simeon, "Said the Holy One, blessed be he: 'If you enter into judgment in the case of an apostate city, I give credit to you as if you had offered a whole burnt offering before me.' "*

[J] *"And it shall be a heap forever, it shall not be built again"—*

[K] *"It should not be made even into vegetable patches or orchards," the words of R. Yosé the Galilean.*

[L] *R. Aqiba says, " 'It shall not be built again'—as it was it may not be rebuilt, but it may be made into vegetable patches and orchards."*

[M] *"And there shall cleave nought of the devoted thing to your hand [that the Lord may turn from the fierceness of his anger and show you mercy and have compassion upon you and multiply you]" (Deut. 13:17).*

[N] *For so long as evil people are in the world, fierce anger is in the world.*

[O] *When the evil people have perished from the world, fierce anger departs from the world.*

[**I**.A]   Said R. Simeon, "This [disposition of the property of the righteous, M. 10:7D] yields an argument *a fortiori*.

[B]   "Now if regarding property, which has no knowledge of either good or evil, because it caused righteous people to make their dwelling with evil ones, the Torah has said that [such property] is to be burned—

[C]   "he who has the intention of misleading his fellow and actually does mislead him from the good way to the evil way—how much the more so [will he be punished]!"

[D]   Said R. Eleazar, "Proof for that proposition is found in the case of Lot, who dwelled in Sodom only on account of his property.

[E]   "He too got out with his skin."

[F]   That is in line with the following verse of Scripture:

[G]   "Make haste, escape there" (Gen. 19:22).

[H]   It is enough for you that you escape with your life.

[I]   It is written, "**In his days did Hiel the Bethelite build Jericho**" (**1 Kings 16:34**).

[J]   **And did not Hiel belong to Jehoshaphat, and Jericho to the district of Benjamin?**

[K]   [And why was the matter blamed on Ahab?]

[L]   **It teaches that they hang guilt on one who already is guilty [T. San. 14:7].**

[M]   [And so it says,] "**With the loss of Abiram his firstborn, he laid the foundation thereof, and with the loss of Segub his youngest son he set up the gates thereof**" (1 Kings 16:34).

[N]   **In the instance of Abiram, he had no [example] from which to learn.**

[O]   **But in the case of Segub, that wicked man had [an example] from which to learn!**

[P]   **They wanted to increase their money.**

[Q]   **Why? Because a curse had affected them and their funds simply continued to decline.**

[R]   This supports Scripture, which says, "According to the word of the Lord, which he spoke by the hand of Joshua the son of Nun, 'Every whit unto the Lord your God . . . And there shall cleave nought of the devoted thing to your hand.' " (1 Kings 16:34) [T. San. 14:9].

[S]   It was taught: R. Simeon b. Eleazar says, "That [Jericho] he did not build, but he built another one. And when it was built, you are permitted to live in it. For it is said, 'And the sons of the prophets which in Jericho drew near to Elisha' " (2 Kings 2:5) [T. San. 14:10].

[T]   R. Yosé and R. Joshua b. Qorha say, "Why does Scripture say, ['Cursed is the man before the Lord who will rise and] build this city, Jericho' [Josh. 6:26]?

[U]   "[Now don't we know that it is called Jericho?]

[V]   "[But the meaning is that] one may not rebuild it and call it by the name of some other town, and that one may not build some other town and call it Jericho" [T. San. 14:6].

[W]   And so it says, "You shall never return (ŠWB) that way again" (Deut. 17:16).

[X]   For the purposes of making a permanent settlement (YŠYBH) you may not return, but you may return to do business, to engage in commerce and to conquer the land.

The homilies, serving M. 10:7 as indicated, include I.Iff., solely because of I.Q. That is, concern for making money caused the catastrophe. Then the entire construction, from I.I–X onward is inserted whole, on account of that one detail.

12 Yerushalmi Sanhedrin
Chapter Eleven

11:1

[A] [30a] *These are the ones who are to be strangled:*

[B] . *He who hits his father or his mother [Ex. 21:15]; he who steals [kidnaps] an Israelite [Ex. 21:16, Deut. 24:7]; an elder who defies the decision of a court, a false prophet, a prophet who prophesies the name of an idol;*

[C] *He who has sexual relations with a married woman, those who bear false witness against a priest's daughter and against one who has sexual relations with her.*

[D] *"He who hits his father and his mother" is liable only if he makes a lasting bruise on them.*

[E] *This rule is more strict in the case of the one who curses than the one who hits them.*

[F] *For the one who curses them after they have died is liable.*

[G] *But the one who hits them after they have died is exempt.*

[I.A] Whence in the Torah do we find a warning against hitting one's father and one's mother?

[B] "Forty stripes may be given him, but not more; [lest if one should go on to beat him with more stripes than these, your brother be degraded in your sight]" (Deut. 25:3).

[C] Now if one who is commanded to flog is commanded not to flog [more than is permitted], he who is not commanded to flog at all [e.g., a court does not assign the son to flog the father]— is it not an argument *a fortiori* that he indeed should be commanded not to flog [under any circumstances at all]? [That is, he should not hit his father or his mother.]

[**II**.A]   *[He is liable] only if he makes a lasting bruise on them:*

[B]   What sort of bruise is under discussion?

[C]   [Is it a] bruise [which is culpable under the law of the] Sabbath, or [is it] a bruise [which is culpable under the law of damages?

[D]   If you say that it is a bruise which is culpable under the laws of the Sabbath, then even if he did not lose [a limb by reason of the son's flogging, the son is liable].

[E]   But if you say that it is a bruise which is culpable under the laws of torts and damages, then [the son is not liable] unless [the parent] actually loses [a limb].

The Talmud's standard operation is to supply a proof test and to clarify Mishnah's rule, and this is what is done at units **I** and **II**, respectively.

11:2

[A]   *"He who steals an Israelite" is liable only when he will have brought him into his own domain.*

[B]   *R. Judah says, "Only if he will have brought him into his own domain and will have made use of him,*

[C]   *"as it is said, 'And if he deals with him as a slave or sells him' " (Deut. 24:7).*

[D]   *He who steals his son—*

[E]   *R. Ishmael, son of R. Yohanan b. Beroqah, declares him liable.*

[F]   *And sages declare him exempt.*

[G]   *[If] he stole someone who was half slave and half free—*

[H]   *R. Judah declares him liable.*

[I]   *And sages declare him exempt.*

[**I**.A]   Whence do we locate the first warning against stealing [that is, kidnapping]?

[B]   "You shall not steal" (Ex. 20:15).

[C]   Whence do we locate the second warning against stealing [that is, property]?

[D]   "You shall not steal" (Lev. 19:11).

[E]   "You shall not steal" for spite [returning the object later on].

[F]   "You shall not steal" planning then to pay double compensation or to pay fourfold or fivefold damages.

[G]   Ben Bag Bag says, "You shall not steal from the thief [even] what belongs to you, so that you will not appear to be a thief."

[**II**.A]   R. Ba, R. Yohanan in the name of R. Hoshaiah: "[The accused] son [of M. 8:3] is liable only if he will steal money [to buy meat for his gluttony]."

[B]   R. Zeira, R. Yohanan in the name of R. Hoshaiah: "He is liable only if he will waste money."

[C]   What do we mean by wasting money?

[D]   If it is a case in which he says to the butcher, "Here are five and give me meat worth three," he is a mere idiot.

[E]   "Here are three and give me [meat worth] five," he is an ordinary person.

[F]   But thus do we interpret the matter: "Here are five, and give me meat worth five," [in this case, having failed to effect a bargain, he has wasted money].

[**III**.A]   What is a thief and what is a robber?

[B]   Said R. Hela, "[If] one stole before witnesses, he is a thief, and if he did so before the owner, he is a robber, [so the criterion is the presence of the owner, which turns a thief into a robber]."

[C]   R. Zeira raised the question: "If so, even if he intended to commit a robbery against the owner, this one is not a robber [if the deed is not done before others]. [That is to say, by Hela's definition, the presence of the witness or the owner is decisive, and without committing the theft in the presence of the witness or the owner, one is no robber.]"

[D]   Then what is meant by a robber in the view of R. Zeira?

[E]   R. Samuel bar Sosetra in the name of R. Abbahu: "Only if one steals an object in the presence of ten men."

[F]   The principal source dealing with the matter is as follows: "The Egyptian had a spear in his hand, but Benaiah went down to him with a staff, and robbed the spear out of the Egyptian's hand" (2 Sam. 23:21).

[IV.A] What is the reason of R. Ishmael b. R. Yohanan b. Beroqah [M. 11:D–E]?

[B]   "If a man is found stealing one of his brethren, of the people of Israel" (Deut. 24:7)—even his son [falls in the category of the people].

[C]   What is the reason of the rabbis?

[D]   "Of his brethren"—excluding his own son.

[E]   What is the reason of R. Judah [M. 11:2G–I]?

[F]   "Of his brethren"—even if he is only partly a brother.

[G]   What is the reason of rabbis?

[H]   "Of his brethren"—only if he is entirely one of his brethren [and this slave is only partially so].

Unit **I** is relevant to M. 11:2A. The rest serves the law of the son who is declared incorrigible, M. 8:3.

11:3 [In Leiden MS and *editio princeps:* 11:3–4]

[A]   *"An elder who defies the decision of a court" [M. 11:1B]—*

[B]   *as it is said, "If there arise a matter too hard for you in judgment, between blood and blood, between plea and plea" (Deut. 17:8)—*

[C]   *there were three courts there.*

[D]   *One was in session at the door gate of the Temple mount, one was in session at the gate of the courtyard, and one was in session in the hewn-stone chamber.*

[E]   *They come to the one which is at the gate of the Temple mount and say, "Thus I have explained the matter, and thus my colleagues have explained the matter.*

[F]   *"Thus I have ruled in the matter, and thus my colleagues have ruled."*

[G]   *If they had heard a ruling, they told it to them, and if not, they come along to that court which was at the gate of the courtyard.*

[H]   *And he says, "Thus I have explained the matter, and thus my colleagues have explained the matter.*

[I]   *"Thus I have ruled in the matter, and thus my colleagues have ruled."*

[J]   *If they had heard a ruling, they told it to them, and if not, these and those come along to the high court which was in the hewn-stone chamber,*

[K]   *from which Torah goes forth to all Israel,*

[L]   *as it is said, "From that place which the Lord shall choose" (Deut. 17:12).*

[M]   *[If] he went back to his town and again ruled just as he had ruled before, he is exempt.*

[N]   *But if he instructed others to do it in that way, he is liable,*

[O]   *as it is said, "And the man who does presumptuously" (Deut. 17:12).*

[P]   *He is liable only if he will give instructions to the people actually to carry out the deed [in accord with the now-rejected view].*

[Q]   *A disciple of a sage who gave instruction to carry out the deed [wrongly] is exempt.*

[R]   *It turns out that the strict ruling concerning him [that he cannot give decisions] also is a lenient ruling concerning him [that he is not punished if he does give decisions].*

[I.A]   ["If any case arises requiring decision between one kind of homicide and another, one kind of legal right and another, or one kind of assault and another, any case within your towns which is too difficult for you, then you shall arise and go up to the place which the Lord your God will choose" (Deut. 17:8).] It is written, "If any case arises . . . which is too difficult for you to judge . . ." (Deut. 17:8)—this indicates that the Scripture speaks of the most distinguished [and senior] member of the court.

[B]   ". . . for you"—this refers to one who is able to advise on intercalation of the year and the declaration of the new moon.

[C]   "A matter"—this refers to a master of lore.

[D]   ["A case requiring decision between] one kind of blood [homicide] and another, [one kind of legal right and another, or one kind of assault and another]" (Deut. 17:8). "One kind of blood and another"—[this is] the difference between the blood of menstruation and hymeneal blood, or between the blood of menstruation and the blood indicating the presence of zibah or ṣaraᶜat.

[E]   "Between one kind of legal right and another" [refers to the difference] between trials for property cases and trials for capital cases.

[F]   "Between one kind of legal right and another" refers to cases in which the death penalty is executed through stoning, burning, decapitation, or strangulation.

[G]   "Between one kind of affliction of disease (negaᶜ) [assault] and another"—this refers to knowing the difference between a meṣoraᶜ who is to be shut up for further inspection, and a meṣoraᶜ who is certified as unclean.

[H]   "Between one kind of affliction and another" [further refers to the difference] between afflictions which affect man and those which affect clothing or houses.

[I]   "Cases of disputes within your gates"—this refers to cases involving the administration of bitter water to a wife accused of adultery, the breaking of the neck of a heifer [in the case of a homicide in which the murderer cannot be found], and the declaring of a meṣoraᶜ to be clean.

[J]   ". . . disputes"—these refer to cases involving valuations, goods declared ḥerem, beasts declared substitutes for sacrifices [and so themselves consecrated], and objects declared consecrated.

[K]   ["Then you shall arise and go up to the place which the Lord your God will choose" (Deut. 17:8).] "You will arise"—from your court.

[L]   "And you will go up"—this refers to the ascent to Jerusalem.

[M]   Another interpretation: "You will go up"—on the basis of this statement we derive proof that the chosen house [the Temple] is to be built only at the highest point in the world.

[N]   What is the Scriptural basis for that statement?

[O]   "And I myself will plant it upon a high and lofty mountain; on the mountain height of Israel will I plant; it, that it may bring forth boughs and bear fruit" (Ez. 17:22–23).

[P]   "*And* you will come"—this encompasses also a court in Yavneh.

[II.A]   R. Zeira says, "In the case of a rebellious elder who gave instructions to carry out [his erroneous ruling]: **if he actually carried out what he said, he is liable.**

[B]   **"But if he gave instruction and did not actually carry out what he said,** he is exempt.

[C]   **"If he gave instruction on the condition of not doing what he said, he is exempt.**

[D]   **"If he gave instruction on condition of actually doing what he said, even if then he did not do it, he is liable"** [T. San. 14:12].

[E]   Said R. Hela, "R. Ishmael taught similarly: '. . . and the man who does . . .' *not* that he will do it."

[F]   R. Huna said, "If [a sage] was teaching a law, and afterward a case came to him in that regard, they do the deed [which he taught was to be done].

[G]   "If the case came to him before he taught that law, then if his decision affects only others, they may follow his decision, but if his decision affects his own case, they may not follow his decision" (PM).

[III.A]   **R. Simeon b. Manassia says, "Beauty, power, wisdom, riches, long life, glory, and children—for the righteous are a benefit to them and a benefit to the world."**

[B]   **What is the Scriptural basis for this statement?**

[C]   **"Old age is a crown of glory. It is gained in a righteous life"** (Prov. 16:31).

[D]   **"Children's children are the crown of old men" (Prov. 17:6).**

[E]   **"The glory of young men is their strength, but the beauty of old men is their gray hair" (Prov. 20:29).**

[F]   And it says: **"Before his elders is honor" (Is. 24:23).**

[G]   It was taught: **R. Simeon b. Gamaliel says, "These are the seven virtues which sages have listed for the righteous, and all of them have been realized in Rabbi and his sons" [T. San. 11:8]**

[H]   R. Yohanan says, "All the seven virtues which sages have listed for the righteous have been realized in Rabbi. Which . . . Rabbi? It is Judah the Patriarch."

[I]   R. Abbahu said, "It is R. Yudan the Patriarch; he is 'Our Rabbi.' "

The verse of Scripture cited in Mishnah is amply parsed at unit I. Unit II takes up the exposition of the liability of the rebellious elder. Unit III presumably speaks of the glory of elders in general, by contrast to the foregoing (if there is reason for its inclusion at all).

11:4 [In Leiden MS and *editio princeps:* 11:5–6]

[A]   *A more strict rule applies to the teachings of scribes than to the teachings of Torah.*

[B]   *He who rules, "There is no requirement to wear phylacteries," in order to transgress the teachings of the Torah, is exempt.*

[C]   *[But if he said,] "There are five partitions [in the phylactery, instead of four]," in order to add to what the scribes have taught, he is liable.*

[D]   *"They put him to death not in the court in his own town or in the court which is in Jabneh, but they bring him up to the high court in Jerusalem.*

[E]   *"And they keep him until the festival, and they put him to death on the festival,*

[F]   "as it is said, 'And all the people shall hear and fear and no more do presumptuously' " (Deut. 17:13), the words of R. Aqiba.

[G]   *R. Judah says, "They do not delay the execution of this one, but they put him to death at once.*

[H]   *"And they write messages and send them with messengers to every place:*

[I]   *"Mr. So-and-so, son of Mr. So-and-so, has been declared liable to the death penalty by the court."*

[I.A]   Associates in the name of R. Yohanan: "The teachings of scribes are more beloved than teachings of Torah and are as precious as teachings of Torah: 'Your kiss is like good wine' [that is, the kiss of the sages is like the good wine of the Torah]."

[B]   Simeon bar Ba in the name of R. Yohanan: "The teachings of scribes are more beloved than teachings of Torah and are more precious than teachings of Torah: 'For your love is better than wine' " (Song 1:2).

[C]   R. Ba bar Kohen in the name of R. Judah bar Pazzi: "You should know that the teachings of scribes are more beloved than the teachings of Torah.

[D]   "For lo, R. Tarfon [at M. Ber. 1:1], had he not recited the *Shema* at all, would have violated only an affirmatively stated commandment of the law. But because he transgressed the teaching of the House of Hillel [in the category of a teaching of scribes], he suffered liability to death,

[E]   "on the count: 'A serpent will bite him who breaks through a wall' " (Eccles. 10:8).

[F]   R. Ishmael taught, "Teachings of Torah are subject to prohibition and are subject to remission, are subject to lenient rulings and are subject to [30b] stringent rulings.

[G]   "But teachings of scribes are solely and completely subject to stringent rulings.

[H]   "You should know that this is so, for lo, we have learned there: *He who rules, 'There is no requirement to wear phylacteries' in order to transgress the teachings of the Torah, is ex-*

*empt. But if he said, 'There are five partitions in the
phylactery, instead of four,' in order to add to what the scribes
have taught, he is liable"* [M. San. 11:4B–C].

[I] Said R. Hinena son of R. Ada in the name of R. Tanhum bar
Hiyya: "More stringent are the teachings of elders than the
teachings of prophets, for it is written, 'Do not preach'—thus
they preach' (Mic. 2:6). And it is said, 'If a man should go
about and utter wind and lies, saying, 'I will preach to you of
wine and strong drink,' he would be the preacher for his people' " (Mic. 2:11).

[J] A prophet and an elder—to what are they comparable? To a
king who sent two senators of his to a certain province. Concerning one of them he wrote, "If he does not show you my
seal and signet, do not believe him." But concerning the other
one, he wrote, "Even though he does not show you my seal
and signet, believe him."

[K] So in the case of a prophet, he has had to write, "If a prophet
arises among you . . . and gives you a sign or a wonder . . ."
(Deut. 13:1).

[L] But here [with regard to an elder]: ". . . according to the instructions which they give you . . ." (Deut. 17:11) [without a
sign or a wonder].

[II.A] The Torah has made the rule that in phylacteries there are four
boxes containing four pericopae. [If] he declared that there
must be five boxes containing four pericopae, he is liable.

[B] R. Ba, R. Yohanan, in the name of R. Hoshaiah: "He is liable
only if he will give instruction in a matter in which the fundamental law is Scriptural, while the interpretation derives from
sages,

[C] "for example, a law dealing with carrion or a creeping thing,
the fundamental law of which derives from the Torah, but the
interpretation for which [e.g., requisite volume for culpability]
derives from scribes."

[D] Said R. Zeira, "Under no circumstances is he liable until he
will deny and give instruction in a matter in which the fundamental law is Scriptural, while the interpretation derives from
sages,

[E]   "for example, a law dealing with carrion or a creeping thing, the fundamental law of which derives from the Torah, but the interpretation for which derives from scribes.

[F]   "But that is so [only] when he diminishes and adds, in a matter in which he adds, he diminishes. [That is to say, liability is incurred only if the rebellious sage diminishes or adds to what the scribes have stated in regard to a law of the Torah. Thus, as **II**.A, if he adds to the number of boxes in the phylactery, he may also diminish the essentials of the law itself. So at issue is not merely differing, but differing within the range of established law, that is, rearranging the established law in some detail]" (PM).

[G]   [With regard to R. Yohanan's citing a saying in Hoshaiah's name,] the face of R. Hoshaiah brightened [because Yohanan had cited him].

[H]   [Yohanan] said to him, "When you are needed, it is pleasure for you. When you are not needed, others have outdone you."

[I]   Thirteen years, [nonetheless, did Yohanan] come before his master, [Hoshaiah], even though he did not require his instruction.

[J]   R. Samuel in the name of R. Zeira, "If it were only this, it was enough for him. But in fact he greeted his master day by day.

[K]   "For whoever greets his master is as if he greets the Indwelling Presence of God."

[L]   R. Berekiah responded [to Zeira's statemnt about adding or diminishing], "And lo, we have learned: *The requisite space of the bright spot is not less than a four-sided Cilician split bean squared. The space of the split bean is nine lentils. The space of a lentil is four hairs. It comes out that they are thirty-six hairs arranged in a square [M. Neg. 6:1].* [Now if the rebellious elder said that the spot need not be squared, but if it covers the relevant area, the person is unclean; even though the spot is not squared, he ends up adding to the measurement at the length and diminishing it at the width. This is a case of someone's diminishing the law by adding to it, as in the case of phylacteries.]"

[M]   Said R. Abbamari, "He who said such a thing [indeed would be within the law, for there is such an opinion stated within the tradition]."

[N]   R. Ba bar Mamal responded: "And lo, it is taught that there are two pericopae in the *mezuzah* [and if one added yet another pericope, the *mezuzah* will be invalid. So the one who adds diminishes]."

[O]   He said to him, "The same law applies to the phylacteries [**II.A**] and to the *mezuzah*."

[P]   R. Hamnuna responded: "And lo, it is taught with regard to the show fringes that they are to be four strands, each of four strings. If one made them three strands of four strings [would we not have a case of one's diminishing by adding]?"

[Q]   He said to him, "Here we have a case in which one diminished but did not add."

[R]   R. Haggai responded before R. Yosé, "And lo, it is taught: [*The flour for the loaves of the thank offering was brought from five seahs by the Jerusalem measure, which are six by the wilderness measure, equivalent to two ephahs, twenty tenths of an ephah, ten tenths of an ephah for what was to be leavened, and ten for what was to be unleavened. Ten for what was to be leavened—a tenth of an ephah for a loaf. And ten for what was to be unleavened. And in the unleavened part are three kinds: loaves, wafers, and oil-soaked cakes. They turn out to be] three and a third tenths of an ephah for each kind, three loaves for each tenth* [M. Men. 7:1A–G]. [Now if the rebellious elder gave instruction to divide equally, instead of putting half into the oil-soaked cakes as is scribes's instruction, that is,] a third for the oil-soaked, a third for the loaves, and a third for the wafers, [do we not have a case to illustrate F]?"

[S]   He said to him, "He [thereby] diminishes oil from the oil-soaked cakes and adds it to the loaves and to the wafers, [and this does illustrate F, above]."

The repertoire on the importance of teachings of scribes in relationship to teachings of Torah, unit **I**, presents no problems. **I**.J–L are attached as part of the already formed materials beginning at F. But the main point—the superiority of the elder, meaning, the sage—is entirely apropos. The focus of discussion at unit **II** is to find a case illustrative of **II**.F, that is, an instruction which a rebellious elder might give in such wise as to add and diminish at one and the same time. If one does not so state the law as to revise existing dimensions, without actually adding to, or subtracting from, them, then he is liable. The successive efforts to give such an example, L, N, P, show that the basic thrust of Zeira's statement, D–F, is to indicate that the law really cannot operate in fact.

11:5 [In Leiden MS and *editio princeps:* 11:7]

[A] *"A false prophet" [M. 11:1B],*

[B] *one who prophesies concerning something which he has not actually heard or concerning something which was not actually said to him,*

[C] *is put to death by man.*

[D] *But he who holds back his prophesy, he who disregards the words of another prophet, or the prophet who transgresses his own words—*

[E] *is put to death by heaven,*

[F] *as it is said, "I will require it of him" (Deut. 18:19).*

[I.A] *He who prophesies concerning something which he has not actually heard* **[M. 11:5B] is such as Zedekiah ben Chenaanah [1 Kings 22:11],** *and one who states something which was not actually said to him* **is such as Hananiah b. Azor [T. San. 14:14].**

[B] R. Joshua b. Levi said, "Hananiah b. Azor was a true prophet.

[C] "But he suffered a period of an intermission of his prophetic gifts, during which his gift of prophesy was null, **and he heard what Jeremiah prophesied in the upper market.**

[D] **"So he went down and he prophesied in the lower market"** **[T. San. 14:14].**

[E] Hananiah b. Azor said, "The entire end of the matter is not so, but, 'When seventy years are completed for Babylon, I will visit you, and I will fulfill to you my promise and bring you back to this place' (Jer. 29:10)."

[F] Now [he calculated] the entire lifespan of Manasseh was only fifty-five years. Deduct from them the twenty years during

which the Heavenly court does not inflict punishment or extirpation, and the two years of Ammon, and the thirty-one years
of Josiah."

[G]   Thus you have that which is written, "In that same year, at the
beginning of the reign of Zedekiah king of Judah, in the fifth
month of the fourth year, Hananiah the son of Azor, the
prophet from Gibeon, spoke to me in the house of the Lord, in
the presence of the priests and all the people, saying, 'Thus
says the Lord of hosts, the God of Israel: I have broken the
yoke of the king of Babylon. Within two years I will bring
back to this place all the vessels of the Lord's house which Nebuchadnezzar king of Babylon took away from this place and
carried to Babylon' " (Jer. 28:1–3).

[H]   Said to him Jeremiah, "You say, 'In two years I shall bring
back . . . ,' but I say to you that Nebuchadnezzar is going to
come and take the rest of the people now here to Babylonia:
'They shall be carried to Babylon and remain there until the
day when I give attention to them . . .' " (Jer. 27:22).

[I]   He said to him, "Give some sort of sign to confirm what you
say."

[J]   He said to him, "I prophesy doom, and I cannot give a sign to
confirm what I say, for the the Holy One, blessed be he, may
form a plan to bring evil, but then reverse it.

[K]   "But you prophesy well, so you give a sign."

[L]   He replied, "No! You're the one who has to bring a sign."

[M]   He said to him, "If so, lo, I shall give a sign and a wonder
through that very person himself [namely, you]."

[N]   In that year he died: "Therefore thus says the lord: 'Behold, I
will remove you from the face of the earth. This very year you
shall die, because you have uttered rebellion against the Lord.'
In that same year, in the seventh month, the prophet Hananiah
died" (Jer. 28:16–17).

[O]   It was another year, and so now do you say so?

[P]   But this teaches that he died on the eve of the New Year.

[Q]   And he commanded his sons and his household to conceal the
matter, so that they should remove his corpse after the New
Year, just so as to falsify the prophesy of Jeremiah.

[II.A]   *But he who holds back his prophesy [M. 11:5D]*—**such as Jonah son of Amittai [T. San. 14:14].**

[B]   Said R. Jonah, "He was a true prophet.

[C]   "You find that when the Holy One, blessed be he, said to him, 'Arise, go to Nineveh, the great city, and cry out against it; for their wickedness has come up before me' (Jonah 1:2),

[D]   "Jonah said, 'I know that these gentiles are nigh unto repentance, and lo, I shall go and prophesy against them, and they shall repent, and the Holy One, blessed be he, consequently will come and inflict punishment on [those who hate] Israel [meaning, on Israel itself].

[E]   " 'So what should I do? [I have no choice but to] flee.'

[F]   " 'But Jonah rose to flee to Tarshish from the presence of the Lord. He went down to Joppa and found a ship going to Tarshish; so he paid the fare, and went on board, to go with them to Tarshish, away from the presence of the Lord' " (Jonah 1:3).

[III.A]   *He who disregards the words of another prophet*—**like Iddo, the seer [cf. T. San. 14:15].**

[B]   Said R. Samuel bar R. Isaac, "This is Amaziah, the priest of Beth El."

[C]   Said R. Yosé, "There was confusion there [lit.: smashed eggs], and who was he [who convinced Iddo to return]? It was Jonathan b. Gershom b. Moses.

[D]   "You find that when David came and found that he was worshipping an idol, he said to him, 'You are the grandson of that righteous man, and yet do you worship an idol?'

[E]   "He said to him, 'I have a tradition from my father's father: "Sell yourself to the service of strange [gods], but do not depend on other people." '

[F]   "He said to him, 'Heaven forfend! He never said such a thing to you.

[G]   "But what he really said was, 'Sell yourself for a kind of service which is alien to you, but do not depend on other people.'

[H]   "When David realized that he loved money, he appointed him superintendent of the treasury of the Temple."

[I]   That is in line with the following verse in Scripture: "And She-buel the son of Gershom, son of Moses, was chief officer in charge of the treasuries" (1 Chron. 26:24).

[J]   It was Shebuel, who returned (shab) to God (el) with all his might, who was chief officer in charge of the treasurers, for he appointed him superintendent of the treasury of the Temple.

[K]   Associates raised the question before R. Samuel bar Nahman: "Can it be that a priest [such as Jonathan b. Gershom] to an idol lived such a long time?"

[L]   He said to them, "Because he was niggardly in the service of his idol."

[M]   And in what way was he niggardly in the service of his idol?

[N]   When someone brought him [30c] an ox, a sheep, or a lamb, for the idol, and said, "Appease the idol for me,"

[O]   Jonathan would say to him, "Why?

[P]   "Now does this thing do you any good? He does not eat or drink, he can do neither good nor bad."

[Q]   So the other would say to him, "What should I do?"

[R]   And he would say to him, "Go and bring a little dish of flour, and ten eggs in it, and I'll go and appease it for you."

[S]   When the other went away, he would eat the whole lot.

[T]   One empty-head came, and he told him [what just now has been reported].

[U]   He said to him, "If it's good for nothing, why do you do what you do here?"

[V]   He said to him, "It's to make a living."

[W]   They replied to R. Samuel bar Nahman, "And lo, it is written, 'And the Danites set up the graven image for themselves; and Jonathan b. Gershom b. Moses, and his sons were priests to the tribe of the Danites until the day of the captivity of the land. So they set up Micah's graven image which he made, as long as the house of God was at Shiloh' " (Judges 18:30–31).

[X]   He said to them, "When David died and Solomon took over, then he changed all of his councillors, and this one went back to his evil ways."

[**IV**.A]   *And a prophet who transgresses his own words*—**this is exemplified by the associate of Micah [T. San. 14:15].**

[B]   This is in accord with the following verse of Scripture: "Now there dwelt an old prophet in Bethel. And his sons came and told him all that the man of God had done that day in Bethel; the words also which he had spoken to the king, they told to their father. And their father said to them, 'Which way did he go?' And his sons showed him the way which the man of God who came from Judah had gone. And he said to his sons, 'Saddle the ass for me.' So they saddled the ass for him and he mounted it. And he went after the man of God and found him sitting under an oak; and he said to him, 'Are you the man of God who came from Judah?' And he said, 'I am.' Then he said to him, 'Come home with me and eat bread.' And he said, 'I may not return with you, or go in with you; neither will I eat bread nor drink water with you in this place; for it was said to me by the word of the Lord, 'You shall neither eat bread nor drink water there, nor return by the way that you came.' And he said to him, 'I also am a prophet as you are, and an angel spoke to me by the word of the Lord, saying, Bring him back with you into your house that he may eat bread and drink water.' But he lied to him. So he went back with him and ate bread in his house and drank water."

[C]   What is the meaning of "he lied to him"? He deceived him.

[D]   "And as they sat at the table, the word of the Lord came to the prophet who had brought him back, and he cried to the man of God who came from Judah, 'Thus says the Lord, because you have disobeyed the word of the Lord and have not kept the commandment which the Lord your God commanded you, but have come back, and have eaten bread and drunk water in the place of which he said to you, Eat no bread and drink no water; your body shall not come to the tomb of your fathers' " (1 Kings 13:11–22).

[E]   "The prophet who was brought back" is *not* written here, but rather, "The prophet who brought him back" [thus the statement was made to the old prophet at Bethel, who had lied].

[F]   Now this matter produces the following argument *a fortiori:*

[G]   Now if one who fed bread to his fellow under false pretenses had the honor of having the word of God addressed in particular to him, he who feeds his fellow bread in truth all the more so!

[H]   It is written, "And a certain man of the sons of the prophets said to his fellow at the command of the Lord, 'Strike me, I pray.' But the man refused to strike him. Then he said to him, 'Because you have not obeyed the voice of the Lord, behold, as soon as you have gone from me, a lion shall kill you.' And as soon as he had departed from him, a lion met him and killed him. Then he found another man and said, 'Strike me, I pray.' And the man struck him, smiting and wounding him. And the prophet departed, and waited for the king by the way, disguising himself with a bandage over his eyes. And as the king passed, he cried to the king and said, 'Your servant went out into the midst of the battle; and behold, a soldier turned and brought a man to me, and said, Keep this man; if by any means he be missing, your life shall be for his life, or else you shall pay a talent of silver. And as your servant was busy here and there, he was gone.' The king of Israel said to him, 'So shall your judgment be; you yourself decided it.' Then he made haste to take the bandage away from his eyes; and the king of Israel recognized him as one of the prophets. And he said to him, 'Thus says the Lord, because you have let go out of your hand the man whom I had devoted to destruction, therefore your life shall go for his life, and your people for his people.' And the king of Israel went to his house resentful and sullen and came to Samaria" (1 Kings 20:35–43).

[I]   It is written, "And the man of God . . . said . . . and he said . . . ," two times. Why two times?

[J]   But in the first time he spoke to him, he said to him, "Should Ben Hadad, king of Aram, fall into your hand, have no pity on him and do not spare him."

[K]   And in the second he said to him, "Because you have let go out of your hand the man whom I had devoted to destruction . . ."

[L]   And how many traps and nets did I prepare for him before I handed him over to you, and you sent him forth and he got away in peace!

[M]   Therefore: "Your life shall go for his life, and your people for his people."

[N]   You find that when Israel went forth to war, of them all only Ahab, king of Israel, alone was the one who died.

[O]   That is in line with the following:

[P]   "But a certain man drew his bow at a venture and struck the king of Israel between the scale armor and the breast plate, and he said to the driver of his chariot, 'Turn about and carry me out of the battle, for I am wounded' " (1 Kings 22:34).

[Q]   And how shall I interpret the statement, "And your people instead of his people"?

[R]   R. Yohanan in the name of R. Simeon b. Yohai: "That single drop of blood which flowed from that righteous man [the prophet of 1 Kings 20:35ff.] effected atonement for all Israel."

The Talmud systematically illustrates the Mishnah's categories with ample biblical references and tales.

11:6 [In Leiden MS and *editio princeps*: 11:8]

[A]   *"He who prophesies in the name of an idol," and says, "Thus did such-and-such an idol say to me,"*

[B]   *even though he got the law right, declaring unclean that which in fact is unclean, and declaring clean that which in fact is clean.*

[C]   *"He who has sexual relations with a married woman"—*

[D]   *as soon as she has entered the domain of the husband in marriage, even though she has not had sexual relations with him—*

[E]   *he who has sexual relations with her—lo, this one is put to death by strangling.*

[F]   *"And those who bear false witness against the priest's daughter and against one who has sexual relations with her"—*

[G]   *for all those who bear false witness first suffer that same mode of execution,*

[H]   *except for those who bear false witness against the priest's daughter and her lover.*

[I.A]   Said R. Yosé b. Hananiah, "All were subject to the single commandment, 'You shall not bear false witness against your neighbor' (Ex. 20:16).

[B]   "Now the one who prophesies in the name of an idol [thus bearing false witness] was singled out [and condemned to death]."

[C]   Whether he gave a sign or did a wonder, whether it had to do with idolatry or any of the other commandments [do not listen to him].

[D]   [Read: **He who prophesies to uproot something which is taught in the Torah is liable. R. Simeon says, "If he prophesied to nullify part and to keep part, he is exempt." But if he prophesied in the name of idolatry, even if he confirms it today and nullifies it tomorrow, he is liable] [T. San.14:13].** Now with regard to idolatry, whether the prophet intended to uproot the whole principle or whether he did not intend to uproot the whole,

[E]   in the view of R. Simeon, they strangle him to death.

[F]   In the opinion of sages, they stone him.

[G]   But with regard to [his preaching against] all the other commandments, if he did not intend to uproot the whole principle, in the view of sages, they stone him.

[H]   In the view of R. Simeon, they exempt him.

[I]   And as to the prophet who began to prophesy, if he gave a sign or did a wonder, they listen to him, and if he did not do so, they do not pay attention to him.

[J]   As to two prophets who prophesied simultaneously,

[K]   or two prophets who prophesied in the same town—

[L]   R. Isaac and R. Hoshaiah—

[M]   one said, "He has to give a sign or do a wonder."

[N]   The other stated, "He does not have to give a sign or do a wonder."

[O]   The one who said that he has to do so objected to the one who said he does not have to do so, "And lo, it is written, 'And Hezekiah said to Isaiah, What shall be the sign that the Lord will heal me, and that I shall go up to the house of the Lord on the third day?' " (2 Kings 20:8).

[P]   He said to him, "That is a special case, because at issue was the resurrection of the dead.

[Q]   " 'After two days he will revive us; on the third day he will raise us up, that we may live before him' " (Hos. 6:2).

[II.A] [Referring to M. 11:6D], said R. Judah b. Pazzi, "Is not the determining factor the marriage canopy? It was not only to the marriage canopy, but even [if she came] to a house in which a marriage canopy was set up, [she is subject to the law of M. 11:6C–E]."

[B]   [Cf. Jastrow, p. 554b, s.v. TRQLYN:] The following construction is required (in order to make the reception of the bride in the triclinium a legal consummation of marriage), a triclinium and a marriage chamber, and that chamber communicating with the triclinium.

[C]   In what regard was the rule stated?

[D]   R. Yohanan said, "It was for the husband to inherit her."

[E]   R. Simeon b. Laqish said, "It was in regard to his power over the annulment of her vows."

[F]   Said R. Zeira, "Even though R. Simeon b. Laqish said that it was for the annulment of her vows, he concedes that the husband does not nullify her vows until she will actually enter the marriage canopy."

[G]   Said R. Huna, "The following verse of Scripture supports the view of R. Simeon b. Laqish: 'For she has wrought folly in Israel by playing the harlot in her father's house' " (Deut. 22:21).

[H]   This then excludes the case in which the agents of the father handed the girl over to the agents of the husband:

[I]   in such a case [if she commits adultery], she will not be punished by stoning, but rather by strangulation [since she is no longer in her father's domain].

[III.A]   **All perjurers and illicit lovers go and suffer the form of death
which they had brought on their victim. Under what circumstances? When they are in the same status as the victim so
as to be subject to that same mode of execution: if the death
penalty attached to the crime is stoning, the accused is
stoned, and the witnesses are stoned; if it was to be burning,
the victim is put to death by burning, and they are burned.**

[B]   **But here he is subject to the death penalty through burning,
while the perjurers are killed through strangulation [T. San.
14:17].**

Unit **I** amplifies M. 11:6A–B, the reason that the one who prophesies in the name of an idol is put to death. Of special interest
is the requirement that a prophet give a sign to validate what
he says. Unit **II** then brings us to the rule, M. 11:6C–E, that as
soon as the woman leaves the father's house, even though the
marriage has not been consummated, she ceases to be subject
to the penalty of stoning in the case of adultery, and now is
punished as is a married woman, by strangling. This interest in
the shift in her status, **II**.C–E, then raises the question of what
rights the husband has prior to the sexual union. Yohanan allows him to inherit, should she die prior to the consummation
of the marriage, and Simeon b. Laqish insists that it refers to
his right to nullify her vows, something the father can no
longer do. Unit **III** then cites Tosefta in connection with M.
11:6G. So, in all, we have systematic analysis of Mishnah.

Makkot

13 Introduction to Makkot

The tractate generates a fair amount of its facts through the exegesis of the verses relevant to its topics, as we shall see in detail. The following are the relevant Scriptural passages.

Ex. 20:16

You shall not bear false witness against your neighbor.

Deut. 5:20

Neither shall you bear witness against your neighbor.

Deut. 19:15–21

A single witness shall not prevail against a man for any crime or for any wrong in connection with any offense that he has committed; only on the evidence of two witnesses, or of three witnesses, shall a charge be sustained. If a malicious witness rises against any man to accuse him of wrongdoing, then both parties to the dispute shall appear before the Lord, before the priests and the judges who are in office in those days; the judges shall inquire diligently, and if the witness is a false witness and has accused his brother falsely, then you shall do to him as he had meant to do to his brother; so you shall purge the evil from the midst of you. And the rest shall hear, and fear, and shall never again commit any such evil among you. Your eye shall not pity; it shall be life for life, eye for eye, tooth for tooth, hand for hand, foot for foot.

Num. 35:9–28

And the Lord said to Moses, Say to the people of Israel, When you cross the Jordan into the land of Canaan, then you shall select cities to be cities of refuge for you, that the manslayer who kills any person without intent may flee there. The cities shall be for you a refuge from the avenger, that the manslayer may not die until he stands before the congregation for judgment. And the cities which you give shall be your six cities of refuge. You shall give three cities beyond the Jordan, and three cities in the land of Canaan, to be cities of refuge. These six cities shall be for refuge for the people of Israel, and for the stranger and for the sojourner among them, that anyone who kills any person without intent may flee there.

But if he struck him down with an instrument of iron, so that he died, he is a murderer; the murderer shall be put to death. And if he struck him down with a stone in the hand, by which a man may die, and he died, he is a murderer; the murderer shall be put to death. Or if he struck him down with a weapon of wood in the hand, by which a man may die, and he died, he is a murderer; the murderer shall be put to death. The avenger of blood shall himself put the murderer to death; when he meets him, he shall put him to death. And if he stabbed him from hatred, or hurled at him, lying in wait, so that he died, or in enmity struck him down with his hand, so that he died, then he who struck the blow shall be put to death; he is a murderer; the avenger of blood shall put the murderer to death, when he meets him.

But if he stabbed him suddenly without enmity, or hurled anything on him without laying in wait, or used a stone, by which a man may die, and without seeing him cast it upon him, so that he died, though he was not his enemy, and did not seek his harm; then the congregation shall judge between the manslayer and the avenger of blood, in accordance with these ordinances; and the congregation shall rescue the manslayer from the hand of the avenger of blood, and the congregation shall restore him to his city of refuge, to which he had fled, and he shall live in it until the death of the high priest who was anointed with the holy oil. But if the manslayer shall at any time go beyond the bounds of his city of refuge to which he fled, and the avenger of blood finds him outside the bounds of his city of refuge, and the avenger of blood slays the manslayer, he shall not be guilty of blood. For the man must remain in his city of refuge until the death of the high priest; but after the death of the high priest the manslayer may return to the land of his possession.

Num. 35:32

And you shall accept no ransom for him who has fled to his city of refuge, that he may return to dwell in the land before the death of the high priest.

Deut. 19:1–13

When the Lord your God cuts off the nations whose land the Lord your God gives you, and you dispossess them and dwell in their cities and in their houses, you shall set apart three cities for you in the land which the Lord your God gives you to possess. You shall prepare the roads, and divide into three parts the area of the land which the Lord your God gives you as a possession, so that any manslayer can flee to them.

This is the provision for the manslayer, who by fleeing there may save his life. If anyone kills his neighbor unintentionally without having been at enmity with him in time past—as when a man goes into the forest with his neighbor to cut wood, and his hand swings the axe to cut down a tree, and the head slips from the handle and strikes his neighbor so that he dies—he may flee to one of these cities and save his life; lest the avenger of blood in hot anger pursue the manslayer and overtake him, because the way is long, and wound him mortally, though the man did not deserve to die, since he was not at enmity with his neighbor in time past. Therefore I command you, You shall set apart three cities. And if the Lord your God enlarges your border, and he has sworn to your fathers—provided you are careful to keep all this commandment, which I command you this day, by loving the Lord your God and by walking ever in his ways—then you shall add three other cities to these three, lest innocent blood be shed in your land which the Lord your God gives you for an inheritance, and so the guilt of bloodshed be upon you.

But if any man hates his neighbor, and lies in wait for him, and attacks him, and wounds him mortally so that he dies, and the man flees into one of these cities, then the elders of his city shall send and fetch him from there, and hand him over to the avenger of blood, so that he may die. Your eye shall not pity him, but you shall purge the guilt of innocent blood from Israel, so that it may be well with you.

Deut. 25:1–3

If there is a dispute between men, and they come into court, and the judges decide between them, acquitting the innocent and condemning the guilty, then if the guilty man deserves to be beaten, the judge shall cause him to lie down and be beaten in his presence with a number of stripes in proportion to his offense. Forty stripes may be given him, but not more; lest, if one should go on to beat him with more stripes than these, your brother may be degraded in your sight.

The outline of the tractate follows.

I. Perjury (1:1–1:10)

1:1   How are witnesses punished as perjurers? They may be flogged.

1:2   Meir: Perjurers may both be flogged and be required to pay compensation. Sages: Whoever pays restitution is not flogged. Flogging on several counts of perjury.

1:3   Witnesses are declared to be perjurers only if they incriminate themselves (not merely if their testimony against the accused is proved false).
Proving several sets of witnesses, in sequence, to be perjured.

1:4   Perjured witnesses in a capital case are put to death only at the conclusion of the trial.

1:5   There is no difference at all between a group of two witnesses and a group of three or more. The same rules apply to any number.

1:6–7   Disjoined testimony (e.g., when a number of witnesses see a crime but do not see one another).

1:8   He whose trial ended and who fled and was brought back before the same court—they do not retry him.

II. The penalty of exile (banishment) (2:1–8)

A. *Those who are sent into exile.* 2:1–3

2:1–2   These are the ones who go into exile (mainly: involuntary manslaughter).

2:3–5   He who throws a stone into the public domain and committed homicide—lo, this one goes into exile. Exposition of Num. 35:23.

B. *The cities of exile.* 2:4–8

2:6   Where do they go into exile? To cities of refuge.
Yosé b. R. Judah: The procedure by which a person flees to a city of refuge and is tried.

2:7   The position of the manslaughterer in the city of refuge.

III. The penalty of flogging (3:1–16)

A. *Those who are flogged.* 3:1–9

3:1   These are the ones who are flogged.
3:2–3   Others who suffer flogging.
3:4   He who removes the dam with the offspring—is he flogged, or may he send away the dam?
3:5–6   The possibility of incurring the penalty of flogging on a number of different counts.
3:7   Triplet of cases in which one incurs flogging on several counts or only a single count.
3:8   There is one who ploughs a single furrow and is liable to flogging on eight counts.

B. *The manner of flogging.* 3:10–14

3:9   How many times do they flog?
3:10   They make an estimate of one's capacity to take the flogging and assign a number divisible by three.
3:11   How do they flog him (narrative)?

C. *Concluding homilies.* 3:15–16

3:12   Flogging remits extirpation, so Hanania b. Gamaliel.
3:13   The Holy One wanted to give merit to Israel. Therefore he gave them much Torah and many commandments.

1:1

[A] [31a] *How are witnesses treated [punished] as perjurers?*

[B] *[If they had said,] "We testify concerning Mr. So-and-so, that he is the son of a divorcee," or ". . . the son of a woman who has performed the rite of removing the shoe," [and had been proved perjurers,]*

[C] *they do not say, "Let this one be declared the son of a divorcee," or ". . . the son of a woman who has performed the rite of removing the shoe."*

[D] *But he is flogged [on account of perjury] with forty stripes.*

[E] *. . . , "We testify concerning Mr. So-and-so, that he is liable to exile,"*

[F] *they do not say, "Let this one go into exile in his stead."*

[G] *But he is flogged with forty stripes.*

[H] *. . . , "We testify concerning Mr. So-and-so, that he has divorced his wife and not paid off her marriage settlement,"—*

[I] *(and is it not so that whether it is today or tomorrow, he certainly is going to pay off her marriage settlement?)*

[J] *they make an estimate of how much a man will be willing to pay [now] for the ownership of her marriage settlement,*

[K] *on the condition that, if [the woman] should be widowed or divorced, [he will take over,] but if she should die, her husband will inherit her [estate, including said marriage settlement].*

[**I**.A]   [The statement which follows explains M. 1:2I–L, which states, *[If witnesses said,]* *"We testify concerning Mr. So-and-so, that he is liable to receive flogging in the measure of forty stripes,"* and they turn out to be perjurers—*"they are smitten eighty times, both on the count of, 'You shall not bear false witness against your neighbor' (Ex. 20:16), and on the count of, 'You shall do to him as he had conspired to do' " (Deut. 19:19), the words of R. Meir. And sages say, "They are flogged only forty stripes."]* Said R. Yosé b. Haninah, "All were subject to the general statement, 'You shall not bear false witness against your neighbor' (Ex. 20:16). The perjured witness then was treated as a special case: 'And you shall do to him as he had conspired to do' (Deut. 19:19).

[B]   "In the case of one in whom you are able to carry out, 'And you shall do to him as he had conspired to do,' you carry out, 'You shall not bear false witness' [punishing on both counts].

[C]   "And in the case of the one upon whom you cannot carry out, 'And you shall do to him as he had conspired to do,' you shall carry out, 'You shall not bear false false witness against your neighbor.' [That is to say, in the case in which one is flogged on the count of 'doing to him as he had conspired to do,' Meir maintains, one flogs him also on the count of 'not bearing false witness.' But if there is no flogging on the one count, there is no flogging on the other.]"

[D]   Another matter: "And you shall do to him"—and not to his descendants. [This explains M. 1:1C, for that judgment would affect his descendants' standing as well.]

[E]   R. Joshua b. Levi said, " 'And you shall do to him . . .'—two matters are handed over to a court. You take hold of only one of them, except for a matter which is in the hands of Heaven. [On this count, the court does not both exact a financial penalty and also impose a flogging, as at M. 1:2, below.]"

[**II**.A]   It is written, "He shall not profane his children among his people [by not marrying a virgin]" (Lev. 21:15).

[B]   I know only that this applies to his seed, which he profanes.

[C]   The woman herself [who is made profane through having sexual relations with him]—how do we know [that that is the case]?

[D]   It is a matter of an argument *a fortiori:*

[E] Now if his seed, which has itself not done any transgression, lo, it is deemed profane,

[F] the woman herself, who has done a transgression—is it not logical that she should be deemed profane?

[G] He himself will prove [that this argument is invalid]. For he has done a transgression and is not profaned.

[H] No, if you have stated that fact in regard to the man, who is never in any event subject to being profaned,

[I] will you say the same of the woman, who indeed is profaned under all circumstances?

[J] Since she is profaned under all other circumstances, it is logical that she should be profaned [in the present case].

[K] And if you should wish to propose:

[L] [Scripture should have written,] "He should not profane [in the Qal construction, YHWL]." When it wrote, "He should not profane [in the Pi'el construction, YHLL]," it refers even to one who was valid and has been profaned [that is, a woman (= C)].

[M] [With reference to M. 1:1C,] Bar Pedaiah says, "He who profanes is not subject to being profaned [so he profanes his seed, not himself]. [So then how can one—the witness—who did not profane, although he wanted to, be profaned]" (PM, QH).

[III.A] Witnesses who were proven to be perjurers—

[B] R. Yohanan said, " 'False,' 'false' [that is, the word occurs twice in context (either Ex. 20:16 and Deut. 19:18 or twice in the latter verse) involving distinct liabilities]."

[C] Witnesses who were proved perjurers, and who again lied [in a property aspect of the same case]—

[D] R. Yohanan said, " 'False,' 'false' [and are flogged and also pay conpensation."

[E] R. Eleazar said, " 'Evil,' 'evil.'

[F] " 'Evil' is stated with reference to those who are liable to the death penalty (Num 35:31), and 'evil' is mentioned in the matter of those liable to flogging (Deut. 75:2).

[G]   "Just as 'evil' which is stated in reference to those liable to the death penalty indicates that a financial compensation is not exacted in the case of a death penalty,

[H]   "so the word, 'evil,' stated with reference to those who are liable to flogging indicates that there is no monetary compensation exacted in the case of flogging [cf. M. 1:2H]."

[IV.A]   Bar Pedaiah said, " 'If anyone kills his neighbor unintentionally . . . ,] he may flee [to one of these cities and save his life]' (Deut. 19:4–5).

[B]   "*He* will flee, but those who perjure themselves against him may not flee."

[V.A]   And they do not pay the whole value of the woman's marriage settlement but they pay the value of making use of such a marriage settlement.

[B]   How so?

[C]   One says, *How much is a man willing to pay now for the right to the marriage settlement of this one, on condition that, if she should die during the lifetime of her husband, [the husband] will inherit it [M. 1:1J–K]*, but if her husband should die in her lifetime, the purchaser then would inherit the value of the marriage contract.

[D]   In accord with such an estimate, does he pay for the value of the marriage settlement [cf. T. Mak. 1:6].

Unit **I** clearly serves M. 1:2, dealing as it does with two distinct elements of that pericope. Unit **II** deals with materials in an entirely other regard. These are explained at the proper place. The reason for the insertion comes at II.M, which makes use of the earlier materials with reference to the present rule. There is nothing to be done to the perjurer, since one cannot render the perjurers (if priests) profaned anyhow. For its part unit **III** serves M. 1:2. Unit **IV** is a brief clarification, relevant to nothing. Only the rather repetitious set at unit **V** pertains to Mishnah.

1:2 [In Leiden MS and *editio princeps:* 1:2–5]

[A]   . . . , "We testify concerning Mr. So-and-so, that he owes his fellow a thousand 'zuz,' on condition that he will pay him in the next thirty days,"

[B]   and the accused says, ". . . in the next ten years,"

[C]   they make an estimate of how much a man is willing to pay for the use of a thousand "zuz," whether he pays them in thirty days or in ten years. [The difference, then, would be owing.]

[D]   . . . , "We testify concerning Mr. So-and-so, that he owes his fellow two-hundred 'zuz,' "

[E]   and they turn out to be perjurers—

[F]   "they are flogged, and they pay up,

[G]   "for the count which brings flogging on them is not the count which brings on them the penalty of restitution," the words of R. Meir.

[H]   And sages say, "Whoever pays restitution is not flogged."

[I]   . . . , "We testify concerning Mr. So-and-so, that he is liable to receive flogging in the measure of forty stripes,"

[J]   and they turn out to be perjurers—

[K]   "they are smitten eighty times, on the count of, 'You shall not bear false witness against your neighbor' (Ex. 20:16), and on the count of, 'You shall do to him as he had conspired to do' " (Deut. 19:19), the words of R. Meir.

[L]   And sages say, "They are flogged only forty stripes."

[M]   They divide up [among the perjurers] a penalty for making restitution, but they do not divide up the penalty of flogging.

[N]   How so?

[O]   [If] they gave testimony about someone that he owes his fellow two-hundred "zuz," and they turned out to be perjurers, they divide up [the two-hundred "zuz"] among them [and make restitution of that amount].

[P]   But if they gave testimony about him that he is liable to receive flogging in the measure of forty stripes, and they turned out to be perjurers, each one is flogged forty times.

[I.A]   R. Ba bar Mamal, R. Amram, R. Mattenah in the name of
Rab: "He who lends funds to his fellow on condition that [the
lender] not lay claim [for return of capital, but the borrower
will pay whenever it suits him]—the Sabbatical year releases
[the debt]." [The point is that Scripture states one should not
exact a debt of his neighbor (Deut. 15:2f.). Now a loan on
these terms cannot be said to be "exacted," that is, it is not an
oppressive debt. Hence one may suppose that the remission of
the Sabbatical year does not apply to such a loan. But Rab
says, that is not the case. The issue then will be debts not collectible at the point at which the Sabbatical year comes into effect, and whether they are or are not remitted, since they are
not to be "exacted" in the stated sense.]

[B]   And lo, we have learned: *He who slaughtered a cow and divided it [among buyers] on the first day of the [eighth] year,
and the month was intercalated [so that that day turned out to
be at the end of the seventh, that is, the Sabbatical, year]—the
debt [incurred by the buyers who bought the meat] is annulled.
But if not, it is not null [M. Shebi. 10:2].*

[C]   And R. Eleazar said, "That is the view of R. Judah [who in M.
Shebi. 10:1 treats credit extended from the seller to the buyer
as a loan and therefore liable to annulment in the Sabbatical
year]."

[D]   And is the debt ever subject to collection on the New Year?!
[Of course not! Therefore this instance of M. Shebi. 10:2 is
similar to a case of extended credit where the seller cannot demand payment at any time.]

[E]   This view accords with that which R. Ba said in the name of
R. Zeira: "[The position of M. Shebi. 10:2 is not in accord
with the theory of Judah, C. Rather, Mishnah's reasoning is in
accord with the following logic:] Since it is a case in which the
debt is subject to claim [at any time], it is as if the seller has
faith in the buyer. Since he has faith, it is as if he can pay off
the debt. Now in this case (M. Shebi. 10:2), since the case is
one in which the purchaser can have paid the money and has
not done so, the first purchase [in a sequence of several] is
deemed tantamount to a debt [in consequence of which the
debt is collectible, the Seventh Year is effective, and the debt is
remitted]. [That is the case even though, in fact, it is the New
Year, and on the festival funds will not be paid out. So this

explains why the debt is deemed in existence, and, consequently, subject to remission.]"

[F]   R. Yosé b. R. Bun in the name of Rab: "He who lends funds
to his fellow on condition that the Sabbatical year not remit the
debt—the Sabbatical year *does* remit the debt. [That is, if the
debt runs for ten years prior to collection, the advent of the
Sabbatical year does not cancel the debt. Rab's view, then, is
that such a clause is null, and the Sabbatical year does nullify
the debt.]"

[G]   And lo, we have learned the following pericope of Mishnah:
. . . *they make an estimate of how much a man is willing to
pay for the use of a thousand "zuz," whether he pays them in
the next thirty days or in ten years* [M. 1:2C]. [It follows that if
the debt is for ten years, the funds in fact will never be paid
back, for the intervening Sabbatical year will nullify the debt.
The force of the testimony would have been to cause the loss of
the whole capital, not merely the use thereof. Consequently, in
line with Rab's view, we must wonder what purpose the stated
estimate is to serve.]

[H]   For can ten years pass without a Sabbatical year?

[I]   [In explanation of this problem,] R. Huna said, "R. Nahman
and R. Sheshet differed on the matter.

[J]   "One said, 'It is a case in which one has made a loan against a
pledge [in which case the effects of the Sabbatical year are
null].'

[K]   "The other said, 'It is a case in which one has made a loan on
the security of a *prozbul* [with the same consequences].' "

[L]   It was taught: "Thirty days—one does not come."

[M]   What is the meaning of this statement: "Thirty days—one does
not come"?

[N]   Samuel said, "[The meaning is:] 'He who lends funds to his
fellow without specification on the length of the term has not
got the right to lay claim on him within the first thirty days of
the loan.' "

[O]   R. Judah entered and stated, "The Scriptural basis for this position is as follows: 'The seventh year, the year of release, is
near' (Deut. 15:9).

[P]   "Now is not the seventh year the same as the year of release?

[Q]   "So why does Scripture specify, as it does, 'The seventh year, the year of release, is near'?

[R]   "It is so that you should not say, 'Throughout the thirty days of the loan [made on unspecified terms], one has not got the power to collect it. After the thirty days have passed, it will be subject to the release of debts so that one cannot collect the debt.' On this account it was necessary to specify, 'The seventh year' and 'the year of release' 'is near,' [that is, to indicate that when there is an unspecified term it is for thirty days]."

[S]   [Now if that is the purpose imputed to the cited verse, how shall we deal with the following problem:] For did not R. Ba bar Mamal, R. Amram, R. Mattenah in the name of Rab say: "He who lends money to his fellow on condition that he will not lay claim on him, [nonetheless] the Sabbatical year remits that debt? [Now if this took place within thirty days of the advent of the Sabbatical year, it is as if the loan was made on condition that the lender has made the condition of not laying claim on the borrower. For through the thirty-day period he cannot lay claim, and afterward the Sabbatical year comes.]"

[T]   The following teaching is available [to account for Rab's position:] R. Ishmael taught, " 'The seventh year, the year of release, is near'—Now is not the seventh year the same as the year of release? So why does Scripture specify, as it does, 'The seventh year, the year of release, is near'?

[U]   "It is so that [a farmer] will not say, 'All six years [prior to the Sabbatical year,] one's vineyard is available, his field is available, [to support him]. Now at the end of six years, funds owing to him are remitted, so that he may not collect them! [If so, how is he supposed to survive?]'

[V]   "On that account it is necessary to say, 'The seventh year, the year of release, is near'—[in reply to this complaint]. [And there is no other lesson to be derived from the cited verse, which simply addresses the stated complaint and yields no further laws.]"

The Talmud serves M. Shebi. 10:2. Its point of contact with the present pericope is at the cited passage, which plays a minor role in the present discourse.

1:3 [In Leiden MS and *editio princeps:* 1:6]

[A]   *Witnesses are declared to be perjurers only if they themselves will be incriminated.*

[B]   *How so?*

[C]   *[If] they said, "We testify concerning Mr. So-and-so, that he killed someone,"*

[D]   *[and] they said to them, "How can you give any testimony, for lo, this one who is supposed to have been killed, or that one who is supposed to have killed, was with us on that very day and in that very place"—*

[E]   *they are not declared perjurers.*

[F]   *But if they said to them, "How can you give testimony, and lo, you yourselves were with us on that very day in that very place"—*

[G]   *lo, these are declared perjurers,*

[H]   *and they are put to death on the basis of the testimony [of the incriminating pair of witnesses].*

[I]   *[If] others came and gave false testimony against them,*

[J]   *and still others came and gave false testimony against them,*

[K]   *even a hundred—*

[L]   *all of them are put to death.*

[M]   *R. Judah says, "This is a conspiracy, [to confuse the judges] and the only ones to be put to death are those of the first group alone."*

[I.A]   [In regard to Judah's view, M. 1:3M, that the first group is put to death,] R. Ba bar Mamal said, "But [that the first group also is put to death, while the others are not] applies in a case in which the first pair of witnesses has already been executed. But if they have not been executed, in such a case we do not apply that rule that we have learned, 'And the only ones to be put to death are those of the first group alone' " [M. 1:3M] (PM).

[B]   [In regard to sages' view, that all of them are put to death,] R. Bun bar Hiyya raised the following question before R. Zeira: "[If] they were standing and giving testimony against the accused that he had killed someone in Lud, and others came and said to them, 'How can you give evidence, for lo, you were with us on the fifteenth in Caesarea,' and yet others came to those and said to them, 'How can you give testimony, for lo, you were with us on the fifteenth day of the month in Sepphoris'—

[C]   "the one who is accused of murder is not put to death.

[D]   "For it may be that the witnesses are perjurers.

[E]   "And the witnesses are not put to death.

[F]   "For [the essence of] what they said may indeed have been the truth."

The point of interest, as is clear, is the extreme positions attributed to sages and Judah in a case of multiple perjury. The point is that once the first set of witnesses is shown to be perjured, the accused is let off. But the witnesses are let go, for the testimony against them itself is not completely without its weak points.

1:4 [In Leiden MS and *editio princeps:* 1:8]

[A]   *Perjured witnesses [in a capital case] are put to death only at the conclusion of the trial.*

[B]   *Now lo, the Sadducees say, "Only when the accused has actually been put to death, since it is said, 'A life for a life' "* (Deut. 19:21).

[C]   *Sages said to them, "And has it not also been said, 'And you will do to him as he had planned to do to his fellow' (Deut. 19:19)? And lo, his fellow is still alive!*

[D]   *"If so, why has it been said, 'A life for a life'?*

[E]   *"For one might suppose that from that very moment at which [the judges] have received their testimony [which is proved to be perjury], they should be put to death.*

[F]   *"Scripture says, 'A life for a life'—lo, they are put to death only at the conclusion of the trial."*

[I.A]   [I translate the text as given at Y. B.Q. 7:3.] [The present discussion pertains to M. B.Q. 7:3, which is as follows: *If one was convicted of theft on the evidence of two witnesses, and was convicted of having slaughtered or sold the beast on the basis of the testimony of two other witnesses, and these and those turn out to be false witnesses, the first pair of witnesses pays twofold restitution, and the second pair of witnesses pays threefold restitution. If the latter pair of witnesses turn out to be false witnesses, he pays twofold restitution, and they pay threefold restitution. If one of the latter pair of witnesses turns out to be false, the evidence of the second one is null. If one of the first pair of witnesses turns out to be false, the entire testimony is null, for if there is no culpable act of stealing, there also is no culpable act of slaughtering or selling.]* Said R. Zeira, "That is to say, A witness proved to be a perjurer is deemed to have given invalid testimony in court only at the point at which the witness himself is proved to be invalid. [That is to say, if the witness is shown to be a perjurer, from that point onward he is invalid. Then, retrospectively, all the testimony he gave even before the point at which he was proved to be perjured also is deemed null. The invalidation is personal.]"

[B]   Interpret the matter to deal with a case of the witnesses giving warning. [The witness must state, "I warned him not to do so and so." Now Zeira deals with the matter of warning and testimony, in the following terms. We have a case in which the act of theft took place on one day, the act of slaughter or sale on another day. Now even though these actions took place at different times, Mishnah does not take account of such differences. The witnesses give evidence in a single act of testimony, even though they speak of different times or days on which the several culpable deeds took place. Consequently, they will have to pay full compensation, should they be proved to be perjurers, e.g., in the matter of slaughter or sale. The proof of perjury thus is deemed to cover the entire testimony, and that is Zeira's observation. From the moment at which the testimony is invalidated, whatever is said thereafter is deemed null as well. Consequently, if the witnesses are shown to be perjurers as regards the theft of the beast, their testimony as regards its slaughter or sale is to begin with of no effect. They will not be assessed damages in that regard. At the point at which they gave evidence about slaughter or sale, the witnesses no longer were valid witnesses at all.]

[C]   And so it has been taught: **Said R. Yosé, "Under what circumstances? That is so in the case of two acts of testimony,**

and in the case of two acts of warning [as explained above]. [That is to say, a witness is deemed to be invalid from the moment at which he was proved invalid, and whatever he says about the case is null and of no effect.] **But if it is a single act of testimony** [as in the case of Zeira's discussion here], **then testimony part of which is invalidated is entirely null** [with the consequence that Zeira's position is effective, as explained] [T. B.Q. 7:23].

[D]   What is the meaning of the statement about nullifying part of a statement in evidence serving to invalidate the entire statement?

[E]   If the witnesses were standing and testifying against a man that on the tenth of Nisan he had stolen an ox on the first of Nisan, [and] on the tenth of Nisan he had slaughtered or sold it, [and] on the fifteenth of Nisan they were shown to be perjurers, all the testimony which they had given in regard to the man's actions from the tenth of Nisan to the fifteenth of Nisan retroactively is deemed null and void. [Since the witnesses testified all at once on these several actions, the entire testimony is deemed null, even though the witnesses spoke of what had been done on different days. It will follow that the witnesses do not pay compensation for their false testimony as to theft, let alone for their false testimony as to slaughter or sale. Once they were proved perjurers, nothing they said is deemed to have had consequences at all (cf. PM).]

[F]   Said R. Ba bar Mamal, "Interpret the statement to apply to a case in which the witnesses were testifying against the accused all at one time. Yosé's view is that, if the witnesses can be shown to have been in some other place at the time at which they allege *one* of the acts of felony to have been committed, then their allegations with regard to the rest of those acts are null. For they will have been shown to have been elsewhere at the time, on a given day, on which one of the deeds was done, and whatever they say about the other deeds will then be null as well.]

[G]   "And there is no further implication to be drawn from that fact. [All parties concur that, as to evidence concerning what happened beyond that point at which the perjurers are shown to have given false evidence, all such evidence is null. As to what they have said about events prior to the act about which they are shown to have been incapable of giving testimony, however, no inference is to be drawn whatsoever from the stated ruling. Nullification of part of the testimony effectively invalidates the whole of it]."

[H] And thus it has been taught that the first set of witnesses is the same as the last, as in the following:

[I] **[If] one held a field in usucaption in the presence of two for one year, in the presence of two in the second year, and in the presence of two in the third year,** *lo, these constitute three distinct acts of testimony, and they count as a single act of witness when the evidence is proved false (M. B.B. 3:4G–H).* **If the testimony [31b] of the first group proved false, lo, one has in his possession [valid evidence about] two years. If the second group proved false, lo, he has in his possession [valid evidence about] one year. If the third group proved false, he has nothing whatever in hand. If the first group and the last group are the same, and they turn out to be false witnesses, if the testimony which turned out to be false concerned the first year, he has nothing at all in hand. If it concerned the second year, lo, he has [valid evidence about] one year in hand. If it concerned the third year, lo, he has valid evidence about two years in hand [T. B.B. 2:9].** [The point of the cited case at T. B.B. 2:9 is that even though the testimony on the first year of usucaption was false, when there is further testimony about later years, that is valid. Thus evidence given concerning events from the point at which the evidence in the case is proved fraudulent and onward is unacceptable. But evidence given concerning what has happened prior to the point at which the testimony is null *still* is valid. Consequently, while the man may not have testimony affecting the second year, he still has evidence regarding the first year. It follows that the whole of the testimony is not nullified retroactively, but only part of it. This brings us to the Talmud's response, as follows.]

[J] How [can we accept the statement of R. Ba bar Mamal above] that "the testimony was given at one time and that no further implication can be drawn from that fact" [and his support for the statement from T. B.B. 2:9 (above, F–I)] (PM)?

[K] The support is dissimilar to his case for [Tosefta] treats only a case in which there were several acts of testimony, [that is, in which there were many acts of giving evidence]. [Each act of testimony governs a single year and is deemed distinct from the others. One can, after all, testify to events of one year and not of some other. The three properly validated years of usucaption then are joined together. It follows that evidence will be acceptable for one year, not nullified by evidence governing some other, later year of the cycle. But evidence as to theft and slaughter or sale concerns a single continuous process.]

[L]   [Following PM, I now translate the version at Y. B.Q. 7:3:] [Now with reference to the statement at M. B.Q. 7:3 concerning conviction of theft on the basis of the evidence of two witnesses, and conviction of having slaughtered on the basis of the evidence of two other witnesses,] up to now we have dealt with a case in which the witnesses concerning theft and those concerning slaughter came simultaneously.

[M]   But if the witnesses concerning theft came and [the judges] did not accept their testimony [for some technical flaw], and afterward witnesses concerning slaughter came along, [and the court] said to them, "You should know that witnesses concerning theft have already come to court, but [the judges] have not accepted them, and it is solely on your account that we shall now accept their testimony as well"—

[N]   then, if the witnesses concerning slaughter turn out to be perjurers, they pay compensation also in behalf of the witnesses to the matter of theft [for their evidence alone is what has had the effect of imposing liability on the accused *both* for the theft and for the slaughter].

[O]   R. Hezekiah did not state matters in that way.

[P]   Rather as follows [did he describe the issue]:

[Q]   "Up to now we have dealt with a case in which the witnesses to the theft and the witnesses to the slaughter came simultaneously.

[R]   "But if the witnesses to the slaughter came, and [the court] did not accept their [testimony], and then the witnesses to the theft came,

[S]   "and [the judge] said to them, 'You should know that witnesses to slaughter have come along, but we did not accept their [testimony], and it is solely on your account that we now accept their testimony as well,'

[T]   "then if the witnesses to the theft turned out to be perjurers they must pay in behalf of the witnesses to the slaughter as well [for precisely the same reason]." [The outcome is no different.]

None of the above discussion concerns the present pericope, and I cannot account for its inclusion here.

1:5 [In Leiden MS and *editio princeps:* 1:13]

[A]   *"At the mouth of two witnesses or three witnesses shall he that is to die be put to death" (Deut. 17:6).*

[B]   *If the testimony is confirmed with two witnesses, why has the Scripture specified three?*

[C]   *But: [the purpose is] to draw an analogy between three and two.*

[D]   *Just as three witnesses prove two witnesses to be false, also two witnesses may prove three witnesses to be false.*

[E]   *And how do we know that [two witnesses may prove false] even a hundred?*

[F]   *Scripture says, "Witnesses."*

[G]   *R. Simeon says, "Just as two are put to death only if both of them are proved to be perjurers, also three witnesses are put to death only if all three of them are proved to be perjurers.*

[H]   *"And how do we know that this applies even to a hundred?*

[I]   *"Scripture says, 'Witnesses.' "*

[J]   *R. Aqiba says, "The mention of the third [witness] is only to impose upon him a strict rule and to treat the rule concerning him as the same as that applying to the other two.*

[K]   *"And if Scripture has imposed a punishment on someone who gets involved with those who commit a transgression precisely equivalent to that which is imposed on those who themselves commit the transgression,*

[L]   *"how much the more so will [Heaven] pay a just reward to the one who gets involved with those who do a religious duty precisely equivalent to that which is paid to those who themselves actually do the religious duty!"*

[M]   *Just as, in the case of two [witnesses], if one of them turns out to be a relative or otherwise invalid, the testimony of both of them is null,*

[N]   *so in the case of three, [if] one of them turns out to be a relative or otherwise invalid, the testimony of all three of them is null.*

[O]   *How do we know that the same rule applies even in the case of a hundred?*

[P]   *Scripture says, "Witnesses."*

[Q]   *Said R. Yosé, "Under what circumstances? In the case of trials for capital crimes.*

[R]   *"But in the case of trials in property litigations, the testimony may be confirmed with the remaining [valid witnesses]."*

[S]   *Rabbi says, "All the same is the rule governing property cases and capital cases."*

[T]   *This is the rule when [both witnesses] warned the transgressor.*

[U]   *But if they had not joined in warning the transgressor, what should two brothers do who saw someone commit homicide?*

[I.A] [Scripture refers to the requirement of two or three witnesses to impose the death penalty, Deut. 17:6. Scripture further states, "Only on the evidence of two witnesses or of three witnesses shall a charge be sustained" (Deut. 19:15). The former deals with capital cases, the latter with property cases. Since both refer to two or three witnesses, the duplication now is explained:] Scripture is required to refer to property cases, and also to capital cases.

[B]   For if it had referred to property cases and not to capital cases, I might have said, In the case of property cases, which are of lesser weight, three witnesses have the power to prove two to be perjurers, but two may not prove three to be perjurers.

[C]   How do I know that that is so even of a hundred?

[D]   Scripture states, "Witnesses."

[E]   Now if reference had been made to capital cases, and not to property cases, I might have said, In capital cases, which are weightier, two witnesses have the power to prove that three are perjurers, but three do not have the power to prove that two are perjurers.

[F] How do I know that that applies even to a hundred?

[G] Scripture says, "Witnesses." [It follows then the Scripture must refer to "two or three" in the context of each matter, since one could not have derived the one from the other.]

The relevance to Mishnah comes at C–D, F–G—which are not pertinent to the issue unfolding at A, B, and E. But whoever made the pericope up certainly followed a single pattern and responded to the Mishnaic passage before us. The point is clear as stated.

1:6 [In Leiden MS and *editio princeps:* 1:14]

[A] *[If] two saw the incident from one window, and two saw it from another window,*

[B] *and one warns [the transgressor] in the middle,*

[C] *when part of one group see part of another, lo, these constitute a single body of testimony [subject to the rules given above].*

[D] *But if not, lo, these constitute two distinct bodies of testimony.*

[E] *Therefore, if one of them turns out to be perjured, he [the transgressor] and those two witnesses are put to death, but the other group of witnesses is exempt.*

[I.A] Said R. Jeremiah, "Note the explanation of what we have learned: *If two saw the incident from one window, and two saw it from another window, and one warns the transgressor in the middle, when part of one group sees part of another, lo, these constitute a single body of testimony. But if not, lo these constitute two distinct bodies of testimony.*

[B] "Lo, if they were *three* [witnesses]?

[C] "The rule does not apply to such a case. [That is, the matter does not depend on the one in the middle. If he sees both witnesses but they do not see one another, they do not form a single group.]"

[D]   Said R. Yosé, "We have learned, 'As to three—three are not subject to the same law.' [If there were three and the one in the middle saw them all, in such a case they do not constitute disjoined groups, as at M. 1:6D.]"

[II.A]   We have learned here what we have not learned in the entire tractate of Sanhedrin:

[B]   *He and those two witnesses are put to death, but the other group of witnesses* [whose testimony is accepted] *is exempt [M. 1:6E].*

Unit **I**'s clarifications are important. The one in the middle does not have the power to join the testimony of individuals who themselves cannot see one another. Unit **II** simply comments on the importance of Mishnah's point.

1:7 [In Leiden MS and *editio princeps:* 1:15]

[A]   *R. Yosé says, "Under no circumstances is one put to death unless both witnesses against him have given warning to him,*

[B]   *"as it is said, 'At the testimony of two witnesses' "* (Deut. 17:6).

[C]   *Another interpretation:*

[D]   *"At the mouth of two witnesses"* [directly]—*that the Sanhedrin should not listen to the testimony through the intervention of a translator.*

[I.A]   R. Hoshaiah taught, "The following verse is stated with reference to two groups of witnesses, 'If a malicious witness rises against any man to accuse him of wrongdoing . . .' (Deut. 19:16)—

[B]   ["Witness"]—this is a perjured witness.

[C]   "To accuse him"—and not the testimony which he gives. [Now we have an allusion to the second group of witnesses, who testify against the accused that he cannot have given the evidence he gave, because he was somewhere else at the time of the event he describes.]

[**II**.A]   As to perjured witnesses, what is the law in respect to their having to be given appropriate warning [prior to their giving testimony? If then, they ignore the warning against giving false witness, they are punished.]

[B]   R. Isaac bar Tablai in the name of R. Eleazar: "Perjured witnesses do not have to be given warning."

[C]   Said R. Abbahu, "Do they then not scruple? [That is, do we assume they would not respond to warning, so that we maintain a warning is not required in their case?]"

[D]   Said R. Jacob bar Dassai, "There indeed are many such cruel people, who see their fellows taken out for execution and know evidence to free them but say nothing."

[**III**.A]   [Leiden MS and *editio princeps:* 1:16] If one has written over his property to two people at one time, and the witnesses to the will are valid for one and invalid for [e.g., relatives of] the other—

[B]   R. Hila said, "R. Yohanan and R. Simeon b. Laqish differed on this matter.

[C]   "One of them said, 'Since they are invalid for this party, they are invalid for that.'

[D]   "The other said, 'They are valid for the one and invalid for the other.' "

[E]   R. Mana did not specify [which party held which opinion, but repeated the tradition in the form just now stated].

[F]   By contrast, R. Abun made explicit [which party held which opinion].

[G]   "R. Yohanan said, 'Since they are invalid for this party, they are invalid for that party.'

[H]   "R. Simeon b. Laqish said, 'They are valid for this party and invalid for that party.' "

[I]   Said R. Eleazar, "The following Tannaitic tradition supports the position of R. Yohanan:

[J]   *"Just as, in the case of two [witnesses], if one of them turns out to be a relative or otherwise invalid, the testimony of both of them is null, so in the case of three, if one of them turns out to be a relative or otherwise invalid, the testimony of all three of them is null. How do we know that the same rule applies even in the case of a hundred? Scripture says, 'Witnesses' " [M. 1:5M–P].*

[K] R. Jacob bar Aha: R. Haninah, the associate of the rabbis, and the rabbis differ:

[L] One said, "R. Eleazar stated matters correctly."

[M] The other said, "R. Eleazar did not state matters correctly."

[N] The one who said, " 'R. Eleazar stated matters correctly,' holds that the testimony is treated as a single act of giving evidence and subject to a single warning, with the result that we invoke the rule, 'Any act of testimony, part of which is nullified, is wholly null' [= G]."

[O] The one who said that R. Eleazar did not state matters correctly maintains that they are treated like two distinct pairs of witnesses, who are then suitable in one case and invalid in another.

Unit **I** presents an exegesis of yet another verse of Scripture. Hoshaiah shows that the cited verse refers to the witnesses against the accused, and yet other witnesses, against the first set. The problem of unit **II** is clear as given. Unit **III** intersects at the indicated point with M. 1:5 and presumably is out of place here.

1:8 [In Leiden MS and *editio princeps:* 1:17]

[A] *He whose trial ended and who fled and was brought back before the same court—*

[B] *they do not reverse the judgment concerning him [and retry him].*

[C] *In any situation in which two get up and say, "We testify concerning Mr. So-and-so that his trial ended in the court of such-and-such, with Mr. So-and-so and Mr. So-and-so as the witnesses against him,"*

[D] *lo, this one is put to death.*

[E] *[Trial before] a Sanhedrin applies both in the Land and abroad.*

[F] *A Sanhedrin which imposes the death penalty once in seven years is called murderous.*

[G] *R. Eleazar b. Azariah says, "Once in seventy years."*

[H] *R. Tarfon and R. Aqiba say, "If we were on a Sanhedrin, no one would ever be put to death."*

[I] *Rabban Simeon b. Gamaliel says, "So they would multiply the number of murderers in Israel."*

[I.A] [Trial before a] *Sanhedrin applies both in the Land and abroad [M. 1:8E],*

[B] as it is written, "And these things shall be for a statute and ordinance to you throughout your generations in all your dwellings" (Num. 35:29).

[C] And why does Scripture say, "You shall appoint judges and officers in all your towns [which the Lord your God gives you]" (Deut. 16:18)?—In the towns of the Land of Israel.

[D] The meaning is that in the towns of Israel they set up judges in every town, but abroad they do so only by districts.

[E] It was taught: R. Dosetai b. R. Yannai says, "It is a religious requirement for each tribe to judge its own tribe, as it is said, 'You shall appoint judges and officers in all your towns which the Lord your God gives you, according to your tribes' " (Deut. 16:18).

[II.A] Rabban Simeon b. Gamaliel taught, "Those declared liable to the death penalty who fled from the Land abroad—they put them to death forthwith [upon recapture].

[B] "If they fled from abroad to the Land, they do not put them to death forthwith, but they undertake a trial *de novo.*"

Since the proof text, **I**.B, yields results contrary to the assumed implications of that at C, D must indicate otherwise. Unit **II** is an independent saying, generally relevant to M. 1:8E.

2:1

[A] [31C] *These are the ones who go into exile:*

[B] *he who kills someone accidentally.*

[C] *[If] he was rolling [the roof] with a roller, and it fell down on someone and killed him,*

[D] *[if] he was letting down a jar [from the roof], and it fell on [a man] and killed him,*

[E] *[if] one was climbing down a ladder and fell down on someone and killed him—*

[F] *lo, this person goes into exile.*

[G] *But: if he was pulling up a roller, and it fell on [a man] and killed him,*

[H] *[if] he was drawing up a jar, and the rope broke, and [the jar] fell on a man and killed him,*

[I] *[if] he was climbing up a ladder and fell on a man and killed him,*

[J] *lo, this one does not go into exile.*

[K] *This is the governing principle: whatever happens en route downward—the person goes into exile.*

[L] *[And whatever happens] not en route downward—the person does not go into exile.*

[I.A] In the cases of M. 2:1C, D,] R. Judah declares [the man] exempt unless he lets the whole rope go.

[B] R. Simeon declares exempt unless he undoes the entire windlass.

[C] What R. Simeon said in regard to the breaking of the rope [accords with the view of rabbis]. [If the rope of the roller broke, even though part of it remained in the man's hand, he goes into exile. It is not necessary to let the entire rope fall from his hand.]

[D] What R. Judah said in regard to the releasing of the windlass [is in accord with the view of Rabbi, M. 2:2, that one is liable only if the entire rope—in this case, windlass—will be released from his hand].

[II.A] R. Jeremiah raised the question before R. Abbahu: "If one was drawing up the roller to himself, and the other party put his head out the window, and the roller hit him [and he died], [what is the law]? [Since this is en route upward (M. 2:1L), perhaps he does not have to go into exile. Or since he was in the process of plastering, it is as if it is en route downward.]"

[B] He said to him, "Going up is the same as coming down [in this case]. [That is, bringing the roller up in this case is tantamount to letting it down, and he goes into exile.]"

[C] R. Jeremiah raised the question before R. Abbahu, "If one was drawing the roller up and a child put out his hand and the roller crushed it [what is the law]?"

[D] He said to him, "Why are you bothering yourself? Going up is the same as coming down [in the present case, as I just said to you]."

Unit **I** links M. 2:2 to M. 2:1, but this is *via* my commentary following PM. Unit **II** clarifies secondary cases in line with Mishnah's generalization at M. 2:1K–L.

2:2

[A] *[If] the iron flew from the heft and killed someone,*

[B] *Rabbi says, "He does not go into exile."*

[C] *And sages say, "He goes into exile."*

[D]   *[If] it flew from the wood which is being split,*

[E]   *Rabbi says, "He goes into exile."*

[F]   *And sages say, "He does not go into exile."*

[I.A] What is the Scriptural basis for the position of Rabbi [at M. 2:2D–E]?

[B]   Here it is stated, ". . . [and the head] slips [from the handle and strikes his neighbor so that he dies . . .]" (Deut. 19:5).

[C]   And later on, the same verb root is used: "[. . . for your olives] shall drop off . . ." (Deut. 28:40).

[D]   Just as the verb root used later means "dropping off," so here it means "dropping off."

[E]   What is the Scriptural basis for the position of the rabbis [at M. 2:2F]?

[F]   Here the verb root "slipping" is used.

[G]   And later on elsewhere we have the following: ". . . and clears away many nations before you . . ." (Deut. 7:1).

[H]   Just as the verb root, clearing away, refers to an [active] blow there, so here too it speaks of an [active] blow [by an object which strikes something, e.g., the ax, not chips of wood].

What the Talmud contributes is the exegetical basis for the argument at M. 2:2D–F. This is implicit in the Mishnah itself.

2:3

[A]   *He who throws a stone into the public domain and committed homicide—lo, this one goes into exile.*

[B]   *R. Eliezer b. Jacob says, "If after the stone left the man's hand, the other party stuck out his head and took [the stone on the head], lo, this one is exempt."*

[I.A] R. Eliezer b. Jacob taught, " '[As when a man goes into the forest with his neighbor to cut wood, and his hand swings the axe to cut down a tree, and the head slips from the handle and] finds [his neighbor so that he dies]' (Deut. 19:5).

[B] "that is to say that the other be available to him at the time at which he kills him, [thus excluding the one who makes himself available by his own action]."

[II.A] And he has every right to throw a stone into the public way, [so why should he be guilty at all]?

[B] Said R. Yosé b. R. Bun, "Interpret the matter to apply to a case in which his wall was unsteady [and the man was tearing it down]. [He had no right to do so in the public way.]

Unit **I** provides an exegetical base for M. 2:3B, and unit **II** treats M. 2:3A. The points are clear as given.

2:4

[A] *[If] he threw the stone into his own courtyard and killed him,*

[B] *if the victim had every right to go into there, [the other party] goes into exile.*

[C] *And if not, he does not go into exile,*

[D] *as it is said, "As when a man goes into the forest with his neighbor" (Deut. 19:5)—*

[E] *just as the forest is a domain in which both the victim and the one who inflicted injury have every right to enter,*

[F] *so the courtyard belonging to the householder is excluded [from reference], since the victim had no right to go there.*

[G] *Abba Saul says, "Just as cutting wood is optional, so are excluded [from punishment those who do their duty, e.g.:] the father who hits his son, the master who strikes his disciple, and the court official [who committed homicide in the doing of their duty]."*

[I.A] Said R. Yannai, "A butcher who was chopping meat, and who smote [someone], whether above or below, goes into exile. [That is, whether swinging the chopper above, backward, or below, downward and forward.]"

[B] And this statement accords with that which R. Huna said, "A butcher who is chopping meat and smote someone in front of him, downward, goes into exile.

[C]   "If it was on an upward stroke [in front of him], he does not go into exile.

[D]   "If it was to the rear, on an upward stroke, he goes into exile.

[E]   "If it was [to the rear] on a downward stroke, he does not go into exile."

[II.A]   Said R. Isaac, "Every sort of case accords with its own context.

[B]   "If one sat on a bed by day, and it is not usual for a baby to be put on the bed by day, he goes into exile.

[C]   "If he sat on the bed by night, and it is usual for the child to be put into bed at night, he does not go into exile [for he should have expected that, at night, the baby would be in the bed].

[D]   "If he sat down on the crib, by day, and it is usual for the baby to be put into the crib by day, he does not go into exile.

[E]   "If he did so by night, and it is not usual for the baby to be put into the crib by night, he goes into exile."

[III.A]   Said R. Yosé b. Haninah, "[If] one was standing and chopping wood in his own courtyard, and a worker came in [with permission] to collect his salary,

[B]   "and a chip of wood flew and injured him,

[C]   "[the householder] is liable.

[D]   "And if [the worker] should die, [the householder does not go into exile [but is tried]."

[E]   And did not R. Hiyya teach, "He is exempt"?

[F]   There is no argument between them.

[G]   That which R. Yosé said applies to a case in which he saw him [and did not take appropriate precautions].

[H]   And that which R. Hiyya said applies to a case in which he did not see him at all.

[I]   If it is a case in which he did not see him, since he said to him, "Come in," he should be liable in any event.

[J]   And did not R. Hiyya teach, "He is exempt"?

[K]   Since he said to him, "Come in," the worker has the duty of taking precautions for himself.

[L]   And there is he who wishes to say, "Since he said to him, 'Come in,' it is like a courtyard belonging to partners."

[M]   For R. Yohanan in the name of R. Yannai said, "Joint holders acquire possession from one another in a courtyard, and they are liable to one another on account of injuries done to one another."

[N]   And did not Rab say, "It is as if the man fills up the entire [31d] public way."

[O]   And does this one fill up the entire public way!? [Why cannot the injured party guard himself properly?]

[P]   He said, "Since it is usual for him to go about in the courtyard, he [the one who caused the damage] is like one who occupies the entire courtyard [and so is liable]."

Unit I seems to me to enrich the interpretation of M. 2:1K–L. I.B–E provide the interpretation of I.A. Unit II's points are clear as stated. When the person had reason to take care and did not do so, he does not go into exile but is tried. When he had no reason to believe he would cause injury or death but has done so, he goes into exile. Unit III, which has its principal locus at M. B.Q. 3:8, takes up the fundamental theme of injuries caused in one's own property, that is, M. 2:4A–F. I have translated the text as it occurs at M. B.Q. 3:8. The main point—that the accident is culpable—is in accord with unit II's main point, that there are accidents which can have been avoided, and for these one does not go into exile but is tried. The point of unit III's discussion is to establish when the householder is liable and why that is the case. The flow of the argument is clear as spelled out.

2:5

[A]   *The father goes into exile because of the son,*

[B]   *and the son goes into exile because of the father.*

[C]   *All go into exile because of an Israelite.*

[D]   *And an Israelite goes into exile on their account,*

[E]   *except on account of a resident alien.*

[F]   A resident alien goes into exile only on account of another resident alien.

[G]   "A blind person does not go into exile," the words of R. Judah.

[H]   R. Meir says, "He goes into exile."

[I]   One who bears enmity [for his victim] does not go into exile.

[J]   R. Yosé b. R. Judah says, "One who bears enmity [for his victim] is put to death,

[K]   "for he is in the status of one who is an attested danger."

[L]   R. Simeon says, "There is one who bears enmity [for the victim] who goes into exile, and there is one who bears enmity who does not go into exile.

[M]   "This is the governing principle: In any case in which one has the power to say, 'He killed knowingly,' he does not go into exile.

[N]   "And if he has the power to say, 'He did not kill knowingly,' lo, this one goes into exile."

[I.A]   Said R. Zeira, R. Shila bar Buna taught, "Since it is said, 'The avenger of the blood shall himself put the murderer to death' (Num. 35:19), lo, he who killed his son—his other son is not appointed avenger of the blood to kill his father.

[B]   "But if a brother killed a brother, another brother is appointed avenger of the blood to kill his brother."

[C]   R. Eliezer b. Jacob taught, "Since it is said, 'The avenger of the blood shall himself put the murderer to death,' lo, he who smote his son—his other son is appointed avenger of the blood to put his father to death.

[D]   "But in the case of a brother who killed his brother, his other brother is not appointed avenger of the blood to put his brother to death."

[E]   And how do we know that even if he said that he cannot find him right off, [he must go in search of him]?

[F]   Scripture said, "When he meets him, he shall put him to death" (Num. 35:19).

[II.A]   A blind person [does not go into exile] [M. 2:5G].

[B]   Said R. Ba, "Who taught that a blind person [does not go into exile]?

[C]   "It is R. Judah.

[D]   "For R. Judah declares him exempt from all of the religious requirements which are stated in the Torah.

[E]   "For we have learned there: *'Whoever has never in his life seen the lights [of heaven] should not recite the Shema'* (M. Meg. 4:6).

[F]   " 'Lo, if he saw them, he does recite it.' "

[**III**.A]   And both of them interpret the same verse [at M. 2:5G–H].

[B]   "[Or if he used a stone, by which a man may die, and] without seeing him [cast it upon him so that he died]" (Num. 35:23)—

[C]   R. Meir says, "The reference to 'not seeing him' is meant to encompass a blind person."

[D]   R. Judah says, "It is meant to exclude a blind person."

[E]   The opinions assigned to R. Judah are reversed.

[F]   There he has said that it serves as an exclusion [at M. 2:5G], and here [at M. Meg. 4:6] he states that it serves to encompass [one who once had sight and lost it].

[G]   Said R. Haninah, son of R. Hillel, "The Mishnah speaks of a case in which one is sitting in a house wholly without light, [and has nothing to do with blindness]."

[H]   Thus do we say, "He who is sitting in a house without light should not recite the *Shema*"?! [Obviously not!]

[I]   But here, the phrase "without seeing" serves to encompass the blind person [as stated].

[J]   How do rabbis [= Judah] interpret the language "without seeing"?

[K]   It is to encompass him who smites someone by night.

Unit **I** deals with M. 2:5A–B, and unit **II**, M. 2:5G–H. The rest is ignored. The main point of unit **II** is to assign the conflicting opinions to differing conceptions of the interpretation of the cited Scripture. I translate the version at Y. Meg. 4:6.

2:6 [In Leiden MS and *editio princeps:* 2:7]

[A]   *Whither do they go into exile?*

[B]   *To the cities of refuge—*

[C]   *to three which are in Transjordan, and to three which are in the Land of Canaan,*

[D]   *as it is said, "You shall set aside three cities beyond Jordan, and three cities you shall set aside in the Land of Canaan" (Num. 35:14).*

[E]   *Before the three in the Land of Israel had been selected [Josh. 20:7], the three which were on the other side of the Jordan [also] did not afford refuge,*

[F]   *as it is said, "They shall be for you six cities of refuge"—*

[G]   *[they do not afford refuge] until all six of them afford refuge at the same time.*

[H]   *And [direct] roads [were prepared] from one to the other,*

[I]   *as it is said, "And you shall prepare the way, and divide the borders of your land" (Deut. 19:3).*

[J]   *And they hand over to him two disciples of sages, lest [the avenger of the blood] should kill him en route.*

[K]   *They will speak to [the avenger of the blood].*

[L]   *R. Meir says, "Also he [the manslaughterer] may speak to [the avenger of the blood],*

[M]   *"as it is said, 'This is the word of the manslaughterer' " (Deut. 19:4).*

[N]   *R. Yosé b. R. Judah says, "To begin with, both the one who kills by accident and the one who kills maliciously go first to the cities of refuge.*

[O]   *"Then the court sends and brings [the murderer] back from there.*

[P]   *"He who is found guilty of death in court they executed.*

[Q]   *"And he who is not found guilty of death they set free.*

[R]   *"He who is found guilty of a crime requiring exile they returned to his place,*

[S]   "as it is said, 'And the community shall send him back to his city of refuge' " (Num. 35:25).

[T]   All the same are [the deaths of] the high priest who is anointed with anointing oil, the one who is consecrated by being clothed in many garments, and the one who has passed from his anointment as high priest—[upon the death of one of these] they bring back the murderer [from the city of refuge, his term having ended].

[U]   R. Judah says, "Also [on the occasion of the death of] a priest anointed for war does one bring back the murderer."

[V]   Therefore the mothers of the priests provide food and clothing for those [who are in the cities of refuge,] so that they will not pray that their sons will die.

[W]   [If] after one's trial has ended [with the sentence of exile], a high priest died, lo, this one does not go into exile.

[X]   [If] it was before the trial had ended that the high priest died and another was appointed in his stead, and afterward his trial came to an end,

[Y]   he comes back only at the death of the next high priest.

[Z]   [If] one's trial ended at a time at which there was no high priest,

[AA]   he who kills a high priest,

[BB]   and a high priest who committed involuntary manslaughter—

[CC]   [none of these] leaves there forever.

[DD]   And one does not leave [the city of refuge] either for giving testimony having to do with a religious duty, or to give testimony having to do with property, or to give testimony having to do with a capital crime.

[EE]   And even if the Israelites need him,

[FF]   and even if he is a general of the Israelite army of the quality of Joab b. Zeruiah,

[GG]   he may not leave there ever,

[HH]   as it is said, "Whither he has fled" (Num. 35:25)—

[II]   there will be his dwelling, there will be his death, there will be his burial.

[JJ]   *Just as the town affords refuge, so the Sabbath limit of the town affords refuge.*

[KK]   *A manslaughterer who went beyond the limit, and whom the avenger of the blood found—*

[LL]   *R. Yosé the Galilean said, "It is a religious duty in the hand of the avenger of the blood [to kill the manslaughterer], and it is an option available to anyone else [to do so as well]."*

[MM]   *R. Aqiba says, "It is an option available to the avenger of the blood, and anyone else bears no liability [if he does so]."*

[NN]   *A tree standing in the Sabbath limit, with its branches extending outside of the Sabbath limit—*

[OO]   *or standing outside of the Sabbath limit, with its branches extending within the Sabbath limit—*

[PP]   *everything follows the location of the branches.*

[QQ]   *[If] one has committed manslaughter in that very town, he goes into exile from one neighborhood to another.*

[RR]   *And a Levite goes into exile from one town to another.*

[SS]   *[Delete: Similarly,] A manslaughterer who went into exile into a city of refuge, whom the townsfolk wanted to honor, must say to them, "I am a manslaughterer."*

[TT]   *[If] they said to him, "Even so," he may accept [the honor] from them,*

[UU]   *as it is said, "This is the word of the manslaughterer" (Deut. 19:4).*

[I.A]   **Three cities [of refuge] did Moses set aside in Transjordan,**

[B]   **and when they came to the Land, they set aside three more.**

[C]   **[But even so,] neither these nor those afford protection until they had conquered and divided up [the Land] [M. 2:6E].**

[D]   **Once they had conquered and divided up the Land, and so had become liable to the tithes and to the laws of the Seventh Year,**

[E]   **both these and those commenced to afford protection [to the manslaughterer] [M. 2:6E–G] [T. Mak. 3:1].**

[F]   **Three cities did they [Joshua] set aside in the Land of Israel,**

[G]   and they corresponded to the three which Moses had designated in Transjordan, like two rows of vines in a vineyard.

[H]   Hebron in Judah corresponded to Boser in the wilderness, Shekem in the Mountains of Ephraim corresponded to Ramot in Gilead, Qadesh in Galilee corresponded to Golan in Bashan.

[I]   Before they had set aside Shekem in the Mountains of Ephraim, it did not afford protection.

[J]   They set aside Qiriat Yearim in its stead, until they had conquered Shekem.

[K]   Before they had set aside Qadesh in Galilee, it did not afford protection.

[L]   So they set aside Gamla in its stead, until they had conquered Shekem [T. Mak. 3:2].

[M]   "And you will divide" (Deut. 19:3)—that they be divided into three parts,

[N]   so that from Hebron to the south is [the same distance] as from Hebron to Shekem and from Hebron to Shekem, is [the same distance] as from Shekem to Qadesh [T. Mak. 3:3].

[O]   [If] one of them fell down, they build it up in the same location.

[P]   And how do we know that they may build it up even in some other location? Scripture says, "Six cities of refuge" (Num. 25:13),

[Q]   that they should be lined up and should afford protection just as do the first ones [T. Mak. 3:4].

[R]   As to these three cities, they do not make them into large cities nor into small towns, but mid-sized cities.

[S]   They build them only at a market town.

[T]   If there is no market town there, they build one.

[U]   They build them only in a place in which there is adequate water.

[V]   [If] they do not have adequate water, they bring water to them.

[W]   And they build them only in a populated area. [If] the population went down, they bring others and settle them in their place.

[X]   If their residents went down in numbers, they add to them priests, Levites, and Israelites [T. Mak. 3:8].

[Y]   "They do not make [in the cities] olive presses or wine presses," the words of R. Nehemiah.

[Z]   And sages permit.

[AA]   And they do not weave ropes in them,

[BB]   and they do not make glass utensils in them,

[CC]   so as not to provide many occasions for the avenger of the blood to go there [T. Mak. 3:9].

[II.A]   R. Yohanan sent to the rabbis over there [in Babylonia]: "Two things you say in the name of Rab and they are not so.

[B]   "You say in Rab's name: 'A beautiful captive woman—permitted in her case is only the first act of sexual relations.'

[C]   "But I say that it is neither the first nor any later act of sexual relations that is permitted, except after all the required preparations have been carried out,

[D]   "as specified as follows: '[When you go forth to war against your enemies, and the Lord your God gives them into your hands, and you take them captives, and see among the captives a beautiful woman, and you have desire for her and would take her for yourself as wife, then you shall bring her home to your house, and she shall shave her head and pare her nails. And she shall put off her captive's garb, and shall remain in your house and bewail her father and her mother a full month;] and after that you may go in to her, [and be her husband, and she shall be your wife]' (Deut. 21:10–13).

[E]   "That is, after the specified deeds.

[F]   "And you say in the name of Rab: 'Joab imagined that the horns of the altar would afford protection to him, but only the roof of the high place at Shiloh affords protection, while that of the Eternal House does not afford protection.'

[G]   "And I say that the altar does not afford protection, nor does its roof afford protection, nor even does that of Shiloh afford protection, nor does the Eternal House afford protection.

[H]   "Only the six cities of refuge alone afford protection."

[I]   Now is it possible that Joab, concerning whom it is written, "A Tahchemonite, chief of the three" (2 Sam. 23:8), should have made an error in such a matter?

[J]   Said R. Tanhuma, "He had fled to the Sanhedrin."

[K]   This is in line with that which you learn:

[L]   As to those put to death by a court, their property goes to their heirs, while as to those put to death by the state, their property goes to the state.

[M]   Consequently Joab thought, "It is better that I should be put to death in court, so that my children may inherit my estate, and let me not be put to death by the king, who then would inherit my property."

[N]   When Solomon heard this, he said, "Do I really need his money?!"

[O]   Forthwith: "[Do as he has said and strike him down and bury him; and thus] take away [from me and from my father's house the guilt for] the blood [which Joab shed] without cause" (1 Kings 2:31).

[P]   The blood had been shed without cause, but his money was not taken away without cause.

[Q]   "Then Benaiah the son of Jehoiada went up, and struck him down and killed him; and he was buried in his own house in the wilderness" (1 Kings 2:34).

[R]   Now was his house really in the wilderness?

[S]   But this is stated to let you know that when Joab died, who had been general of the Israelite army, Israel was turned into a wilderness.

[T]   [He had enriched the community.] If you say that he would take spoil and with it build for the Israelites public baths and watering places, it is a matter of praise.

[U]   If you say that he would take spoil and support sages and their disciples, it is the greatest praise of all.

[V]   Now how do we know that the great Sanhedrin was located near the altar [on account of which Joab was said to be near the altar]?

[W]   It is written, "And you shall no go up by steps to my altar" (Ex. 20:26).

[X]   And thereafter it is stated, "Now these are the ordinances which you shall set before them" (Ex. 21:1).

[III.A]   It was taught: R. Eliezer b. Jacob says, "Refuge . . . ,' 'Refuge. . . ,' is stated [two times] at the crossroads,

[B]   "so that the manslaughterer may see that which is written and know in which direction to go."

[C]   Said R. Abun, "There was a sign shaped like a hand, showing them the way."

[IV.A]   Said R. Phineas: " 'Good and upright [is the Lord; therefore he instructs sinners in the way]' (Ps. 25:8).

[B]   "Why is he good? Because he is upright.

[C]   "And why is he upright? Because he is good.

[D]   " 'Therefore he instructs sinners in the way'—that is, he teaches them the way to repentance."

[E]   They asked wisdom, "As to a sinner, what is his punishment?"

[F]   She said to them, "Evil pursues the evil" (Prov. 13:21).

[G]   They asked prophecy, "As to a sinner, what is his punishment?"

[H]   She said to them, "The soul that sins shall die" (Ez. 18:20).

[I]   They asked the Holy One, blessed be he, "As to a sinner, what is his punishment?"

[J]   He said to them, "Let the sinner repent, and his sin will be forgiven for him."

[K]   This is in line with the following verse of Scripture: "Therefore he instructs sinners in the way" (Ps. 25:8).

[L]   "He shows the sinners the way to repentance."

[V.A]   It is written, "Like a sparrow in its flitting, like a swallow in its flying, a curse that is causeless does not alight" (Prov. 26:2).

[B]   Can you say so [that is, M. 2:6V]? [For the prayer will do no harm, in line with A.]

[C]   Interpret the statement to apply to a case in which it was the right time [for such a prayer].

[D]   This is in line with that which R. Yosé b. Halafta said, "There are times for prayer.

[E]   "Said R. David before the Holy One, blessed be he, 'Lord of all worlds, when I pray before you, may it be an acceptable time, as it is written, 'But as for me, my prayer is to thee, O Lord. At an acceptable time, O God, in the abundance of thy steadfast love answer me' " (Ps. 69:13).

[VI.A]   R. Samuel bar Nahman in the name of R. Jonathan, "At every point at which 'speaking' is mentioned, there is a new point there made by Scripture."

[B]   And is it not written, "And God spoke . . ."?

[C]   This is in line with what the exegesis which the sages provided [the passage is not completed].

[D]   What is the meaning of, "Then the Lord *said* to Joshua, 'Say to the people of Israel, Appoint the cities of refuge . . . and give him a place, and he shall remain with them' " (Joshua 20:1–4)?

[E]   The rabbis of Caesarea in the name of R. Shiloh: "If he was a disciple of a sage, they organize a meetinghouse for him."

[VII.A]   **Three cities [of refuge] did Moses set aside [32a] in Trans-jordan, and when they came into the Land, they set aside three more.**

[B]   **And in the time to come, they will set aside three more in each case, thus there are six, *"and yet three more"*, (Deut. 19:9) lo, nine, as it is said, "Three . . . three . . . three . . . ," lo, nine.**

[C]   **Abba Saul says, "Three for the three, lo, six, and another three, lo, nine, for the three, thus twelve" [T. Mak. 3:10].**

[D]   R. Nehorai says, " 'Three . . . ,' 'three. . . ,' 'three . . . ,'—lo, nine. 'And more'—lo, twelve. 'In addition to the three . . . ,' lo, fifteen."

[E]   It is written, "And the cities which you give shall be your six cities of refuge" (Num. 35:13).

[F]   The meaning is that all six of them should afford protection simultaneously [cf. M. 2:6E].

[G]   And you say thus (C–D)?

[VIII.A]   [M. 2:6T, treating priests consecrated in different ways as equivalent:] And this is in accord with that which R. Samuel said in the name of R. Aha: "In five ways the latter Temple was less than the former temple, as it is written, 'Go up to the hills and bring wood and build the house, that I may take pleasure in it and that I may appear in my glory, says the Lord' (Haggai 1:8).

[B]   " 'And I shall appear in my glory' is written, lacking the expected *he*, referring to the five ways in which the latter temple was less than the former temple.

[C]   "And these are they:

[D]   "Fire, ark, Urim and Thummim, anointing oil, and Holy Spirit."

[IX.A]   Said Abbaye, "A disciple of a sage has to make himself known.

[B]   "How so?

[C]   "A man who knew one tractate, and he who went to a place and they paid him honor as if he knew two tractates has to tell them, 'I know only one tractate.' "

[D]   R. Huna said, "He says so in a pleasant manner and with the right hand open to accept repayment."

[X.A]   What is the Scriptural basis for the position of R. Yosé [at M. 2:6LL]?

[B]   "Lest the avenger of blood in hot anger pursue the manslayer and overtake him" (Deut. 19:6) [which indicates it is his religious duty to do so].

[XI.A]   Said R. Abbahu, "And the manslaughterer returns when the third of the three dies [if the second dies as did the first]" [cf. M. 2:6Y].

[XII.A]   Said R. Abbahu, "If they need him for something [M. 2:6DD], they send and bring him back from there. [So Mishnah's rule is narrowly construed.]"

[B]   Said R. Yosé, "The Mishnah does not say so.

[C]   *"But even if the Israelites need him, and even if he is a general of the Israelite army of the quality of Joab b. Zeruiah, he may not leave there ever, as it is said, 'Whither he has fled . . .' "* (Num. 35:25) [M. 2:6EE–HH].

Unit **I** simply presents a repertoire of materials from Tosefta relevant to Mishnah. I assume that the reference at M. 2:6 to Joab, FF, and the general theme of taking refuge account for the inclusion of the whole of unit **II**. The connection to Mishnah is slight. **II**.A–H should be understood as assigned to Yohanan, citing and differing from Rab, as indicated. The theme of Joab then is carried forward to the end of the unit. Unit **III** presents further information, along the lines of unit **I**. Unit **IV** then turns to an elaborate discourse on the importance of repentance, the relevance of which is unclear to me. Unit **V** turns to the curse on the high priest on the part of those condemned to live in the cities of refuge, M. 2:6V. **VI**.C is unclear; it is an abbreviation, not spelled out. The main point comes at **VI**.D–E. **VII**, in general, is relevant to M. 2:6A–G, but the purpose is to indicate there will be more than six such cities in the world to come. **VIII** accounts for the fact that priests may be consecrated in differing ways and points to the consecration not with anointing oil as a trait of high priests in the Second Temple, when such oil was unavailable, as Aha explains. Unit **IX** is relevant in a general way to M. 2:6SS–UU, that is, the notion of informing people of one's true character before accepting honor from them. Units **X**, **XI**, and **XII** present brief but important clarifications of the rules of the Mishnah, as specified.

2:7

[A]   *"[Refugee manslayers] paid Levites a rental,"* the words of R. Judah.

[B]   *R. Meir says, "They did not pay them a rental."*

[C]   *"And [the manslayer] returns to the office which he had held before,"* the words of R. Meir.

[D]   R. Judah says, "He did not return to the office which he had held before."

an animal and offers it up outside of

assover;

does an act of labor on the Day of

ting oil like the anointing oil of the Tem-
ncense like the incense of the Temple, or
f with anointing oil;

r terefah-meat, forbidden things or creep-

n which tithes had not been removed at all,
h heave offering had not been removed,
ecrated food which had not been redeemed,
ing].

hich had not been tithed at all does one eat

Any amount at all."

An olive's bulk."

Simeon, "Do you not agree with me in the
eats an ant, however small, that he is liable?"

n, "It is because that is how it has been

n, "Also a single grain of wheat is precisely in
ich it has been created."

to flogging are:] he who eats first fruits over
as not made the required declaration:

Things outside the Temple veils, Lesser Holy
econd tithe outside the wall [of Jerusalem].

eaks the bone of a Passover offering which is in a
anness—lo, this one is flogged with forty stripes.

[I.A]   [As to the rights of possession accruing to the Levites in the cities of refuge,] it was taught: R. Judah says, "They were given [to the Levites] for division [as their permanent possession in the Land]."

[B]   R. Yosé says, "They were given for dwelling [but not as a permanent possession and inheritance]."

[C]   The view of R. Yosé [at Y. M.S. 5:5] is in accord with the opinion of R. Meir, and that of R. Judah is consistent with what he has already said [at M. 2:7A].

[D]   For we have learned, "They pay Levites a rental," the words of R. Judah. R. Meir says, "They do not pay them a rental."

[II.A]   Raba in the name of R. Judah, R. Zeira in the name of Mar Uqba: "[M. Erub. 5:4:] They measure only with a rope fifty cubits long [in order to establish the sabbath boundaries of a town]."

[B]   R. Zira in the name of R. Hisda says, "They do not measure by level distance [between two places separated by mountains, but include the mountain in ground measure] [for the purpose of adding to the Sabbath limits of a town] either in the towns of the Levites [to determine its borders] or in the location of a heifer whose neck is broken [to determine which city is closer]."

[C]   And this view accords with the opinion of him who said, "A thousand cubits constitute the outskirts of a village, and two thousand, the Sabbath limit" [M. Sot. 5:3]. [That is, for the cities of refuge no measure by level distance was taken, but for the establishment of the Sabbath limit, they did survey by level distance.]

[D]   But in accord with the one [Eleazar b. R. Yosé the Galilean] who said, "A thousand are the outskirts, and two thousand encompass the fields and vineyards of a town" [M. Sot. 5:3], did they not derive the rule for the Sabbath limit from the boundaries of the towns of the Levites? [That is, we know the Sabbath limit's measurement from that specified for the cities of refuge. Thus from this viewpoint would it follow that] if for the main point of interest they do not make a survey by level distance, for the secondary point of interest, will they make a survey by level distance [that is, for the Sabbath limit]? [Obviously not! So the authority of B is C, not D.]

[**III**.A]   And how do we know from Scripture that they do not bury the dead in the Levites' towns?

[B]   R. Abbahu in the name of R. Yosé bar Haninah: " 'The cities shall be theirs to dwell in, and their pasture lands shall be for their cattle and for their livestock and for all their beasts' (Num. 35:3).

[C]   "For that which is alive have the pasture lands been given over, and not for burial of the dead."

Unit **I** serves M. M.S. 5:5 and draws upon our pericope to elucidate the positions of the authorities of that one. Unit **II** is relevant to M. 2:6NN–PP, the Sabbath limit of the city of refuge and how it is measured. **II**.B makes that surmise virtually certain. What Hisda means to say is that the extraordinary exercise in adding to the clear limits is not undertaken in these cities. The point of **II**.B–D is to align B with the known authorities of M. Sot. 5:3. Since Num. 35:4, 5 specify the boundaries of the city of refuge at a thousand cubits around the walls for fields, and two thousand cubits as pasture, what we want to know is whether the fact that we do not make a survey of a Levitical town of refuge, B, is because the Scripture already has specified that measure for the Sabbath limit, as C maintains. That is, C's view is that the two thousand cubits specified by Scripture constitute the Sabbath limit. Hence one does not make such a survey of a Levitical town, because it is not necessary to do so. It follows that it is the law governing the Levitical town's Sabbath limit which provides the analogy for other towns, C. If, however, we do *not* interpret the stated verse to refer to the Sabbath limit, D, then what sense can we make of B? For, as D says, if the rule for the Sabbath limit derives from the Levitical boundary, then, if we do not make a survey for the Sabbath limit of such a town, there surely will not be a survey for some secondary purpose. So D cannot accord with B, but C can and does (PM). What all this has to do with our tractate is not self-evident. Unit **III**, finally, provides an exegesis for the same set of verses as are under discussion at unit **II**.

[C]   [a priest] who slaughters
the Temple;

[D]   he who eats leaven on P

[E]   and he who eats or who
Atonement;

[F]   he who prepares anoin
ple, he who prepares
he who anoints himse

[G]   he who eats carrion o
ing things.

[H]   [If] one ate food fro
first tithe from whic
second tithe or cons
[he is liable to flogg

[I]   How much food w
so as to be liable?

[J]   R. Simeon says, '

[K]   And sages say, "

[L]   Said to them R.
case of one who

[M]   They said to hi
created."

[N]   He said to the
the form in wh

3:3

[A]   [Also subjec
which one h

[B]   Most Holy
Things or

[C]   He who b
state of cl

[E

[F]

3:

[A]   [Als
in th
uncle

[B]   he wh
overnig
intentio

[D]   But he who leaves over meat of a clean Passover offering or who breaks the bone in the case of an unclean one is not flogged with forty stripes.

3:4

[A]   He who removes the dam with the offspring—

[B]   R. Judah says, "He is flogged, and he does not have to send the dam away."

[C]   And sages say, "He sends the dam away, and he is not flogged.

[D]   "This is the governing principle: In the case of any negative commandment which involves doing a positive deed, one is not liable."

3:5

[A]   He who makes a baldness on his head [Deut. 14:1], he who rounds the corners of his head and mars the corners of his beard [Lev. 19:27], or he who makes a single cutting for the dead [Lev. 19:28] is liable.

[B]   [If] he made a single cutting on account of five different corpses,

[C]   or five cuttings on account of one corpse,

[D]   he is liable for each and every one of them.

[E]   For [cutting off the hair of] the head, he is liable on two counts, one for each side of the head.

[F]   For cutting off the beard, he is liable on two counts [32b] for one side, two counts for the other side, and one count for the lower part.

[G]   R. Eliezer says, "If he removed all of it at once, he is liable only on one count."

[H]   And he is liable only if he will remove it with a razor.

[I]   R. Eliezer says, "Even if he removed it with pinchers or with an adze, he is liable."

3:6

[A]   *He who tattoos his skin—*

[B]   *[if] he made a mark but did not tattoo it in,*

[C]   *tattooed it in but did not make a mark,*

[D]   *he is not liable—*

[E]   *unless he makes a mark and tattoos with ink or with eyepaint or with anything which lasts.*

[F]   *R. Simeon b. Judah says in the name of R. Simeon, "He is liable only if he will write the name [of a god],*

[G]   *"as it is written, 'Nor will you tattoo any marks on you, I am the Lord' " (Lev. 19:28).*

3:7

[A]   *A Nazirite who was drinking wine all day long is liable on only one count.*

[B]   *[If] they said to him, "Don't drink, don't drink!" yet he continued to drink,*

[C]   *he is liable on each count.*

[D]   *[Leiden MS and editio princeps: 3:8] [If a Nazirite] was contracting corpse-uncleanness all day long, he is liable on only one count.*

[E]   *[If] they said to him, "Do not contract corpse-uncleanness! Do not contract corpse-uncleanness!" yet he continued to contract corpse-uncleanness,*

[F]   *he is liable on each count.*

[G]   *[Leiden MS and editio princeps: 3:9] [If] he was shaving himself all day long, he is liable on only one count.*

[H]   *[If] they said to him, "Don't shave! Don't shave!" yet he continued to shave,*

[I]   *he is liable on each count.*

[J]   [Leiden MS and *editio princeps:* 3:10] *If someone was wearing a garment of diverse kinds [Lev. 19:19, Deut. 22:11] all day long, he is liable on only one count.*

[K]   *[If] they said to him, "Don't put it on? Don't put it on!" yet he took it off and then put it on, he is liable on each count.*

3:8 [In Leiden MS and *editio princeps:* 3:11]

[A]   *There is one who ploughs a single furrow and is liable on eight counts of violating a negative commandment:*

[B]   *[specifically, it is] he who ploughs with an ox and an ass [Deut. 22:10], which are both Holy Things, in the case of [ploughing] mixed seeds in a vineyard [Deut. 22:9], in the Seventh Year [Lev. 25:4], on a festival [Lev. 23:7], and who was both a priest [Lev. 21:1] and a Nazirite [Num. 6:6] [ploughing] in a graveyard.*

[C]   *Hanania b. Hakhinai says, "Also: He is [ploughing while] wearing a garment of diverse kinds" [Lev. 19:19, Deut. 22:11].*

[D]   *They said to him, "This is not within the same class."*

[E]   *He said to them, "Also the Nazir is not within the same class [as the other transgressions]."*

3:9 [In Leiden MS and *editio princeps:* 3:12]

[A]   *How many times to they flog him?*

[B]   *Forty stripes less one,*

[C]   *as it is said, "By number, forty" (Deut. 25:2, 3)—a number close to forty.*

[D]   *R. Judah says, "He is flogged a full forty times."*

[E]   *And where does the additional one fall?*

[F]   *Between the shoulders.*

3:10 [In Leiden MS and *editio princeps:* 3:13]

[A]   *They make an estimate of his capacity to take flogging [without being irreparably injured or killed] only by a number divisible by three.*

[B]   *[If] they estimated him as able to take forty, [if] he then received part of the flogging, and they said that he cannot take all forty, he is exempt.*

[C]   *[If] they estimated him as able to take eighteen, [and] once he has received the flogging [of eighteen] they said that he can take all forty, he [still] is exempt from the rest.*

[D]   *[If] he committed a transgression on which he is liable on two counts of violating negative commandments, and they make a single estimate [of what he can take, covering both sets],*

[E]   *he is flogged and exempt [from the other].*

[F]   *And if not, he is flogged and allowed to heal, and then goes and is flogged again.*

3:11 [In Leiden MS and *editio princeps:* 3:14]

[A]   *How do they flog him?*

[B]   *One ties his two hands on either side of a pillar,*

[C]   *and the minister of the community grabs his clothing—*

[D]   *if it is torn, it is torn, and if it is ripped to pieces, it is ripped to pieces—*

[E]   *until he bares his chest.*

[F]   *A stone is set down behind him, on which the minister of the community stands.*

[G]   *And a strap of calf hide is in his hand, doubled and redoubled, with two straps that rise and fall [fastened] to it.*

[H]   *[Leiden MS and editio princeps: 3:15] Its handle is a handbreadth long and a handbreadth wide,*

[I]   *and its end must reach to his belly button.*

[J]   *And he hits him with a third of the stripes in front and two thirds behind.*

[K]   *And he does not hit [the victim] while he is either standing or sitting, but bending low,*

[L]   *as it is said, "And the judge will cause him to lie down" (Deut. 25:2).*

[M]   *And he who hits him hits with one hand, with all his might.*

[N]   [In Leiden MS and *editio princeps:* 3:16] *And a reader reads: "If you will not observe to do . . . the Lord will have your stripes pronounced, and the stripes of your seed" (Deut. 28:58ff); "And you will observe the words of this covenant" (Deut. 29:9); [and he finishes with, "But he is full of compassion and forgave their iniquity" (Ps. 78:38),] and he goes back to the beginning of the passage.*

[O]   *And if the victim dies under the hand of the one who does the flogging, the latter is exempt from punishment.*

[P]   *[But if] he added even a single stripe and the victim died, lo, this one goes into exile on his account.*

[Q]   *If the victim dirtied himself, whether with excrement or urine, he is exempt [from further blows].*

[R]   *R. Judah says, "In the case of a man, with excrement; and in the case of a woman, with urine."*

3:12 [In Leiden MS and *editio princeps:* 3:17]

[A]   *"All those who are liable to extirpation who have been flogged are exempt from their liability to extirpation,*

[B]   *"as it is said, 'And your brother seem vile to you' (Deut. 25:3)—*

[C]   *"once he has been flogged, lo, he is tantamount to your brother," the words of R. Hananiah b. Gamaliel.*

[D]   *[Said] R. Hananiah b. Gamaliel, "Now if one who does a single transgression—[Heaven] takes his soul on that account,*
       "he who performs a single religious duty—how much the more so that his soul will be saved for [handing over to] him on that account!"

[E]   *R. Simeon says, "From its own passage we may learn that,*

[F]   "for it is written, 'Even the souls that do them shall be cut off'
        (Lev. 18:29).

[G]   "And it is said, 'Which if a man do he shall live by them' (Lev.
        18:4).

[H]   "Lo, whoever sits and does no transgression—they give him a
        reward like that which goes to one who [goes and] does a reli-
        gious duty."

[I]   [Leiden MS and editio princeps: 3:18] R. Simeon b. Rabbi says,
        "Lo, it says, 'Only be sure that you do not eat the blood, for
        the blood is the life' (Deut. 12:23).

[J]   "Now if blood, which the soul of man despises—he who keeps
        away from it receives a reward,

[K]   "robbery and fornication, which the soul of a man desires and
        after which he lusts—he who keeps away from them how much
        more will attain merit—

[L]   "for him, and for his descendants, and for the descendants of
        his descendants, to the end of all generations!"

3:13 [In Leiden MS and editio princeps: 3:19]

[A]   R. Hanania b. Aqashia says, "The Holy One, blessed be he,
        wanted to give merit to Israel.

[B]   "Therefore he gave them abundant Torah and numerous
        commandments,

[C]   "as it is said, 'It pleased the Lord for his righteousness' sake to
        magnify the Torah and give honor to it' " (Is. 42:21).

Abbreviations and Bibliography

Alloni: Nehamya Alloni. *Geniza Fragments of Rabbinic Literature.* Jerusalem, 1973. Pp. 70–71.

Appointed Times: Jacob Neusner. *A History of the Mishnaic Law of Appointed Times.* Vols. 1–5. Leiden: E. J. Brill, 1980–83.

Assis: Moshe Assis. "A Fragment of Yerushalmi Sanhedrin." *Tarbiz* 46 (1977): 29–90.

b.: *Babli, Babylonian Talmud.* Alt.: *ben,* "son of."

B.B.: Baba Batra.

B.M.: Baba Mesia.

B.Q.: Baba Qamma.

Bekh.: Bekhorot.

Ber.: Berakhot.

Chron.: Chronicles.

Damages: Jacob Neusner. *A History of the Mishnaic Law of Damages.* Vols. 1–5. Leiden: E. J. Brill, 1984–.

Deut.: Deuteronomy.

Ed.: Eduyyot.

Editio princeps: *Talmud Yerushalmi, Venezia.* Reprinted with no place or date. Originally printed by Daniel Bomberg, 1523–24.

Ex.: Exodus.

Ez.: Ezekiel.

Francus: Israel Francus. *Talmud Yerushalmi. Massekhet Besah. Im perush Eleazar Azkari.* New York: Feldheim, 1967.

Gen.: Genesis.

Ginzberg: Louis Ginzberg. *Yerushalmi Fragments from the Genizah.* Vol. 1. *Text with various readings from the editio princeps.* New York: George Olms Verlag, 1909. Reprint. New York and Hildesheim: Georg Olms Verlag, 1970.

Holy Things: Jacob Neusner. *A History of the Mishnaic Law of Holy Things.* Vols. 1–6. Leiden: E. J. Brill, 1978–79.

Hor.: Horayot.

Hos.: Hosea.

Is.: Isaiah.

Jastrow: Marcus Jastrow. *A Dictionary of the Targumim, the Talmud Babli and Yerushalmi, and the Midrashic Literature.* Vols. 1–2. Reprint. New York: Pardes Publishing House, 1950.

Jer.: Jeremiah.

Jos.: Joshua.

Ker.: Keritot.

Ket.: Ketubot.

Krauss: Samuel Krauss. *Griechische und Lateinische Lehnwörter im Talmud, Midrasch, und Targum.* Berlin, 1899. Reprint. Hildesheim: George Olms Verlagsbuchhandlung, 1964.

Leiden MS: *The Palestinian Talmud.* Leiden MS. Cod Scal. 3. A facsimile of the original manuscript. Vols. 1–4. Introduction by Saul Leiberman. Jerusalem: Kedem Publishing, 1970.

Lieberman, Caesarea: Saul Lieberman. *The Talmud of Caesarea.* Jerushalmi Tractate Nezikin (supplement to *Tarbiz* II.4, in Hebrew). Jerusalem, 1931.

Lieberman, "Fragments": Saul Lieberman. "On the New Fragments of the Palestinian Talmud." *Tarbiz* 46 (1977): 91–96.

Lieberman, TR: Saul Lieberman. *Tosefeth Rishonim.* A Commentary. Based on Manuscripts of the Tosefta and Works of the Rishonim and Midrashim in Manuscripts and Rare Editions. Vols. 2–4. Jerusalem: Mossad Rabbi Kook Press, 1939. In Hebrew.

Lieberman[n], YK: Saul Lieberman[n]. *Ha-Yerushalmi Kiphshuto.* A Commentary based on Manuscripts of the Yerushalmi and Works of the Rishonim and Midrashim in Mss. and Rare Editions. Vol. 1. *Sabbath, Erubin, Pesahim.* Jerusalem: Darom Publishing Co., 1934. In Hebrew.

Ma.: Maaserot.

Mak.: Makkot.

Mal.: Malachi.

Marshall: J. T. Marshall. *Manual of the Aramaic Language of the Palestinian Talmud.* Grammar, vocalized text, translation, and vocabulary. Edited by J. Barton Turner. Introduction by A. Mingana. Leiden: E. J. Brill, 1929.

Meg.: Megillah.

Melammed: E. Z. Melammed. *An Introduction to Talmudic Literature.* Jerusalem, 1973. In Hebrew.

Mic.: Micah.

Mid.: Middot.

Ned.: Nedarim.

Neg.: Negaim.

Neh.: Nehemiah.

NY: *Noam Yerushalmi.* Joshua Isaac Salonima. *Sefer Noam Yerushalmi. Vehu beur 'al hayyerushalmi.* Vols. 1–2. Vilna, 1868. Reprint. Jerusalem, 1968.

Par.: Parah.

Pes.: Pesahim.

PM: Pené Moshe. Moses Margolies (d. 1780). *Pene Moshe.* Amsterdam, 1754; Leghorn, 1770. Reprinted in the Yerushalmi Talmud.

Prov.: Proverbs.

Ps.: Psalms.

Purities: Jacob Neusner. *A History of the Mishnaic Law of Purities.* Vols. 1–22. Leiden: E. J. Brill, 1974–77.

QH/QE: *Qorban ha'edah.* David Frankel. *Qorban Ha'edah.* Dessau, 1743; Berlin, 1757, 1760–62. Reprinted in the Yerushalmi Talmud.

Qoh.: Qohelet [Ecclesiastes].

Rabbinowitz: Louis I. Rabbinowitz, "Talmud, Jerusalem." In *Encyclopaedia Judaica.* Vol. 15. Jerusalem, 1971. Pp. 772–79.

Ratner: B. Ratner. *Ahawath Zion we-Jeruscholaim.* Varianten und Ergänzungen Textes des Jerusalemitischen Talmuds nach alten Quellen und handschriftlichen Fragmenten ediert, mit kritischen Noten und Erlauterungen versehen. Vilna: Wittwe and Gebr. Romm et al. I, *Berakhot* (1901); II, *Shabbat* (1902); III, *Terumot, Hallah* (1904); IV, *Shebi'it* (1905); V, *Kilayim, Ma'aserot* (1907); VI, *Pesahim* (1908); VII, *Yoma* (1909); VIII, *Rosh Hashshanah, Sukkah* (1911); IX, *Megillah* (1912); X, *Besah, Taanit* (1913); XII, *Pe'ah Demai, Ma'aser Sheni, 'Orlah, Bikkurim* (1917). No number, *Sheqalim, Hagigah, Mo'ed Qatan.* Jerusalem, 1967.

R.H.: Rosh Hashanah.

Sam.: Samuel.

San.: Sanhedrin.

Schwab: Moise Schawb. *Le Talmud de Jérusalem.* Traduit pour la premiere fois en francais. Reprint. Paris, 1960.

Shab.: Shabbat.

Shebi.: Shebiit.

Shebu.: Shebuot.

Sheq.: Sheqalim.

Sot.: Sotah.

T.: Tosefta.

Toh.: Tohorot.

Women: Jacob Neusner. *A History of the Mishnaic Law of Women.* Vols. 1–5. Leiden: E. J. Brill, 1979–80.

Y.: Talmud Yerushalmi (repr. of ed. Romm., New York, Montreal, Tel Aviv, 1949: Gilead Press).

Yeb.: Yebamot.

Zech.: Zechariah.

Zeph.: Zephaniah.

Zuckermandel: M. S. Zuckermandel. *Tosephta.* Based on the Erfurt and Vienna Codices with Parallels and Variants. Reprint. Jerusalem: Wahrmann Books, 1963.

Zussman, Beth Shean: Jacob Zussman. "An Inscription of a Legal Character from the Beth Shean Valley." *Tarbiz* 44 (1973–74): 88–158, 193–95. In Hebrew.

Index of Biblical and Talmudic References

General Index

Abba bar Kahana, death penalty, 344
Abba Saul: death penalty, 308, 325; exile or banishment, 422; judicial jurisdiction, 53; political crimes, 53
Abba bar Zimna, death penalty, 240
Abbahu: capital cases, procedures in, 139, 143; death penalty, 193, 197–99, 207, 209, 220, 224, 226, 229, 252, 262, 265, 268, 276, 288, 296, 311, 358, 371, 375; exile or banishment, 420, 435, 438; judicial jurisdiction, 11, 13, 15, 17, 21, 23, 33, 47, 52, 60, 62; perjury, 416; political crimes, 52; priests and king in court system, 71; property cases, 104, 106–7, 119
Abbamari, death penalty, 378
Abbaye, exile or banishment, 435
Abemakhis, property cases, 131
Abin: capital cases, procedures in, 143, 159; death penalty, 188, 219, 252–53, 347; judicial jurisdiction, 41
Abina, property cases, 115
Abudimi, death penalty, 179
Abun: death penalty, 239; exile or banishment, 433; perjury, 416; priests and king in court system, 66
Abuna: judicial jurisdiction, 40; property cases, 108
Aha: capital cases, procedures in, 151; death penalty, 190–91, 315, 317, 322, 331, 336; exile or banishment, 435–36; judicial jurisdiction, 15, 31; priests and king in court system, 67, 78, 88, 90
Ahi, capital cases, procedures in, 139

Ami: judicial jurisdiction, 15, 17, 28, 44; property cases, 108
Ammi: capital cases, procedures in, 137; property cases, 117
Amram, perjury, 403, 405
Aqiba: death penalty, 209, 221–24, 226–29, 257–58, 306–8, 312, 320, 355, 357, 365, 376; exile or banishment, 429; judicial jurisdiction, 12, 23, 37, 42; perjury, 412, 418; property cases, 111, 120

Ba: death penalty, 267, 275, 370, 377; exile or banishment, 426; judicial jurisdiction, 13, 15, 42, 55; property cases, 116, 119, 124
Ba bar Hiyya: capital cases, procedures in, 157; judicial jurisdiction, 27
Ba bar Kahana: judicial jurisdiction, 46; priests and king in court system, 82
Ba bar Kohen, death penalty, 376
Ba bar Mamal, perjury, 403, 405–6, 409–10
Ba bar Mamel, death penalty, 230, 379
Ba bar Samuel, property cases, 122
Ba bar Yasa, capital cases, procedures in, 145
Ba bar Zabeda: death penalty, 316, 322; judicial jurisdiction, 28–29; property cases, 106–7
Ba bar Zamina: death penalty, 188; property cases, 109
Bar Kappara, death penalty, 314
Bar Nahman, death penalty, 316